D1171951

LORD DERBY AND VICTORIAN CONSERVATISM

LORD DERBY

AND

VICTORIAN CONSERVATISM

by

WILBUR DEVEREUX JONES
Assistant Professor in the Department of History
in The University of Georgia

THE UNIVERSITY OF GEORGIA PRESS
ATHENS
1956

PUBLISHED IN GREAT BRITAIN BY
BASIL BLACKWELL, OXFORD

PRINTED IN GREAT BRITAIN

Matri et Uxori meis

ACKNOWLEDGMENTS

The writer's thanks are due to the following publishers and agents for permission to quote from the works following their names: A. P. Watt & Son and Hodder & Stoughton, Publishers (Lady Gwendolen Cecil, *Life of Robert, Marquis of Salisbury*, 1926); the Dowager Countess of Airlie, G.C.V.O., G.B.E., and Hodder & Stoughton, Publishers (Countess of Airlie, *Lady Palmerston and Her Times*, 1922); Captain R. V. Walling and Cassell & Co. (R. A. J. Walling, *The Diaries of John Bright*, 1913); the Earl of Derby (Edward Stanley, *Journal of a Tour in America, 1824-1825*, 1930); Ernest Benn, Ltd. (*Early Correspondence of Lord John Russell, 1805-1840*, 1913); Edward Arnold (Publishers), Ltd. (Sir Herbert Maxwell, *The Life and Letters of George William Frederick, Fourth Earl of Clarendon*, 1913); John Murray, (Publishers) Ltd. (A. C. Benson and Viscount Esher, *The Letters of Queen Victoria*, 1907. G. E. Buckle, *The Letters of Queen Victoria*, 1926. The Duke of Argyll, *Duke of Argyll, Autiobiography and Memoirs*, 1906. W. F. Monypenny and G. E. Buckle, *The Life of Benjamin Disraeli*, 1916. C. S. Parker, *The Life and Letters of Sir James Graham, 1792-1861*, 1907); Longmans, Green & Co., Ltd. (A. E. Gathorne-Hardy, *Gathorne Hardy, First Earl of Cranbrook, A Memoir*, 1910. Lord Edmond Fitzmaurice, *The Life of Granville, George Leveson Gower, Second Earl of Granville, 1815-1891*, 1899. *The Later Correspondence of Lord John Russell 1840-1878*, 1925); Messrs. Halsey, Lightly and Hemsley (L. Strachey and R. Fulford, *The Greville Memoirs*, 1938); Williams & Norgate, Ltd. (A. Aspinall, *Three Early Nineteenth Century Diaries*, 1952).

CONTENTS

INTRODUCTION

THE fact that no recent biography of Great Britain's first three-term Prime Minister, Lord Derby, has been written was pointed out to me by my friend and former teacher, Donald Grove Barnes, of Western Reserve University. This lack of attention to his career can possibly be traced to two sources; viz., the often unflattering contemporary accounts of Derby, and the tendency to overemphasize the relative importance of his lieutenant, Disraeli. One has only to thumb through the pages of Charles Greville's *Diary* to find evidence of the first, and to examine the card catalogue of almost any library to confirm the second. Perhaps the prominence of Disraeli was inevitable because of the 'human interest' aspects of his career. Disraeli struggled for his place; Derby was born to his. As his successive and able biographers elaborated on Disraeli's colourful career, Derby, like the proverbial old soldier, simply faded away into the background.

In undertaking a short political biography of Lord Derby, this writer consulted all the secondary sources he could find on this side of the Atlantic, and such original sources as were made available to him in England. With regard to the latter, it was a keen disappointment to discover that certain important collections were not available for study, but the project was by then so far advanced that the writer was deeply interested in going on with it. The very large number of Derby letters and papers, however, which were found to be available for this study give some assurance of its reasonable completeness and accuracy.

In writing Derby's political biography, the writer felt he had a responsibility both to his subject and to the readers who might be interested in Derby's story. To omit what might be called the 'Greville side' of Derby's personality would be to create a myth; to overemphasize it would be to do less than justice to a statesman who had a serious, reflective and sensitive side to his personality. In this situation, a reasonable compromise was the only possible solution.

In spite of his love for racing and the company connected with it, Lord Derby in his private life was by no means out of place in the Victorian Age. He appears to have been a very sincerely religious man, a faithful husband and a devoted father. As a public official he guided the Conservative Party for more than two decades. Under his leadership it never achieved a majority in the Commons, and whether this situation resulted from defective leadership, or was due to conditions Derby could not possibly overcome, is certainly a major question of his political career. This writer, within the physical limitations of the work due to publication costs, has tried to present the evidence for both of these interpretations, and has summarized briefly his own conclusions towards the end of the book.

The writer desires to acknowledge with sincere appreciation the financial assistance of the Carnegie Grants-in-Aid programme of Atlanta, of the University Center in Georgia, and of Dean George H. Boyd of our Graduate School; and to acknowledge the courtesies of the National Trust, the British Museum and the Public Record Office in England. Thanks also go to Dr. E. Merton Coulter for his encouragement, to my old friend Warren Haenny for his careful study of the manuscript, and to my wife for her help in preparing it.

He desires also to acknowledge with the deepest appreciation the suggestions and criticisms of M. G. Brock of Corpus Christi College and Professor Asa Briggs of Leeds University. Neither bears any responsibility for the opinions or statements made in the work, but their suggestions not only greatly improved the manuscript, but made more confident an American who could not help feeling somewhat presumptuous in attempting a work of this nature and scope.

WILBUR DEVEREUX JONES

The University of Georgia
Athens, Georgia
August 30th, 1954

REFERENCE FOOTNOTES AT END OF CHAPTERS

The following abbreviations, referring to documentary sources, are used:

Aberdeen Papers* — *AP*	Gladstone Papers* — *GP*
Cardwell Papers — *CP*	Home Office Papers — *HOP*
Colonial Office Papers — *COP*	Peel Papers* — *PP*
Disraeli Papers — *DP*	Ripon Papers* — *RP*
Ellenborough Papers — *EP*	Russell Papers — *RUSP*

The above sources marked with an asterisk are found in the British Museum, and in these cases the abbreviation will be followed by the reference number of that institution (e.g., '*RP*, BM 40863'). Those not marked with an asterisk are found at the Public Record Office, and bear the reference of that institution (e.g., '*COP*, CO 138/55'), with the exception of the Disraeli Papers, which are found at Hughenden and are here identified according to the writer and the box number (e.g., '*DP*, Derby XII'). In a few cases involving printed works which are used with considerable frequency, this writer has taken the liberty of abbreviating both the names of the authors (or editors) and the titles (e.g., 'B&E, *Victoria*') in citing references in A. C. Benson's and Viscount Esher's well-known publication of Queen Victoria's letters.

CHAPTER I

YOUNG STANLEY'S ENGLAND

THE year was 1799, and the place, Knowsley, the seat of the aristocratic Stanley family, the Earls of Derby. Located in the countryside near Liverpool, the manor house was substantial, but not massive, befitting a family which traced its title to the budding Renaissance of the fifteenth century, rather than to the dim recesses of the Middle Ages. Similar strongholds of the great land magnates were common enough in England, but to the people of Lancashire Knowsley was the great house of the locality, and, therefore, of their world. Knowsley was synonymous with Stanley, and Stanley with Lancashire, into which the family had deeply thrust its roots, taking from the county a princely income, and exercising political and social influence far beyond the limits of their actual proprietorship.

The Countesses of Derby had usually been thoughtful enough of family fortunes to provide male heirs, and rarely did the sucession seem more secure than in 1799. On March 29th the birth of Edward George Geoffrey Smith Stanley raised to three the generations of direct male heirs to the title. The village church bells rang out to celebrate the event, and the good fortune of the newcomer. To be born into the ruling class of any nation any time is generally an excellent start in life, but to be born into such a group in the most important and powerful nation in the world, fills the cup of destiny to overflowing. For much of the world at that time, or shortly thereafter, existed for the better living of the British, and the mass of British themselves to some extent existed for the benefit of that upper crust of their people, who directed their political life and participated most fully in the fruits of national triumphs. So this was by no means an ordinary birth. The infant was one of the greatest expectations.

At the time of Young Stanley's birth the patriarch of the family was the 12th Earl of Derby, a pudgy, undersized man, with a pleasant face and happy disposition. In contemporary politics he was a leading spirit of the liberal Whigs, and in the sporting world he gave his title to the greatest of horse races. His restless energy, and an unhappy marriage to the daughter of the Duke of Hamilton, caused the 12th Earl to seek numerous and varied interests outside the home. For a time he was attracted to the theatre, and once played 'Lovemore' in the comedy *Way to Keep Him* at Richmond House. This interest led to his meeting the beautiful and talented actress, Elizabeth Farren, the daughter of a bankrupt father, but a purposeful woman who carefully avoided the snares set for those in her profession.[1] She won the Earl's heart, and, following the death of his first wife, they were married. This happy union added three children to the two the Earl had previously begotten, and Young Stanley was to grow up in the same generation as his grandsire's second brood.

Edward Stanley's parents lacked the colour of the older generation, but they were substantial people well fitted to open a century distinguished for lofty moral aspirations. His father, a blue-eyed, rosy-cheeked man, was fated to live in the shade of those around him. The 12th Earl, who lived until 1834, guided family activities during the best years of his son's life, and when he passed on, the 13th Earl already found himself in the shadow of his son's growing reputation. Though he served in the Commons for many years, his main interest was in zoology. A huge zoo, covering a hundred acres of land and seventy of water, was created at Knowsley, and, even in their comfortable circumstances, its expense taxed the family budget. For a wife he chose his cousin, Charlotte Hornby, a brunette with an aquiline nose and serious countenance. A daughter of the Rector of Winwick, her background contrasted sharply with that of her stepmother-in-law.

No doubt each of these four people held out certain hopes for Young Stanley, and these mirrored their own personalities and ideals. Charlotte Hornby wished, above all, that her son would be a God-fearing man, and a pillar of the Established Church; while her husband hoped his son would develop intellectual interests in common with his own. Elizabeth Farren, who still in memory heard the applause of countless delighted audiences, thought no greater experience could possibly await him than to take the centre of the stage and toy with the emotions of eager listeners. No doubt, however, the 12th Earl wished the hardest. He had fashioned his son into a Whig, though, unfortunately, not a very brilliant one, and he was determined to do the same favour for his grandson. Party was almost an obsession with him, and he could foresee no more satisfying future than to have Young Stanley lead the Whigs in successful onslaughts against the Tories. But wishing could not make it so. Of the four, the little Earl was the only one to be disappointed.

When he was old enough to notice such things, Edward Stanley realized that his grandfather and father were highly important men in the neighbourhood. Nearby Preston was referred to by them as if it were a parcel of the estate. Sometimes the Earl spoke of his position as Lord Lieutenant of the County and on occasion he wore the uniform of a colonel of the Lancashire militia. The squires of the county, some of whom were seeking commissions for their sons, fawned when they met the Earl, while the common folk, on such occasions, adopted an attitude of exaggerated humility.[2]

The family's holdings were scattered over four English counties as well as in Ireland.* They had the finest coaches, the proudest horses, and the most exclusive people were their guests. The Prince of Wales found his way to Knowsley on occasion, and the Comte d'Artois, later to be Charles X of France, visited there.[3]

In fact, Stanley could hardly remember a day during his youth at Knowsley when he was alone with his parents. Elizabeth Farren loved crowds, being at her best when she could sweep through the room acting the lady of fashion before the curious mixture of people she numbered among her friends. And in this respect Lord Derby was a perfect mate. Nothing pleased him more than to have his relatives move in, bag and baggage along with their servants, to stay for indefinite periods. During the

* In 1876 the Derbys owned some 47,269 acres in Lancashire, 9202 in Cheshire, 92 in Flint and 35 in Kent, but, rather strangely, no land at all in Derby. John Bateman, *The Acre-ocracy of England* (London: Basil Montagu Pickering, 1876), p. 56. Their estates in Ireland were apparently extensive, and located in Limerick. *Hansard* (third series), CXCVI, 719. Some income was derived from city property in Liverpool. G. E. Cokayne, *Complete Peerage of England, Scotland and Great Britain* (London: George Bell & Sons, 1890), III, 77.

Lord Derby's income was usually estimated at about £60,000 a year. Lytton Strachey and Roger Fulford, *The Greville Memoirs* (London: MacMillan and Co., 1938), V, 320. *Diary*, May 11th, 1846. (Hereinafter cited as 'S&F, *Greville*'). Disraeli once stated that Derby's 'clear' annual income was £110,000. *Disraeli Papers* XVII, Miscellaneous Observations §76. This seems a little high, even though Derby was involved in some business ventures, and managed his estates well.

summer and most of the autumn, forty to a hundred people dined daily, and Mondays were especially crowded, for on that day Derby received as many of the citizens of Liverpool as cared to call on him. While Elizabeth Farren carried on small talk with the admiring male visitors, the little Earl flitted among the young ladies and brought blushes to their cheeks as he inquired into the more intimate aspects of their love lives. In the mornings the men, clad in splendid costumes, rode off to hunt, to return for lunch and a ride with the ladies in the afternoon.[4] Even into the gloomiest recesses of the old manor the warmth of the Earl's personality seemed to penetrate. They were good days, those days of busy idleness!

Few visitors to Knowsley made much of an impression on Young Stanley, but one misshapen and ugly man was outstanding, chiefly because he seemed to dominate the little Earl. When the two chatted, his grandfather did most of the listening and agreeing. Stanley's recollection of the man was intensified by the memory of one gloomy day he later dated to 1806. Rarely was his grandfather so depressed and out of sorts, and his mother explained it was due to the death of the peculiar-looking man. In the family circle, Derby discoursed at length about the virtues of the deceased, and coldly ignored Charlotte Stanley's observation that Charles James Fox's personal life had done little to recommend him to God-fearing people.

Gradually the conversational topics of his elders became more intelligible to Stanley. Ireland, frequently the subject of table talk, was represented as a dreary place inhabited by a violent, un-English people. Atrocity stories stemming from the recent rebellion there were never-to-be-forgotten memories. Quite as interesting were the references to the French Revolution. Lord Derby spoke warmly of the French,[5] and of his own efforts to keep civil liberties alive in England during the frightened 1790s.* But as time went by, the conversation on this subject became more guarded. Napoleon's aggression in Europe made it increasingly difficult for patriotic Englishmen to take his part,

* The intimate political connection between the 12th Earl of Derby and Charles James Fox is noted in many places. Lord Derby was a 'liberal' in the sense that he opposed war with France in 1793, on grounds that it would burden the poor, and in his opposition to the abridgment of civil liberties during the war. See: *Annual Register* (1793), pp. 128-30; Ibid. (1794), pp. 143-4; Ibid. (1795), pp. 153-5; Ibid. (1796), pp. 44-5, 154-5. On the other hand, Derby opposed free trade.

though Derby, perhaps in compensation, was critical of Wellington.[6] Young Stanley finally concluded that in Napoleon's times the French had distorted the noble ideals of liberty, equality and fraternity to serve their own selfish ends.[7] At the same time, however, he felt some attachment to French idealism, and was proud that his grandfather maintained a reputation for liberalism. Neither Stanley nor his grandfather, however, had insight enough to imagine how the new ideology of the lower classes was to be later expressed in English politics.

The practical education Stanley received at home was supplemented by formal study at those places which were the special preserve of his class, first Eton, and then Christ Church, Oxford. His chief mark of scholastic distinction was the Chancellor's prize in Latin verse which Stanley received for a composition called *Syracuse*, but he left Oxford without a degree. Latin and Greek remained with him as a life interest, but Stanley also cultivated the use of the English language, helped, no doubt, by his step-grandmother. During his student days Stanley was considered to be a youth of considerable potentialities, but his tendency to be at once headstrong and sensitive to criticism did not enhance his personal popularity.[8]

In 1817 the death of his step-uncle, a youth of Stanley's age, in April was followed by the passing away of his mother two months later. Knowsley was in deep mourning, and the intimate visitation of death in his family perhaps stimulated in Stanley a desire to leave the stuffy environs of formal education to enter the world outside. Life, he discovered, was tragically finite, and it was perhaps wise to begin to live as soon as possible.

Life, at the same time, was fascinating. Each day brought new evidence that the reconstruction of the old order by the Congress of Vienna would not be long-lived. There were numerous stories of unrest and violence on the Continent, where, under the glittering foam of reaction, the French revolutionary ideas still fermented. But one did not have to go so far afield to find such evidence. In nearby Liverpool Stanley could see the prosperous, middle-class industrialists whom the war and the Industrial Revolution had elevated to a position of financial well-being comparable to that of the oldest aristocratic families in all England. They were aggressive, vigorous individuals, men full of confidence in their own abilities. How much longer would they be content to leave political control, and with it the direction of national economic life, in the hands of the landed nobility?

And what of the poor? The war's end brought the city masses high prices, unemployment and short rations. A mass meeting at Spa Fields in 1816 had been a warning, and the march of the unemployed to London the following year reminded the government of its neglect. Then in 1819 came the affair at St. Peter's Fields. Henry 'Orator' Hunt, who was to cause Stanley much embarrassment a decade later, stirred up the poor, and the cavalry cut them down. At the moment the Whigs seemed no more sympathetic than the Tories, and Stanley was confused to find that both his father and grandfather approved the atrocity.[9] Perhaps the ineptitude of the older generation would provide an opportunity for the new. So these were fascinating times, indeed.

Though he was not yet twenty-one, Stanley could discuss the possibility of his entering Parliament, and people took him seriously. No one doubted his facile intelligence, which enabled him to understand a problem in a very short time,[10] nor his ability to express himself clearly. Such precocity was so rare among members of his class that Stanley was sometimes mentioned as the only 'brilliant eldest son produced by the British peerage for a hundred years'.[11] Furthermore, Whig fortunes continued in the doldrums. The party could use an able young man, especially one with the backing of the Derby prestige.

But the little Earl hesitated to give his consent. Stanley had certain disturbing qualities. Self-confidence was a quality essential for success in the Commons, but mature judgment was equally important, and the little Earl was not sure his grandson had developed the latter as markedly as he had the former. And, though Stanley professed to be a Whig Liberal, he showed enough intellectual independence to raise a suspicion that he might not be a 'good party man'. In 1820, however, Derby purchased the seat for Stockbridge for his grandson, whose career, like that of many other British statesmen, owed its inception to the rotten borough system.*

Stanley's Tory predecessor at Stockbridge vacated the seat

* *Hansard* (third series), CLXXXVIII, 1775-6. Stanley later in life said that a wealthy Whig peer who was anxious to increase his political influence prevailed on him to take the seat. The unidentified peer may have been Lord Lansdowne.

early in the session, and introduced Stanley to his newly bought constituents. The new candidate spoke well on the occasion, but his grandfather was quick to point out that the successful hustings orator might win little acclaim in the Commons, where logic was as important as eloquence.[12] Stanley was cautioned to listen closely to the great speakers of the time, to the compelling oratory of George Canning and the cold precision of Sir Robert Peel, before rising to make his maiden speech.

So, once elected to Parliament, Stanley sat night after night in the Commons without venturing to speak, and, as time went by, the hurdle seemed to become ever higher. In 1823, however, he was appointed to a committee on gaslighting, and he studied the subject until he was convinced, if he could ever speak on anything, it would be on that. Nevertheless, the celebration of his twenty-fifth birthday was ruined by the prospect of the ordeal which confronted him the following night.

When he went to his place in the Commons that evening of March 30th, 1824, Stanley felt like a doomed man ascending the steps of the gallows. When he arose to address the House, his voice, coming through parched lips, seemed to have the thin, halting quality of a scale as performed by a beginning violinist. Though the words came more easily after a time, Stanley experienced a keen sense of failure when he finally concluded.*

To his surprise Sir James Mackintosh, the next speaker, had kind words for his effort.[13] Stanley's disappointment was supplanted by a feeling of double triumph. Obviously he had spoken well, but, what was equally important, his nervousness had not been apparent. Towards Mackintosh he felt a keen sense of gratitude. In later years Stanley was to perform a similar act of thoughtfulness for young William Ewart Gladstone, who never ceased to be thankful for it; and was to ignore the maiden speech of another orator, Benjamin Disraeli, who, perhaps, never forgot it either.

After this modest success Stanley felt capable of discussing a subject more important than gas lights in Manchester, and the opportunity shortly appeared. The prominent Radical, Joseph

* As late as 1831 Stanley confessed: 'My throat and lips, when I am going to speak, are as dry as those of a man going to be hanged.' G. Otto Trevelyan, *The Life and Letters of Lord Macaulay* (New York: Harper & Bros., 1875), I, 219-20. (Macaulay to Hannah M. Macaulay, August 29th, 1831).

Hume, introduced a motion to inquire into the income of the Irish Church to determine if it were excessive. The Irish Church, supported partly by the unwilling contributions of Catholics, was an anomaly liberals found increasingly difficult to defend, but from 1824 to the end of his days Stanley made defence of the Established Church both in Ireland and England the cornerstone of his political philosophy.

So Stanley answered Hume, and, to the delight of the Tories, opposed the appointment of a commission likely to be hostile towards the Church. The speech revealed Stanley's considerable knowledge of Church affairs, and it also emphasized his willingness to put his views above party regularity. Stanley was glad to find his father agreed with him and helped vote down the motion, but their lofty course found no sympathy in the top circle of the household. Lord Derby was at a loss to explain the traitorous conduct of both his son and grandson and became ill through brooding over the incident.[14]

The Knowsley atmosphere was still somewhat strained in June 1824 when Stanley and three other 'Fashionables' boarded a five hundred ton packet at Liverpool bound for the United States.* Stratford Canning had recommended the young men to Daniel Webster, and the trip was intended both for diversion and to further their political education.[15] This tour dwarfed, in extent at least, Stanley's European excursion of 1822.†

Being well provided with servants to see to his needs, Stanley was comfortable enough *en route*, and in three weeks reached New York.‡ There, not without complaining, Stanley climbed three flights of stairs to a room in the City Hotel on Broadway, and faced eight months of sightseeing in the new and prospering Republic.

* Wrote a contemporary: 'The scheme was thought very wild, and much disapproved of by the West End of the town; and disappointment and disgust were universally predicted.' It was later acknowledged to have turned out very well. Lady Seymour, ed., *The Correspondence of John Whishaw and His Friends* (London, 1906), p. 250.

† When in Naples Stanley is said to have knocked down an officer who used violent language to him, and to have spent a day in the black hole and thirteen in jail as a result. A. Aspinall, ed., *Three Nineteenth Century Diaries* (London: Williams & Norgate, 1952), p. 344. (Littleton's Diary, July 7th, 1833).

‡ The following account is based on: Edward Stanley, *Journal of a Tour in America 1824-1825* (London: Privately printed, 1930).

The young tourists had an eager desire to see everything. Beginning with a tour of New York State, they went up to Canada, down through New England, across Pennsylvania, West Virginia and Ohio, south through the Mississippi Valley to New Orleans, north-east through the Deep South and so on to Washington. In many ways the society differed from that of England. The upper and lower classes dressed in the same fashions; the shopkeepers treated the young aristocrats like ordinary folk and ex-President Adams was found to live 'on the lowest scale of a country gentleman'. The casual American attitude at first offended Stanley, but being young and adaptable, and after studying the ways of the people, he concluded there was more genuine hospitality in the Republic, though of a different sort, than in England.

Once he forgot the quality of his pedigree, Stanley thoroughly enjoyed himself. In Ohio he attended a meeting of the Shakers; in Kentucky he went to a barn dance where he drank corn whisky with a local judge; in the Deep South he watched the slaves do a 'hardly altogether strictly decorous' Congo dance. While he met such prominent Americans as James Fenimore Cooper, Daniel Webster, John Adams and John C. Calhoun, Stanley did not avoid contact with the 'lower orders' and thus gained a well-rounded impression of American society. He admired especially the New England system of education, and the religiousness of the people there. Distasteful to him, however, were the slavery of the South and the moral laxity of the South around New Orleans.

For one who believed, as he did, in the monarchical constitution of England, the contrast between Canada and the United States was somewhat painful, but Stanley did avoid a conclusion which seemed self-evident. Royal Canada was listless and backward, and Stanley concluded that few would prefer it to the United States and its free institutions. He seems to have fully appreciated the strengths as well as the weaknesses of the American way of life. 'If I left the United States without much admiration for the attractive qualities of their citizens,' he wrote, 'I left them also with feelings which I would fain hope are gaining ground in England of respect for much of solid and sterling merit, and with a full persuasion of the firmness of the foundation on which their political structure is built.'[16]

His Journal also revealed something of Stanley himself. On one occasion he and a friend explored the wild country near the Mississippi River. After a time they came upon a shanty in a thicket and were amazed to find three small children, whose parents had been away for three days, living alone. Stanley wrote:[17]

> They showed us their bed with two deerskins thrown on it, and requested our assistance in carrying it into a log hut, as they said it was very cold in the shanty; we afterwards cut up a large tree at their request for firewood and left these young children of Independence.

Thus the scion of one of England's most aristocratic families bent his back and raised blisters on his hands to aid some unknown waifs in the wilderness of the great American frontier. This side of Stanley's personality was never revealed to the general public, and only his most intimate friends were ever aware of its existence.

In Stanley's Journal a note explains that the tour of America was cut short by the receipt of some letters, which necessitated his return to England. They may have been written by Emma Caroline, second daughter of Edward Bootle Wilbraham, for Stanley married her shortly after his return to England in April 1825. Stanley then acquired his closest, and perhaps only real confidante and partner of the next half-century. Emma Stanley was the patient listener to all the complicated political problems of the early Victorian era, played hostess on countless occasions, and acted on occasion as her husband's confidential secretary.* If she lacked, as Disraeli later charged, artistic tastes, her husband nevertheless provided the best of everything for her, and it made no difference to him. Apart from his love of Shakespeare and the classics, Stanley himself was not of an artistic turn of mind.

Turbulent Ireland – of all places – was chosen for a home following their marriage. Because he condemned the evil of absenteeism and wanted to establish a partial residence in Ireland,[18] Stanley built a house on the family estates and settled down

* Disraeli's description of Lady Derby, written in 1864, was not very flattering: 'No one has more splendid horses and equipages than Lady D. He looks after this. She has a weakness for "great folles" seems never to catch anything of the taste & splendour of their lives. "Did you ever see such china in a room," exclaimed Lady Chesterfield. "It's what you wd. put in your still room in the country." ' *Disraeli Papers*, XVII, Miscellaneous Observations §66. Lord Redesdale called her parties 'of a dullness as depressing as a London fog'. Lord Redesdale, *Memories* (New York: E. P. Dutton & Co., n.d.), II, 534.

to what he later described, possibly with exaggeration, as a pleasant enough association with the Irish people. He often walked through the neighbourhood carrying a thick stick, wearing a slouched hat, and rarely noticing those who crossed his path. His neighbours termed him the 'odd gentleman from England', and after a time probably ignored him also. No doubt Stanley, in his off-hand way, was studying the problems of Ireland, but he could not, as in America, enter into the daily life of the people, and thus his conclusions had to be based on rather imperfect evidence. Nevertheless, the facts he gleaned were to stand him in good stead later.

In 1826 Stanley bade farewell to his corrupt constituents at Stockbridge. On June 26th he succeeded to the seat for Preston, occupied by his father for many years and controlled by the Earl of Derby through an agreement with the corporation. The change was therefore no indication of Stanley's growing popularity, or of his ability as a candidate.* Later Stanley was to learn to his sorrow that Preston was not so deep in the Earl's pocket as had been supposed.

The same year also saw an event of high importance in Stanley's domestic life. His first son was born on July 21st, and, like many of the earls of previous generations, the child was named Edward. Celebration was in order at Knowsley as the beaming little Earl assembled the next three generations of Derbys around him. But this time he was not so sure the Whig Party would be the gainer by the blessed event.

Meanwhile a new era was opening in British political life. Castlereagh, who was associated with the reaction following the Napoleonic Wars, committed suicide, and George Canning, aided by some liberal Tories, became the leading spirit in the Cabinet. A period of cautious reform brought greater freedom of trade,

* Some indication of Stanley's feelings on the subject of candidacy and the obligations of the successful candidate to his constituents can be found in a speech of 1834. He said that voters elected men in whom they had confidence to represent their interests faithfully, saying in effect: 'Go to the House of Commons, watch over our welfare, protect our interests, act as our Representative, not as our delegate, go as one of the Representatives of the country and blend our interests with those of the empire at large.' But '. . . if with regard to every question that came before the House, I was to be subjected to the examination and cross-examination of my constituents, and to have no free will upon any, I would not submit to it.' *Hansard* (third series), XXIII, 1068-79.

improvements in the criminal code, and an easing of restrictions on working men's unions. When Lord Liverpool was replaced by Canning in 1827 the section of the Tory Party headed by the Duke of Wellington and Sir Robert Peel refused their support, and Canning had to look elsewhere for aid.

Canning had been a rather irregular party man, and, especially in foreign affairs, was considered liberal. His record induced a section of the Whig Party, especially the Lansdowne faction to which Stanley belonged, to join the Government. After a period of negotiations, Lansdowne finally entered the Cabinet. One of his minor requests was that Sir James Mackintosh and Stanley also be given posts so that '... there is respect for the past and hope for the future'.[19] Stanley, however, received only a Lordship of the Treasury, which he considered a 'mere initiation' into the routine of business. He justified crossing party lines on grounds that Canning's principles were similar to his own.[20]

On August 8th, 1827, Canning suddenly died and an interim Government was headed by Lord Goderich, previously the Chancellor of the Exchequer. Few Cabinet changes were made, but Lansdowne managed to secure the Under Secretaryship of the Colonies for Stanley.[21] Though Stanley had yet to prove his administrative ability, some Whigs felt his background entitled him to an even more important position.[22] Goderich's Government survived only until January 8th, 1828, when the Duke of Wellington was called in to form a High Tory Government.

When Parliament opened in 1828 Stanley thought his views regarding Wellington's Government important enough to be explained in some detail. Asserting his independence of all statesmen save those with whom he was united in principle, Stanley professed adherence to the 'certain line of liberal policy' of Canning. While he noted that the 'old and stubborn spirit of Toryism is at last yielding to the increased liberality of the age', he charged that Ireland and the Catholics could expect little from the new Government, and said he would support Wellington only if he followed Canning's principles.[23] With this speech Stanley, in effect, thrust himself forward as the potential leader of a new faction. Later in the year his friend, Sir James Graham, advocated a coalition between moderate Whigs and liberal Tories under Stanley's leadership, but the project was premature.[24]

During these years Stanley's speeches sometimes emphasize the 'liberality of the age', indicating that he was imbued with the Whig liberal tradition. His votes were likewise in support of liberal legislation. In 1826 he spoke in favour of an emergency corn importation measure designed to relieve the distress of the poor, and he criticized the agricultural interest for their unsympathetic attitude towards the poor and unemployed of the manufacturing districts.[25] Wellington's alteration of the Corn Laws he attacked as being inferior to Canning's,[26] and in 1830 he favoured the reduction of duties on certain items.[27]

Stanley was also quite friendly towards the Catholics during these years — at least to the extent of supporting their interests in Parliament. He voted for Catholic Emancipation in 1825, 1827, 1828 and 1829. When the bill came up for the last time, he resisted Wilmot Horton's amendment to exclude Catholic members from voting on ecclesiastical matters. In 1823 he voted against renewing the Irish Insurrection Act, and in 1827 he supported a motion to inquire into Orange activities in Ireland.[28] He also came to the aid of Daniel O'Connell, who claimed to have spent thousands of pounds during the past twenty-five years to keep agitation alive, by speaking against the outlawing of the Catholic Association in 1829,[29] and by voting with him to amend the Vestry Act in 1830.[30]

In colonial policy Stanley also leaned strongly towards liberalism. He proposed that Britain should employ the 'most unfettered liberality' in its treatment of Canada, noting it was possible to pursue a more liberal course there than in England where there were 'previous interests and existing prejudices'.[31] When the Clergy Reserves (large areas reserved for the support of the Church in Canada) there were discussed in 1827, Stanley condemned the Reserves for blocking agricultural and internal improvements and doing absolute mischief.[32]

In some small ways Stanley aided the manufacturing interests of Great Britain. During the debates on the East Retford disfranchisement bill in 1828 Stanley supported the claims of Birmingham and Manchester to representation in opposition to the agricultural interest.[33] He spoke on behalf of the canals and stage-coaches against the railways, and in 1830 brought in a petition from the Manchester Chamber of Commerce against the East India Company.[34]

Many of his early speeches contain the enthusiasm of the

reformer, and Stanley was particularly effective in speaking on behalf of the poor. On some of the issues he was later, however, to hold rather different language. Two decades in the future found Stanley the friend both of the East India Company and the Clergy Reserves, and cautious about introducing democratic institutions into the colonies. He was to be the premier spokesman for the agricultural interest, and, to some extent at least, hostile towards the manufacturers. And he later became considerably more cautious on the question of Catholic rights. Granted these changes of opinion, it must be added that Stanley always recognized the individual's right to change his mind.*

A closer look at Stanley's utterances during this period goes far towards dispelling the notion that he was a really ardent reformer. This is particularly noticeable in his remarks on the subject of Reform.† When the Marquis of Blandford introduced a rather radical Reform measure in 1830, calling for disfranchisement of the rotten boroughs, and creating a 'scot and lot' franchise along with payment for members of Parliament, Stanley joined Sir Robert Peel in voting against the bill.[35] Althorp, Brougham and Russell all supported the measure, but Sir James Graham joined Peel and Stanley, foreshadowing the realignment which was to take place in the 1830s.

Stanley supported Catholic Emancipation and continued to speak well of it until his contests with O'Connell caused him to have some doubts on the subject. There was never any question, however, about his stand on the Church. When Lord John Russell in 1828 proposed that he join a Committee for Promotion of Religious Liberty, Stanley replied cautiously that he was not willing to exempt the Catholics from contributing to the Established Church, which, he admitted, might be some people's notion of religious liberty.[36] During 1828-30 he worked closely with

* Commenting on Peel's change of position on Catholic Emancipation, Stanley said he had shown himself '... superior to that feeling of pride, which would dignify a pertinacious adherence to an opinion once expressed, by the name of consistency and showed that he was not afraid to be thought to have been bullied or intimidated'. *Hansard* (new series), XX, 202-6.

† Stanley believed that Reform should be accomplished piecemeal, by disfranchising boroughs whenever it could be shown they were corrupt. He voted to investigate the Leicester election in 1827, and to disfranchise Penryn borough the same year. He described this gradual Reform as follows: '*Utor permisson caudaeque pilos ut equinae Paulatim vello; et domo unum, demo etiam unum, dum cordat elusus ratione ruentis acervi.*' Ibid., XIX, 806.

the Irish Bishops in an effort to improve the leasehold system in Ireland, and his bill on the subject later had the support of Peel.[37]

His attitude towards the Corn Laws during this period was likewise cautious. In supporting the corn importation measure in 1826, one of his leading arguments was that the 'agricultural interest' must demonstrate its interest in the poor.[38] In the 'abstract', he favoured a fixed permanent duty which would protect both producer and consumer against price fluctuations, but he supported the sliding scale proposed by Canning because it would permit agriculture a 'fair profit' and still keep prices low. He was not enthusiastic about the measure of 1828.

One could hardly, then, class Stanley as a reformer with Lord John Russell. It seems clear that he had deep humanitarian instincts which made him wish to alleviate human misery whenever possible, and that he was interested in eliminating the 'inveterate abuses' in various British institutions. But, by and large, he was interested in putting traditional British institutions on a sounder footing and thereby strengthening particularly the Church and his own class. Certainly Stanley was never the prophet of some 'new order' of society.

During 1830 the death of George IV in June and the subsequent dissolution of Parliament rendered the confused political situation even more disordered. Wellington's Catholic Emancipation and corn measure had alienated the Ultra-Tories, and, without help from the Canningites, he could not continue in office. To some extent the July Revolution in France, which caused new concern among the British aristocracy, operated in favour of the Duke, and caused some conservative Whigs to consider joining him. Lord Palmerston bargained with both Whigs and Tories right down to the meeting of Parliament in November. Stanley and Graham were both ready to support Wellington if some compromise could be reached on Parliamentary and Church Reform.[39] While dropping hints which he hoped would reach the Duke, Stanley also negotiated with the Whigs. Later in the year Stanley reached some sort of understanding with his own party, but the line to Wellington was apparently not altogether cut until November 1st.[40]

The meeting of Parliament of November 2nd found the Duke standing squarely at the crossroads. He could adopt a conciliatory attitude and seek support from the Whigs and liberals in general, or he could appeal to the prejudices of the most conservative section of his own party. To the consternation of the liberals, the Duke chose the latter course and stood out against Reform.

Stanley viewed the situation with mixed emotions. At the time the Duke symbolized for him all that was reactionary and out of date, and he had a Whig's dislike for the man who added such lustre to the Tory Party. Yet there was something admirable about a man who stood staunchly by his beliefs in the crisis, and dared his enemies to attack him. For, in effect, the Duke was daring the Whigs to overthrow him and face themselves all the complicated problems of the day. His opponents accepted the challenge. On November 15th the Iron Duke was overwhelmed by a concerted attack from all sides and on all flanks, and he retired from the field, leaving the problems of reconstruction after the victory to the forces which had dislodged him.

NOTES

[1] *Public Characters of 1799-1800* (London, 1799), pp. 465-73. Lady Theresa Lewis, ed., *Extracts of the Journals and Correspondence of Miss Berry* (London: Longmans, Green & Co., 1865), I, 254-5, 328, 392, 429. (*Diary*, November 13th, 1790, August 1791, September 29th, 1793, December 14th, 1793).

[2] *The Times* (London), October 25th, 1869.

[3] Richard Edgcumbe, ed., *The Diary of Frances Lady Shelley, 1787-1817* (New York: Charles Scribner's Sons, 1912), pp. 16-24. See also: Lewis, *Miss Berry*, II, 471. (*Diary*, March 22nd, 1811).

[4] Edgcumbe, *Lady Shelley*, pp. 12-13.

[5] Lewis, *Miss Berry*, I, 429. (*Diary*, December 14th, 1793).

[6] Countess Granville, ed., *Lord Granville Leveson Gower, Private Correspondence* (London: John Murray, 1917), II, 412.

[7] Edward Stanley, *Journal of a Tour in America, 1824-1825* (London: Privately printed, 1930), p. 2.

[8] Sir Herbert Maxwell, *The Life and Letters of George William Frederick Fourth Earl of Clarendon* (London: Edward Arnold, 1913), II, 222-3. (Emily Eden to Clarendon, 1860).

[9] Graham Wallas, *The Life of Francis Place, 1771-1854* (New York: Alfred A. Knopf, 1919), p. 144. (Place to Hodgskin, September 8th-12th, 1819).

[10] *The Times* (London), October 25th, 1869.

[11] Ibid.

[12] Sir Herbert Maxwell, ed., *The Creevey Papers* (New York: E. P. Dutton & Co., 1904), p. 382. (Derby to Creevey, August 10th, 1822).

[13] *Hansard* (new series), XI, 13-14.

[14] Maxwell, *Creevey*, p. 418. (Creevey to Ord, May 12th, 1824).

[15] Claude Moore Fuess, *Daniel Webster* (Boston: Little, Brown & Co., 1930), I, 346-7.

[16] Stanley, *Journal*, p. 336.

[17] Ibid., pp. 240-1.

[18] *Hansard* (third series), XV, 607-14.

[19] Edward Herries, *Memoir of the Public Life of the Rt. Hon. J. C. Herries* (London: John Murray, 1880), I, 178.

[20] *Hansard* (new series), XVIII, 517-24.

[21] Lewis Melville, ed., *The Huskisson Papers* (New York: Richard R. Smith, 1931), p. 238. (Huskisson to Lansdowne, September 1st, 1827).

[22] Maxwell, *Creevey*, p. 470. (Creevey to Ord, September 18th, 1827).

[23] *Hansard* (new series), XVIII, 517-24.

[24] Charles Stuart Parker, *Life and Letters of Sir James Graham* (London: John Murray, 1907), I, 70-1. (Graham to Stanley, July 15th, 1828).

[25] *Hansard* (new series), XV, 977-8.

[26] Ibid., XIX, 23-35.

[27] Ibid., XXIII, 919.

[28] Ibid., IX, 239; Ibid., XVII, 151.

[29] Ibid., XX, 202-6.

[30] Ibid., XXIV, 104.

[31] Ibid., XIX, 339.

[32] Ibid., XVI, 586-9.

[33] Ibid., XIX, 1544.

[34] Ibid., XV, 90-2; Ibid., XXII, 429 and Ibid., XXIV, 672.

[35] Ibid., XXII, 724.

[36] Rollo Russell, ed., *The Early Correspondence of Lord John Russell 1805-1840* (London: T. Fisher Unwin, 1913), I, 282-3. (Stanley to Russell, October 22nd, 1828).

[37] *Hansard* (new series), XXI, 131-4.

[38] Ibid., XV, 977-8.

[39] Sir Herbert Maxwell, *The Life of Wellington* (Boston: Little, Brown & Co., 1899), II, 253. See also: Parker, *Graham*, I, 98.

[40] George M. Trevelyan, *Lord Grey of the Reform Bill* (New York: Longmans, Green & Co., 1920), p. 221. (Durham to Grey, October 4th, 1830). Charles S. Parker, *Sir Robert Peel* (London: John Murray, 1899), II, 164-5. (Arbuthnot to Peel, November 1st, 1830).

CHAPTER II

CONCESSIONS IN SEASON

WITH the fall of the mighty Duke of Wellington, Lord Grey formed a government of the most exclusive Whig aristocrats of his time. It included not only the older Whigs, such as Grey himself, who had endured the extended period of Tory rule, but there was an infusion of younger blood, men like Lord John Russell, who was identified with Parliamentary Reform, the serious-minded Sir James Graham and Edward Stanley, all of whom brought with them some of the fire and drive of youth. Stanley was made Chief Secretary for Ireland, a position of importance because of the intricate and pressing problems of the country, but it still was not one of full Cabinet rank. Though his personal reputation had increased considerably during the past few years, so much so that the ill-fated William Huskisson had called him the 'Hope of the Nation' a year before,[1] there were many men with better claims, based on political experience, than his, and the prominent Canningites, as well as the Whigs, had to be rewarded through recognition in the Cabinet. Nevertheless, the Irish Secretaryship was a stepping-stone to something better.

The satisfaction Stanley felt with his new appointment was quickly submerged by a major embarrassment. Having accepted a post in the Government, Stanley was forced to stand for re-election at Preston, and on this occasion the unsettled times encouraged the demogogic Henry 'Orator' Hunt to run against him. Both candidates campaigned vigorously, feelings running so high that Stanley once barely escaped being manhandled by a Tory mob,[2] but when the results were posted, it was found that the Preston constituents had preferred, by a slight margin, Hunt's radicalism to Stanley's aristocratic liberalism. While Stanley convinced himself that the defeat was due, not to the will of the voters, but to the corrupt practices of Hunt's supporters,* the

* Stanley charged that Hunt's backers all voted a number of times. S&F, *Greville*, II, 94. (*Diary*, December 19th, 1830). For other explanations see: G. Barnett Smith, *The Prime Ministers of Queen Victoria* (London: George Routledge & Sons, 1886), pp. 181-2, and *The Times* (London), October 25th, 1869.

Derby crest had fallen considerably. The Earl of Derby wrathfully withdrew his patronage from the borough, and Stanley vainly sought to unseat Hunt on grounds of corrupt election practices.[3]

Even before Stanley's defeat was confirmed Lord Grey sought aid from King William, who controlled the borough of Windsor. Complicated negotiations followed. Under pressure from the King and Grey, the member for Windsor, Sir Hussey Vivian, agreed to vacate the seat in exchange for a post in Ireland. Sir William Freemantle was persuaded to give up his desire to represent Windsor, and Sir John Byng agreed to accept Vivian as his second in command and successor in Ireland. Once the seat was vacated Stanley stood for it, and quieted the fears of some of his friends by winning the election.[4] In thus aiding Stanley William IV was interested in demonstrating his support of Grey's Government; Grey probably was largely motivated by his need for the Derby prestige and aid in dealing with the problem of Reform.[5]

Stanley's new position brought with it the problem of Daniel O'Connell, the mighty orator who was the soul of reviving Irish nationalism. The goal towards which O'Connell struggled was the independence of Ireland and it was one which the British of the nineteenth century felt they could not possibly concede. Each concession that O'Connell won was not, for him, a new basis for mutual understanding, but a quickly forgotten triumph to be followed by agitation on another issue. Conciliatory gestures were interpreted by him as signs of weakness promising more concessio s in the future.

As he had helped to overthrow Wellington, O'Connell hoped to be included in the Government. Grey soothed him somewhat by reappointing the popular Marquis of Anglesey as Viceroy of Ireland,[6] but he had no intention of admitting the Irishman into his exclusive inner circle of advisers. A very minor position was tendered O'Connell, but he emphatically turned it down,[7] and was therefore free to agitate without the restraining influence of a formal connection with the Government.

The contest between O'Connell and Stanley during 1831-32 was one of the most bitter struggles in British parliamentary history. The irresistible force from nationalist Ireland met the immovable object from aristocratic, imperial Britain, and, to make it worse, the two men, who apparently never exchanged a word outside the halls of Parliament, had violently clashing personalities. O'Connell had been on bad terms with Stanley's predecessor, and was to have a low opinion of the man who succeeded him,[8] which indicates it was his policy to dislike Irish Secretaries. Stanley, on the other hand, in spite of a real concern for the welfare of Ireland,* had little love for the Irish people.

Arrogant and haughty Stanley found he could send O'Connell into a Gaelic frenzy by interrupting his speeches, or by sneering contemptuously while listening to them.[9] O'Connell used various techniques to discredit his opponent. One was suddenly to ask a question in Parliament on some minor Irish occurrence concerning which Stanley would be forced to confess his ignorance.[10] With artful cunning he capitalized on Stanley's impetuousness and aristocratic bearing to create in him a symbol of greedy British imperialism in Ireland, using him as American Democrats used Herbert Hoover, and the Republicans used Dean Acheson to personify certain discredited policies. He capitalized on the racial issue by continually referring to Stanley as 'the Saxon'.[11]

To evaluate the activities of either man on the moral basis of right and wrong is perhaps to cloud the issue between them. Both fought for their national causes – as they saw them – as best they could, using with brutal effectiveness the great weapons of intellect and oratory they both possessed. Stanley at times pricked O'Connell's pride unmercifully, but the latter was never without mighty bludgeons with which to retaliate. On Stanley's behalf, the observation of a contemporary should be quoted: 'If he said sharp things, he was willing to be paid back on a footing of perfect equality.'[12]

Ireland was more than usually restless when Stanley entered upon his career as Irish Secretary. Daily the mails brought reports of outrages and plots from various British officials in Ireland, as well as numerous unofficial reports, usually from Irish gentry, telling of election violence and demonstrations calling for various reforms.[13] After reading the accounts, Stanley sent them to Lord Melbourne at the Home Office. Melbourne, never a positive leader, appealed to Stanley for advice, but found

* Stanley always insisted upon this, and stressed his kind treatment of his tenants in Ireland. *Hansard* (third series), CXCVI, 719.

little offered to him.[14] Stanley saw the figure of O'Connell lurking amid the unrest and was convinced there could be no peace in Ireland while the Liberator was at large.

As a means of quieting Ireland, Lord Anglesey issued proclamations restricting public meetings there. O'Connell quickly fell foul of the law, and on January 19th, 1831, was imprisoned on thirty-one counts of conspiring to violate and evade the proclamations. Stanley was gleeful. 'I think he may be dealt with and *transported*,' he wrote, 'and, if he were, I really hope Ireland would be tranquil.'[15] O'Connell, on the other hand, found new reasons to hate the Irish Secretary.*

But the case against O'Connell was not pressed, and on February 14th the Marquis of Chandos asked in Parliament if a direct or indirect compromise had been made by the Government with the Irish leader.[16] Stanley replied that O'Connell's friends had tried to make terms for him, but the Government '. . . could not, in this affair, recede one single inch'.[17] Two weeks later O'Connell called upon Stanley to explain the implications of his statement, and a hot exchange followed with O'Connell threatening to make Stanley answer for his actions before the Reformed Parliament, and Stanley challenging him to carry out the threat.[18] Both denied that any understanding had been reached between the Government and the Liberator.

The Government, however, dropped the seventeen counts against O'Connell which charged breach of the Common Law. On fourteen counts of violating the Proclamations O'Connell at first demurred, but the King's Bench allowed him to change his plea to not guilty.[19] The weeks went by without further action against O'Connell, and with the dissolution of Parliament in April 1831 the case against him expired. When the new Parliament opened, Stanley insisted that the Government had meant to press the case, but admitted that they considered passing a Reform Bill more important than imprisoning O'Connell.† His words did

* Some seventeen months later O'Connell said: 'The right honourable Gentleman should recollect, that he was Secretary for Ireland when common thief-takers were sent to his house to drag him from the bosom of his family — and the right honourable Gentleman should also remember that pains were taken to pack the Jury who had to try him.' *Hansard* (third series), XIII, 805.

† See: J. A. Roebuck, *History of the Whig Ministry of 1830 to the Passing of the Reform Bill* (London: John W. Parker & Son, 1852), II, 177. According to Roebuck, Stanley's remarks on this occasion gave the deepest offence to O'Connell.

not dispel the suspicion that the Government purposely let the case die in order to secure O'Connell's support in Parliament.

Thus, far from discouraging the Liberator, the abortive legal action had merely strengthened his position, and demonstrated the Government's need for his support. On the other hand, Stanley's position was considerably weakened, and he could not help feeling that the peace of Ireland had been sacrificed for the sake of British Reform.*

In 1831 Ireland was in the throes of one of its periodic food crises. The harvest of 1830 in general had been scanty, and the potato crop, on which the Irish poor relied, had partly failed. Famine conditions prevailed in two baronies of County Mayo, and severe food shortages were felt in Galway, Sligo and Clare. Crowded on tiny plots of endlessly subdivided estates, hungry and poverty-stricken, the Irish poor hardly needed O'Connell to tell them that widespread reforms were in order.

Like most statesmen of his generation, Stanley thought relief should come from private rather than public funds, and he was chary of promising in Parliament any programme of aid which might discourage private donations. But he did what he could to alleviate the distress.[20] The Government seems to have sent enough food to Ireland in the spring of 1831 to force hoarders to put their food stocks on the market, but this move was kept secret.[21] For the record Stanley announced that the Government would intervene to save life only when private charity was exhausted.[22]

Public works provided another means for Irish relief. Stanley, in June 1831, proposed that £500,000 in exchequer bills be loaned for public works, and that £50,000 be granted outright for distribution to districts which would match the Government aid.[23] O'Connell approved the grant, but felt it was too small. A commission to supervise the projects undertaken under the loan was attacked by some as a patronage device,[24] and the loan system itself was criticized. 'Ireland might as well obtain £500,000 from the Jews in the Minories,' one member observed, 'and could obtain it on as easy terms.'[25] Stanley's attempts to relieve the

* Before dissolution Stanley is quoted as saying: '. . . he would go out if they dissolved — he would no longer be responsible for Ireland'. Aspinall, *Three Diaries*, p. 80. (Lord Ellenborough, April 18th, 1831).

distress of the Irish poor thus did little to enhance his popularity.

A reform related to public works in Ireland was the Grand Jury Bill outlined by Stanley to the Commons in September 1831. Irish Grand Juries not only dealt with criminal matters, but decided upon, and taxed the people to pay for, public works. As these juries met for only brief periods, they lacked time to deal properly with the many important matters brought before them. Stanley therefore suggested that the Irish Magistrates screen the proposed projects before they were presented to the Jurors, that the Jurors deliberate upon public matters in open court, and that contracts for public works be given to the lowest bidders.[26] But many Irish members wanted to turn public works over to county boards elected by taxpayers, which Stanley opposed on grounds that politics would thereby become involved in the system. Nothing was done that year.

Stanley brought up the matter again in 1833, shortly before leaving Ireland. He still opposed elective boards at that time, but agreed that rate-paying farmers should be given some opportunity to express themselves regarding public works.[27] His plan met such a cool reception that he carried it no further. Undoubtedly his proposals would have improved the system then operating; they failed simply because the Irish section considered them too conservative.

The Irish Secretary was more successful in another of his reforms of 1831. Irish Magistrates were usually recommended for appointment by local politicians whom they supported, and they had a reputation for inefficiency. Stanley proposed to extend government control over them by appointing Lord Lieutenants to the Irish counties with power both to recommend and to supervise the work of the Magistrates.[28] O'Connell saw in this another patronage scheme, and declared that the Lord Lieutenants would be outside Roman Catholic influence.[29] But the 'Thirty Tyrants Bill', as he called it, was passed, and the Lord Lieutenants were duly appointed. While some of the appointments were criticized, the Whigs selected some Catholics and individuals opposed to the Government politically for the new positions.[30]

During 1831-32 much of Stanley's time was devoted to the immense problems of Reform both in England and Ireland.

While he was much more responsible for the terms of the latter than the former, Stanley's part in the passage of the great Reform Bill of 1832 cannot be overlooked. The principle which he applied to Reform in general is summed up in his statement: 'Sharing in the Government is not an abstract right which any man can claim, but at the same time it is a right which no Government can withhold from a man, except upon this principle, that the class to which he belongs is not capable of being trusted for the discreet exercise of such a right.'[31]

When he first learned of the terms of the English Reform Bill in 1831, he is said to have 'burst into an incredulous laugh'.[32] But Stanley recovered his composure and gave full support to the measure perhaps for two reasons. 'Seasonable concession,' he said on one occasion, 'is the only means by which you can either put down just or prevent unjust demands.'[33] At the same time he took comfort from the fact that this was to be a 'complete and final measure'.[34]

The story of the passing of the Reform Bill is too well known to need recounting here, and it remains only to state briefly Stanley's share in it. After the failure of the Reform Bill in 1831, Stanley was among those who sought to reach an understanding with the Tories on the subject for the coming session.[35] Stanley all through his career showed a willingness to reach secret understandings with the gentlemen of the Opposition if he thought the common good was thereby served. When Wellington came to power briefly in 1832 Stanley spoke violently against the partisanship of the King, but was willing to take a Reform measure from the Duke.[36] On the other hand, Stanley agreed with the peer-making plan as a last resort.*

Stanley's great services during the debates on the Reform Bill are attested to by almost all of the contemporary writers and diarists, and he should probably be considered to have outshone

* Stanley agreed to a moderate peer-making plan early in January 1832. Charles S. Parker, *Life and Letters of Sir James Graham 1792-1861* (London: John Murray, 1907), I, 134-5. (Stanley to Graham, January 2nd, 1832). He seems simply to have advised moderation. Lord Brougham, *The Life and Times of Henry Lord Brougham* (New York: Harper & Bros., 1872), III, 305. (Holland to Brougham, January 2nd, 1832). See also: S&F, *Greville*, II, 240. (*Diary*, January 24th, 1832). Stanley also supported the plan in his speeches. *Hansard* (third series), XI, 765. Like many other Whigs Stanley reasoned that the Crown held the balance between the two Houses and at times must coerce the Lords. This reasoning was based on the delusive assumption that the Crown was a free agent.

all his contemporaries during these bitterly-fought contests. He sometimes warned anti-Reform members they would lose their seats, and on one occasion he announced that a certain constituency had offered them their seat in order to oust their anti-Reform representative.[37] The reasonable nature of the bill also received stress, but on one occasion he almost upset his own case against the rotten boroughs. 'He would repeat his determination,' Stanley said, 'not to enter into the question whether it might or might not be expedient to preserve places for securing admission to the House of Commons of the Officers of the Crown without imposing upon them the necessity of courting a mob. . . .'[38] The speaker who followed him observed: 'The right hon. Gentleman's own case was a proof that nomination boroughs were not useless in this respect . . .'[39] Stanley's oratory was, of course, colourful. He called Croker's speech on the third reading of the 1831 measure the 'funeral oration over the dying efforts of the opposition'.[40] Whatever were his own misgivings about both measures, Stanley boldly described the measures of 1831 and 1832 by quoting Ovid: *Matre pulchra filia pulchrior!*[41]

Stanley spent so much time defending the English Reform measures that he was accused of neglecting Ireland.[42] While there were no 'Old Sarums' in Ireland, eighteen of the thirty-one boroughs with members in Parliament had less than a hundred electors, and the borough of Belfast was controlled completely by the Marquis of Donegal. Stanley's problem was to revise the Irish system so that it would be liberal enough to satisfy O'Connell, but still be conservative enough to reserve some political influence for the Irish Protestants. Eliminating the boroughs with small constituencies struck a blow at the latter.

Stanley discussed his Reform Bill in March and June of 1831, but the general political situation prevented action that year. In January 1832 he explained his measure at some length.[43] He offered Ireland five additional seats, four to the great boroughs and one to the University of Dublin, not because of her increased population, but because important 'borough interests' merited representation. In the counties he offered the vote to leaseholders with a beneficial interest of £20 and a lease of fourteen years, and £10 leaseholders with leases of sixty years. In county cities the vote went to the £10 freeholders, and in the boroughs to £10 householders. Stanley thus sought to keep the county electorate conservative and Protestant, while making some concessions to the Catholics by liberalizing the borough franchise.[44]

In Committee both Protestants and Catholics condemned the bill.* Lord Castlereagh said the bill would give Ireland to the Catholics, and allow O'Connell to hold the balance of power between the two parties.[45] O'Connell – who had seemed fairly well satisfied during the discussions in 1831 – demanded more seats for Ireland in view of her increased population, and demanded the vote for the 40s. freeholders who had lost it at the time of Emancipation. Stanley would not admit that seats should be granted on the basis of numbers, and declared the 40s. freeholders were subject to undue influence. The only concession he offered during the bitter debates was to extend the £10 freehold franchise to leaseholders with twenty-year leases who occupied their holdings.[46]

As presented to the Lords, the Irish Reform Bill gave the county vote to leaseholders of sixty years at £20 rent, of twenty years at £10 rent, and fourteen years at £20 rent, added to the old £50 annual value franchise. The county cities had the £10 freehold and leasehold franchises, and the boroughs the £10 household franchise. The Lords made a minor change in favour of the Protestants, but otherwise the bill stood. While the borough franchise was more favourable to the Catholics, the county franchise was limited to a select group of about 30,000 voters.

While the bill was condemned as being more conservative than the English, it opened the door to moderate gains by O'Connell. At the election of 1832 about eighty-two liberal members were returned for Ireland, forty-five of whom were pledged to repeal of the Union, and the rest supported considerable reforms, especially with regard to the Established Church.[47]

Of all the complicated questions with which Stanley had to deal the one most intimately associated with him was that of the Irish Church. Involved were two of Stanley's most strongly held ideals – Protestantism and private property, for he felt the fate

* Amid the conflict between O'Connell and Stanley over this bill, the Protestant opposition might be overlooked. Stanley was caught between two fires. The Earl of Roden's speech, which called Stanley's Protestantism into question, illustrates this point. See: *Hansard* (third series), XIV, 763-71. On the other hand, O'Connell called his measure a 'bill to restore Orange Ascendency in Ireland'. Ibid., XIII, 119-20.

of the Church of England, control of Ireland, and the rents and properties of landlords were united closely with the preservation of the Irish Church. Defending the Church also won him the affections of the 'No Popery' section of the British public, and he may have had some other motives also.*

One of the many questions centred around the Irish Church was the Vestry Act, which, among other things, taxed Catholics for the building and repair of Anglican churches. In 1830 Stanley had supported O'Connell's demand for a revision of this Act, and one of his first acts as Irish Secretary was to bring in a bill on the subject. But it did not satisfy O'Connell, and so he withdrew it.[48] In 1831 he also referred the question of the First Fruits to the Irish Law Officers, seeking a revaluation of Irish benefices to provide funds for building purposes, but the Officers decided such a valuation could not be made and the project fell through.[49]

Much more pressing was the Tithes question. An organization called the 'Hurlers' was formed in a Kilkenny parish to resist tithe payments, and a passive resistance movement spread to Carlow, Queen's County, Wicklow, Wexford, Tipperary, King's County, Longford and Westmeath during 1831. Because the resistance was largely passive, it was the more difficult to deal with, and in July 1831 some Irish clergy petitioned Parliament for aid in collecting their tithes.[50] Stanley replied he would receive suggestions on the subject, but had no plan to offer. Then James Gratton threw out the proposal that was eventually to carry Stanley out of the Whig Party — that some of the Church's income should go to the relief of the Irish poor.[51] Not long thereafter Stanley declared that Church property was beyond the reach of Parliament, and denied its right to divert Church property to purposes other than its own business.[52] O'Connell immediately replied: 'The Church Establishment was founded on Act of Parliament and could be altered by the same authority.'[53]

On December 15th, 1831, Stanley in a very able speech moved that a select committee be formed to consider the tithes question. His announcement was so timed that discussions would take place between the autumn and spring tithe collections. The committee

* During a debate in 1832 Sheil charged Stanley was 'chained to the Church by a golden link, which it would be preposterous to require of him to break'. *Hansard* (third series), XII, 592. Stanley replied the charge was unworthy of notice, and unfortunately Sheil did not elaborate on it.

was formed, but Stanley carefully excluded Catholics from it, a policy which tended to discredit the committee as an organ of conciliation. By early 1832 Stanley had drawn up and circulated among the Cabinet his Confidential Report on Tithes of 1832.

Before reforming the tithes system, Stanley was determined to force payment of outstanding tithes. So on March 13th he presented five resolutions to the Commons calling for recognition of the plight of the clergy due to the resistance to tithes, and for financial aid to them from the consolidated fund. He asked that the Government be empowered to levy the amount of arrears of tithes or tithes composition for the year 1831, and promised a revision of the system by a commutation in lieu of the tithes.[54]

On April 6th, 1832, Stanley moved the second reading of his Arrears of Tithes (Ireland) Bill. Acts of 1787, 1788 and 1799 provided some of the ideas for this measure. To avoid the difficulties of process serving, the bill provided that arrears notices could be posted on the doors of the Catholic chapels in defaulting areas, giving the defaulters a month to settle their accounts. Such settlements would be made with due consideration being given to the incomes of the individuals involved,* but, if no settlement was reached, the Government was empowered to use all means at its disposal to collect the tithes. Stanley maintained that the measure was not aimed at the Irish poor, but at affluent tenants who intentionally withheld their tithes.[55] In practice the measure fell short of being a success.†

Having made some provision for collecting the tithe arrears, Stanley introduced his Tithe Composition Bill of 1832 (Ireland) the following July. While Stanley used the phrase the 'total and entire extinction of tithes' in connection with the measure, this was obviously not its purpose. He called for an extension of the Tithe Composition Bill to make it permanent and compulsory. The value of the composition was to be determined every seven

* Irish tithes were still often paid in kind. Stanley estimated they amounted to about 1/15 of the rent of a holding. Compared with England where tithes were about 1/5 of the rent of a holding (which was, in turn, 1/5 of its produce), Irish tithes were not heavy, but they were placed on even tiny holdings. Ibid., XI, 146.

† O'Connell estimated that it cost the Government £15,000 to collect £12,000 worth of tithes the first year this bill was in operation. They evidently used units of the armed forces in some cases. Ibid., XVIII, 1075-7. Stanley, however, did not lose faith in coercion as a means of collecting the tithes, and blamed Althorp for stopping the process when it was on the point of succeeding. John Morley, *The Life of William Ewart Gladstone* (New York: The MacMillan Co., 1903), I, 133.

years on the basis of the average selling price of produce – a sort of 'sliding scale' for tithe compositions, and it was to be collected as part of the rent charge.[56]

While his plan never went beyond the above, he also outlined the process which would bring about the extinction of the tithes. The Bishop and beneficed clergy of each diocese were to form a corporation for receiving and distributing the tithes. These corporations would be encouraged to sell out their tithe rights to local landlords at the price of sixteen years' value. Money would be advanced to landlords who desired to make such purchases and thereby increase the value of their lands. With the money received from selling out their tithe rights the Church corporations would purchase lands whose rental value would replace the tithes.

Before introducing his bill Stanley sought to enlist Peel's support by sending him a copy of his confidential report on the subject.* But this, of course, did not influence the attitude of the Irish members, who were very testy. James Gratton denounced the bill; Sheil called it a mockery, and O'Connell took this occasion for a scathing review of Stanley's career in Ireland.[57] The Liberator correctly accused Stanley of playing 'with a loaded die' – for he had plenty of votes to pass the measure. In August it went to the Lords, where it was welcomed. In final form the bill made tithe compositions uniform, compulsory and permanent, and created commissions to create compositions on the basis of the annual value of the tithe over a seven-year period. In old leases the immediate lessor had to collect the tithe; but in future leases the landlords made the tithe part of their rent charge. Ireland united to keep the plan from working.[58]

In the final analysis Stanley's changes in the former Tithe Composition Act were not too important. But Stanley could not abolish the tithe because he considered it a species of private property. As he saw it, even if tithes were removed, the prices of produce would fall proportionally, or the slack would be taken

* Peel's marginal notes show he was not very enthusiastic over the plan. *Peel Papers*, BM 40403 (Stanley to Peel, April 22nd, 1832). In the confidential memorandum Stanley made a number of interesting points. He had high praise for the Tithe Composition Act, and identified the principal objectors to it as landowners whose parks and grazing lands, hitherto exempt from the tithe, came under the composition. He also noted that some landlords encouraged resistance to the tithe so that they might collect higher rents. Stanley thought the payment of the clergy should be put on the landlords, who owned 70 per cent of Ireland, rather than the occupiers.

up in higher rent. By turning the collections over to non-churchmen he hoped at once to placate the feelings of the Catholics who made the payments, and to save Anglican clergymen both embarrassment and trouble.

These tithe measures were but a preliminary to the reform of the Irish Church as a whole. As it was a government measure, the Church Temporalities (Ireland) Bill was introduced by Althorp, rather than Stanley, in February 1833.[59] Althorp estimated the annual income of the Irish Church as £800,000, but pointed out that 200 Irish benefices received less than £100. The problem involved providing supplements for the smaller livings, and raising funds for the building and repair of churches. The first had been hitherto provided for by the First Fruits Tax, which worked badly; the second by a variable tax known as the Church Cess, which was levied every Easter by the Protestant vestries and was much hated by the Catholics.

The Temporalities Bill proposed to substitute a graduated tax on Irish benefices ranging from 15 per cent on the larger livings down to 5 per cent on the smaller. It also proposed that the salaries of the great Irish bishops, beginning with the primate, the Bishop of Armagh, be reduced, and that all Deans and Chapters without duties should receive assignments or be abolished. The number of bishoprics was to be reduced by consolidation from twenty-two to ten. The savings thus made would permit the abolition of the Cess, while the graduated tax would provide a supplement for the smaller livings.

Various objections were raised to the measure. The Bishop of Armagh did not oppose the abolition of the Cess, but felt the consolidation was too drastic.[60] The Duke of Wellington claimed the bill violated the spirit of the Coronation Oath.[61] Sir Robert Peel felt the graduated system of taxes on church benefices was comparable to the Radical income tax. On the other hand, the Irish and Radicals first approved the measure, hoping that the surplus revenues of the Church might be devoted to secular purposes. O'Connell was quick to suggest that the surpluses should be devoted to Irish hospitals and asylums.[62]

As the bill went through committee, however, it became apparent the Government planned to use the surpluses to help the smaller benefices and for church and glebehouse building. Clause 147 was hotly contested. The bill permitted the bishops' tenants to secure perpetual instead of the former twenty-one year leases at a somewhat higher rent. This surplus over the old rent created by the change in the lease-law was a sort of 'unearned increment' resulting from the measure, and the Government at first planned to place it at the disposal of Parliament. But they later, much to O'Connell's disgust, abandoned the clause.

In the Lords a few changes were made. Greater latitude was given the Church Commission created by the Act to make decisions on the suppression of benefices and on church building. In its final form it had the support, if not uniformly enthusiastic, of the moderates of both parties, and a combination of Irish, Radicals and extreme Conservatives formed the minority on the third reading. Though it offered Ireland relief from the Cess, O'Connell observed at that time: 'He would record his vote against the third reading of the Bill, and he repudiated it on the part of the people of Ireland.'[63] Stanley, who had done much to fashion the measure and to secure its passage, viewed the result with lasting satisfaction, but it was apparent to everyone in the Cabinet that his views on reform by this time differed sharply from those of some other prominent members of the Government.

Still another reform was carried by Stanley during his term as Irish Secretary. When Spring Rice made a motion in September 1831 to grant £30,000 for Irish education, Stanley discussed the schools system there at some length.[64] The Kildare Street Society had been receiving annual grants from the Government which had gradually increased from £6000 to £25,000, and by 1830 they had set up 1620 schools with an enrolment of 133,896 pupils in Ireland. While the progress of the society was impressive, two-thirds of the benefits of the system went to Protestant Ulster.[65]

Stanley concluded that Catholics refused to attend these schools because they featured daily Bible readings, without interpretation or comment by the students. He proposed, therefore, to make the schools available to Catholics by separating the literary and religious instruction and by transferring control of them to a board composed of Protestants and Catholics. The new national schools, as Stanley planned them, were based on ideas drawn from the Kildare Street Society, from Dr. Doyle's Catholic School, and from reports of parliamentary commissions which had studied the question in 1812, 1824 and 1825.

O'Connell and the Catholics received his plan very favourably, but the reaction of some Protestants, especially the Presbyterians, was quite hostile. The Presbyterian Synod of Ulster sponsored a large petition against the National Education System which was presented to the Commons in March 1832. Their main point was that they considered the Bible the basis of education, and that their faith demanded that students use the whole Bible. Stanley tried to quiet their fears, but the Irish Reform Bill and the National Education System combined to make him unpopular in Ulster.

Nevertheless, early in 1832 a considerable number of schools petitioned to become part of the new system, and the plan got under way. A board of five Protestants and two Catholics was set up to screen the books used in the schools. Books used in mixed classes could contain moral subjects, uncontroversial sections of the Bible, and also illustrative material from Holy Writ. Protestant religious instruction was carried on either before the Catholic children arrived, or after they departed.[66] Stanley hoped that the period of joint instruction would impress the children with their similarities rather than their points of difference.[67]

Being a compromise, the system was never wholly satisfactory. At first it was opposed chiefly by the Presbyterians, but later the Irish Catholics lost their enthusiasm for the schools, which they thought dulled Irish nationalism. Nevertheless, the schools, with modifications, survived Stanley and educated, if they did not reconcile, Ireland.

Stanley's programme for Ireland was a combination of reform and force, of concession and coercion. In September 1831 he proposed a modification of the White Boy Acts,* 'every step of which,' according to O'Connell, 'has been trod in blood'.[68] Because the Protestant celebration of the battle of the Boyne in 1831 caused riots, Stanley introduced his Religious Processions Bill in 1832 in an attempt to prohibit religious demonstrations likely to cause ill feeling. But O'Connell, who had demanded the Government put a stop to such demonstrations back in 1831, on this occasion joined the Orange faction in voting against the bill.[69]

* These Acts fixed the death penalty for malicious injuries to property, sending threatening letters, and other normally lesser crimes. Breaking of outhouses, if done at night, was a capital offence; if done by day, only a misdemeanour. Stanley proposed transportation in lieu of the death penalty. *Hansard* (third series), VII, 487-8.

To avoid the charge that he was directing his bill primarily at the Orange group, Stanley did not press it until later in the session.

Stanley's concessions to Ireland, his Reform Bill, the abolition of the Cess, his National Education and relief projects, were always accompanied by an actual or implied threat of coercion. Just when he became convinced coercion was necessary in Ireland is not too clear. In 1829 he agreed to the assumption of extraordinary powers – which he would oppose as a permanent policy – by the Tory Government in dealing with Ireland, and only demanded that conciliation (Emancipation) should follow quickly. The order of these two is significant. Stanley demanded that the governmental authority be demonstrated before blessings were bestowed, for he conceived of government as a stern, though just and conciliatory father, whose *potestas* could not be questioned. His veering towards a 'high tone of government', especially in Ireland, together with his dislike of Radicalism and defence of the Anglican Church indicate that Stanley was moving away from the Whig position, which stressed civil and religious liberty, towards Toryism.* Stanley, however, insisted that he followed Whig tradition even after his break with the Grey Government.

Being a Protestant and an Irish landowner, Stanley might be expected to sympathize with the Irish Yeomanry, the Protestant militia which had aided the Government at the time of the Act of Union. In 1831 they composed a force of perhaps 27,000 poorly equipped men, who could be called out, as citizens rather than soldiers, to preserve the peace whenever the local magistrates saw fit. Though the Yeomanry contained many men of substance and high ideals, it could easily become an instrument for oppressing the Catholics. In February 1831 Stanley was chary about utilizing the militia. 'Matters are becoming critical,' he wrote, 'and the Yeomanry shd. be the last resource.'[70]

To what extent he was influenced by the Irish gentlemen, and even some Irish Members of Parliament who usually attacked him in the Commons,† is not clear, but evidently Stanley quickly

* This writer is indebted to M. G. Brock of Corpus Christi College for this analysis of Toryism.

† In explaining, not justifying, Stanley's conversion to coercion, it should be pointed out that many from the propertied classes of both faiths in Ireland were increasingly alarmed by the violence there. The case of Richard Lalor Sheil is in point. In February 1834, Althorp accused him of supporting the Coercion Bill in private and condemning it in public. Sheil indignantly denied the charge, and the

changed his mind regarding using the Yeomanry. Arms were furnished to them, and in June 1831 the Government asked for £19,290 to support them. While Stanley gave assurances in July that no arms would be issued thereafter, the promise was evidently not entirely kept.[71]

The same summer Stanley was guilty of a discrediting blunder in connection with the Arms (Ireland) Bill. This measure, which forbade keeping arms without a licence and made violations misdemeanours subject to fines, came up for renewal, and Stanley proposed to change the penalty clause to make violators in disturbed areas subject to seven years' transportation.[72] This Draconian proposal was particularly untimely because the Government had been arming the Protestant Yeomanry, and its reception was so hostile that Stanley reverted to the renewal of the original measure. Peel rightly chid him for his 'levity' in dealing with the problem.[73]

While Stanley consented to use the Yeomanry, he still hesitated to call for a bona fide coercion law. In March 1832, in rejecting the plea of some Irish Magistrates to renew the Insurrection Act, Stanley declared: 'If, indeed, any such measure was to be the chief instrument in putting down disturbances, the mischief attendant upon its adoption would be greater than the evil it was intended to remedy . . . Unless every other measure failed, he would not resort to the Insurrection Act.'[74] In May 1832 Stanley '. . . distinctly disavowed any intention whatever . . . of introducing the Insurrection Act into Ireland'.[75] But about the same time Stanley authorized Irish Magistrates in a circular letter to disperse Irish meetings and laid himself open to attack by O'Connell who demanded the right of people to gather peacefully for purposes of petition.[76]

By mid-1832 Stanley's relations with O'Connell had reached a crisis. In July the Irish leader announced he would personally bring up charges of impeachment against Stanley in the Reformed Parliament on grounds of his gross misconduct of Irish affairs.[77] Stanley, of course, was contemptuous of the threat, but his reply

exchange became so spirited that a duel seemed probable. Both, in fact, were temporarily taken into custody by the Sergeant-at-Arms. See: *Hansard* (third series), XXI, 119-26. The Le Marchant diary seems to support Althorp's case. See, in particular, Aspinall, *Three Diaries*, pp. 278-9, and pp. 313-14. If many Irish members were frightened at the condition of Irish affairs, Stanley could find considerable justification for strong measures.

indicated the direction of his thoughts. 'If the continued resistance of the people should render stronger measures necessary, he would then come to Parliament for additional powers to support the authority of the laws.'[78] The following month his old enemy, 'Orator' Hunt, collected 4913 signatures in Preston to a petition calling for Stanley's removal because of his Irish Reform Bill, his Registration of Arms Bill, and his Arrears of Tithes measure. Sheil introduced it into Parliament, and Stanley disdainfully insisted that it be printed.[79]

By the autumn of 1832 the Government was badly divided in its opinions regarding Ireland. Some, such as Russell and Durham, supported to some extent by Brougham,* favoured concessions to Ireland, including some adjustment of Church property, and opposed a coercion measure. Stanley would not hear of alienating Church property, and backed coercion. At times both Russell and Stanley were ready to quit the Government.[80] Anglesey, the Lord Lieutenant of Ireland, differed so widely from Stanley on Irish policy that the two avoided mentioning the subject to each other![81] Lord Grey leaned heavily on Stanley's advice,[82] and badly needed Stanley in the Commons. As one observer put it, Stanley had an intuitive knowledge of parliamentary tactics, and 'It has generally happened that, whenever the Ministerial side of the House was in any difficulty, it seemed to rely on the right hon. Secretary to get them out of it.'[83] Grey was able to prevent a major break in the ranks of the Government at the moment, and the victory went to Stanley.

This was apparent at the meeting of Parliament in February 1833 when the Government sought additional powers to deal with Ireland. Stanley said they would resist to the death any attempts to dissolve the Union, for that would lead to the dissolution of the British Empire.[84] Stanley took a very severe tongue-lashing during the debate on the Address, and he was much gratified when Peel unexpectedly sprang to his defence.† But, content with his

* When Stanley appeared in public life Brougham observed that at thirty he was by far the cleverest young man of the day, and that at sixty he would be the same. Morley, *Gladstone*, III, 160. See Macaulay's similar observation in: Trevelyan, *Macaulay*, II, 218. (*Diary*, February 3rd, 1849).

† *Hansard* (third series), XV, 370. Stanley expressed his thanks in a note 'for the handsome & flattering terms in which you were good enough to speak of me last night . . .' *Peel Papers*, BM 40403 (Stanley to Peel, February 8th, 1833). Althorp once defended Stanley against O'Connell, whom he said Stanley often worsted in

victory, Stanley's own speeches were quite conciliatory. 'He did not,' Stanley said on February 12th, 'and never had entertained any ill feeling towards any one of those who had crossed his path, or endeavoured to obstruct his measures.'[85] According to Le Marchant: '. . . the defence of himself was followed by the most tumultuous cheering I ever heard in the House . . . Even O'Connell touched his hat, bowed, and joined in the applause.'[86]

O'Connell, who privately had said the speech was '. . . the most bloody and brutal Speech ever delivered by a King – and it's Stanley's writing,' took his first opportunity to reply to Stanley's gesture. 'He begged the right hon. Gentleman to understand that he should deeply regret if any expression directed against the statesman should have, for a moment, sounded like want of courtesy to the Gentleman.'[87] This extraordinary exchange, which took place at the time the reform of the Irish Church was under discussion, may have been prompted by the knowledge that Stanley was about to leave Ireland, coming from him as a valedictory, and from O'Connell in relief in being rid of him.

On February 27th, 1833, the Coercion Bill, a sort of successor to the Insurrection Acts,* was introduced into the Commons. Althorp's introduction was spiritless and reflected his dislike of the bill. The impression was so bad that the bill was placed in jeopardy, and Sir James Graham and others prevailed on Stanley to speak, though he had not planned to do so until the next evening. The result was evidently one of the greatest speeches of the era.† Forty years later Lord John Russell retained a vivid

* The Insurrection Act was passed in 1807 and renewed yearly till 1811. It was revived in 1814 and passed at intervals thereafter. It empowered the Lord Lieutenant to proclaim districts outside ordinary law, suspending jury trial and making it an offence to be out of doors between sunset and sunrise.

† As the speech is quoted in *Hansard* in the third person, it is difficult to find representative quotations which would do it justice. For contemporary reactions to it see: Macaulay in *Hansard* (third series), XV, 1326. Lord Campbell in Hon. Mrs. Hardcastle, ed., *Life of John, Lord Campbell* (Jersey City: Frederick D. Linn & Co., 1881), II, 88. Lord Ellenborough in Aspinall, *Three Diaries*, p. 309; and Le Marchant in Ibid., p. 313. The remarks in the last source are particularly interesting. 'Had it been (Abercrombie said) the old House, I should have quietly walked home and put on my nightcap under the conviction that Stanley would in a few weeks be Prime Minister and remain so as long as he pleased, and that he would govern us on Tory principles, for the whole speech was imbued with the deepest spirit of Toryism.'

---

debate (*Hansard*, third series, XIX, 52-3), but his colleagues came to Stanley's defence but rarely and this probably intensified his gratitude at Peel's action. It may have been a very shrewd move on Peel's part.

impression of it. 'In the midst of the storm which his eloquence had raised,' he wrote, 'Stanley sat down, having achieved one of the greatest triumphs ever won in a popular assembly by the powers of oratory alone.'[88] Its effect was apparently overpowering – 'The cheers, or rather yells of the House,' wrote Ellenborough, 'were astounding.'[89]

The bill was much in need of eloquent defence. It empowered the Lord Lieutenant to prohibit and disperse meetings, to proclaim a district and to establish courts martial to replace civil courts in such a district. The military tribunals were directed to investigate disturbances by the terrorist Whitefoot organization, outrages, burglaries, houghing of cattle, and violations of property rights carried out by organized intimidation which made ordinary legal practices ineffective. In disaffected areas a curfew was to be enforced, and steps were taken to protect witnesses and to permit the searching of houses. Perhaps the most objectionable part of the measure did away with jury trial in some cases, and this part was apparently the work of Melbourne, who did not trust Irish juries to bring in honest verdicts, rather than Stanley.[90]

As might be expected the drastic measure was sharply contested by the Irish. Sheil, who may have been insincere, bitterly observed that Stanley 'trampled on the Irish with his English majorities'.[91] O'Connell, who considered it worse than the Insurrection Acts, called it 'a bill to collect tithes by the aid of Courts-martial'.[92] Stanley denied the Act would be used to collect tithes or rent, but admitted it would help protect the property of the Church.[93] There was again sharp work between O'Connell and Stanley, who, according to Hume, made 'every subject under discussion a personal matter between himself and the hon. and learned member for Dublin'.[94] By the time the bill was read for a third time on March 29th, Sheil admitted it had been modified and mitigated considerably,[95] so O'Connell's fight was not wholly fruitless.

Even before the Coercion Bill passed, Stanley had quit as Irish Secretary. All during 1832 there had been rumours of Cabinet changes,* but it was February 1833 before Stanley demanded flatly that he be released. About that time the fiery Lord Durham,

* In 1832 there was some discussion of sending Lord Althorp to the Lords, and in March Stanley was sounded regarding his taking the leadership in the Commons. Stanley was much against it, perhaps because of his unpopularity with many members in the Commons. See: Aspinall, *Three Diaries*, p. 211. (Le Marchant's Diary, March 10th, 1832).

alienated by the Irish policy, quit the Government and vacated the office of Privy Seal. After much persuasion both by the Government and the King, Lord Goderich, tearfully it is said, took the office of Privy Seal and left the Colonial Office for Stanley.[96]

Stanley observed Goderich's grief with concern, and on March 28th wrote him:[97]

> I did not like to speak to you yesterday upon the subject of the pending changes, which I know must between us be one of considerable delicacy. I cannot, however, refrain from writing to you, as the matter is definitely arranged, to tell you how deeply I feel, in common with our Colleagues, the obligations which we, & I more especially owe to you, for the great personal sacrifice which I am aware you have made to the convenience of the Government; and how sincerely I regret that any difficulties in which I might appear to be personally involved, should have been productive of any pain or annoyance to you.

Goderich replied that this had been the 'most painful sacrifice that I was ever called on to make', but promised to try not to 'cherish excited or angry feeling'.[98] Goderich (who became Lord Ripon) lived up to his word, and Stanley diplomatically consulted him on patronage and legislative matters. Just what were Stanley's 'difficulties' is not too clear, but it is certain he wanted the Colonial Office – just at that time!*

Waiting at the Colonial Office was a major question whose solution was certain to win renown for the man who solved it, and perhaps this helps explain Stanley's eagerness to return there. This question involved liberating the slaves of the British Empire, a step demanded by the quickening conscience of the western world and by the Abolitionist 'Saints' who represented that conscience in the Commons.

With the removal of much of the influence of the West Indian planters in Parliament by the destruction of the rotten boroughs, the Government in 1833 was in a better position to deal with the subject than before. Stanley opposed slavery for religious reasons, but, at the same time, the planters were part of the aristocracy,

* A note in Ellenborough's diary of March 30th, 1832, anticipated almost exactly these Cabinet changes of a year later. Ibid., p. 217. (Ellenborough's Diary, March 30th, 1832).

and the slaves were a species of property. He felt he could not honestly advocate emancipation without some form of compensation.[99] His thinking on the subject was apparently influenced by a number of British contemporaries,* and perhaps also by John C. Calhoun, who had once shown him how properly controlled slavery might be used as a civilizing stage between barbarism and civilization.[100]

To the consternation of James Stephen, legal counsellor for the Colonial Office, and occasionally to the detriment of efficiency, Stanley actually assumed active control of affairs at the Colonial Office.[101] His immediate task was to prepare the West Indies for the coming liberation. Jamaica had lately been the scene of a slave uprising, and this presaged ill for the tranquillity of the country once the news of the abolition debate reached there. Stanley ordered the Lords Commissioners of the Admiralty to dispatch a fast man-of-war to the West Indies with the warning '. . . on Tuesday the 14th of this month a discussion in Parliament will take place, the account of which, when received in Jamaica, is likely to produce great irritation and excitement'.[102] The naval forces were alerted, and a regiment of soldiers was sent to the island and housed in deserted plantations, mute evidence of the insurrection horrors.[103]

On May 14th Stanley introduced five resolutions into Parliament. They called for the emancipation of the slaves within a year's time, and a twelve-year apprenticeship thereafter during which their wages would be collected by the Government as

* Just how much of the final Emancipation Act should be attributed to Stanley is not clear. Stanley was a man who followed certain principles, but was not an original thinker, and thus utilized the ideas of others to accomplish his ends. If it cannot be proved that he originated the ideas of apprenticeship and compensation, he nevertheless made them a part of the bill and to that extent, it is Stanley's. Various writers vary widely on this question. Le Marchant wrote: 'Whatever merit may be found in the plan is due to Stanley, for the clerks in the office from Stephen downward . . . gave him no assistance . . .' Aspinall, *Three Diaries*, p. 329. But many writers assert that Stephen wrote the bill after Stanley confessed his inability to do so. See: Paul Knaplund, *James Stephen and the British Colonial System, 1813-1847* (Madison: University of Wisconsin Press, 1953), p. 98. Stanley himself acknowledged his debt to Canning in his approach. *Hansard* (third series), XVII, 1194-6. Another writer says that Graham helped Stanley draw up a 'safe' bill. H. W. C. Davis, *The Age of Grey and Peel* (Oxford: Clarendon Press, 1929), p. 242. On the other hand, Stanley differed considerably on the subject from Goderich and Howick. William L. Mathieson, *British Slavery and Its Abolition* (London: Longmans, Green & Co., 1926), pp. 229-40. It might be safest to conclude that Stanley drew up the resolutions, but that the bill itself was fashioned by Stephen.

reimbursement for a £15,000,000 'loan' granted the slaveholders in compensation. This apprenticeship was also to serve as a means of transition by which the slaves would gradually adapt themselves to freedom. Slave children under six years of age, not being economically valuable property, were to be freed without delay.

Neither the planters nor the Abolitionists liked the scheme, the former because they objected to abolition, the latter because they thought apprenticeship smacked of slavery and because the compensation seemed too high. During the next few weeks Stanley negotiated with the representatives of the planters, and on June 10th introduced a bill which made concessions to both sides. He increased the compensation to £20,000,000 as an outright gift to the planters (this had been necessary to secure their unanimous consent), and he reduced the apprenticeship to seven years. Under these conditions the slaves received their freedom on August 1st, 1834.

Many details remained to be ironed out. As the price and quality of slaves varied from island to island, the problem of distributing the compensation was quite involved, and by the terms of the Abolition of Slavery Act, special commissioners were appointed to cope with it.[104] To these officials Stanley referred the applications and inquiries which came to his office.

While Stanley desired to free the slaves, he was by no means a radical abolitionist. Over Stephen's objections he approved a franchise law for St. Kitts which was designed to exclude the ex-slaves from voting, and later he approved changes in the Jamaican law to strengthen the hand of the aristocracy there.[105] He also approved Stephen's policy for a White Australia.[106] Stanley also favoured preferential duties to help the West Indian planters, and was quite disappointed that the ex-slaves did not show gratitude for their emancipation by working hard.[107] The problem of a West Indian labour supply was to be with him again when he returned to the Colonial Office a number of years later.

Whether the West Indian plantations could have continued to prosper under a system of forced labour of rebellious slaves is a moot point. But it seemed at the time that their system was wrecked first by the Reform Bill of 1832, then Emancipation, and finally by Free Trade. Stanley saw the signs of changing times in these vicissitudes. An aristocratic society was being levelled — and by what? Apparently by the power of ideas translated into

Acts of Parliament. And he felt a little nervous even in 1833 that these hazy and indefinite forces might strike nearer home.

The business of the 1833 session had rested heavily on Stanley's shoulders. The Coercion Act, Church Temporalities, Abolition, these controversial matters had sapped his physical strength considerably, and, when Stanley took time off to pursue his favourite pastime on the Turf his many detractors found in such excursions evidences of irresponsibility. Autumn was later to be Stanley's season of danger, and late in 1833 he paid for these months of prolonged excitement with a period of illness. The attacks of that year were vaguely described as 'fainting fits', and were traced to his stomach, that organ that responds so irritably to continued nervous tension.[108]

In addition to the business of his office and the demands of party politics, Stanley had another problem to deal with—his own personality.* His was a positive personality which never left a negative impression on anyone. With members of his own class he was most agreeable, a welcome addition to any party or gathering, but those outside his set might as well have moved in another world for all they could associate with Stanley. Though a politician by choice, and because he enjoyed politics, Stanley could never muster that attractive, if frequently affected, intimacy of manner in dealing with people which was to become increasingly a part of the successful politician's repertory. Guided always by a sense of the fairness and rectitude of his own policies, Stanley depended on them rather than personal contacts to win the support of the rank and file. If Stanley could have retained his own intelligence and ability, and added to them Althorp's winning

* Stanley's unpopularity at this time was considerable, due largely to his arrogant disregard for the feelings of those of lower class or lesser ability. Lord Campbell found him 'very courteous and agreeable', and could not account for his unpopularity in Ireland 'till I saw the excessive *brusquerie* of his manner with strangers, and his carelessness about the opinion of others'. Hardcastle, *Campbell*, II, 87. Creevey thought Stanley would make an excellent Commons leader 'if he had only common sense and common manners'. Sir Herbert Maxwell, ed., *The Creevey Papers* (New York: E. P. Dutton & Co., 1904), p. 637. (Creevey to Ord, November 12th, 1834). Political opponents, of course, were even less favourable to him in their comments. In his own time these traits of personality cost him many supporters who otherwise would have accepted his lead, and his contemptuous treatment of the famous diarist, Charles Greville, who left many unflattering references to him in his diary, helped to undermine his reputation with later generations.

ways, he might well have been the outstanding political figure of the early Victorian era.

During 1833 and early 1834 the Grey Government was held together largely by Grey's ability to reconcile temporarily the clashing points of view in his Cabinet, and by the willingness of the reform element to make concessions to Stanley.* While favouring reform of the municipal corporations and of the discipline of the Church of England, Stanley by 1834 was ready to take a rest from reforming, and to let the country adjust itself to those reforms already accomplished. Though he considered himself liberal, Stanley had generally adopted a middle-of-the-road position, and a small group in the Government, chiefly Sir James Graham and Lord Ripon, supported his views. But another faction led by Lord John Russell, whose ancestral political legacy was to support the movement party, desired to promote further reforms. At Cabinet meetings Stanley was often at odds with his colleagues, and his support for a measure usually had to be purchased by a modification of any radical provisions in it.[109] Lord Grey realized that this situation could not last indefinitely, but his fondness for Stanley caused him to postpone a Cabinet reorganization.

The most immediate and pressing point of difference among the Cabinet members involved the revenues of the Irish Church. Stanley wholeheartedly supported the property rights of the Church, for, if her property could be alienated by act of Parliament, what could prevent later the alienation of the property of the Church of England, or, for that matter, of the landlords?† Russell, on the other hand, took a less legalistic view. He thought

* The division lists in *Hansard* indicate that the major personalities in the Government supported Stanley's measures quite faithfully. They voted together on the divisions on the Coercion Act, including the courts martial clause; in downing a motion that the Coercion Act should not be applied to tithe collections; on the removal of the 147th clause of the Church Temporalities Act, and on the section of the Slave Emancipation Bill which increased the compensation from £15,000,000 to £20,000,000. The incident mentioned in Greville (S&F, *Greville*, II, 397. *Diary*, July 18th, 1833) was apparently exceptional.

† Many years later Stanley (then Derby) wrote Disraeli: 'You know I have always entertained a very strong opinion, adverse to the Right of Parliament to alienate any part of the property of that [the Irish Church] or any other Corporation — and this was the main ground of our successful opposition to the Appropriation Clause . . . It seems to be generally assumed that this position is no longer tenable — but the moment you depart from it you will find yourself involved in inextricable difficulty.' *Disraeli Papers*, Derby XII. (Derby to Disraeli, March 3rd, 1868).

the income of the Irish Church was in excess of its need, and that, in justice to Ireland, it should be thoroughly investigated and any surplus discovered should be appropriated for secular purposes. Beyond his desire to protect private property, Stanley was motivated by his devotion to the Church, and perhaps by a half-formed plan to win the political support of moderates in both the Whig and Tory Parties. Russell perhaps also had a motive beyond his desires to do justice to Ireland and to aid the 'movement' party. While he liked and admired Stanley as a friend, he saw in him also his greatest competitor for the leadership of the Whig Party, and his own political future would be brighter with Stanley eliminated. The stage was thus set for the dramatic occurrences of May 6th, 1834.

The Government had advanced a large sum to the Irish Church in lieu of the tithes which had not been collected during the preceding three years, and they planned to force the Irish people to reimburse the Crown. Much to Stanley's disgust, the Government, fearful of losing Irish support, had not forced the payment of tithes,[110] and instead offered a new tithe measure designed to help the Government recoup its losses and to settle the problem for the future.

The night of May 6th the temper of the Irish section of the House was more than usually bad. Stanley smiled superiorly when Ronayne rose to speak, and the Celt commented acidly concerning Stanley's habit of propping his legs 'upon the table like a man in a North American Coffee-house'.[111] Disregarding the challenge, Stanley spoke so mildly that Peel later expressed disappointment at his attitude.[112] He refused to discuss the broader aspects of the measure, and promised, after certain changes were made, to support it.* Lord John Russell interpreted Stanley's speech to pledge the Government to maintain the revenues of the Church undiminished, and felt called upon to point out that Stanley did not speak for the whole party.[113] Though six months before he had decided a 'long and patient

* Russell later wrote that he could not locate the part of Stanley's speech that offended him in *Hansard*. Lord John Russell, *Recollections and Suggestions* (London: Longmans, Green & Co., 1875), p. 120. Nor have I found it, but there is Peel's expression of disappointment at Stanley's mildness (S&F, *Greville*, III, 34-5) to substantiate the interpretation that Stanley's speech was not one of his stronger pronouncements.

investigation' should be made before a diminution of the Church revenues should be recommended,[114] Russell expressed his own opinion that the revenues were larger than necessary, and cheers broke from the Irish section of the House. Some of those present did not fully grasp the implications of this exchange, but Stanley did, and hastily wrote a note to Graham: 'John Russell has upset the coach. We cannot go on after his declaration that "if ever a nation had a right to complain of any grievance, it is the people of Ireland of the Church of Ireland".'[115]

Russell's statement was not in itself sufficient cause for Stanley to resign from the Government, but the situation was immediately complicated by a motion of the Radical, Henry G. Ward, to pledge the Commons to a reduction of the revenues of the Irish Church. Such a question, if it came to debate, was bound to reveal the split in the Government. Whether this situation was arrived at through chance, or was brought about intentionally by certain Whigs to oust Stanley from the party is an interesting question. Palmerston believed that Durham was behind an intrigue against Stanley.[116] On the other hand, Stanley himself traced the situation to Lord Russell, whose 'violence & independence' upset the coach.* By this time Stanley's position in the Cabinet had become so uncomfortable that he was not very sorry to leave it, particularly on an issue which had considerable national appeal.†

* *Ripon Papers*, BM 40863. (Stanley to Ripon, November 20th, 1834). Stanley repeated this interpretation a quarter century later in a scathing review of Russell's career. *Hansard* (third series), CLIII, 1270. For some confirmation of his position see: Parker, *Graham*, I, 187; Spencer Walpole, *The Life of Lord John Russell* (London: Longmans, Green & Co., 1889), I, 200. It is possible that Russell, in making his remarks, sought to drive Stanley, his greatest competitor, from the Party.

† While the Ward Motion brought the Cabinet differences to a crisis, it seems probable that Stanley would have had to resign sooner or later anyway, for it was quite apparent he was out of place with the Whigs. The hostile Greville called him 'half a Tory' (S&F, *Greville*, II, 3[illegible]. *Diary*, June 26th, 1833), and many others shared this opinion. In a letter [illegible] March 1833, the prying Princess Lieven said the King believed 'That before [illegible] Mr. Stanley and Sir R. Peel will form a ministry. Stanley is the most Tory member of the actual Government — Peel the most moderate of the Tories.' Lionel G. Robinson, *Letters of Dorothea, Princess Lieven* (London: Longmans, Green & Co., 1902), pp. 336-7. Mrs. Arbuthnot wrote to Charles Arbuthnot in February 1833: '*Everybody* I find are turning their minds & their hopes to a junction of Brougham & Stanley with the Duke, & certainly I think it our best hope.' A. Aspinall, ed., *The Correspondence of Charles Arbuthnot* (Camden Third Series, Vol. LXV, 1941), p. 165. In drawing up a proposed 'Peel

At the Cabinet discussion of Ward's motion on May 7th, Stanley offered his resignation as a way out of the dilemma, but Grey threatened to retire if Stanley persisted in this course.[117] Brougham and some others urged that they avoid debate on Ward's motion by moving the previous question, and the Cabinet tentatively agreed on this tactic as a short-term solution of their problem.[118] But on May 25th another Cabinet meeting was held after the members had had a chance to study the likelihood of carrying the previous question, and Lord Holland and Ellice now doubted the possibility of success.[119] Lansdowne, Palmerston and some others, however, stood by the plan, and Stanley, who once again offered his resignation and expressed doubts about the scheme, was again persuaded to stay on.[120]

At the Palace on the afternoon of May 27th Stanley talked and joked with Russell and Melbourne in a manner which seemed to indicate a break had been averted,[121] but this exhibition of camaraderie had no political significance whatsoever, for it was a point of honour with Stanley not to allow political differences to interfere with his friendships. But by this time Grey had changed his position and explained to Stanley that certain Cabinet officers felt his resignation should be accepted.[122] Both Stanley and Graham, who supported Stanley during the whole crisis, agreed that this was the wisest course, and said as much in an interview with the King. The King agreed to accept their resignations if Lord Grey would consent to it.[123] Though he protested that he never advocated such a course, Grey finally acquiesced.[124]

News of the schism reached Althorp at the Commons while Ward was introducing his motion, and he immediately put through an adjournment, which allowed the Government six days to reorganize. Some of the Whig liberals were happy to be rid of Stanley and Graham; some other members of the party took the secession more seriously, but all, no doubt, expected that it would have taken place sooner or later.[125] Both his father and grandfather approved Stanley's course, and held that the seceders acted according to true Whig principles.[126] Once replacements were

Government' in March 1833, Lord Ellenborough placed Stanley at the Colonial Office! Aspinall, *Three Diaries*, p. 311. (Ellenborough Diary, March 4th, 1833). Thus it seems that observers of different party affiliations noticed Stanley's growing 'Toryism' and he could hardly have been unaware of it himself even though he occasionally insisted upon his attachment to the Whigs.

found, the Government disposed of Ward's motion rather easily.*

Confident that his course was both honourable and politically wise, Stanley felt a sense of relief that the crisis was passed. True, Russell obtained what he wanted – a field clear of major competition, but Stanley felt no resentment towards his friend. He, Stanley, was rid of O'Connell for one, and, though he still remained in the Whig Party, he had gained a new freedom of action. Perhaps he would not long be on the outside. Surely many of the Whigs would follow him for the sake of principle, and perhaps his moderate ideas might appeal to many of the Tories. With luck his faction might grow enough to be a third party. Let Russell have the Whig leadership – perhaps he had not won after all!

NOTES

[1] Maxwell, *Creevey*, p. 545. (Creevey to Ord, November 1st, 1829).

[2] T. A. Kebbel, *Life of the Earl of Derby* (London: W. H. Allen & Co., 1893), p. 18.

[3] Sir Herbert Taylor, *The Correspondence of the Late Earl Grey with His Majesty King William IV and with Sir Herbert Taylor* (London: John Murray, 1867), I, 32-3. (Grey to Taylor, December 22nd, 1830). (Taylor to Grey, December 23rd, 1830).

[4] Ibid., p. 20. (Taylor to Grey, December 10th, 1830); Ibid., p. 127. (Taylor to Grey, February 12th, 1831).

[5] Trevelyan, *Lord Grey*, p. 250.

[6] Robert Dunlop, *Daniel O'Connell and the Revival of National Life in Ireland* (New York: G. P. Putman's Sons, 1900), p. 246.

[7] Ibid., p. 247. (O'Connell to N. Bennett, undated).

[8] Ibid., p. 245.

[9] *Hansard* (third series), V, 1129; Ibid., XIII, 563.

[10] Ibid., V, 1122-4.

[11] Ibid., XIII, 780.

[12] Hon. Mrs. Hardcastle, *Life of John, Lord Campbell* (Jersey City: Frederick D. Linn & Co., 1881), II, 87.

[13] *HOP* 100/236. (Stanley to Melbourne, February 25th, 1831).

[14] Ibid. (Stanley to Melbourne, February 25th, 183[illegible] [illegible]anders, *Melbourne*, pp. 173-5. (Melbourne to Stanley, January 13th, 183[illegible]

[15] *HOP* 100/236. (Stanley to Melbourne, Jan[illegible] [illegible]th, 1831).

[16] *Hansard* (third series), II, 490-1.

[17] Ibid.

[18] Ibid., pp. 1006-20.

* Althorp proposed that a lay commission be appointed to study the Church revenues, and requested that Ward drop his motion. Ward persevered in it and was beaten 120-396. *Hansard* (third series), XXIV, 11-86. While Greville says the defeat came as a surprise, Palmerston, for one, had been confident all along that Ward could be beaten. See: S&F, *Greville*, III, 44 (*Diary*, June 3rd, 1834) and Evelyn Ashley, *The Life and Correspondence of Viscount Palmerston* (London: Richard Bentley & Son, 1879), I, 305. (Palmerston to Temple, June 27th, 1834).

[19] *HOP* 100/236. (Stanley to Melbourne, February 2nd, 1831). (Anglesey to Stanley, February 5th, 1831).

[20] *Hansard* (third series), IV, 802.

[21] Ibid., pp. 223-7.

[22] Ibid., p. 802.

[23] Ibid., pp. 573-4.

[24] Ibid., V, 257-9.

[25] Ibid., VI, 46.

[26] Ibid., VII, 837-45.

[27] Ibid., XV, 955-64.

[28] Ibid., VI, 22.

[29] Ibid., pp. 334-7.

[30] Ibid., VIII, 142-5.

[31] *Speech of E. G. Stanley at Lancaster Castle on his Nomination as a Candidate of the Northern Division of Lancashire* (Manchester: C. Wheeler & Son, 1832).

[32] Lord Broughton, *Lord Broughton, Recollections of a Long Life* (New York: Harper & Bros., 1872), IV, 93.

[33] *Hansard* (third series), IX, 55.

[34] Ibid., XV, 244.

[35] Lytton Strachey and Roger Fulford, *The Greville Memoirs* (London: The MacMillan Co., 1938), II, 214 *et seq.* (*Diary*, November 19th and 28th, 1831). (Hereinafter cited as 'S&F, Greville').

[36] A. Aspinall, ed., *Three Early Nineteenth Century Diaries* (London: Williams & Norgate, 1952), p. 251 and footnote 3; Parker, *Graham*, I, 143.

[37] *Hansard* (third series), III, 1648.

[38] Ibid., V, 618.

[39] Ibid., p. 620.

[40] Ibid., VII, 359-67.

[41] Ibid., IX, 519.

[42] Ibid., V, 1040-1.

[43] Ibid., IX, 595-606.

[44] Ibid., p. 623; Ibid., XIII, 119-25.

[45] Ibid., pp. 125-37.

[46] Ibid., pp. 1010-15.

[47] G. Shaw Lefevre, *Peel and O'Connell* (London: Kegan Paul, Trench & Co., 1887), pp. 132-3.

[48] Ibid., III, 486; Ibid., VI, 768-9.

[49] Ibid., III, 413, 429; Ibid., VII, 292.

[50] Ibid., IV, 1092.

[51] Ibid., p. 1095.

[52] Ibid., VI, 949.

[53] Ibid.

[54] Ibid., X, 136-55.

[55] Ibid., XII, 579-83.

[56] Ibid., XIV, 95-112.

[57] Ibid., pp. 117-38, 360-74.

[58] J. A. Roebuck, *History of the Whig Ministry of 1830 to the Passing of the Reform Bill* (London: John W. Parker & Son, 1852), II, 379-81, 420; *Hansard* (third series), XIX, 47-8.

[59] Ibid., XV, 561-77.

[60] Ibid., XIX, 550-1, 749-50.

[61] Ibid., p. 552.

[62] Ibid., XV, 577-8.

[63] *Hansard* (third series), XVIII, 1075-7.
[64] Ibid., VI, 1249-61.
[65] Ibid.
[66] Ibid., XIII, 405.
[67] Ibid., CXIX, 1136.
[68] Ibid., XIII, 266; Ibid., VII, 487-8.
[69] Ibid., IV, 802; Ibid., XIII, 1037-8.
[70] *HOP* 100/236. (Stanley to Melbourne, February 25th, 1831).
[71] *Hansard* (third series), IV, 388; Ibid., V, 1183-4, 1194-5.
[72] Ibid., IV, 618, 976.
[73] Ibid., VII, 581-3.
[74] Ibid., XI, 247-50.
[75] Ibid., XIII, 272-3.
[76] Ibid., XIV, 547-54.
[77] Ibid., p. 547.
[78] Ibid., p. 554.
[79] Ibid., pp. 1084-8.
[80] Russell, *Early Correspondence*, II, 35-6. (Holland to Russell, October 26th, 1832); Parker, *Graham*, I, 180. (Graham to Stanley, November 18th, 1832); Ibid., pp. 175-9. (Grey to Graham, November 3rd, 1832). (Graham to Stanley, November 3rd, 1832). (Graham to Stanley, November 18th, 1832).
[81] Maxwell, *Creevey*, p. 607. (Creevey to Ord, November 3rd, 1833).
[82] Lord Brougham, *The Life and Times of Henry Lord Brougham* (New York: Harper & Bros., 1872), III, 165, 178. (Grey to Brougham, December 4th, 1832). (Grey to Brougham, January 1st, 1833).
[83] *Hansard* (third series), XXI, 185.
[84] Ibid., XV, 184.
[85] Ibid., pp. 607-14.
[86] Aspinall, *Three Diaries*, p. 300.
[87] Ibid., p. 296. (Littleton's Diary, February 5th, 1833); *Hansard* (third series), XV, 877-8.
[88] Lord John Russell, *Recollections and Suggestions* (London: Longmans, Green & Co., 1875), p. 113.
[89] Aspinall, *Three Diaries*, p. 309. (Ellenborough's Diary, February 28th, 1833).
[90] Sanders, *Melbourne*, pp. 188-9. (Melbourne to Stanley, December 20th, 1832).
[91] *Hansard* (third series), XV, 1311.
[92] Ibid., XVI, 750.
[93] Ibid., pp. 607-8.
[94] Ibid., p. 624. See also: John C. Fitzpatrick, *The Autobiography of Martin Van Buren* (Washington: Government Printing Office, 1920), II, 475-6. In *Annual Report of the American Historical Association for the Year 1918*, II.
[95] *Hansard* (third series), XVI, 773.
[96] S&F, *Greville*, II, 366-7. (*Diary*, March 29th, 1833); Brougham, *Life*, III, 255.
[97] *RP*, BM 40863. (Stanley to Goderich, March 28th, 1833).
[98] Ibid. (Goderich to Stanley, March 28th, 1833).
[99] *Hansard* (third series), XVIII, 539.
[100] Stanley, *Journal*, pp. 286-8.
[101] Paul Knaplund, *James Stephen and the British Colonial System* (Madison: University of Wisconsin Press, 1953), pp. 30, 107.
[102] *COP*, CO 138/55. (Lefevre to Barrow, May 10th, 1833).
[103] Ibid. (Lefevre to Stewart, June 8th, 1833).
[104] Ibid. (Stanley to St. Vincent, June 29th, 1833). (Lefevre to Little, December 24th, 1833).

[105] Knaplund, *Stephen*, pp. 118 (and footnote 50), 122.
[106] Ibid., p. 25 (and footnote 42).
[107] *Hansard* (third series), XI, 949-52; Ibid., XIX, 1202.
[108] Maxwell, *Creevey*, p. 611. (Sefton to Creevey, November 26th, 1833).
[109] Aspinall, *Three Diaries*, p. 350. (Littleton's Diary, July 21st, 1833); S&F, *Greville*, II, 383. (*Diary*, June 26th, 1833).
[110] John Morley, *The Life of William Ewart Gladstone* (London: Macmillan & Co., 1903), I, 133.
[111] *Hansard* (third series), XXIII, 623-4.
[112] S&F, *Greville*, III, 34-5. (*Diary*, May 12th, 1833).
[113] Russell, *Recollections*, p. 120.
[114] Spencer Walpole, *The Life of Lord John Russell* (London: Longmans, Green & Co., 1889), I, 197.
[115] Parker, *Graham*, I, facing p. 187.
[116] Sidney L. Bulwer, *The Life of Henry John Temple, Viscount Palmerston* (Philadelphia: J. B. Lippincott & Co., 1871), II, 176. (Palmerston to William Temple, June 27th, 1834).
[117] Maxwell, *Creevey*, p. 617. (Creevey to Ord, May 8th, 1834).
[118] S&F, *Greville*, III, 43. (*Diary*, June 2nd, 1834).
[119] Parker, *Graham*, I, 190. (*Graham's Minute*, May 27th, 1834); S&F, *Greville*, III, 39. (*Diary*, May 27th, 1834).
[120] Ibid.
[121] Walpole, *Russell*, I, 201.
[122] Parker, *Graham*, I, 190-2. (*Graham's Minute*, May 27th, 1833).
[123] Ibid.; Aspinall, *Three Diaries*, pp. 378-80.
[124] Parker, *Graham*, I, 190-2. (*Graham's Minute*, May 27th, 1833).
[125] S&F, *Greville*, I, 189. (*Diary*, June 1st, 1834); *The Wellesley Papers* (London: Herbert Jenkins, 1914), II, 239. (Brougham to Wellesley, May 1834); Bulwer, *Palmerston*, II, 176. (Palmerston to William Temple, June 27th, 1834); Brougham, *Life*, III, 248-9. (Brougham to Grey, May 25th, 1834).
[126] Parker, *Graham*, I, 195-6. (Lord Stanley to Graham, June 1st, 1834). (Graham to Lord Stanley, June 4th, 1834).

CHAPTER III

THE DILLY STOPS AT THE CARLTON

LOOKING around him towards the end of May 1834, Stanley weighed the strength of his forces, and the result was not unimpressive. Among his cohorts, and certainly the most important, was the quietly efficient, reserved, Sir James Graham, who had served with distinction at the Admiralty, a man of proven worth and ability, and of all, Stanley felt, the one most devoted to him personally. He was Stanley's *alter ego*, perhaps the only statesman, apart from Malmesbury, whom he met later, in whom Stanley had implicit confidence. In the House of Commons, as well as in party administration, Graham was an invaluable ally. In the Upper House was Lord Ripon, a man of fading influence, but nevertheless, because of his background, a statesman of distinction. That he had accepted without rancour his removal from the Colonial Office was the acid test of his loyalty and attachment. The Duke of Richmond, who had once been a Tory, had shown his adhesion to Stanley's political ideas by giving up his position as Postmaster General, and he was not an unimportant figure in the House of Lords. In addition to the seceders from the Grey Government, there were some others, Gally Knight, Stratford Canning, Sir Matthew Ridley and Lord George Bentinck,[1] whose support could be expected. Of these, Bentinck was the most interesting, a rather violent, unpredictable gentleman with a passion for the Turf, but one who had politically powerful friends and important social connections. Though Stanley did not realize the fact in 1834, he was later to form a government with less political material at his disposal.

At the same time, Stanley took stock of himself. Looking in the mirror he saw an attractive man in the prime of life, with brown wavy hair, a firm chin and full lips, and his mother's aquiline nose. It was an aristocrat's face, the image people conjure up in their minds when they think of nobility, and its only fault was its youthfulness. This priceless gift was, and was to be,*

* Disraeli wrote years later: 'Ld. Derby looks very thin & pale, but I think improved — he looks so very young.' *Disraeli Papers*, VII. (Disraeli to Wife, December 12th, 1853).

a source of mild annoyance to Stanley, for it caused people to think of him in terms of the future rather than the present. But both his looks and family position were distinctly in his favour, and by this time that winded feeling no longer interfered with his speaking in the Commons. No one there, indeed, could match his agility of mind, grace and ease of delivery, for, at thirty-five, Stanley emerged as one of the greatest orators in British history.* Stanley realized that his many strengths were spoiled in the eyes of some by the casual attitude he affected towards politics. Yet to change was impossible, for it was not meet for one of his station, constantly in association with social inferiors, to wear his deeper feelings on display, and to become intimate with the rank and file would be to deny the aristocratic principle for which he stood. Besides, his illustrious background was one of his major claims to leadership, and tradition demanded that he be an aristocrat first, an individual second, and third, a party man.

Stanley was somewhat amused at the compliment paid him by the Tories, who, at the time of his resignation, proclaimed the dissolution of the Government.[2] But he had no desire to see this, for it was much better to keep Grey, who agreed with him on Irish affairs,[3] at the head of the Government while the Tithes and Coercion measures were pending. Nevertheless, it appeared expedient to aid the Tories against the Government in the solution of these matters for the Whigs were under Irish influence. Sir

* There is a mass of evidence to support this conclusion. Lord Aberdeen, whose memory spanned many decades, remarked that Stanley, at his best, excelled orators such as Fox, Pitt, Grenville and Whitbread. G. B. Smith, *Prime Ministers*, pp. 202-3. The great American orator, Daniel Webster, visiting the Commons in 1839, wrote that Stanley made the best speech he had ever heard, and this in the day of great American orators! George Ticknor Curtis, *Life of Daniel Webster* (New York: . Appleton & Co., 1870), II, 10. (Webster to Davis, June 24th, 1839). The Duke of Argyll, who opposed Stanley politically, wrote in 1841 that Stanley was the only orator in either House of Parliament at that time. Duchess of Argyll, ed., *Duke of Argyll Autobiography and Memoirs* (London: John Murray, 1906), I, 157. Lord Campbell, a liberal, wrote: 'Stanley is a host in himself. He has marvellous acuteness of intellect and consummate power in debate. There is no subject which he cannot master thoroughly and lucidly explain. His voice and manner are so good that no one can hear him without listening to him.' Hardcastle, *Campbell*, II, 324. See also: Sir Francis Hastings Doyle, *Reminiscences and Opinions* (New York: D. Appleton & Co., 1887), pp. 171-2; J. A. Roebuck, *History of the Whig Ministry of 1830 to the Passing of the Reform Bill* (London: John W. Parker & Son, 1852), pp. 359-60. The second of these was very hostile towards Stanley, but nevertheless admitted his great powers. Stanley's supporters, of course, had an even higher opinion of his speaking ability.

James Graham was most anxious to adopt such a course, and he acted as the go-between for Stanley and Peel in their co-operation.[4] When the governmental forces met on June 2nd, Stanley indicated displeasure with their attitude towards Irish affairs by staying away from the meeting.[5]

Early in July, Littleton, the Irish Secretary, introduced into the Commons some new resolutions regarding the tithes which threatened the income of the Irish Church. Meeting on July 3rd, Graham and Peel decided that Stanley should attack the resolutions as subverting the original principles of the Tithes Bill, and a battle would be waged to preserve the bill in its original form.[6] Had Stanley needed any further prodding, it was given him by O'Reilly's speech, just preceding his own, calling for the total abolition of the tithes.[7] In unusually fine form, Stanley dropped a bombshell on the Commons with his famous 'Thimblerig', or, in American terms, 'shell-game', speech in which he compared Ministers to the sharpers at race tracks and county fairs, and accused them of seeking to plunder the Church.[8] Grey especially was offended by this implied charge of dishonesty, and he forgave Stanley only after receiving a penitential letter which reaffirmed the allegiance of his former Colonial Secretary.[9] In spite of his attacks on the resolutions, however, Stanley wanted a tithe bill, and wrote lengthy and specific instructions to Ripon for amending the measure in the Lords.[10] Their Lordships, however, voted it down, and the tithe question remained unsettled.

Hard on the heels of the Thimblerig incident, Lord Grey resigned, worn out by the conflicts and dissensions in his Government, and the task of dealing with his more radical colleagues. The King called in Lord Melbourne and revealed his conservative leanings by suggesting that the new Prime Minister seek a coalition with Wellington, Peel and Stanley.[11] Though it was a highly doubtful procedure, Melbourne contacted them, and received refusals, though Stanley reaffirmed his adherence to Lord Grey and his principles.[12] At this time Stanley learned from an authoritative source that Peel and Wellington were very favourable towards him personally, and that Peel was ready to take office without requesting a dissolution.[13] On July 10th Melbourne, while expressing a warm affection for Stanley, advised the King that the proposed coalition was impossible, and the old Government, save for Grey, continued in office.

So long as the Government of which he had been a part remained in office, Stanley hesitated to launch a vigorous third-party movement, but his friend, Sir James Graham, was very active in this cause. Late in September he wrote that Melbourne was anxious to retain their friendship, but was unwilling to reach a definite understanding with them; and Stanley, in reply, criticized Melbourne's obsequious attitude towards O'Connell.[14]

In November, however, their position changed suddenly. When Lord Althorp, the leader in the Commons, succeeded to a peerage, another reorganization of the Government was necessary. Lord John Russell appeared to be the logical successor to Althorp, but his appointment would seem to presage a swing towards more radical policies. Neither the King nor Melbourne desired such a shift, and the latter was relieved of his problem in November when the King suddenly decided that the Government was too weak to continue. As Palmerston put it, they were '. . . all out; turned out neck and crop'.[15] For the moment, thanks to the King, conservatism had triumphed, and Stanley wondered if the King might not all along have been carrying on an intrigue with the Tories in hope of restoring them to power.[16] Such speculation, however, was pointless. Why waste time when Fortune suddenly seemed to wear a new and promising smile?

In October 1834, the 12th Earl of Derby p[illegible]sed away, and thus did not live to see the denouement of the ser[illegible] of events which was pushing his grandson ever further from [illegible] party of his forefathers. Stanley – now called Lord Stanley [illegible]was saddened by the event. His mother, Elizabeth Farren, and [illegible]w the little Earl, the people who had influenced him most de[illegible] were all gone, and his father was in uncertain health. The ev[illegible]brought him even closer to the Church, and he drew a solace [illegible]n that source possible only for those who both by instinct and c[illegible]e are anchored in the bed rock of revealed religion. In spite [illegible] the demise of the Whig patriarch, politics went on as usual.

The news of Melbourne's dismissal caused Stanley to survey the political situation carefully. In spite of his Whig's dislike for arbitrary monarchy, Stanley was rather glad that the King had refused to accept Russell's elevation, and saw some justification for it because Russell had 'upset the coach'.[17] Writing to Ripon, he predicted that Peel would aid 'the Beau' (as he called Wellington) in forming a government which would bid for popularity with a reform programme.* His own group, Stanley felt, should refuse to join any government of which Wellington, whom they had often attacked, was a part, but they should give the Tories an opportunity to introduce a programme. After writing Ripon, Stanley felt troubled. Perhaps he had put it a little strongly in condemning the Tories for carrying reform measures 'in defiance of their own principles'. Following such reasoning to its logical conclusion would mean the Tories would be unable to introduce any measure, for almost any measure meant change, and the Tories were opposed to change. Did it follow, then, that the numerous Tory Party could not, under any circumstances, carry on the Government? Such a conclusion certainly was not logical, and it was quite confusing. So many terms which he understood so well in 1830, now seemed a little hazy. He was a liberal, but what was a liberal? So was Johnny Russell a liberal, and yet they were drifting further and further apart. If he found it impossible to define liberalism, how was it possible for him to decide what was or was not honourable for the Conservatives?

On November 21st came a letter from Graham, who seemed convinced that he, Stanley, might form a liberal government. Richmond had been contacted on the project, and had shown himself favourable to it, but he suggested that all who might support such a scheme should declare themselves without delay.[18] The immediate problem for the seceders, however, was not to form a government but to formulate a policy towards the Tories and especially towards an offer of coalition from them. The three, Stanley, Graham and Richmond met together late in Novembe[r] and decided to adopt Stanley's plan to remain aloof from an[y] government wherein the Duke of Wellington sat. At the same tim[e] they put the third party on a firmer ideological basis by adoptin[g] a party platform, which they called the 'Knowsley Creed'. Th[e] two main planks therein were Church and municipal reform.[†]

* Stanley wrote: '. . . thus a good set of measures may be carried without i[n]creasing my confidence in, or good opinion of men who carry them in defiance [of] their own principles'. *Ripon Papers*, BM 40863. (Stanley to Ripon, November 20th, 1834).

† The same two subjects, Church and municipal reform, were the heart of Peel's platform, the *Tamworth Manifesto*. Parker, *Graham*, I, 219. (Graham to Ripon, December 23rd, 1834). See also: Ibid., pp. 227-8. (Graham to Stanley, January 12th, 1835).

Having thus set their house in order, the members of the third party began a period of watchful waiting.

The Duke of Wellington had meanwhile passed on to the sturdy shoulders of the brilliant Peel the onerous task of heading a Tory government, with the advice that Peel try, if possible, to secure the aid of Stanley's group.[19] Acting on the suggestion, Peel wrote Stanley an earnest letter in which he stressed the similarities of their political ideologies, and offered to thresh out any points at a personal meeting.[20] Stanley's refusal was both prompt and polite. The third party could not join a government which bore the impress of Wellington's name and principles, and it would not be politically wise for them to join the party they had opposed so long. Stanley hoped this would soften the refusal, and throw 'it more on his own crew'.[21] He also promised to give his independent support to Peel in a 'temperate improvement' of national institutions.[22] Graham, who apparently hoped to absorb Peel into their third party, did his best to dispel any impression that the Stanleyites were hostile towards him.[23] But Peel was bitterly disappointed, and suspected that Stanley's refusal to join him might have been partly based on his own desire to form a government.[24]

Peel's Government obviously could not carry on in the Commons as then composed, so there was a dissolution, and January 1835 brought a canvass by all parties. Realizing that their political influence depended on creating a Stanleyite bloc which would hold the balance of power between Whigs and Tories, the third party put up candidates wherever possible. Stanley harangued his constituents of North Lancashire, but their response defied analysis. Applause greeted his declaration of allegiance to the Whig Party; cheers followed his characterization of Peel as 'frank, open and manly'; and his assertion that Peel's Government did not inspire the confidence of men of liberal opinions was likewise greeted with enthusiasm.[25] About all that he could be sure of was that he personally had their confidence.

Campaigning in Cumberland, Graham was chagrined to discover it was necessary to play down his connection with Stanley in order to win the approval of the voters there.* In some other

* Graham wrote an explanatory letter on the subject, to which Stanley replied: 'It is clear that I am not a popular character on a Cumberland hustings, and that you have to deal with a much more Radical constituency than I have.' Parker, *Graham*, I, 228-31. (Stanley to Graham, January 21st, 1835). See: A. B. Erickson, *The Public Career of Sir James Graham* (Oxford: Basil Blackwell, 1952), p. 122.

places also the augury for the Stanley party was not favourable. Lord George Bentinck found it difficult to secure a Stanleyite candidate for Lynn, where the patronage of the Duke of Richmond offered the prospect of a seat.* As it turned out, the third party suffered an election setback, for, though the Whigs lost some seats and the Tories gained, the Stanley party did not hold the balance of power.

In January 1835, the middle of the political road, down which Stanley hoped to lead a coalition of moderate reformers, was rather crowded. Peel was there ahead of him, and Whig leaders, such as Melbourne and Grey, hoped to dislodge Peel from the position. The question was – who would lead the parade, Peel, Melbourne or Stanley? Ideologically, little separated these men, but party lines prevented a coalition, save between Melbourne and Stanley. Stanley's identification of himself as a Whig during the campaign seemed to confirm an impression he gave on numerous occasions – that, once the question of the Irish Church was solved, he meant to rejoin the Whigs.[26] Grey wanted him back, and Palmerston did not see how he could abandon family tradition and transplant 'himself into the Tory nursery'.[27] Melbourne, who disliked both the radical Whigs and the Irish, hoped to secure Stanley in a moderate government.[28]

The Irish Church did, indeed, stand between Stanley and a return to the Whigs, but so also did Russell's tactic of winning Irish and Radical support, which would further alienate Stanley, secure his own political future, and insure a majority in the Commons. And so it was, as the time for Parliament drew near, the political skies were overcast with clouds of doubt, the rooms of Brooks's and the Carlton Club alike were filled with speculation. The only thing certain in the situation was that Peel would lead his inadequate forces into an ambush.

The prelude to Peel's 'Hundred Days' was an Opposition plot to vote down the Conservative candidate for the Speakership, Manners Sutton, in favour of their own candidate, Abercromby. Stanley was fully informed of the manœuvre, and had already decided by late January to support Peel's candidate.[29] If the Opposition sought to oust Peel, he felt they should try a vote of

* S&F, *Greville*, III, 126-7. (*Diary*, December 24th, 1834). Stanley's elder son was later to represent the Lynn constituency for many years.

no confidence, and not attack an individual whose reputation might thereby suffer. While this Whig tactic annoyed him, disturbing also were the Tory efforts to detach Graham from the third party. The Governor-Generalship of India was offered to Graham, and the Tories were also ready to support him for the Speakership, thereby hoping to fuse the Stanley faction into the Tory Party.[30] Graham, however, waived these chances for advancement for the good of the third party, and Stanley, more than ever, felt confident of his friend's loyalty.

The cold, closing days of January brought to Stanley a letter in a familiar hand. It was from Lord John, who was cautiously exploring the possibility of securing his aid in disposing of Sutton. Busy little Johnny! Regardless of the past, or, for that matter, what might lie ahead of them, Stanley felt that he would always trust Russell's sense of honour to keep any confidences. Taking a pen, he scribbled:[31]

> I am sorry to find that we are likely to be at issue on the very first day of the meeting of Parliament, for though you say you do not expect me to tell you what line I mean to take, I think it only fair to say that I cannot support Abercromby, whose nomination, indeed, has a good deal surprised me. What may be the case to be made against Manners Sutton I have no means of knowing. . . .

The Whigs, then, could go on or give up the project, as it pleased them, without his aid. They were now quite aware of his own sentiments in the matter.

As he had predicted, Stanley and Russell were at odds when Parliament met on February 19th. Speaking at some length, Stanley did his best to get Peel past the initial obstacle by condemning the plot and announcing his intention to divide with the Tories. Lest his enemies take this as evidence of growing conservatism, however, Stanley emphatically declared he would yield to no man in his attachment to liberal principles.[32] The speech was not very effective, and, according to Greville, he won over but a single vote.[33] Russell did much better, and Abercromby won by ten votes. Seldom had a government got off to a more unpromising beginning.

Desperately seeking aid, Peel sent Graham a copy of the Speech from the Throne. A preview would have permitted Stanley and Graham to prepare an effective defence of the Government, but they thought to accept it would compromise the position of their party. Graham, therefore, sent the packet back to Peel, unopened. Twenty years later, however, Stanley and Russell gave such previews to each other regularly.*

It was apparent that the debate on the Address would bring another attack on the Government, and Stanley, who avoided doing so before lest the smallness of their numbers become generally known, decided to hold a Stanleyite rally. On February 24th Graham managed to lure some members from another meeting to Stanley's house, and about forty were present.[34] Little was accomplished save to schedule another conclave for the next day. At this second meeting, it was obvious both to Stanley and Graham that the third party was so largely Whig in its attachments that any sign of cordiality towards Peel on their part would spell the doom of the budding organization.† The situation was both difficult and discouraging. When Howick dropped by after the debate on the Speakership to sound him on his course, Stanley was almost ready to return to his old, familiar associates.[35] Nevertheless, Stanley did his best to convince a group with no confidence in the Government that they should not vote against it, and also to make Peel aware of his support without actually collaborating with him. Emma accomplished the latter purpose for him. She wrote of Stanley's activities to her uncle, Sir Herbert Taylor, the King's Secretary, who communicated the information to His Majesty, and His Majesty turned it over to Peel.‡ In turn, the King tried to induce Stanley to drop his neutrality and to come out openly for Peel.[36]

The existence of the third party was unostentatiously announced by Stanley on February 25th in his speech against the Morpeth Amendment to the Address:[37]

In saying this, allow me to add, that I speak not only my own

* See: S&F, *Greville*, VI, 369. (*Diary*, November 11th, 1852). The diarist explained that Derby, in November 1852, though anxious to keep the details of the Speech secret, sent Russell a copy before the meeting of Parliament because the latter had always given him a preview of his own Speeches.

† Emma Stanley wrote: 'At a meeting of about fifty Members here today, they pressed such an entire want of confidence in Ministers that if he had shewn more cordiality towards them, or led his friends to imagine there was the slightest appearance of understanding with the Government, he could not have attained his end, and carried their votes.' *Peel Papers*, BM 40303. (Emma Stanley to Herbert Taylor, February 25th, 1835).

‡ On this point see: Ibid. Emma Stanley's letters to Taylor of February 24th and 25th, Taylor's replies of February 25th, Taylor to Peel of February 26th, and Peel to Taylor of February 26th.

> sentiments, but the sentiments of a body of Gentlemen, not insignificant either in point of numbers or station in this House, who, bent upon the sure but steady attainment of certain measures of Reform, are determined to effect our object by no party course of proceeding, but by such a course as in our own unbiased judgment we may deem most conducive to the end in view.

The speech was an appeal to all moderate reformers who were anxious to resist the Whig-Irish-Radical attacks on the Irish Church. Some Whigs he hoped might be attracted by the offer. On the other hand, Stanley appealed to the more progressive Tories by emphasizing the improbability of their effecting reforms through a party which, in its Address, hesitated even to use the term 'reform'. It was only a moderate success. A number of those who attended his meetings offered congratulations and promised to follow him in resisting the Morpeth Amendment,[38] but only a few newcomers enlisted in his cause. Peel was disappointed and peeved at Stanley's tone. The following day he wrote Taylor that considering 'the sentiments which Lord Stanley expressed last night towards the Duke (if you should receive any more communications of a similar nature to the enclosed) I think upon the whole, I had better not see them'.*

O'Connell felt the announcement of the thir[illegible] party should not pass without a comment. He could be confiden[illegible], even cocky, for the Whigs were becoming increasingly friendly to [illegible]him. 'What are we to call that section of the House . . . over which [illegible]he noble Lord presides?' he asked the House. 'It is not a p[illegible]rty – that he denies; it is not a faction, that would be a harsher ti[illegible]. I will give it a name – we ought to call it the tail.'[39] The 'Tail', [illegible] observed contemptuously, was too weak to save Peel, and, refle[illegible]ng on the smallness of the third party, O'Connell went on to qu[illegible] a short poem:

> Down thy hill, romantic Ashbourne, glides
> The Derby dilly, with his six insides.

Why he quoted the poem is understandable; why he misqu[illegible] it is not so clear.† Nevertheless, in so doing he fastened a nam[illegible]on

* *Peel Papers*, BM 40303. (Peel to Taylor, February 26th, 1835). Stanley's references to the Duke, as found in *Hansard*, do not seem offensive. *Hansard* (third series), XXVI, 257-8. In this case it seems probable that Stanley deleted them.

† The quotation was taken from 'The Loves of the Triangles, A Mathematical and Philosophical Poem', which reads as follows:

Stanley's party,* which the founder himself accepted. O'Connell then levelled his barbs at Peel. Peel had stood by the rotten boroughs, exemplified by Old Sarum and Gatton, to the last, and who could trust a man with such a Reform record? On the division, the Government was beaten again, 302-309, maddeningly close, but nevertheless a telling defeat. The Dilly, as O'Connell predicted, could not save Peel.

The position of the Stanley party rapidly became untenable. As Ellice wrote at the time: 'Stanley's conduct is more capricious and unaccountable than ever. Why abuse the people, and support them?'[40] Many of the Dilly began to ask themselves that question, and it was most difficult to answer. Stanley had hoped to study the first few divisions, and to learn from them which members might be expected to support a centre party. Instead, the first few divisions merely upset the theory on which the Dilly was founded. Meant to be a centre party between two extremes, its success depended upon the Whigs appearing to be radical, and the Tories, reactionary. In his role of moderate reformer, Peel prevented defections from his own party, and this was a hard blow to the Dilly. It also appeared probable that the conservative Whigs, such as Melbourne and Grey, would be able to control the radical elements attached to their party. The only refugees from either party whom Stanley could hope to attract were those unusually sensitive on the subject of the Irish Church. Even at that, had the Stanley group secured the balance of power at t[illegible]e election, their ranks would have been swollen by many mod[illegible]ate men who could see a future in the party. As it was, St[illegible]ley had the greatest

* The name 'tail', which O'Connell sugges[illegible]r the group seems never to have caught the popular fancy. One meets it oc[illegible]lly in Greville. See: S&F, *Greville*, III, 170, (*Diary*, March 4th, 1835). O[illegible]ther hand, the term 'Dilly' was used on numerous occasions.

So down thy hill, r[illegible] Ashbourn, glides
The Derby dilly, [illegible]g *Three* Insides
One in each co[illegible]s, and lolls at ease,
With folded [illegible] propt back, and outstretch'd knees;
While the pres[illegible] *Bodkin*, punch'd and squeezed to death,
Sweats in t[illegible] midmost place, and scolds, and pants for breath.

Poetry of the Anti-J[illegible]obin, 2d. ed. (London, 1800), pp. 128-9. The poem stresses the number 'three' [illegible]hroughout, and it would hardly have been possible for one who had read it to m[illegible]ke such an error. O'Connell may have been misquoted in *Hansard*, but this seem[illegible] doubtful. Probably he had in mind the half-dozen members most closely asso[illegible]iated with Stanley when he changed the wording.

difficulties in holding his heterogeneous followers together. At a meeting early in March, he found that one faction of the Dilly wanted to join in a no confidence motion against the Government; while some others demanded additional guarantees that Peel would be supported.[41] Under these conditions Stanley found himself both attacking and supporting the Government. By early March a half-dozen of the Dilly had returned to the Whig camp, and during the month a considerable number decided to hop on Russell's bandwagon.[42] Even the growing intimacy between Russell and the Irish failed to stop the defections.

Stanley, however, stood by his original decision to support Peel. By March he had overcome his earlier scruples and entered into correspondence with Peel not only on subjects of policy, but of tactics. They consulted on the Malt Duties Bill, which did not become a party issue, and it was passed through Parliament.[43]

Once again the Irish Church and its revenues loomed as a major hurdle. When Peel consulted him on the subject, Stanley replied in a letter which indicates the closeness of his co-operation with the Tory leader:[44]

> Your course is just what I expected, and . . . I entirely concur in the propriety of it. The alliance of O'Connell & the Radical Party was formally declared at the dinner last night, and so far places matters on a new footing. Graham left me a short time before your note arrived – he is quite prepared also to take the high line . . . He will speak early in the Debate, and will not immediately follow John Russell – indeed I conclude that some member of Your Government will take that post. If the debate lasts two nights, as I conclude it will, at least, I will try to speak late tomorrow night. I suppose you wish to wind up the whole debate, subject to Lord John's reply.

Stanley was usually careful of his timing, and in this case he hoped to make a strong appeal to the waverers shortly before the division. But the preparations were wasted.

Early in April, Russell managed to secure a majority in the Commons for the principle of 'appropriation', i.e., the use of surplus funds from the Irish Church for the education of the Irish people. To Stanley's way of thinking, this defeat was decisive, and Peel should have resigned, but the unwanted Prime Minister still clung to his post. Stanley compared him with a 'hunted fox, who, instead of dying gallantly before the hounds in the open, skulks along the hedgerows, and at last turns up his legs in the ditch'.* Two more defeats, however, caused Peel to give up. After this brief interruption, the Whigs resumed office to finish out the decade they had so ably begun.

The change-over returned the weak Lord Melbourne to be Prime Minister with Lord John Russell, the keystone of the new Whig-Radical-Irish alliance, achieving the leadership in the Commons. Peel was beaten, but not discredited, and was bending his efforts to increase the membership of the new Conservative (he preferred this designation to 'Tory') Party. The Dilly, however, had fallen on evil days. When Peel's fall became certain, large numbers of the Stanley party, looking to their own political futures, deserted and voted against the Conservative Prime Minister.[45] Graham, who had given unstintingly of his time and energies to the Dilly, was deeply discouraged, and he was inclined to blame Stanley's lack of serious concentration for their failure.† Much as he admired his colourful friend, and appreciated his sincere convictions and sense of honour, Graham felt a growing attraction to Peel, whose personality was more like his own, grave, responsible and stable. To Graham it became increasingly clear that the Dilly should end its separate existence and fuse with the Conservative Party.

When the new Parliament assembled, Stanley and Graham, who had been undecided for a time,[46] chose to retain their old places with the Whigs. In spite of this they tended to support the Opposition rather than the Government.[47] The inconsistency of

* S&F, *Greville*, III, 185-8. (*Diary*, April 3rd, 1835). This is one of Stanley's many colourful remarks, and quite unfair, though he probably did not realize it at the time. Peel was ready to resign much earlier, but continued under pressure from his Party and the King. Charles S. Parker, *Sir Robert Peel* (London: John Murray, 1899), II, 292-7. (*Cabinet Paper*, March 25th, 1835). (Wellington to Peel, March 25th, 1835). (William to Peel, March 28th, 1835).

† Greville recorded his conversation with Graham in some detail, and quoted him as saying: 'With great talents, extraordinary readiness in debate, high principles, unblemished honour, he [Stanley] never had looked, he thought he never would look, upon politics and political life with the seriousness which belonged to the subject; that he followed politics as an amusement, as a means of excitement, as another would gaming or any other very excitable occupation . . .' While Graham admitted Stanley's character was 'very peculiar', he thought his 'eminence' was inevitable. S&F, *Greville*, III, 192-4. (*Diary*, April 9th, 1835). In evaluating this statement, it is only fair to remember that one of Stanley's acknowledged enemies is quoting a man recently disillusioned at political developments.

their position was quickly noted by the Government press, and frequently the party regulars around them made remarks which, Stanley once menacingly observed, in private life would not have been passed over.[48] One night, following a division in which he had sided with the Opposition, Graham was greeted by the jeers of his former associates and the question: 'Why don't you stay there?' Stung, Graham crossed the floor. The following day Graham pointed out a newspaper attack made on Stanley to his friend, and invited him to follow his example. Stanley quietly acceded to Graham's suggestion, and took a seat with the Opposition.[49]

O'Connell, who always followed Stanley's career with interest, on June 2nd needled the young nobleman into an explanation of his conduct.[50] Stanley strongly denied that the change of position entailed any change of opinions. He said that the seat he occupied formerly had been chosen purposely to imply a neutrality towards the Peel Government, and that he had retained it after the change of Ministries in order to indicate a similar neutrality towards Melbourne. The attitude of the men around him there, however, and the attacks of the press, caused him to seek more hospitable surroundings.[51] Following the speech, Lord John Russell, who had achieved his purpose, asserted: 'No part in politics which his noble friend might take would ever induce him to believe that he acted from any other motive than his own sense of honour.'[52] Russell was to repeat almost the same opinion thirty-four years later, after more than three decades of political conflict with Stanley.

Four other members of Parliament, George Bentinck, Gally Knight, Stratford Canning and Matthew Ridley joined Graham and Stanley in their new position, and the 'six insides' were all accounted for.[53] Thereafter the third party was little more than a small faction of men attached to Stanley, but it still retained some semblance of independence, if not neutrality. Stanley preferred to have it that way. There was some satisfaction in being head of a party, however small, which would be lost if he threw in his lot with the growing numbers of the Conservative Party.

In the autumn of 1835 the political outlook seemed dark and discouraging to Stanley. His old party was apparently taken over by the Radicals, and one Whig aristocrat even mixed socially with O'Connell, whom, Stanley thought, 'no gentleman would willingly associate with'.[54] The Liberator now openly advocated the most radical changes in British institutions, and it appeared probable that the House of Lords would be attacked. Some of his Irish tenants, taking heart in this situation and expecting abolition, refused to pay the tithes.* While Stanley expected the Whigs would be able to contain the assault on the Lords, their attitude encouraged radicalism, and especially attacks on the Irish Church.[55] Yet, at the same time, these Whigs secretly opposed appropriation.[56] Their inconsistencies were all the more apparent to Stanley because, even after leaving the party, he was still a Whig socially, and he constantly learned of their real views.[57] Under such circumstances, the possibility of his ever rejoining them became increasingly remote.

Peel sensed, if he did not fully understand, the difficulties of Stanley's position. As the time for Parliament drew near, he predicted Stanley would not aid in attacking the Address, nor in any way commit himself to the Tory Party, and Peel decided not to try to hurry Stanley or to force his hand.[58] When Parliament assembled, however, he was pleased to find that Stanley took a seat near to him.[59] There was no real need for Peel to apply pressure, for a community of interest was obviously bringing them together. A Government proposal to reform the Irish corporations found Peel and Stanley in agreement that the measure would throw the town councils into Catholic hands.[60] So Stanley supported Peel in the attempt to amend the Address, but they failed by some forty votes. After the division an old Whig wrote: 'What say you to our own Stanley? Was there ever such a case of suicide? I really think if I saw him in the street I should try to avoid him to save his blushes; yet perhaps such things are unknown to him.'[61]

The opening battle set the pattern of co-operation between Stanley and Peel for the session. At first Graham acted as the go-between, co-ordinating their parliamentary operations, helping to iron out minor differences of opinion, and, incidentally, trying

* In a letter to Ripon Stanley noted that there had been a meeting on an 'isolated part' of his property, and resistance to the tithes had been agreed upon. In most cases he had been unable to add the tithe to the rent charge during the current term of his tenants' leases, but he anticipated no difficulty in adding the charge when the leases were renewed. *Ripon Papers*, BM 40863. (Stanley to Ripon, October 13th, 1835).

to convince Stanley that it was not they, but the Whigs, who had deserted their principles.[62] However, in March Stanley and Peel began to correspond regularly, met frequently, and in almost all cases Stanley acted with him.[63] In late summer he wrote Peel: 'I am glad however to hear from Graham that the Muster Roll at present promises a still further decrease in the Government majority.'[64]

A pattern of opposition to the Melbourne Government was likewise established on the Irish Municipal Reform question. After Peel and Stanley were defeated on the issue in the Commons, the bill faced the keen blade of Wellington in the Lords. After carving out those points unacceptable to his friends in the lower house, Wellington sent the bill back to the Commons. There Russell rejected the Lords' amendments, but the Lords insisted on them and Russell finally moved and carried a rejection of the mutilated bill.[65]

Even more objectionable to Stanley and the Conservatives was Russell's new Tithe Bill which contained the too familiar appropriation clause. A battle of statistics ensued. The Government claimed that only 1250 of the 1385 Irish benefices were necessary, and showed that by eliminating the others, the Church would need only £361,938 of its £459,550 income. They proposed to give the saving to Irish education.[66] When the Government moved the bill on June 1st Stanley proposed an amendment to allow him to bring in his own bill on the subject, providing for the conversion of the tithe into a rent charge, for the redemption and better distribution of the tithes, and omitting the appropriation clause. Stanley denied there was a surplus to be appropriated. He showed that there were 852,000 Anglicans in Ireland, that benefices covered thirteen to fourteen square miles each and served an average of 615 people. The average income of the benefices was only £255, hence better distribution, not reduction, was in order.[67] Russell struck back, and as Greville put it: 'There was very sharp work between Stanley and John Russell, who left off *noble friending* and took to *noble lording* him.'[68] O'Connell, of course, supported Russell, and Peel came to Stanley's aid. While most of the debating power was on the side of the Opposition, the Government had the weight of votes, and passed their appropriation clause by twenty-six votes.

But Wellington lay in wait in the Lords. Unsheathing his sword a second time he pruned out the appropriation clause and returned a less objectionable bill to his friends in the Commons. However, Russell was more resourceful this time. Noting that the appropriation clause involved money, he declared the Lords' action involved a question of privilege and violated the Commons' authority over money bills. Peel quickly detected the weaknesses of this argument, and challenged Russell to rest his case on the question of privilege. When the Speaker ruled this was not a money bill in the sense suggested by Russell, the latter dropped the measure entirely.[69] Their Lordships' bold action no doubt stemmed from the knowledge that the British public backed them on the issue. Had Melbourne resigned on the question and held an election, the electorate might have returned a Conservative majority.[70] On the appropriation question, in fact, a majority of English members voted with the Opposition.

When the 1837 session opened, the Government could muster 332 votes to the Opposition's 319, and thus were never too sure of their majorities. The Conservative party, however, still was not in winning form. The Reform controversy still had not died out completely, and animosities still lingered from the days of Catholic Emancipation.[71] Furthermore, Stanley still hovered on the sidelines, unwilling to join the team, but on coming to London late in January 1837, he sat in on party strategy conferences, and even dined with his old political *bête noire*, Wellington.[72] In spite of this Peel stills sometimes hesitated to invite him to party meeting.[73]

During the session, as Peel and Stanley became more intimate, a basic difference in political philosophy between them appeared. Stanley felt that party lines should not prevent men of like minds from collaborating, or working through a common friend, in the solution of difficult questions. Peel, on the other hand, had very orthodox notions regarding party regularity. On one occasion, Stanley wanted to warn the King against a certain project of his Ministers, only to find that Peel objected to the tactic, strongly implying that it was unethical.[74] Stanley, however, was not discouraged, and strongly advocated that indirect tactics be employed in solving the twin problems of the Irish tithes and corporations. The latter question almost disrupted the Conservative Party, for some, including Stanley and Graham, felt that uncompromising opposition to the creation of Irish corporations could not be permanently maintained, while the Ultra-Tories, especially in the Lords, would not hear of creating them.[75] Stanley's next proposal, then, must have tempted Peel, though it did not shake him.

In May 1837 Stanley explored the possibilities of a *sub rosa* agreement between the Whig Prime Minister, Melbourne, and the Conservative leaders, and detailed his friend, Richmond, to sound Melbourne concerning a general agreement on the tithes and the municipal corporations of Ireland. On May 12th Richmond, having contacted Melbourne, suggested that Stanley request permission from Peel and Wellington for a face to face conference with the Prime Minister.[76] Stanley thereupon forwarded Richmond's letter to Peel, observing:[77]

> ... I am convinced that Melbourne has made up his mind to accept any reasonable terms of agreement, and pass the two Bills — and I am led to believe that if personally satisfied himself of the reasonableness of the proposal, and of its being such as he could accept without loss of character, he has both the will & the power to compel the acquiescence of his Cabinet. This however is a matter of such extreme delicacy, that I need hardly say I could not discuss it — nor have I hinted nor shall I hint to any human being except yourself, the idea of such a step as a confidential communication with L.M. If however you think it in any way practicable to open a communication, I think it might be done indirectly through Wharncliffe & Richmond. Melbourne has expressed a readiness to see me, and to tell me unreservedly his views — but this of course I have not felt myself authorized or entitled to accept.

To which Peel replied:[78]

> It appears to me that it would not be advisable to have any Communication with the Government, or with any members of it, in respect to the course to be taken on the Irish Municipal Bill or the other Bills.
>
> The course has not yet been sufficiently considered to warrant such a communication were it on no other grounds, free from objection, but I should object, on principle, to make a Communication, from its tendency to perplex the Relation between a Government and its opponents, and to fetter the entire freedom of action which it is so desirable to maintain and particularly to shake the Confidence of a Party in its Leaders . . . Lord Wharncliffe sent me his memorandum of his conversation with Lord Melbourne,

> and it has, I confess, strongly confirmed the objections which I entertain, in principle, to such Confidential Communications as those which it details. What must Lord John Russell think of a Colleague, who talks to a political opponent of 'his petulant Folly' and holds the Language which Lord Melbourne holds with regard to the Appropriation Clause and the readiness to abandon it. I cannot see how a Government could remain united, or Lord Melbourne at the Headship were that Memorandum known to the Membership.

Deeply concerned with the solution of the two Irish questions, Stanley read Peel's answer with a feeling of disappointment. He replied stiffly: 'I was certainly desirous of obtaining your *individual* opinion, in strict confidence, as to the practicability of any ulterior communications. You have given it very distinctly, and I at once acquiesce.'[79] The death of William IV in June 1837 removed Sir Herbert Taylor, Stanley's confidential contact with the Crown, from his secretarial position. Stanley congratulated him on being able to drop out of politics, observing: 'It is a villainous *métier* at the best of times, and I do not think it likely to improve in these.'[80]

The same year brought serious political difficulties to Graham, whose removal from the Whig Party cost him the support of many in his constituency. Before the contest he wrote Stanley that his re-election was doubtful, but he felt he must allow his constituents to pass on his political conduct. Stanley replied cynically that he saw no reason why Graham was honour-bound to go through with it if the contest was a hopeless expenditure and vexation.[81] For a time Graham's prospects seemed good,[82] but he was beaten and temporarily without a seat in Parliament.

During his entire political career Stanley followed a code of honour which was his own. His indirect methods which offended Peel, and the disagreement with Graham over the demands of honour, illustrate this, and the numerous occasions when his outspokenness in Parliament offended other members perhaps point it up. Feeling that birth and social position entitled him to be an arbiter in matters concerning honour, he followed his own code and refused to alter it to suit other people. He was an aristocrat and an individual as well as a politician. As a noble he was above party lines, associating with and sometimes freely confiding in members of his own class who were his political opponents. As an individual he demanded complete freedom of action, and expected his constituents to vote for him as a man of character who would do what he thought was right for them and the country. As a politician, he followed the game because he enjoyed it, and because he thought it an obligation of one of his class. These attitudes, of course, do not necessarily set Stanley apart from his contemporaries of the same social level. It seems possible, however, that Stanley became increasingly restless in representing a constituency in the Commons and came to look longingly at the freedom of action that came with sitting in the Lords.

That year, 1837, brought Stanley a new associate who was to be year in, year out, save for Graham, his closest friend. The Earl of Malmesbury recorded their meeting briefly: 'Arrived at Chillingham, where Lord and Lady Stanley came, and I made his acquaintance for the first time. He is very amusing, and with his high spirits and cleverness kept a large party in roars of laughter.'* Three days later Malmesbury added: 'I think we have taken a decided liking to one another.'[83]

A man of many acquaintances, Stanley had less than a handful of intimate friends, and Malmesbury was one of them. Never a brilliant statesman, Malmesbury was always in the shade of his friend, but the association was one of great stability. Every year, usually around November, Malmesbury appeared at Knowsley where, in the fields surrounding the estate, the two indulged their favourite sport of *battue* shooting.[84] Their expeditions were on a grand scale. Stanley always had his beloved dogs with him,[85] and the nearby town furnished sometimes two or three hundred men to act as beaters. Malmesbury dubbed Stanley the 'keenest' sportsman he had ever seen, and their love of the hunt never dimmed. Later, when too infirm to do any shooting himself, Stanley went along with the crowd and instilled spirit into the game.[86] Malmesbury was also enthusiastic, and it is easy to understand the closeness of their friendship. There was something magnificently English about Stanley and Malmesbury, in their unflagging pursuit of pleasures traditional for many generations, in their attachment to the little worlds bounded by their estates.

* Earl of Malmesbury, *Memoirs of an Ex-Minister* (London: Longmans, Green & Co., 1884), I, 82. (*Diary*, September 1837). But see: Ibid., I, 17, 40. There is some doubt when he first met Stanley.

Neither would have wished to have been born at another time, and certainly not in any other place. Yet, even in their day, there was also something anachronistic about their way of life in rapidly industrializing England.

In December 1837, after more than three years of leading a faction, Stanley formally joined the Tory Party. The Derby Dilly had at long last stopped at the Carlton, and Stanley, who had jealously guarded his independence, now lost it to a considerable extent. It was quite time that he did. He had previously sat in on party conferences, concerted his parliamentary activities with those of Peel, and even requested influence in patronage matters from the Conservative leader.* That he had hesitated so long, however, is perhaps understandable. Sitting on the front bench beside Peel he was only a heart-beat away from the leadership, but it was a strong beat, that of a man in the most vigorous period of his life. Barring an accident, or some strange twist of fate, he was now doomed almost indefinitely to the ranks. However, in May [illegible]38 Stanley and Peel paid their respects to each other at a l[illegible] public dinner at Merchant Taylors' Hall. Of the three [illegible]ndred and thirteen party members, some three hundred turned out to hear Peel lay down Conservative pol[illegible]es, and to refer to the accession of Stanley and Graham as [illegible] union not the result of conferences, not the offspring of ne[illegible]iations, but originally brought about by the force of circ[illegible]stances and afterwards cemented by mutual co-operation, b[illegible]reciprocal confidence and respect'.[87] And they heard Stanle[illegible]eply that his alliance was 'founded on the strongest moti[illegible] which could act on private feeling, or influence public con[illegible] — it was founded on a sense of danger, on a conviction of [illegible]ommon interest'.[88] These statements sealed the union of S[illegible]ey with the party he was to serve and later to govern for the [illegible]ainder of his life.

Almost at this same ti[illegible]ame warnings that his most vigorous years lay behind him. S[illegible]ey's grandfather had been periodically incapacitated by go[illegible]nd his father's health was uncertain. Thus, in falling ill, S[illegible]ley was following in the footsteps of his forefathers. In December 1837 he experienced swelling and inflammation, and was put to bed in company with a dozen

* See his letter to Peel on behalf of one of his relatives. *Peel Papers*, BM 40425. (Stanley to Peel, November 25th, 1837).

leeches. Early in 1838, he was again attacked, this time apparently by his ancestral infirmity, the gout.[89] With the onset of this illness, Stanley became increasingly cautious in political affairs, and the impetuousness of his youth rapidly became a fading memory.

When Parliament opened in 1838 the Conservative Party was stronger than it had been for many years. On its benches sat Peel, Stanley and Graham, a hard-driving trio, and young Gladstone was near by. To their rear was an affected young man, loud in dress and great in ambition, but at the moment quite insignificant. Two years before he had sought to stir the political world by publishing his anonymous *Runnymede Letters*, which showered praise on Peel and Stanley.

Peel apparently saw some possibilities in the newcomer, but Stanley, possibly because of a tiff between Disraeli and a member of the Stanley clan, was set against him.[90] At the time Stanley and Disraeli had nothing in common, and the former no doubt regarded him as one of the social horrors of the reformed Parliament. Stanley, for some reason, stood aside at Disraeli's request when he made his disastrous maiden speech,* but the two statesmen, in 1838, were a world, rather than a few benches, apart. At the moment they were members of a party in a pleasant position. As Lord Campbell once put it: 'The most delightful political position is to be a member of a powerful and united party out of office, eagerly attacking a falling Ministry.'[91]

The opportunity for a strong assault on the Melbourne Government was presented by a minor rebellion in Canada in 1837. The Conservatives toyed with the idea of censuring government policy, then suddenly found themselves placed in a most embarrassing position by the Radicals. Molesworth, a Radical, gave notice of a motion of no confidence in Lord Glenelg, Secretary of State for the Colonies, and the Conservatives faced the alternatives of voting with the Radicals, which they objected strongly to doing, or with the Government, whose course in Canada they did not entirely approve. After extended correspondence among Peel, Wellington and Stanley, the Conservatives managed to have a vote taken on

* The only remark in Stanley's speech, following Disraeli's ordeal, that might be interpreted as being sympathetic towards the latter was the observation: 'He was aware how difficult it was at that hour to command the attention of the House.' *Hansard* (third series), XXXIX, 807.

their own motion censuring the Government as such, and this repelled Radical support. During the incident, Stanley received communications from sources outside of his Party, but, remembering Peel's attitude towards such collaboration, he did not encourage the writers.*

On another issue, however, the Conservatives lent a helping hand to the Government. The question of the Irish tithes had been hanging fire so long that most members of Parliament were anxious to get rid of it. In May 1838 Stanley demanded that Russell explicitly renounce the appropriation idea,[92] and, as an inducement for him to do so, Peel later promised the co-operation of his party in settling the problem.[93] Though a tithe bill without appropriation did not sit well with the Irish wing of his party, Russell at length produced one, and, with the aid of the Conservatives,† passed it. For thirty years the question was allowed to rest, and this was no doubt the most gratifying victory of Stanley's early career. He had sacrificed his career with the Whigs for the sake of the Irish Church, and it was to live, and to die, with him.

The victory of the Conservatives on the tithe question had caused further disorganization in the decaying Melbourne Government, and by autumn 1838 Stanley could ask the question: 'Is it possible that O'Connell and the Government should still hold together?'[94] At the moment the tide was turning in favour of the Tories. Not only was the Government split between the Radicals, who blamed their losses in 1837 on the vacillation of the Whigs, and the Whigs, who felt that the Radicals frightened as many electors as they pleased, but the rise of Chartism was causing Conservatives of various economic backgrounds to look to Peel as a dam against radicalism.[95]

Colonial affairs brought about a crisis. The legislature of Jamaica became involved in a quarrel with the Home Government, and Melbourne sought to coerce them by introducing a bill to

* One letter was from Lord Brougham; the source of the other is not identified. In connection with the latter Stanley wrote Peel: 'I thought it better to answer at once and not consult you, as I know you are not very fond of these communications . . .' *Peel Papers*, BM 40425. (Stanley to Peel, February 17th, 1838). (Stanley to Peel, January 8th, 1838).

† Russell got in touch with Stanley indirectly and urged him to bring as many Conservatives as possible for the division, as he was afraid of his own Party. Ibid. (Stanley to Peel, August 10th, 1838).

suspend their constitution for five years. Stanley was deeply interested in the situation and spoke at some length against the Government.[96] As the attack on the Jamaican constitution also alienated the Radicals, the governmental majority on the suspension bill sank to five votes, and, concluding they could not carry the bill through committee, the Government, on May 7th, resigned.

The day following Peel held a meeting of his inner council to construct a government. Both Stanley and Graham were offered Secretaryships of State; Wellington was to have the Foreign Office. On May 9th a former member of the Dilly called at Stanley's residence in St. James's Square* to request recognition, and Stanley reported Ripon's request to Peel.† Emerson Tennent and Lord Wilton also sought to contact Peel through Stanley. Stanley himself was busy selecting the subordinate personnel for the Colonial Office, and recommended George Hope for the Under Secretaryship, but all of them were doomed to disappointment. Unable to secure an indication of the confidence of the Queen, Peel refused to take office. Melbourne and his entourage again returned to power. Stanley was wholly satisfied with Peel's decision,[97] and so were most members of his party. Disraeli, however, was one of the few who disagreed. Office, to him, was sweet almost under any conditions, and this divergence of opinion between him and Stanley was later to be a source of misunderstanding between them.

Stanley was, in fact, rather relieved that they had not taken the government while still in a minority in the Commons. Their near capture of control, however, had excited the rank and file of the Conservative Party, and, while Stanley did not favour a new attack at the opening of the next Parliament, for fear that a failure would dishearten the party, he realized that one might have to be made to satisfy them.[98] The Duke of Wellington agreed with Stanley, but both Peel and Graham were ready for a fight. An attempt to

* Stanley's house in St. James's Square was previously occupied by the Elder Pitt, and later by William E. Gladstone. Today it is marked with a plaque. Disraeli was not impressed by the place. 'He has also one county seat to keep up,' Disraeli wrote, 'Knowsley, wh: wd. be the ugliest house in England, were it not for his "family mansion" in St. James Sqre. That is furnished like a second-rate lodging house & in itself essentially mean: all this not from stinginess, but from sheer want of taste.' *Disraeli Papers*, XVII, Miscellaneous Observations §66.

† *Peel Papers*, BM 40426. (Stanley to Peel, May 9th, 1839). Stanley also noted that Spring Rice would not stand for the Chair and wanted to avoid 'further communication'. This indicates that Stanley had perhaps been delegated to contact him on the subject of the Speakership.

unseat the Government, therefore, was made in January 1840, and Stanley in his speech declared Ministers had the confidence of O'Connell and few others, but the division belied his words, for the Government triumphed by twenty-one votes.

On February 25th Stanley introduced a measure into Parliament which was to spearhead the attack not only during the 1840 session, but also during the year following. When he introduced his Irish registration bill, he carefully noted that it was designed merely to overhaul the registration procedure, and did not pretend to deal with the franchise itself. Stanley found many faults with and abuses in the current method of registering voters. Registration was quarterly and not annual as it was in England, and a voter was kept on the list for a period of eight years without a reinvestigation of his qualifications. After registration, the voter received a certificate, and it often fell into the hands of unauthorized persons. Sufficient time was not allowed to challenge those who were registered. So faulty, indeed, was the procedure that Stanley showed how a single voter might obtain fifteen voting certificates during a seven and one-half year period, and distribute the extras to his friends. Stanley's case was very strong, but his remedy was bitterly opposed. Certificates were to be abolished, and registrations were to be held annually. The assistant barristers were allowed to continue to determine the qualifications for voting, but, in cases of appeals, the assize judges would have the final determination. Slight fines were to be imposed on those who made frivolous claims to the franchise, and also on those who entered objections without good reason.[99]

Russell bitterly opposed the bill, noting: 'I say that the noble Lord has compounded with that which was wholesome food, so much poisonous matter of his own introduction, that I must reject the whole concoction . . .'[100] The main objection to the bill was its tendency to restrict the franchise, which would decrease the influence of the small Catholic voters who served O'Connell. 'Scorpion' Stanley, as the Liberator privately called his Conservative opponent,[101] was trying to increase the influence of the landlords over their tenants, and he denounced both the bill and its author.[102] The measure was an admirable instrument of party warfare, for it forced the Government to defend the obvious abuses of the registration system, or risk offending their Irish supporters. Stanley carried the second reading by sixteen votes in a very full

House, and thereafter the Government could only resort to delaying tactics. Introduced in February, the bill was still in committee early in July and only five of its forty-six clauses had been discussed. Stanley, therefore, withdrew it for the session, but had the satisfaction of having seen the Government beaten on nine out of ten divisions on the measure.[103]

When Parliament convened in January 1841 Stanley again had his registration measure with him, this time slightly revised to meet the approval of the Ulster Liberal Society. Presented on January 26th, Stanley outlined some revisions he had made for the protection of the voter. Once registered, a voter was qualified for life, save if an objector proved his disqualification. A maximum fine was fixed for frivolous or vexatious appeals, and some other minor alterations were suggested. Hard pressed, the Government on February 4th introduced a rival bill by Lord Morpeth, which was similar to Stanley's, save that a rider broadened the Irish franchise. To wriggle off the horns of the dilemma, then, the Government thus proposed to meddle with the dangerous question of Reform.[104] Hoping for a compromise, Lord Howick contacted Stanley in February. Stanley, however, rejected the overture, and, complaining of gout in his hand, had Emma Stanley write Lady Howick that he disagreed entirely with her husband on the subject.[105]

Failing to secure a compromise, the Government faced its opponents in a great parliamentary battle. Stanley attacked Morpeth's bill in a very long and excellent speech, in which he considered in detail all the complicated aspects of the difficult problem.[106] Peel and Graham also committed their oratorical powers to the massive verbal onslaught. The debate continued for four nights, and, when the time came for the division, both sides brought 'down the sick and dying without remorse'.[107] Again the Conservatives were unsuccessful in a major attempt to unseat the Government, for the second reading of the Morpeth bill, which now had the right-of-way over Stanley's measure, was carried by five votes. The margin, however, was so slim that Russell, aided by O'Connell, again resorted to delaying tactics, and they managed to keep the question out of committee. When they finally were forced to submit the Morpeth bill to this closer inspection of the House membership, they were beaten a number of times, and the Prime Minister decided to withdraw it.[108]

The Irish registration struggle thus ended without correcting the abuses of the system, for Morpeth's bill had consumed so much time that Stanley was unable to press his own measure. But the question had served party purposes admirably. The Whig reformers had been forced to defend the corrupt practices in Ireland, had been made to contradict themselves on the question of the Irish franchise, and had been beaten on so many divisions that their Administration was seriously weakened. Once he became Prime Minister, Peel announced that he would not reintroduce Stanley's bill, but would seek to reform the registration by other means.[109] Whether or not he could have carried the measure had he chosen to try is questionable, but the fact that Peel dropped it so readily gave credence to Lord Campbell's observation that: 'The object of its promoters being gained, it is now thrown like a worthless weed away.'[110]

With the prize of office at their finger-tips, the nerves of many of the Conservative leaders became increasingly frayed. During one debate Stanley and Peel were both guilty of making unintentional misstatements of fact,[111] and in March Stanley let drop a remark in Parliament which offended Peel.* That same evening he wrote his chief, declaring that he would not intentionally utter:[112]

> . . . a single word which would give a moment's pain to one, with whom, on every account, I desire to maintain relations of the most unreserved confidence; for whom, personally, I entertain a very sincere regard, and of whose acknowledged friendship I feel justly proud.

Peel, with all his virtues of ability and mind, was deeply sensitive to criticism, and his feelings, once wounded, were not readily assuaged. Men such as Stanley and Wellington,† who were his social superiors, found it rather difficult at times to serve under

* The debate concerned a minor issue, the Stafford and Rugby Railway. On the division, Peel and Stanley voted on opposite sides and the latter won. The statement made by Stanley to which Peel objected is quoted as follows: 'His right hon. Friend had said, with all the ingenuity and art with which he knew so well how to dress up a statement for that House . . .' *Hansard* (third series), LVII, 324.

† One finds all sorts of quotes concerning Peel attributed to Wellington. Campbell noted in his memoirs: 'I know from Lord Wellesley that the Duke said he had so much disliked being under Peel during the hundred days, that if Lord Melbourne would only behave tolerably well he would sooner support him than return to office as a subordinate.' Hardcastle, *Campbell*, II, 220.

him. Receiving Stanley's apology, Peel replied the following morning:*

> The impressions of your informant with respect to the effect of some expressions which fell from you last night, must have arisen from the purport of the expressions themselves and from the manner in which they were received by those who sit opposite & not from any observations made by me.
>
> I have not opened my lips on the subject to anyone.
>
> Nothing could be more natural than that with your opinions and in your position you should offer every opposition in your power to the Bill which was under discussion, and urge in the strongest manner you could the objections to it. It would be absurd indeed if I could feel any surprise or annoyance at this—but I do not think it was at all necessary for the maintenance of your own opinions to speak of 'the art and ingenuity with which I am in the habit of dressing up statements for the House'.
>
> [As the expressions certainly were in appearance at least of an unfriendly rather than an unparliamentary character, I thought it much better to let them pass without notice or mplaint—and without incurring the Risk of there being the .
>
> I can assure you however that I place implic nfidence in your declaration that there was no intention on y part to give pain by the use of those expressions, and even wi out that declaration I would have attributed them to the challe s of debate, and not to any settled feeling. . . .

Upon reading this reply Stanley felt his ology had not been wholly acceptable, so he wrote another let denying he had used the expression quoted by Peel, or impl that Peel habitually misrepresented facts. He continued:[113]

> What I thought I said was 'the art d ingenuity with which you know so well how to dress up ar *gument* addressed to the House', by which I meant no more than that which every debater aims at doing, presenting his argument in the point of view most likely to conciliate and convince his hearers. Whichever the expression were, if it gave you a moment's uneasiness, I repeat my regret at having used it, and trust it will have no further impression on your mind. On reflection, I am aware of the point, wholly unexpected and unintended by me, given to the expression

* This quotation is from a draft letter in the Peel collection. The paragraph in brackets was crossed out in the original, but perhaps indicates Peel's feelings better than the rest of the letter. *Peel Papers*, BM 40467. (Peel to Stanley, March 18th, 1841).

by the cheers from those who are politically opposed to us, and would gladly see a breach between us; and I wish at the moment I had been sufficiently alive to the import of that cheer, to have qualified my expression.

Thereafter the incident was closed, but probably not forgotten.* During their years of political intimacy, Peel and Stanley worked together effectively and neither could blame the other for failure to co-operate. Their conflict remained in the background, but was nevertheless present, and perhaps formed a part of a greater overall picture. While the British patricians shared political power with members of great plebeian families, it was difficult for them to become subordinates of the newcomers. Few statesmen were more ready, save on a few questions, to modify their opinions to suit the wishes of the other party leaders than Stanley, but, in spite of this, deep in his consciousness was the feeling that, for reasons of the prestige of his House rather than from a desire for personal glory, he, rather than a *novus homo* like Peel, should lead the Party. Stanley, though he always acknowledged Peel's outstanding ability, could not eradicate this feeling, and Peel, perhaps sensing that it was there, never felt wholly at ease in the presence of his noble subordinate.

While the Government was still weak from the body-blows inflicted by defeats on the Irish Registration, Peel, on May 27th, moved a motion of no confidence. A rigorous five nights' debate followed, interrupted only by the Whitsun recess, and the division took place at three in the morning of June 5th. No stone was left unturned to secure votes, and the Whigs even brought in Lord Douglas Haliburton, who, though in a state of 'drivelling idiocy' and unaware of what was taking place, was wheeled past the tellers.[114] Even this effort was inadequate, however, and the Government lost by a single vote. They were allowed to continue for a short time to pass some necessary legislation, then Parliament was dissolved and the parties appealed to the country.

During the campaign the Conservatives attacked the Government on its record of the past few years, and the Whigs, who had

* Shortly after the incident described above Stanley criticized Peel for being too 'thin-skinned'. Morley, *Gladstone*, I, 234. (*Diary*, April 3rd, 1841). After the reorganization of the Peel Government in 1845 Lord Campbell wrote: 'Peel was greatly delighted when he had patched up his Cabinet, inducing all whom he really liked to remain with him. He was not sorry to get rid of Stanley, with whom he was never cordial . . .' Hardcastle, *Campbell*, II, 260.

little hope of securing a majority, promised future blessings. About the middle of July Russell conceded defeat in a letter to Stanley, who forwarded it on to Peel.[115] After some discussion of the tactic which would enable their opponents to be defeated quietly,* the Conservatives finally decided on an amendment to the Address. Lord Ripon in the Lords and J. S. Wortley in the Commons offered such amendments, which were carried by large majorities. The decade of Whig leadership had at long last come to an end.

In resigning his leadership of the Commons, Russell made a sportsmanlike speech, expressing the hope that no personal bitterness would arise between him and his opponents, and Stanley responded with compliments for Russell's zeal, ability and talents.[116] Throughout the period they had remained on cordial terms, and during the debates Stanley would sometimes toss notes across the table to Russell making humorous observations on proceedings.[117] 'Stanley and Graham are two men for whom I shall always retain cordial feelings of attachment,' wrote Russell. 'I cannot, when I part from a friend, go to St. James's coffee-house and get a new one. I hanker after old affections, and am very slow with my new ones.'[118] Though the Dilly stopped at the Carlton, its leader more than once thereafter dropped by at Grillion's to renew his acquaintance with old Whig associates.

NOTES

[1] S&F, *Greville*, III, 219. (*Diary*, July 3rd, 1835).
[2] Hardcastle, *Campbell*, II, 107.
[3] S&F, *Greville*, III, 43. (*Diary*, June 2nd, 1834).
[4] Parker, *Graham*, I, 206-7. (Stanley to Graham, undated). (Graham to Stanley, July 3rd, 1834).
[5] S&F, *Greville*, III, 44. (*Diary*, June 3rd, 1834).
[6] Parker, *Graham*, I, 206-7. (Graham to Stanley, July 3rd, 1834).
[7] *Hansard* (third series), XXIV, 1145-6.
[8] Ibid., pp. 1146-8.
[9] S&F, *Greville*, III, 58-9. (*Diary*, July 12th, 1834).
[10] *RP*, BM 40863. (Stanley to Ripon, July 25th, 1834).
[11] Arthur Aspinall, *Lord Brougham and the Whig Party* (Manchester: University Press, 1927), p. 291. (Brougham to Wellesley, undated).
[12] Maxwell, *Creevey*, p. 626. (Creevey to Ord, August 12th, 1834).

* *Peel Papers*, BM 40467. (Stanley to Peel, July 18th, 1841). (Stanley to Peel, July 29th, 1841). Russell told Stanley he would take a defeat on the Address as decisive. Stanley felt that his plan to put an objectionable paragraph in the Speech to invite amendment would be disrespectful to the Crown. In 1868, however, he was to suggest a similar course to Disraeli, who at that time resigned before meeting Parliament. *Disraeli Papers*, Derby XII. (Derby to Disraeli, November 22nd, 1868).

[13] *RP*, BM 40863. (Stanley to Ripon, July 22nd, 1834).

[14] Parker, *Graham*, I, 208-10. (Graham to Stanley, September 26th, 1834). (Stanley to Graham, September 30th, 1834).

[15] Bulwer, *Palmerston*, II, 186. (Palmerston to Temple, November 16th, 1834).

[16] *RP*, BM 40863. (Stanley to Ripon, November 20th, 1834).

[17] Ibid.

[18] Parker, *Graham*, I, 214. (Graham to Stanley, November 21st, 1834).

[19] Peel, *Memoirs*, II, 29-30. (Wellington to Peel, November 30th, 1834).

[20] Ibid., pp. 33-5. (Peel to Stanley, December 9th, 1834).

[21] Parker, *Graham*, I, 218.

[22] Peel, *Memoirs*, II, 36-42. (Stanley to Peel, December 11th, 1834).

[23] *PP*, BM 40405. (Peel to Salisbury, December 13th, 1834). (Peel to Becket, December 13th, 1834). Parker, *Graham*, I, 219. (Graham to Ripon, December 23rd, 1834).

[24] Parker, *Peel*, II, 277-8. (Croker to Peel, January 8th, 1835). (Peel to Croker, January 10th, 1835).

[25] *Stanley's Speech at Lancaster*, January 12th, 1835. (C. Wheeler & Son, 1835).

[26] See, for instance: S&F, *Greville*, III, 51-2. (*Diary*, July 6th, 1834). Maxwell, *Creevey*, p. 626. (Creevey to Ord, August 12th, 1834). *Hansard* (third series), XXIV, 11.

[27] Ashley, *Palmerston*, I, 315. (Palmerston to Temple, March 10th, 1835).

[28] Sanders, *Melbourne*, pp. 237-8. (Melbourne to Grey, January 23rd, 1835).

[29] Parker, *Graham*, I, 231. (Graham to Stanley, January 23rd, 1835).

[30] Ibid., pp. 225, 231-2. (Graham to Stanley, January 23rd, 1835). (Stanley to Graham, January 30th, 1835).

[31] Rollo Russell, ed., *The Early Correspondence of Lord John Russell, 1805-1840* (London: T. Fisher Unwin, 1913), II, 83-4. (Stanley to Russell, January 31st, 1835).

[32] *Hansard* (third series), XXVI, 28-31.

[33] S&F, *Greville*, III, 160. (*Diary*, February 20th, 1835).

[34] *PP*, BM 40303. (Emma Stanley to Taylor, February 24th, 1835). Parker, *Graham*, I, 233-4. Ibid., pp. 231-3. (Stanley to Graham, January 30th, 1835).

[35] Russell, *Early Correspondence*, II, 100. (Grey to Russell, February 23rd, 1835).

[36] *PP*, BM 40303. (Taylor to Emma Stanley, February 25th, 1835).

[37] *Hansard* (third series), XXVI, 257.

[38] *PP*, BM 40303. (Emma Stanley to Taylor, February 25th, 1835).

[39] *Hansard* (third series), XXVI, 397.

[40] Aspinall, *Brougham*, pp. 292-3. (Ellice to Brougham, March 5th, 1835).

[41] S&F, *Greville*, III, 170. (*Diary*, March 5th, 1835).

[42] Ibid., pp. 174-5, 183, 185-8. (*Diary*, March 15th and 29th, 1835, April 3rd, 1835).

[43] *PP*, BM 40416. (Stanley to Peel, March 6th, 1835).

[44] Ibid., BM 40418. (Stanley to Peel, March 29th, 1835).

[45] S&F, *Greville*, III, 185-8. (*Diary*, April 3rd, 1835).

[46] *Hansard* (third series), XXIX, 201-2. Parker, *Peel*, II, 313. (Hardinge to Peel, April 23rd, 1835).

[47] Ibid.

[48] *Hansard* (third series), XXIX, 202.

[49] S&F, *Greville*, 219-20. (*Diary*, July 3rd, 1835).

[50] *Hansard* (third series), XXIX, 199-200.

[51] Ibid., pp. 201-2.

[52] Ibid., p. 203.

[53] S&F, *Greville*, III, 219. (*Diary*, July 3rd, 1835).

[54] *RP*, BM 40863. (Stanley to Ripon, October 13th, 1835).

[55] Ibid.

[56] *PP*, BM 40422. (Stanley to Peel, March 21st, 1836).

[57] S&F, *Greville*, III, 275-6, 279. (*Diary*, February 3rd and 7th, 1836).

[58] Louis J. Jennings, ed., *The Correspondence and Diaries of the Late Right Honourable John Wilson Croker* (New York: Charles Scribner's Sons, 1884), II, 102-3. (Peel to Croker, January 12th, 1836). See also: Parker, *Peel*, II, 318. (Peel to Goulburn, January 3rd, 1836).

[59] S&F, *Greville*, III, 277. (*Diary*, February 5th, 1836).

[60] Parker, *Graham*, I, 243-4.

[61] Maxwell, *Creevey*, p. 651. (Creevey to Ord, February 15th, 1836).

[62] Parker, *Peel*, I, 244, 248. (Graham to Peel, February 12th, 1836). (Graham to Stanley, August 30th, 1836).

[63] *PP*, BM 40422. (Stanley to Peel, March 21st, May 26th, June 24th and 25th, 1836).

[64] Ibid. (Stanley to Peel, July 28th, 1836).

[65] *Annual Register* (1836), pp. 52-3, 64.

[66] Ibid., pp. 66-9.

[67] Ibid., pp. 72-4.

[68] S&F, *Greville*, III, 295. (*Diary*, July 9th, 1836).

[69] *Annual Register* (1836), pp. 99-110.

[70] S&F, *Greville*, III, 304-5. (*Diary*, August 21st, 1836).

[71] *PP*, BM 40423. (Peel Memorandum, July 4th, 1837).

[72] *PP*, BM 40423. (Stanley to Peel, January 28th, 1837). Jennings, *Croker*, II, 111. (Croker to Hertford, February 8th, 1837).

[73] John Morley, *The Life of William Ewart Gladstone* (New York: The MacMillan Co., 1903), I, 139.

[74] *PP*, BM 40423. (Stanley to Peel, April (?) 1837). (Peel Memorandum, (?) 1837).

[75] Ibid. (Peel Memorandum, July 4th, 1837).

[76] Ibid. (Richmond to Stanley, May 12th, 1837). (Stanley to Peel, May 14th, 1837).

[77] Ibid. (Stanley to Peel, May 14th, 1837).

[78] Ibid. (Peel to Stanley, May 19th, 1837).

[79] Ibid. (Stanley to Peel, May 21st, 1837).

[80] Ernest Taylor, ed., *The Taylor Papers of Lt. Gen. Sir Herbert Taylor* (London: Longmans, Green & Co., 1913), p. 412. (Stanley to Taylor, August 24th, 1837).

[81] Parker, *Graham*, I, 249. (Stanley to Graham, December 17th, 1836).

[82] *PP*, BM 40423. (Stanley to Peel, July 7th, 1837).

[83] Earl of Malmesbury, *Memoirs of an Ex-Minister* (London: Longmans, Green & Co., 1884), I, 83. (*Diary*, September 21st, 1837).

[84] Ibid., p. 42.

[85] *PP*, BM 40427. (Stanley to Peel, October 2nd, 1839).

[86] *DP*, Lennox XIII. (Lennox to Disraeli, November 28th, 1863).

[87] *Annual Register* (1838), p. 116.

[88] Ibid., p. 119.

[89] *PP*, BM 40425. (Stanley to Peel, December (?) 1837). (Stanley to Peel, February 14th, 1838).

[90] W. F. Monypenny and G. E. Buckle, *The Life of Benjamin Disraeli* (London: John Murray, 1929), I, 520. (Hereinafter cited as 'M&B, *Disraeli*').

[91] Hardcastle, *Campbell*, II, 121.

[92] *Annual Register* (1838), pp. 122-3.

[93] S&F, *Greville*, IV, 63. (*Diary*, June 3rd, 1838).

[94] *PP*, BM 40425. (Stanley to Peel, November 29th, 1838).

[95] See: *History Today* (August 1951), pp. 33-40. M. G. Brock, 'George Canning'; Ibid. (May 1953), pp. 329-38. M. G. Brock, 'Politics at the Accession of Queen Victoria'.

[96] *Annual Register* (1839), pp. 103, 117-18.
[97] Parker, *Peel*, II, 400. (Graham to Peel, May 13th, 1839).
[98] *PP*, BM 40427. (Stanley to Peel, December 18th, 1839).
[99] *Annual Register* (1840), pp. 117-19.
[100] Ibid., p. 125.
[101] Ibid.
[102] Ibid., p. 120.
[103] Ibid., pp. 127-8.
[104] *Annual Register* (1841), pp. 38-42.
[105] S&F, *Greville*, IV, 354. (*Diary*, February 12th, 1840).
[106] *Annual Register* (1841), pp. 42-5.
[107] S&F, *Greville*, IV, 356. (*Diary*, February 27th, 1841).
[108] *Annual Register* (1841), pp. 52-62.
[109] Ibid., p. 216.
[110] Hardcastle, *Campbell*, II, 202.
[111] S&F, *Greville*, IV, 384. (*Diary*, June 12th, 1841).
[112] *PP*, BM 40467. (Stanley to Peel, March 17th, 1841).
[113] Ibid. (Stanley to Peel, March 18th, 1841).
[114] S&F, *Greville*, IV, 383. (*Diary*, June 6th, 1841).
[115] *PP*, BM 40467. (Stanley to Peel, July 18th, 1841).
[116] *Annual Register* (1841), p. 198.
[117] Walpole, *Russell*, I, 305-6.
[118] Parker, *Graham*, I, 271. (Russell to Tavistock, November 19th, 1838).

CHAPTER IV

BURDENS OF THE EMPIRE

THERE was no novelty in returning to the Colonial Office. For Stanley, it was a twice-told tale. The challenge was quite gone, but the rather uninspiring routine remained. There were always numerous applications from the needy in the colonies for relief from Her Majesty's Bounty,* and many pleas from the British poor who sought funds to help them start life anew in the colonies. At the same time the colonies had to be protected from emigrants who landed penniless, and taxed the small relief funds which were derived from a small tax on passengers.[1] Save for paupers aided under the Poor Law, money for emigration purposes was scarce, and Stanley thought it should be reserved for those who migrated to distant colonies.[2]

Then there was the daily, deadly routine of examining the acts passed by colonial legislatures,† but, save in unusual cases, this task was assigned to James Stephen, who had long experience in the office, and who, with George W. Hope, formed the inner circle of advisors. Russell, Stanley's predecessor, had been more interested in the Commons than colonial affairs, and had left behind a considerable correspondence, concerning such uninviting topics as pickled fish, for his successor to answer. Some problems had been hanging fire for some time, such as the case of Mr. Crook, who still sought indemnification for his vessel, the *Lord Nelson*, which was seized by the United States prior to the War of 1812.[3]

Another bequest of the previous Administration was the war with China. Begun late in 1839, the prospects for its conclusion were very uncertain. As Secretary of State for the War Department

* Stanley was by no means callous to such pleas. On one occasion he wrote Peel: 'Is there no fund, or other public money to go to in such a case as this? If not, I must see what a private subscription will do . . .' *Peel Papers*, BM 40467. (Stanley to Peel, October 6th, 1841). In some cases he could use the Royal Bounty. *Colonial Office Papers*, CO 43/102. (Hope to Waddilove, November 10th, 1842).

† In 1841 Stanley wrote: 'I cannot conclude this dispatch without the general remark that . . . the Legislative System of Nova Scotia admits of, & requires, some considerable amendments . . . Their Statute Book is annually receiving an Augmentation scarcely inferior in bulk to that of the annual statutes of this Kingdom . . .' *Colonial Office Papers*, CO 43/143. (Stanley to Falkland, December 31st, 1841).

the supervision of the war in China fell to Stanley, and, having a patent dislike for war, Stanley was hardly equipped to give inspirational leadership in the undertaking.* The overlapping of various civil and military jurisdictions made the conduct of supply and operations difficult. Any decisions Stanley made had to have the approval of the Cabinet, and especially of Aberdeen at the Foreign Office. Then there was the Governor General of India, who had a hand in military operations, but between him and Stanley stood the Board of Control. There was also the Admiralty to consider, and, in supply questions, the Victualling Department. Add to this the tedious slowness of communications with China, and Stanley's problem of supervising the war becomes apparent.

Though he believed the China war could have been prevented, Stanley thought that Britain should receive economic concessions from it. British war aims were stated in a letter to the President of the Board of Control:[4]

> . . . the only objects which Her Majesty desires to obtain, are satisfaction for the injuries to which Her subjects have been exposed, and for the insults which have been offered to Her Crown, and the establishment of peaceful & friendly Commercial relations with China, upon such a footing as shall afford permanent and effectual security against a recurrence of similar misunderstandings in the future. Her Majesty desires no acquisition of territory nor any advantages for Her own subjects which should not equally be shared by other nations; and to the attainment of these objects and these alone the efforts of Her Majesty's Forces are to be directed.

This letter probably reflects the opinion of the whole Cabinet as of late 1841. Britain was then not fighting to win the opium trade, Chinese territory, or special advantages. Events, however, caused a modification of these aims.

Stanley's immediate problem was to devise a military campaign for 1842, and to provide for the Army and Navy. The weeks of late

* In 1842 Stanley observed: 'The country he was sure would look to China with no satisfaction and with little pride; they would, on the contrary, regard it as a subject exciting much pain; they would believe it to be a war of doubtful character, and unnecessarily brought on — a war against an unwarlike people, who were slaughtered without glory and almost without resistance.' *Hansard* (third series), LXIV, 1081. But see: A. C. Benson and Viscount Esher, eds., *The Letters of Queen Victoria* (New York: Longmans, Green & Co., 1907), I, 552-3. (Stanley to Victoria, November 23rd, 1842). (Hereinafter cited as 'B&E, *Victoria*').

1841 went by without any word later than the preceding August being received from the fighting front. Stanley wrote the Board of Control on December 31st that under the circumstances the plan of campaign must be left largely to the Governor General, but he suggested that the island at the intersection of the Grand Canal and the Yangtze River be seized as a means of putting pressure on the Peking Government to make peace.[5] This letter was hardly written when letters dated September 10th and October 21st from the Governor General arrived at the Board of Control and were forwarded to the Colonial Office. Stanley studied them and sent his supply plan to the Board of Control within forty-eight hours. The Governor General should supply the native troops; the Colonial Office would provide for the Europeans.[6] To facilitate the process, Stanley directed the Governor General to send his future requisitions for supplies directly to the Colonial Office. Planning the campaign, however, took longer than dealing with the problem of supply, and it was early February before Stanley submitted the military advice of the Government.[7]

The primary concern of the Government was to 'overcome the obstinacy of the Court of Pekin' by frightening the Emperor, and at the same time to avoid exposing the 'hitherto unvaried success of the British arms to any serious hazard of reverse or failure . . .'[8] Two plans were suggested by Stanley. The first was the seizure of Chinkiang* at the intersection of the Yangtze and the Grand Canal which would cut off a troublesome Chinese force south of Peking, and strike a blow at the internal commerce of China. It was felt this step might alarm the Emperor and perhaps end the war, but it seemed possible the Chinese might adopt a passive resistance programme which would prove 'very embarrassing'. Seeking to avoid new sources of ill feeling, the Government countermanded an alternative plan advanced by their predecessors which involved blowing up the locks of the Grand Canal.† The second plan, which the Government felt involved considerable risk, was to advance up the Pei-ho River and to take Tientsin, near the capital, a move

* Stanley mentions the island of 'Kin-Shan'. *Ellenborough Papers*, PRO 30/12 68. (Stanley to Lords Commissioners of the Admiralty, February 4th, 1842).

† The instruction reads as follows: 'It appears to Her Majesty's Government that such a measure would be one of uncalled for and gratuitous cruelty, inflicting incalculable injury upon unoffending inhabitants, and naturally exciting feelings of the bitterest hostility against the British name.' Ibid.

designed to bring a speedy end to the war.* The decision was left to the field commanders, Sir William Parker of the Fleet, and Sir Hugh Gough, of the Army.

Thus a small British force, numbering about ten thousand,† set off in 1842 to bring Imperial China to her knees. Thereafter, save for an occasional letter from Ellenborough, Stanley was out of touch with the war. The armed forces, however, followed the first of the plans and seized Chinkiang in July. The following month the Emperor signed the Treaty of Nanking, opening five ports, ceding the island of Hongkong, and, among other things, paying for the opium that had been destroyed. Two months after the treaty was signed Stanley and Aberdeen were pessimistic about the war and the former was ready to stop it.‡

When news of the British victory and the acquisition of Hongkong arrived, not all members of the Government were jubilant over the latter. Aberdeen had written earlier:[9]

> It was always with much reluctance that I looked to the possibility of a permanent settlement on the coast of China. The certain expense, the nature of our Relations with that Strange Empire & the probable embarrassment it would create with other Powers, made it desirable not to encourage such a project.

Stanley foresaw that they might have to keep Hongkong – 'all classes, Military, Civil and Mercantile are conspiring to force us into its adoption'.[10] Not only the value of the property there, but a desire to protect the Chinese people who had sided with Britain during the war weighed heavily on the side of keeping the island. Stanley continued:[11]

> I should much prefer the establishment of a legitimate trade with China based on Treaty to the occupation of a Chinese Gibraltar or two . . . and if we could bring the Emperor to terms

* This alternative plan was used with some success in 1858.

† Stanley thought the force quite adequate. 'I assume that the forces available for 1842 will be an army of nine thousand to ten thousand men, of which there will be five British regiments, amounting to four thousand men, and a Company of British Artillery, combined with a naval force of three ships of the Line and a Fleet including thirteen or fourteen Steamers, of about forty Sail.' Ibid.

‡ Stanley decided that, if the campaign of 1842 failed, as seemed likely, he would advocate calling off the war and entering into commercial relations with the Chinese people without the consent of the Emperor. *Aberdeen Papers*, BM 43072. (Stanley to Aberdeen, October 17th, 1842).

> this year [1842], I should still be prepared to give up Hong Kong, notwithstanding the outcry which I know would be raised against it.

Want it or not, the island fell to Britain and Stanley had to worry about it. His first suggestion was to put Hongkong under the Home Government rather than to treat it as a dependency of India, and in this Peel concurred.[12] Later he submitted a detailed plan to Aberdeen. British law should be established, and a judge appointed to try both civil and criminal cases. As existing and probable conditions were not favourable to representative government there, he suggested the colony be put under a governor and his council. True to his original aims in this respect, Stanley suggested that Hongkong be made a free port, so that it would become an 'entrepot' for all nations.[13] However, all the land should be retained by the Crown, and the income from the increasing value of the site would defray the expenses involved in operating the port and administering the colony.* To bind the locale with additional cultural bonds, Stanley suggested that an Anglican clergyman be sent there immediately. When opportunity presented itself he recommended that a man 'strongly in favour of the absolute exclusion of opium' replace the British official who controlled the island after the war, and who favoured the opium trade.[14] In these ways Stanley provided for setting this new jewel in the crown of Victoria. Though never an imperialist, Stanley foresaw the potential importance of the island, and tried to make it more habitable for settlement.[15]

Canada also presented a considerable problem. Discontent in both Lower and Upper Canada had brought a revolt in 1837, and demands by the colonists to control the executive branch of their government. Stanley thought that the muddled Whig Canadian policy had brought on the rebellion, but he was aware there was no easy solution to Canada's problems.

Before their defeat the Whigs took steps to restore the loyalty of the colonists. In 1840 Upper and Lower Canada were united, and the colonists were given some voice in their government through an elective lower chamber, the Assembly. At the time the Whigs

* *Peel Papers*, BM 40426. (Stanley to Peel, December 22nd, 1842); *Aberdeen Papers*, BM 43072. (Stanley to Aberdeen, December 30th, 1842). (Aberdeen to Stanley, December 31st, 1842). The land plan described above was apparently originated by Stanley.

hoped this reform would give the Canadian English a preponderant voice in legislative matters over the Canadian French,* and they did not intend that the elective Assembly should control the Governor. Lord Sydenham, the Governor, had managed to hold the Assembly in check, largely through promises of future concessions in legislative matters,[16] and when the Conservatives came to power, they had to iron out the details of the relationship between the Governor and the Assembly.

Stanley realized that they would have difficulty in replacing the able Sydenham, and time bore out the truth of his fears. Casting around for a man with enough political ability to control the Canadian Assembly by private communications with its members, they finally came up with a relative of the Duke of Wellington, Sir Charles Bagot. Knowing that Bagot was not a very able politician, Stanley tried to secure the services of Lytton Bulwer, as his assistant, but he was unsuccessful. Thereafter, Bagot's departure became a comedy of errors. First, he demanded and received a new outfit, and then a secretary.† After a late start, the ship carrying Bagot encountered storms and was driven back to Cork, and had to be repaired. By that time the season was so far advanced that the new governor had to go through New York in order to pass on to Quebec, and this at a time when British-American relations were severely strained. Fate seemed determined to prevent Bagot's going to Canada – and his death.[17]

Though Sydenham had predicted that a two to one majority for the Government would be forthcoming, Bagot found a discouraging political situation in Canada. In a letter to Stanley he explained that there were five parties, representing the Government, the residents of Upper Canada, the Conservatives of Upper Canada, the Montreal British party and the French party, with the last of these holding the balance of power.[18] In this situation, Stanley could only advise that Bagot act as a mediator, and try to lure members from the other parties to that of the Government. Bagot exceeded considerably the intentions of the Home Government in the policy of

* 'The main argument for the Union,' wrote Stanley in 1842, 'was the hope of converting the British minority in the Lower Province into a majority by the infusion of the British majority of the Upper Province . . .' *Peel Papers*, BM 40426. (Stanley to Peel, August 27th, 1842).

† Stanley felt these concessions should be made in order to encourage Bagot to go to Canada '. . . more especially as I do not know where we should turn if he does not'. Ibid. (Stanley to Peel, Tuesday, 1841).

conciliation, and early in October 1842 Stanley learned that he had given the French party a place in the Government. Stanley always gave support and encouragement to his colonial officials, and in this case he assured Bagot of the support of the Home Government, even though certain members of the Cabinet, especially Wellington, strongly objected to the admission of a party 'tainted with treason'. At first the Duke was quite disturbed over what he considered a tame surrender, but after a special Cabinet on Canada early in November, it was decided to go along with Bagot. The gesture might be expected to create a new sympathy in Canada for the Home Government.[19]

Stanley hoped further to conciliate the restless Canadians by making some economic concessions to them. This could be done, he thought, by establishing a form of imperial preference, which would permit the shipment of corn to the mother country.[20] Early in March 1842, he wrote Bagot explaining that he would like to admit Canadian produce, but as Canada might simply become the intermediary for American-grown wheat, a relaxation of the tariff in her favour was impossible.[21] The Canadians interpreted his letter to promise that, if Canada laid a tariff on American corn, Britain would then relax the Corn Laws in her favour.[22] When Canada had imposed this duty, Stanley faced the task of selling both to the Cabinet and his party* the unpopular idea of relaxing the Corn Laws. As he pointed out to one member, who had difficulty in explaining the change to his suspicious constituents, the Canadian duty of 3s. on American wheat plus a colonial duty of 1s. gave the British farmer a 4s. protection against American wheat via Canada, and this was considerably higher than the usual duty on American wheat shipped direct to England.[23] Under the force of his arguments, and desiring to accommodate the Canadians, the Conservative Party went along with the change.[24]

The Administration of Stanley and Bagot of Canada was preeminently conciliatory, but the team was broken up shortly thereafter. Suddenly in December 1842, Stanley received alarming

* Louis J. Jennings, ed., *The Correspondence and Diaries of the Late Right Honourable John Wilson Croker* (New York: Charles Scribner's Sons, 1884), II, 314-15. (Stanley to Croker, June 20th, 1847). Stanley apparently had to overcome considerable resistance in the Cabinet to his plan, and his letter to Bagot of March 1842 may have been intentionally vague. The action of Canada forced the Cabinet to adopt his views. Stanley, however, was sure that the change contemplated would not injure British agriculture or the Corn Laws.

accounts of Bagot's health together with his resignation, and on the last day of the year he learned that there was no hope of Bagot's recovery.[25] Sir Charles Metcalfe, who had some colonial experience as Governor of Jamaica, replaced Bagot in March 1843, and in May the former Governor died. On its way to Britain, the remains of Bagot passed through the territory of the United States, and the citizens of Oswego courteously paid their respects. Stanley responded to this goodwill gesture by requesting the American authorities in Washington to tender thanks to them.[26]

On taking office Metcalfe sought to ingratiate himself with the colonists by exercising his discretionary powers to pardon some Canadians, deeply implicated in the 1837 revolt, who had been transported to Van Diemen's Land. For fear their return to Canada might bring new unrest, Stanley had been against pardoning these men, but, faced with a *fait accompli*, he favoured pardoning all rebels who would take the oath of allegiance.[27] Peel, however, demurred on grounds that a mass pardon might appear to be a British admission that the revolt was justified.[28] The Prime Minister's views prevailed, and the pardons of both Canadian and American prisoners came by individual applications.*

Some months later, a leading Canadian agitator, who helped start but did not participate in the revolt, demanded his back pay, and, hoping to help Metcalfe, Stanley went along with the demand.[29] By February 1844 Peel's patience was wearing thin. He wrote angrily: 'We shall soon have to tell these factious people there is one limit to our concessions. We will not govern you in a manner discreditable to us and injurious to you.'[30] Stanley agreed: 'It is in truth a struggle whether the Royal Authority shall exist, or virtually be set aside.'[31] The remainder of his term of office was marked by constant bickerings between the Home Government and the colony over various matters.

The struggle with Canada during these years was overshadowed by the diplomatic wranglings between Britain and the United States over boundary problems. Stanley feared American expansion to the north, and relied on the American South, which was tied

* Stanley asked that American prisoners be included in the general amnesty, but, on the advice of Peel, they were pardoned in the same way as the Canadians. By May 1845 most of the American prisoners had been released. See: *Colonial Office Papers*, CO 43/104. (Stephen to Addington, May 3rd, 1844). (Stephen to Addington, May 25th, 1844); CO 43/105. (Stephen to Addington, May 8th, 1845). (Stephen to Addington, June 20th, 1845).

economically to Britain, to restrain American northern expansion.[32] Nevertheless, late in 1841, it appeared that war between Britain and the United States might result from the Maine Boundary problem, and a number of minor sources of international irritation.

Stanley's knowledge of American affairs proved useful at this time. In November 1841 he received a dispatch from the Lieutenant Governor of New Brunswick proposing that the boundary question be settled through a convention between New Brunswick and Maine. Transmitting the dispatch to the Foreign Office, Stanley observed:[33]

> With regard to the proposed Convention with the State of Maine, Lord Stanley directs me to remark that that state has no more authority to conclude any arrangement on the subject which would be binding, than the Lieutenant Governor of New Brunswick. The Convention, if necessary, must be between Great Britain and the United States. . . .

Regarding the boundary itself, Stanley agreed with Wellington that a communications route between Quebec and New Brunswick should be maintained, at the cost of a 'very liberal concession to the westward'.[34] As interest in the subject quickened, the Colonial Office became a collecting point for old maps of the disputed area, some offered gratis, others for a price.[35]

Stanley, like Peel and Aberdeen, was anxious to remove all possible sources of conflict with the United States. He urged that the *Caroline* problem be settled, that the question of fugitive slaves who had come to Canada be solved, and he displayed little sympathy for Alexander McLeod, whose arrest brought Britain and the United States to the brink of war in 1841, twice rejecting his applications for indemnification.[36] Stanley also sought to avoid new sources of difficulty with the United States. In November 1841 a memorandum from the British Minister in Mexico was sent to him, which suggested that a 'Company of Adventurers' occupy Upper California, establish their 'sovereignty' there, and then be taken under the protection of the Crown. Stanley replied:[37]

> His Lordship directs me, in answer, to acquaint you . . . that he is not anxious for the formation of new and distant colonies, all of which involve heavy direct and still heavier indirect expenditure, besides multiplying the liabilities of misunderstandings and collisions with Foreign Powers . . . he cannot advise any encourage-

ment being given to the scheme of Colonization sketched by Mr. Pakenham.

Stanley's objections helped give the quietus to a plan which might have had serious international repercussions.

The tension between the United States and Britain eased for a few months following the signing of the Webster-Ashburton Treaty.* Stanley suggested to Aberdeen that the British naval force on the Great Lakes, strengthened at the time of the revolt, be cut down to the size agreed upon with the United States in 1817.[38] Aberdeen concurred, and Stanley advised the Admiralty of their decision.[39] About the same time Stanley contacted the American minister with a plan to allow free American negroes to go to the West Indies under contract as labourers.[40] But the Anglo-American rapprochement was ruined by the rising tension over the Oregon question, and in 1844 the Government was concerned to learn the United States was strengthening her force on the Great Lakes.[41]

The question of the Canadian frontier defence was but one aspect of the whole colonial defence problem. In many places the fortifications were very inadequate. The Australian colonies had no artillerymen at all until a few were sent there in 1845.[42] Periodically the Duke called attention to these weaknesses, but his views did not impress a Prime Minister whose primary interest was balancing his budget, a Foreign Secretary who was a pacifist, and a Colonial Secretary who opposed imperialism. 'There is nothing I dread more,' wrote Peel, 'than [illegible] Ordnance Report on the defence of any place . . .'[43] T[illegible]s Stanley replied: 'I entirely partake your feeling of ala[illegible] at an Ordnance Report upon Defences. . .'[44] Along this line, Stanley's only real interest at the time was in Malta, which was obviously important as a naval base.

By and large these men trusted in the wooden walls of Great Britain, and in the reasonableness of other nations. Diplomacy in their hands was not an instrument for winning transient successes which made good newspaper reading, but a means for establishing peace. Moderation, patience and compromise – these, they knew, were the key to peace, and by using them they guided Britain

*A discussion of the British interest in Maine can be found in: *The Mississippi Valley Historical Review* (December 1953), pp. 477-90. Wilbur Devereux Jones, 'Lord Ashburton and the Maine Boundary Negotiations'.

through a most critical period in her relations with the United States.

On hearing rumours that the United States was rearming the Lakes, Stanley wrote to Metcalfe in Canada for a report on the situation, and learned that American forces on Lakes Erie and Ontario were being augmented. He turned this information over to the Foreign Office, and a remonstrance was sent to Washington. The American reply was evasive, but it was not clear whether steamers had been included in the 1817 convention, or if Britain were thus justified in charging the United States with breaking the agreement. Peel wondered whether or not Britain might be fairly charged with setting a precedent for the non-observance of the Convention when she increased her Great Lakes force some years before. At the moment nothing was done to meet the American move.[45]

Behind the defence question lay Oregon, an issue which became increasingly menacing during 1845, and by late summer the Duke of Wellington was thoroughly out of patience with the governmental inactivity. Unable to secure support for what he considered adequate defence expenditures, or to interest Stanley in his plan for colonial defence, the Duke, on August 7th, wrote Peel and threatened to send an 'official protest' to Stanley.[46] Peel replied tactfully, and turned the correspondence over to Stanley for his information. The Colonial Secretary agreed that the Duke's defence plan, reviving an idea dating back to 1826, would practically ruin the country financially.[47]

While they were trying to reassure the Duke, another dispatch arrived from Metcalfe, who was quite alarmed, and toyed with the idea of an offensive war against the United States. Peel was astonished at the suggestion, and Stanley, to keep the dispatch out of the Duke's hands, sent it to Aberdeen with the comment that offensive operations against the United States were impracticable and impossible, but that some steps be taken for defence.[48] Peel also took a new interest in the defence question, and requested a report from Stanley,[49] who replied that there were large forces in Canada on paper, but that the Canadian legislature was uncooperative, and the militia could not be called up.[50] Pursuing the question further, Stanley drew up a Minute on Canadian defences on September 1st, and this reflected the majority opinion of the Cabinet. Preparations should be defensive rather than offensive, they should seek a naval superiority on the Lakes, and Quebec, Montreal and Kingston should be fortified. Before the Cabinet appropriated funds for Canadian defence, they demanded that Canada improve her militia, which must be a vital element in her defence.[51]

A few days later Peel wrote gloomily of the prospects in the 'Cold War':[52]

> What is to be the result in a financial point of view of being prepared for attack on all important points on which attacks, in the event of war, are possible & not improbable contingencies, I know not. It will make peace so expensive — that many will think actual war a more tolerable evil than such a state of burdensome and anxious suspense. After all our labours and all our Expenses there will be some vulnerable point which will probably be the object of attack.

Stanley had greater confidence in their defence plans, but what bothered him most was the attitude of the Canadian people. After outlining the defence plan, Stanley added: 'This done, I shall feel very easy about the defence of Canada, if the Canadians wish to be defended.'[53]

In January 1846 Aberdeen skilfully combined a conciliatory attitude with a threat of force, and these caused the Americans to withdraw from their advanced position and seek a compromise solution of the Oregon issue.* The Maine and Oregon compromises reflected great credit both on Lord Aberdeen and the Government of which he was a part.

Around the world from Britain, about six months away by mail, lay New Zealand, which was to cause Stanley some of his most embarrassing moments at the Colonial Office. It was acquired in 1840 by a treaty with the Maoris, the natives there, and shortly thereafter the New Zealand Company began to send settlers to the island. Their colonization efforts were strongly opposed by the Church Missionary Society, which sought to shield the simple natives from what they considered to be the evil effects of white civilization. Before long Stanley was to find himself in the midst of the struggle between these two organizations.

* For a discussion of Aberdeen's skilful diplomacy see: *Pacific Historical Review* (November 1953), pp. 353-64. Wilbur Devereux Jones and J. Chal Vinson, 'British Preparedness and the Oregon Settlement'.

It is perhaps an understatement to say that Stanley was not favourably disposed towards the New Zealand Company. He was lacking in that imaginative daring which caused the British to send their people to remote areas of the world, and, as in the cases of Hongkong and Upper California noted above, Stanley opposed the planting of distant colonies. Furthermore, the headship of the Company was composed largely of Whigs and Radicals, two groups which Stanley opposed politically. Finally, much of the information Stanley received on the situation in New Zealand was interpreted for him by James Stephen, the Under Secretary at the Colonial Office, who was a prominent member of the Church Missionary Society and deeply prejudiced against the Company.

On the other hand, the Company itself was not wholly blameless for the conflict that followed Stanley's assumption of the direction of New Zealand affairs. The survey work carried on by the Company in New Zealand was badly managed, and the arriving colonists did not set to work immediately upon arrival, but wasted their time and money in town. They were guilty also of what is usually considered a well-nigh unpardonable crime in frontier areas – selling arms and ammunition to the natives. There is some evidence also that the Company sought to distribute 'profits' from the venture before it was really well under way.* Finally, Stanley assumed control of the New Zealand situation at a most inopportune moment, when the funds brought from England by the settlers were approaching exhaustion, and before the colony had found export products to pay its way along.

Late in 1843 Stanley sent Captain Fitzroy to become Governor of the struggling colony. Fitzroy was directed to raise funds for administration purposes from tariffs rather than direct taxation, to uphold the Treaty of Waitangi under which the Maoris ceded New Zealand to Britain in 1840, and to act as mediator in cases of

* Stanley claimed that they paid large dividends to themselves as shareholders. *Peel Papers*, BM 40468. (Stanley to Peel, February 11th, 1845). An authority on the subject, however, feels that the dividends were not excessive. J. S. Marais, *The Colonization of New Zealand* (London: Humphrey Milford, 1927), pp. 76-8. Marais is particularly critical of Stanley, and blames him, rather than James Stephen, for carrying on a running battle with the Company. The case against Stanley can be found in Chapter VII of the above work. An older authority treats Stanley much more tenderly. G. W. Rusden, *History of New Zealand* (London: Chapman & Hall, 1883), pp. 271, 493. James Stephen's most recent biographer (Paul Knaplund, *James Stephen and the British Colonial System*) unfortunately does not treat this controversy in detail.

land disputes between the colonists and the Maoris.[54] The second of these instructions became a point of vital importance. Under the terms of that treaty Britain guaranteed to the Maoris the 'full, exclusive, and undisturbed possession of all their lands and estates, forests, fisheries, and other properties . . . so long as it is their wish and desire to retain the same in their possession'. The Company felt the guarantee applied only to the lands actually occupied by the Maoris; the missionaries, and Stanley, were convinced it included all of the lands of New Zealand. The latter, in theory at least, were apparently right.*

It is quite important to note that Fitzroy, whose appointment was greeted with the warmest approval by the Company,[55] was more or less on his own once he reached New Zealand, for the place was so distant that he could not expect to receive specific instructions from the Home Government to meet day-to-day situations. Upon arrival there, Fitzroy discovered that a very difficult situation had developed. A number of settlers, including a prominent official of the Company, had been killed by the Maoris at the Wairau River in a dispute over land claims.† The settlers, of course, sought the punishment of the guilty natives, but they had many other grievances also. They wanted the capital, far to the north at Auckland, moved to Wellington in the south.[56] They wanted an improved police force, and restraint to be placed on the hostile activities of the missionaries, who tried to discourage the settlement of the island. But their most pressing need was the clearing up of land claims which would permit them to occupy definite holdings and get to work.

As the settlers had been unable to take over much land for cultivation, their resources were rapidly depleted by the need to import food and supplies from Sydney and Valparaiso. Land was absolutely necessary to the life of the settlement, but it had to be obtained under terms satisfactory to the Maoris, who were armed and able to defend their rights. William Spain had been

* See: Marais, *New Zealand*, pp. 100-1.

† '. . . all the accounts I have received,' Stanley wrote Peel, 'lead me to believe that that catastrophe was wholly attributable to the Colonists, and that they were in the wrong throughout'. *Peel Papers*, BM 40550. (Stanley to Peel, September 5th, 1844). The *Morning Chronicle* said the massacre resulted from Stanley's unwillingness to settle the land claims in favour of the Company. 'His wrongful quarrel with the New Zealand Company has been voided in the massacre at Wairau.' *New Zealand Journal*, August 17th, 1844. (Reprint from the *Morning Chronicle*).

sent to New Zealand while Russell was still in office to settle the land claims in the Company's district, but the job took him three years and satisfied no one.

Fitzroy tried to satisfy both sides, but ended up by alienating both. In March 1844 he decided to allow the settlers to purchase lands directly from the natives, subject to government approval, and upon the payment of a small fee. These direct negotiations led to numerous disputes between the settlers and the Maoris, who had their own land laws which were almost incomprehensible to the British. By this time money had become so scarce that Fitzroy reduced sharply the government fee for land purchases, and, hoping to save the local bank and the precarious financial structure of the colony, he allowed debentures to circulate as money.[57]

But the Governor was equally, if not more, favourable towards the Maoris. He took the word of a Maori chief that the whites had precipitated the Wairau massacre, and refused to prosecute the Indians implicated in it. When Spain finally made his award, Fitzroy set it aside on grounds that it was too favourable to the settlers, and he went so far as to drop his plan to create a militia, lest this offend the Maoris. And when, in violation of his instructions, he lifted the tariff wall and substituted a property tax for it, this was collected only from the whites. But his appeasement did not work. Egged on by the missionaries,* the Maoris became so troublesome that Fitzroy had to request military aid from New South Wales. For their difficulties, the colonists blamed Fitzroy, Stephen and Stanley in about that order.†

During these crucial months Stanley was almost wholly out of touch with the colony. The Company, of course, advised him of its difficulties in a series of letters, which he answered in the same combative tone in which they were written. Stanley, however, consented to having a parliamentary investigating committee study the New Zealand situation in April 1844. The Company apparently outmanœuvred Stanley in the selection of members of this committee. 'The moment they had ascertained I would con-

* Even Stanley, who favoured the missionaries, admitted they sought to oppose the colonization. *Peel Papers*, BM 40550. (Stanley to Peel, September 5th, 1844).

† Sentiment against Stanley grew as the situation deteriorated. In August 1844, the *New Zealand Journal* traced its difficulties to Stephen; six months later, to Stanley. See: *New Zealand Journal*, August 17th, 1844, February 15th, 1845. During that time Stanley had little direct influence over the situation in the colony.

sent to the appointment of one,' wrote Stanley, 'they prepared a list of names, studiously selected from *our* side of the House, but previously thoroughly imbued by Charles Buller with the views of the Co: and before obtaining my assent, rendered it most difficult to object, by saying that each of them had consented and wished to serve.'[58] When the report of the committee was published, the Company's interpretation of the Treaty of Waitangi was affirmed, and its position was strengthened on almost all points at issue.

Stanley refused to accept the report of the committee on the land question. He offered to give the Company all of the land to which the Crown had title, but refused to include in this lands which had not been relinquished by the natives. 'They are well-armed, & warlike,' wrote Stanley in December, 'and number above 100,000. Our settlers are dispersed, not above 10,000 in number, and our Military force for the whole Island is under 150 men . . . With these facts, I would ask whether I use too strong an expression when I say, setting aside considerations of justice and good faith, I *dare* not act on the principles laid down by the Company, and apparently supported by the Committee . . .'[59] He explained to Peel that he had at first sought to co-operate cordially with the Company, but that their 'small trickery' had alienated him. His hostility to it as of December 1844 is shown in his observation: 'The Company has been, from the first, a great bubble, the bursting of which, but for the immediate consequences to the settlers, I should rejoice at, and consider eminently advantageous to New Zealand.'[60] Both of these motives, fear of the natives and dislike of the Company figured in Stanley's thinking at this time.

During 1844 many of the newspapers took up the cause of New Zealand against the Colonial Office. The *Morning Chronicle* made the following observation regarding Stanley: 'Lord Stanley is the best hand in the world at a party speech, when such things are wanted. But his possession of this quality is no reason for entrusting him with the fortunes of our Colonies, of which he has no time to understand the many wants, while his best energies are devoted to breeding horses for Liverpool and Goodwood races.'[61] Stanley shortly found himself in a most embarrassing position, even though Peel wrote in December 1844: 'I will do whatever you wish in this matter. I think you were quite right throughout.'[62]

The cause of the embarrassment was the strange silence of

Fitzroy, from whom Stanley expected to receive information which would refute some of the charges made against his administration. In a dispatch of February 3rd, 1845, Stanley complained that it was four months since he had heard from the Governor. That same month he was unable to answer one of the questions asked by Peel on the subject, and it was a most important question. Stanley did not know why the conditional grants of land had not been made. Undoubtedly Stanley's impatience grew apace, for on March 1st he wrote Fitzroy: 'I am unwilling to suppose that you have really been silent during the whole of that period: but should that have been the case, I cannot conceal from you that I should regard such silence as a dereliction of duty so serious, as to render it impossible for me to advise the Queen to continue to you her confidence in so distant a Government.'[63] What Stanley did not know, officially at least, at this time included most of the important decisions that Fitzroy had made. Fitzroy had not explained his tax proposals, why he had made debentures legal tender, why he had called in troops from New South Wales, why he had pardoned a certain Maori chief, and why he had set aside the awards made by Spain.*

Just how completely out of touch Stanley had been with New Zealand affairs was revealed to all who were not aware of it before when a member of Parliament called for a variety of papers on the subject of New Zealand. The Government was able to supply information on only two of the six returns from Fitzroy's dispatches

* Stanley charged in his dispatches to Fitzroy that the Governor's dispatches had not covered these important matters as late as March 1st. The tax changes and making debentures legal tender had taken place in May 1844; calling in the troops and the pardon of the chief (Heke) took place in the summer of 1844: Fitzroy's setting aside of Spain's award apparently occurred somewhat later in the year. It would seem that Fitzroy had both the time and opportunity to explain in detail to Stanley why he acted as he did in these cases, for the Company had information on these subjects long before Stanley had. Stanley wrote that Fitzroy had sent three series of dispatches during this period: those written January 11th-15th, 1844 (received on June 11th, 1844), those written March 26th-April 15th, 1844 (received on September 17th, 1844), and those written April 18th-September 28th, 1844 (received on March 29th, 1845). They were all evidently rather defective. After receiving all of them Stanley complained that Fitzroy had not fully explained his financial transactions, had 'scarcely noticed' the incident involving bringing troops from Australia, and, most important, had written practically nothing regarding the settlement of land claims. Stanley's case against Fitzroy, both for failing to adequately inform the Colonial Office regarding his activities, and for violating instructions, seems to be very strong. *Peel Papers*, BM 40468. (Stanley's Confidential Statement on New Zealand, April 11th, 1845).

and could answer the third from information from other sources. On three of the subjects the Government had to confess its ignorance.[64] While both Peel and G. W. Hope defended the Colonial Office as best they could, the impression that there was something radically wrong with Stanley's administration of colonial affairs could hardly be avoided.

To extricate himself, Stanley could place the blame on Fitzroy, and he undoubtedly had some cause to do so. He submitted a report to the Cabinet on April 11th, shortly after receiving the third set of unsatisfactory dispatches from Fitzroy, and advised that the Governor be recalled. This course was supported by the rest of the Cabinet, and in a dispatch of April 30th Stanley advised Fitzroy of his dismissal.[65] In a dispatch of May 14th Stanley explained his reasons in greater detail – that Fitzroy had not adequately informed the Government of his activities, that he had violated Stanley's 'express wishes' in substituting direct taxation for customs duties, that Fitzroy had shown arbitrariness and indecision in settling the land claims, that he had violated his instructions in not raising a militia force, and because he had put the Government in a position of 'almost inextricable embarrassment'.[66]

The recall of Fitzroy, however, by no means halted the attacks on the Government's conduct of colonial affairs. In May Stanley sought to quiet the Company by buying out its interests in New Zealand, but his offer was rejected.[67] The following month Charles Buller asked the House to consider the state of New Zealand, and the case of the New Zealand Company, and Peel, who considered the move as an attempt further to discredit his Colonial Secretary, opposed the motion.[68] During the three nights' debate that followed, Stanley's friends defended him as best they could, but they did not do too well. Graham, for example, refused to admit that Stanley had erred, but went on to explain that, if he had, it was based on the highest motives.[69] Peel was able to secure a majority against Buller only by making the issue a party question.

Meanwhile in New Zealand disaster followed disaster. Fitzroy's appeasement policy did not prevent a Maori insurrection. Chief Heke, whom Fitzroy had once pardoned for a revolt, turned on the Governor and sporadic fighting followed. With settlers and Maoris up in arms, with attacks at home both on his party and himself, Stanley lived through some trying days in 1845. At length a new Governor, George Grey, was sent to the islands and the situation there was gradually restored.

Stanley's conduct of New Zealand affairs is the worst blot on his record as a colonial administrator. His obvious dislike of the New Zealand Company, his partisan sympathy for the missionaries who were guilty of many indiscretions, and the fact that he did not keep a closer watch over the situation in New Zealand in 1844 are all points against him. On the other hand, it should be remembered that he assumed direction of affairs there in a most trying period, and inherited a most difficult situation particularly with regard to the land claims. It might, with some justice, be asked why the New Zealand Company did not wait until the land situation was completely cleared up before bringing settlers into the area. If Stanley was wrong in not pressing Fitzroy to settle quickly the land claims, which were the most important factor in the whole situation, the Company was equally wrong in assuming that the Government would interpret the Treaty of Waitangi in its favour.

One cannot doubt that Stanley acted according to his own sense of Christian justice throughout the incident, and it is indeed unfortunate that his lofty motives led to such tragic results. New Zealand suffered, and so did Stanley's reputation as a statesman. Having gone to the House of Lords, he was unable to defend himself in the Commons, and he was not too happy with the manner in which Peel handled the controversy.[70] But the affair was merely an incident compared with the great issue in which he was shortly to be involved.

NOTES

[1] *COP*, CO 43/103. (Hope to Lord Provost of Glasgow, May 15th, 1843).
[2] Ibid.; *Annual Register* (1843), pp. 67-9.
[3] *COP*, CO 43/105. (Stephen to Addington, June 7th, 1845).
[4] *EP*, PRO 30/12 68. (Stanley to President of the Board of Control, December 31st, 1841).
[5] Ibid.
[6] Ibid. (Stanley to President of the Board of Control, January 3rd, 1842).
[7] Ibid. (Stanley to the Lords Commissioners of the Admiralty, February 4th, 1842).
[8] Ibid.
[9] *AP*, BM 43072. (Aberdeen to Stanley, October 15th, 1842).
[10] Ibid. (Stanley to Aberdeen, October 17th, 1842).
[11] Ibid.
[12] *PP*, BM 40426. (Stanley to Peel, November 27th, 1842).
[13] *AP*, BM 43072. (Stanley to Aberdeen, December 30th, 1842).
[14] Ibid. (Stanley to Aberdeen, December 23rd, 1843).

[15] *PP*, BM 40426. (Stanley to Peel, December 22nd, 1842).

[16] Ibid., BM 40467. (Peel to Stanley, October 5th, 1841).

[17] Ibid. (Stanley to Peel, Tuesday Night). (Stanley to Peel, September 20th, 1841); *COP*, CO 43/100. (Hope to Moore, November 13th, 1841); *AP*, BM 43072. (Stanley to Aberdeen, September 16th, 1841).

[18] *PP*, BM 40426. (Stanley to Peel, August 27th, 1842).

[19] Ibid. (Stanley to Peel, August 27th, October 3rd and 21st, 1842). (Peel to Stanley, October 17th and 26th, 1842).

[20] Jennings, *Croker*, II, 313-16. (Stanley to Croker, June 20th, 1847).

[21] *Annual Register* (1842), pp. 335-7. (Stanley to Bagot, March 2nd, 1842).

[22] *PP*, BM 40426. (Stanley to Peel, November 22nd, 1842).

[23] Ibid., BM 40468. (Stanley to Worsley, April 17th, 1843).

[24] Jennings, *Croker*, II, 358. (Bentinck to Croker, December 27th, 1847).

[25] *PP*, BM 40426. (Stanley to Peel, December 22nd and 31st, 1842).

[26] *COP*, CO 43/103. (Stephen to Canning, June 22nd, 1843).

[27] *PP*, BM 40468. (Stanley to Peel, August 30th, 1843).

[28] Ibid. (Peel to Stanley, August 31st, 1843).

[29] Ibid. (Stanley to Peel, December 26th, 1843).

[30] Ibid. (Peel to Stanley, February 2nd, 1844).

[31] Ibid. (Stanley to Peel, January 18th, 1844).

[32] Ibid. BM 40425. (Stanley to Peel, January 8th, 1838). (Stanley to Peel, December 7th, 1838).

[33] *COP*, CO 43/100. (Stephen to Canning, November 13th, 1841).

[34] *AP*, BM 43072. (Stanley's Notes on Aberdeen's Papers regarding the Maine Boundary, 1842).

[35] *COP*, CO 43/100. (Stephen to Canning, April 5th, 1842); Ibid., CO 43/102. (Hope to Addington, March 24th, 1843).

[36] Ibid., CO 43/101. (Stephen to Addington, June 1st, 1842); Ibid., CO 43/105. (Stephen to Addington, June 9th, 1845).

[37] Ibid., CO 43/100. (Hope to Canning, November 23rd, 1841).

[38] Ibid., CO 43/102. (Stephen to Addington, February 10th, 1843).

[39] Ibid. (Stephen to Barrow, February 18th, 1843).

[40] *AP*, BM 43072. (Stanley to Aberdeen, November 12th, 1842). (Stanley to Everett, November 8th, 1842). (Stanley's Memorandum, November 11th, 1842). (Aberdeen to Stanley, November 13th, 1842). (Stanley to Aberdeen, November 14th, 1842).

[41] *COP*, CO 43/104. (Stephen to Addington, May 22nd, 1844).

[42] *PP*, BM 40468. (Stanley to Peel, November 28th, 1845).

[43] Ibid. (Peel to Stanley, November 7th, 1844).

[44] Ibid. (Stanley to Peel, November 11th, 1844).

[45] Ibid. (Stanley to Peel, September 5th, 1844). (Peel to Stanley, September 7th, 1844). (Peel to Stanley, August 14th, 1845). (Stanley to Peel, August 18th, 1845); *AP*, BM 43072. (Stanley to Aberdeen, August 18th, 1845); *COP*, CO 43/104. (Stephen to Addington, May 22nd and June 3rd, 1844).

[46] Parker, *Peel*, III, 201-6. (Wellington to Peel, August 7th, 1845).

[47] *PP*, BM 40468. (Peel to Stanley, August 11th, 1845). (Stanley to Peel, August 12th, 1845). (Peel to Stanley, August 13th, 1845).

[48] Ibid. (Peel to Stanley, August 13th, 1845). (Stanley to Peel, August 18th, 1845); *AP*, BM 43072. (Stanley to Aberdeen, August 18th, 1845).

[49] *PP*, BM 40468. (Peel to Stanley, August 14th, 1845).

[50] Ibid. (Stanley to Peel, August 18th, 1845).

[51] Ibid. (Stanley's Minute on the Defence of Canada, September 1st, 1845).

[52] Ibid. (Peel to Stanley, September 5th, 1845).

[53] Ibid. (Stanley to Peel, September 12th, 1845).

[54] Ibid. (Stanley to Peel, December 17th, 1844). (Stanley's Confidential Report on New Zealand, April 11th, 1845); Ibid., BM 40571. (Stanley to Fitzroy, March 1st, 1845). (Stanley to Fitzroy, May 14th, 1845).

[55] Ibid., BM 40468. (Stanley to Peel, December 17th, 1844).

[56] *New Zealand Journal*, February 3rd, 1844.

[57] *PP*, BM 40468. (Stanley's Confidential Statement on New Zealand, April 11th, 1845).

[58] Ibid. (Stanley to Peel, December 17th, 1844).

[59] Ibid.

[60] Ibid.

[61] *New Zealand Journal*, August 17th, 1844.

[62] *PP*, BM 40468. (Peel to Stanley, January 15th, 1845).

[63] Ibid. BM 40571. (Stanley to Fitzroy, March 1st, 1845).

[64] Ibid. (Stanley to Fitzroy, March 14th, 1845).

[65] Ibid. (Stanley to Fitzroy, April 30th, 1845).

[66] Ibid. (Stanley to Fitzroy, May 14th, 1845).

[67] J. S. Marais, *The Colonization of New Zealand* (London: Humphrey Milford, 1927), pp. 190-1.

[68] Ibid., pp. 191-6.

[69] *Hansard* (third series), LXXXI, 929.

[70] Morley, *Gladstone*, I, 298. (*Diary*, July 24th, 1846).

CHAPTER V

THE GREAT CONSERVATIVE SCHISM

UNAFFECTED by the diplomatic tensions with America or the Maori uprisings in New Zealand, Stanley's domestic life followed its usual pattern. His father continued in uncertain health, and his wife and sometime secretary, Emma, frequently fell ill. There was another birth in January 1841. Occurring two weeks sooner than was expected, the event found Stanley away, and his second son was already squalling by the time he hurriedly appeared at St. James's Square.[1] They named him Frederick Arthur. The family grew to include two boys, both later to inherit the title, and a girl, Emma, named for her mother.

On quiet evenings nothing pleased Stanley more than to read Shakespeare to his family in that same rich tenor with which he regaled the Commons.[2] By midsummer he was always impatient for the adjournment of Parliament so that he might return to Knowsley, where he supervised the making and selling of drain tile to his tenants,[3] partook of the pleasures of the hunt, and awaited the visits of Malmesbury, Graham and others. There were good seasons and bad ones – when game was abundant, and when it was scarce. But even during this period Stanley was unable to stand the rigours of outdoor life as well as before. In 1841, 1843 and 1845 he was stricken with gout, and at times could not bear to set his foot on the ground. Once, after a walk with Peel, he found his foot so swollen he could not put a shoe on it.[4] The physicians blamed his condition on his sedentary life in London, but there was no cure, and periodically Stanley was forced to hobble around on crutches.[5]

Even though he was not Prime Minister, Stanley could take pride in the Government of which he was a part, and many years later Graham was to look back on the Cabinet and call it a 'happy accident'.[6] Apart from Peel, the Government could boast of two ex-Prime Ministers, and three Prime Ministers of the future. Had Disraeli been successful in securing a post, the list of Ministers would look, in retrospect, even more impressive, but his earnest pleas to Peel for recognition were turned down. There was a story that Stanley, and not Peel, was responsible for the snub, and that Stanley told Peel '. . . if that scoundrel were taken in he would not remain himself'.[7] Whether or not this is true, Disraeli treasured up his grievance against Peel until the time arrived when he could take revenge and simultaneously advance his own career.

Such an illustrious group was bound sometimes to experience dissensions. Wellington at times proved difficult, and Peel handled his eminent subordinate very carefully. On more than one occasion Stanley also had an encounter with the Duke. Ever careful of rewarding his followers and the officers of his department, Stanley tried his best to expand the membership of the Order of the Bath so that workers in colonial fields might be recognized with the honour. The Duke opposed such an expansion of the membership, and the controversy continued for more than a year without result.[8] When he sought a peerage for Metcalfe in Canada, Peel balked, but finally yielded to Stanley.[9] Patronage caused another minor unpleasantness between Peel and Stanley late in 1841,* but such incidents were the exception rather than the rule. Unless the issue involved a major question of principle, Stanley was ready to follow Peel or anyone else in the Cabinet in reaching decisions. 'For my own part,' he wrote Gladstone in 1844, 'I should prefer that course which seems necessary for the government, even though I might not think it best in itself.'[10]

During these years of triumphant conservatism, Stanley watched with interest Peel's operations in the realm of finance and economics. In 1841 Stanley, who never pretended to be an authority on economics, acknowledged the possibility of combining the removal of economic restrictions with an increase in revenue, and he hoped that such a plan would obviate the necessity of an income tax, which he strongly opposed.[11] However, when Peel decided upon an income tax, Stanley swallowed his objections and spoke in its favour.[12] He was aware that England could compete successfully with any nation in a free market, so he had suggested that

* *Peel Papers*, BM 40467. (Peel to Stanley, November 10th, 1841). (Stanley to Peel, November 10th, 1841). There are also evidences that their relationship was not unpleasant. Early in 1844, Peel requested that Stanley sit for a portrait for his collection and Stanley seemed flattered. It turned out so well that Emma Stanley had a copy made from it. Ibid., BM 40468. (Peel to Stanley, January 15th, 1844). (Stanley to Peel, January 15th, 1844). Ibid., BM 40541. (Emma Stanley to Peel, March 2nd, 1844). This is apparently the portrait now hanging in the National Portrait Gallery.

Hongkong be made a free port, and wrote regarding Liberia: '. . . the great interests there are commercial interests, and . . . with fair play, we can beat any other Nation in the World in the influence to be obtained through such means'.[13]

In relaxing trade restrictions, Stanley contemplated a sort of Imperial Preference such as that in his Canadian Corn Bill. On the other hand, as a consistent opponent of slavery, he demanded that the tariff be used to aid the free labour sugar-producers against slave-grown sugar competition.* In 1844 the Government appeared to be heading for defeat on a hotly-contested sugar bill until at a crucial moment Stanley made a ringing speech on its behalf. The admiring Gladstone noted he never thereafter struck 'such a stroke as this'.[14]

This speech was a fitting swan song to the House of Commons. By 1844 Stanley was convinced his health demanded an easing of his routine, and he had become dissatisfied with the Commons wherein 'every year more time is wasted, and business done more unsatisfactorily'.[15] As there was little interest in colonial affairs, Stanley was not often needed in debate, and was merely an onlooker who cast a vote on divisions. In the Lords the Duke was ageing, Ripon was often ill, Lyndhurst seemed unwilling to debate, and there was a genuine need for Stanley's talents.† There, also, the routine would be less pressing, and he would find relief from the 'drudgery' of the Commons.

On July 27th, 1844, Stanley wrote Peel requesting his elevation to the Upper House. Peel consulted Wellington, who agreed that Stanley would be of service in the Lords, and then the Queen, who expressed her surprise at the request, but gave her consent to it. Thereafter Peel replied in a warm letter, noting that he would be losing his 'right arm', but he agreed to the change. 'Nothing could be kinder', Stanley wrote Ripon, 'than the manner in which my request was acceded to by Peel.'[16] To Peel he extended thanks, and expressed the hope that there would be a 'long continuance' of their association in the public service.[17]

* *Annual Register* (1844), p. 161; Ibid. (1845), pp. 59-60. See, for example, Stanley's opposition to the Portuguese Slave Treaty. *Aberdeen Papers*, BM 43072. (Stanley to Aberdeen, September 28th, 1842).

† Greville noted it was 'high time' Stanley went to the Lords. '. . . there is nobody there who can speak, and they have therefore been obliged to hire Brougham by the night'. A. H. Johnson, ed., *The Letters of Charles Greville and Henry Reeve* (London: T. Fisher Unwin, 1924), pp. 95-6. (Greville to Reeve, September 5th, 1844).

Some details still had to be arranged. The Radicals were strong in Stanley's election district — another reason for his requesting the change – and he felt they could be better defeated at a by-election than a general election. His father helped him time the announcement of his retirement from the seat so that the Radicals would have little opportunity to prepare themselves for the contest.[18] Late in September, Stanley had still not received his writ of summons, and was somewhat worried lest the opening of Parliament 'find myself between two Houses, with a seat in neither'.[19] But the summons came in October, and he was raised to the peerage as Lord Stanley of Bickerstaffe.

Stanley's elevation, Gladstone later observed, changed the whole course of English politics. But, in 1844, Stanley could not foresee that Ireland and a potato blight were about to shake the very foundations of the British party system. Nor could he foretell that the opportunity for leadership he had sought so long was suddenly to present itself, and to find him in the wrong house of Parliament.

To the landed aristocracy and squires of England the Corn Laws, which preserved the home market for them against foreign competition, seemed to be the beam undergirding their economic life. Without them, foreign grains might flood the country, bring prices to a low level, and impoverish both their own class and the tenants and farm labourers who worked their lands. For many years their monopoly had gone virtually unchallenged, but during the 1830s a new theory of economics sponsored by the Radicals was brought to bear against them.

The Free Traders advocated the removal of all impediments to the free play of economic forces, and looked askance at the Corn Laws, which they felt maintained high living costs and high wages, and thus took money from the manufacturers' and workers' pockets and placed it in the purses of the landlords. Thus, there were two points of view on the subject, one of the country, the other of the city, and they were shortly to be personified in the persons of Sir Robert Peel, whose fortune came from industry, and Stanley, whose substance arose from the land.

In 1838 Charles Villiers introduced a motion into Parliament that the House resolve itself into committee for the purpose of reviewing the Act of 9th George IV, c. 60, the Corn Laws. The motion was easily disposed of, but yearly it returned with added strength behind it. The powerful Anti-Corn Law League and the workers both agitated in favour of repeal. Richard Cobden, Stanley observed, was in particular a 'worrying man' on corn, and argued his point of view quite intelligently.[20] The idea enlisted increasing numbers to its banner, and during the election of 1841 Russell tried to make a fixed duty, rather than the sliding scale, the chief issue. At that time the men of substance rallied around Sir Robert Peel, as an antidote for Radicalism, and his efficient Party was wafted into office. He opposed the fixed duty, which he said could not be permanent,[21] and many Conservatives, like Stanley, thought Peel was 'quite strong' for the Corn Laws at this time.[22] At the same time, however, he was aware that Peel had friends in the Anti-Corn Law League.[23]

The idea of Free Trade had a humanitarian, as well as an intellectual and economic, appeal. The plight of undernourished workers' families huddled in the squalor of dirty manufacturing towns was miserable enough to make thoughtful men pause and seek means of remedying the situation. Abolition of the Corn Laws might well be expected to be a boon to the lowly. Which of these considerations, the intellectual, economic or the humanitarian, loomed largest in Peel's mind is debatable, but it is clear that he became an increasingly less strong supporter of the Corn Laws. His Budgets all pointed to a removal of trade restrictions. An alteration of the Corn Laws in 1842 slightly reduced duties on corn and meat, but the change had the consent of the agricultural interest, and Stanley agreed to it because the change brought Protection rather than absolute exclusion.[24] Two minor members of the Government, Lords Buckingham and Hardwicke, however, resigned over the change. Had the others seen Graham's letter to Peel of December 1842, many might have followed their example. 'In truth', Graham wrote, 'it is a question of time. The next change must be to open trade . . . But the next change must be the last; it is not prudent to hurry it.'[25] While Graham and Peel thus secretly left the ranks of the Protectionists,* this does

* About the time Graham wrote the above to Peel, he was persuading Croker to write an article in favour of Protection. Jennings, *Croker*, II, 368. (Croker to Graham, September 23rd, 1847). The rank and file of the Conservative Party obviously were in the dark about their leader's change of policy until the crisis was well advanced. Lord Campbell described the situation in 1843 as follows: 'The Prime Minister, having as yet given no intelligible intimation that he meant to depart

not mean they were hostile towards the agriculturists, for they felt that efficiently-run British farms could compete with foreign producers.

Stanley, while he was quite aware of Peel's proneness to experiment with the tariff system, was not taken into his or Graham's confidence on the subject of the Corn Laws. He was reluctant to bring up the sensitive subject again, but in 1843 he introduced his Canadian Corn Bill and carried it largely because it represented the fulfilment of a promise made to Canada, and because he could convince his friends of his own attachment to the Corn Laws. The fact that he did reassure his friends of his belief in the protective system at this time probably made Stanley even more reluctant to go along with Peel late in 1845.

Though they might by using ambiguous language conceal the conclusion to which their thinking had led them, Peel and Graham were increasingly less able to conceal the direction of their thought from the Commons. In 1843, after listening to Peel advocate buying in the cheapest market, Stanley nervously observed to Gladstone: 'Peel laid that down a great deal too broadly.'[26] Stanley himself always experienced difficulty in speaking on economic topics, and after his own speech during the debate he was quite disgusted with himself.[27]

Peel's pronouncements in favour of Protection became ever weaker as the months went by. Early in 1845 he said the Corn Laws ought not to be abolished, but it was far from being a strong statement.[28] He and Graham spoke so cautiously when Villiers brought up his annual motion in June that Lord Howick, noting their indecision, observed that both might have backed the motion if it had called for gradual abolition. Many Conservatives, who interpreted Peel's ambiguous language in their own way and perhaps read into his speeches promises which were not there, continued to have faith in Peel.

During the summer of 1845 Peel and Graham were deeply interested in the weather. Since the end of 1843 there had been reports of a new potato disease which had found its way to the

further from the Protectionist principles which he had professed when assailing the late Government, continued to possess the confidence of the great bulk of the Conservative party . . .' Hardcastle, *Campbell*, II, 240. Disraeli wrote that, while his colleagues knew the direction of Peel's economic thinking, they did not challenge him so long as he kept his views in the theory stage. Benjamin Disraeli, *Lord George Bentinck* (London: G. Routledge & Co., 1858), p. 14.

British Isles, and as early as 1844 Stanley had investigated the progress of the blight. This was a particularly bad summer, cold, rainy and disagreeable. On August 12th Stanley reported to Peel that the crops had suffered in certain areas, but in others the prospects seemed to be satisfactory. Graham wrote on August 21st that the potato disease had seriously injured the crop in southern England, but as yet there were no reports from the north or from Ireland. Shortly thereafter he visited Stanley and was pleased to find his old friend had recovered from the gout. During the balance of the month the reports received by Graham concerning Irish agriculture were generally favourable, but the English wheat yield was deficient and the country faced the prospect of high food prices.[29]

Suddenly, early in October, the disease struck Ireland a heavy blow. Stanley wrote Peel on October 14th: 'I am sorry to say I have a private letter from Westport, in Mayo, announcing the almost total failure of the Potato Crop in that neighbourhood, from disease, which has appeared suddenly within a few days. If this be at all general the consequences will be frightful.'[30] Even before he had received this information from Stanley, Peel had decided how best to cope with the situation. Probably he had hoped to keep the Corn Laws until the next election, but the situation in Ireland caused him to change his plans.[31] Writing to Graham on October 13th, he declared: 'The removal of impediments to import is the only effectual remedy.'[32] In a letter of October 17th Graham agreed that they might be driven to a suspension of the Corn Laws, and that the laws hardly could be re-enacted thereafter.[33] By October 19th, then, both Peel and Graham were ready to open the ports.

Peel, knowing his views, was somewhat nervous about Stanley's attitude toward his remedy, and he feared that the Protectionists at this time might even be strong enough to form a government in which Stanley would figure prominently.[34] He notified Stanley of a Cabinet meeting on October 31st, and a few days later sent him some frightening reports on the state of Ireland which he hoped might influence his attitude.[35] Stanley agreed that the prospects for Ireland for the coming winter and spring were melancholy; even in his neighbourhood the farmers were digging up their potatoes as fast as they could and bringing them to market.[36] When Malmesbury arrived at Knowsley on October 30th, anticipating the pleasures of the hunt, he was disappointed to find that his friend had already gone to London.

In the Cabinet Peel proceeded cautiously.[37] After recommending some measures for the relief of Ireland, public works, and precautions to be taken against disease, he suggested they anticipate the coming agitation on the subject, and suspend the operation of the Corn Laws, which, he admitted, would cause a reconsideration of the whole question. Stanley immediately demurred. As the crop was not yet dug up, it was impossible to determine the condition of the Irish food supply, and, if there were a widespread failure of it, a suspension of the laws would not prevent starvation. Absolute means of purchase, rather than a mere reduction in price, would be needed, and the admission of foreign grain would simply lower the value of other crops, such as oats. Stanley was ready to support a temporary suspension of the Corn Laws, but he feared Peel meant to go further than that. Finding that only Graham, Aberdeen and Herbert supported him, Peel closed the meeting with a suggestion that they decide whether the Government should maintain, modify, or suspend the Corn Laws.

Stanley was deeply disturbed. Had Peel suggested the Corn Laws be suspended to a definite date, when they would automatically become operative again, he would have reluctantly agreed, but it seemed clear that Peel sought their abolition. Taking pen in hand, he wrote a lengthy memorandum on the subject, enclosing it with a letter to Peel.*

> I find it difficult to express to you the regret with which I see how widely I differ in opinion with Graham and yourself as to the necessity of proposing to Parliament a [suspension] repeal of the Corn Laws. . . . I foresee that this question, if you persevere in your present opinion, must break up the Government, one way or the other: but I shall greatly regret indeed, if it should be broken up, not in consequence of our feeling that we had prepared measures which it properly belonged to others to carry, but in consequence of differences of opinion among ourselves.

Peel realized that public opinion was not yet enough aroused to deter the Protectionists from forming a government, so he chose

* *Peel Papers*, BM 40468. (Stanley to Peel, November 3rd, 1845). The word in brackets was crossed out in the original.

to mislead Stanley regarding his intentions. After reading the memorandum, he passed it on to Graham, who was 'touched' by some of the expressions it contained, but not convinced by it.* Then Peel wrote:†

> I must however observe that [you have assumed I think too hastily] that I have not proposed to the Cabinet that we should [that we should unite in] recommend[ing] to Parliament the Repeal of the Corn Laws [or in addressing] still less that we should offer our advice to the Queen that the Corn Laws ought to be abandoned.

Peel now recommended the appointment of a commission to study conditions in Ireland, and at a Cabinet meeting on November 6th he modified his earlier proposal to suspend the laws. He suggested they lower the tariff by an Order in Council, call on Parliament to sanction the order, and give notice that they would present a bill modifying the Corn Laws after Christmas.[38] A suspicious Cabinet refused, however, to go along with these suggestions.

Peel and Graham began to work feverishly in an effort to bring the waverers in the Cabinet over to their point of view. Graham visited and wrote to Stanley on several occasions, sent a memorandum of his own to each member of the Cabinet, and circularized among them the minute of a conversation he and Peel had had with a Professor Lindley. But time was running out. Lord John Russell, whose ear was always to the ground to learn the direction of the majority, published a letter in which he abandoned the fixed duty on corn. This declaration forced the Government to do nothing about the Corn Laws, or, in proposing alterations, to give the appearance of following Russell. Peel, of course, had been prepared to go much further than this weeks before.

At a Cabinet on November 25th Peel offered another alternative, this time that they should suspend the operation of the Corn

* At his request, the paper was returned to Stanley, and it was probably the same one sent to Croker with similar instructions in 1847. (See: Jennings, *Croker*, II, 315). Parker, who was permitted to use the Knowsley papers in writing his work on Graham, could not find this memorandum. (Parker, *Graham*, II, 25). That it was long is apparent from Stanley's reference to page '48' in a letter to Croker. (Jennings, *Croker*, II, 315).

† *Peel Papers*, BM 40468. (Peel to Stanley, November 5th, 1845). The words in brackets were crossed out, and seem to indicate that Peel intentionally strengthened the tone of the letter to mislead Stanley.

Laws by an Order in Council. Stanley remained unyielding. On November 29th he wrote Peel:[39]

> I am strongly inclined to think that the best thing, for our own credit and for the country, would be that we should agree to differ. I never was more perplexed in my life than by reading Mr. Lincoln's Pamphlet, which at your desire I have just been reading. All that one can say is that figures will prove anything . . . but the book is cleverly written — and the result in my mind is that the alternative is between full protection, if protection be right, or no protection, if protection be wrong.

That evening Graham visited him again, and reported to Peel: 'His judgment and wishes are opposed to the opening of the Ports; and as to the future, he sees no alternative but the maintenance or the abandonment of the Principle of Protection.'[40] While they failed to move Stanley, Peel and Graham won a major victory when Wellington, a staunch advocate of the Corn Laws, nevertheless agreed to support Peel. When the news of the Duke's action reached Stanley, he was still unmoved, and observed that only the Duke could support a government whose measures he disapproved.[41] The Duke noted that Stanley could not possibly have pursued a similar course.[42]

Meetings of the Cabinet were held on December 2nd and 3rd. Lord Wharncliffe offered a peace proposal, but it received scant attention. For a time Peel felt that a victory was in sight,[43] but Stanley and the Duke of Buccleuch held out and on December 5th Peel tendered his resignation to the Queen. At his interview the following day the Queen asked why, with a majority of a hundred votes in the Commons, Peel could not carry on. Peel replied that half of Scotland would follow Buccleuch, and that Stanley had great influence in the Lords. There was also the unpleasant possibility that the Radicals, angered at his appropriation of their favourite measure, might join the Protectionists to oust him. The possibility of a Stanley administration was discussed briefly, but they agreed the mass of people might be led to riot against an aristocratic administration which kept food prices high. So Russell was called in, and Peel agreed to support him.[44] Knowing that his action had not found favour at Court, Stanley wrote the Queen on December 11th and explained that he could not sacrifice his principles and the expectations of his followers by supporting an abolition of the Corn Laws, but he promised to do whatever possible to allay the excitement which would result from the change of policy. The Queen replied coldly, but gave Stanley credit for having disinterested motives.[45]

Russell encountered some difficulties in forming a cabinet, and he was not unwilling to turn the government back to Peel, knowing that this meant the destruction of the Conservative Party. For a time Peel considered the possibility of having the Queen offer the government to Stanley, who, he knew, was unable to form a government, but at length he decided against it. Stanley was now without a sizeable following, and could not begin to construct a cabinet. As Peel had hoped, public sentiment prevented the Protectionists from attempting to form a government. So Russell had tried and failed, the Protectionists were unable to try to form a government, and his own position was greatly strengthened.

Peel now gave up the idea of an Order in Council, and decided to bring in a bill to be accepted or rejected. Feeling supremely confident, Peel, on December 21st, demanded that his Cabinet give him a free hand to draw up and present the measures he felt were needed.[46] Just what his plan would involve was not definite, but it was clear that the Corn Laws were to be considerably altered. Stanley immediately announced his decision to resign, commenting that he felt the Corn Laws should be, and might have been, preserved.[47] They could not, as he had observed before, 'do this as gentlemen'.[48] The Duke of Buccleuch wavered, and, after a period of consideration, decided to go along with Peel. So Peel had been eminently successful. In October, he and Graham had been the only ones in favour of abolishing the Corn Laws; two months later, the whole Cabinet, save Stanley, had decided to support him unreservedly. In Gladstone, they had a very capable replacement for Stanley, and, after a conversation with Stanley on the subject, the future Prime Minister decided to accept the Colonial Office.

On December 22nd Stanley wrote his last letter to Peel as a member of his Government. He expressed satisfaction that Gladstone had decided to succeed him, and had no hard feelings towards the Duke of Buccleuch for finally deciding to remain in the Government. Concluding, he wrote:[49]

> If I do not hear further from you I shall meet you at the Railway Station at 1 o'clock, prepared to give up the Seals of my Office, not without some causes for regret, but hoping not to have forfeited

> the friendship of those whom I must call my late Colleagues, and on my part without the least abatement of the sincere regard with which I am, My dear Peel, very sincerely yours. . . .

This had been a hard test of his rule of conduct, that differences of political opinion should not be followed by resentment or ill-feeling. In one case, he found it impossible to follow this rule at all.

The night before, Graham, urged by Peel, visited Stanley in an endeavour to prevent his 'unintentionally prejudicing' Gladstone against accepting the Colonial Office. At this meeting with the man who had shared his political fortunes for so long, the question arose of Stanley's future. Graham observed that it would be Stanley's fate to become Prime Minister at the head of a High Tory government, or at least become their accredited leader.[50] Knowing that Graham was aware of Emma Stanley's ambitions for him in that direction,[51] Stanley sensed an implication that he, Stanley, had quit the Government in order to advance his own career. Things were never again the same between them. But when the door closed behind Graham that night, Stanley suddenly felt very much alone.

While Stanley broke with the Conservative Government solely over the question of the Corn Laws, there were perhaps other reasons at the back of his mind. The middle class was crowding into the Stanley preserve in Lancashire, decreasing their prestige and power there, and changing the old order.[52] Though head of the Conservative Party, Peel in recent years seemed to lean towards the middle class and to have less patience with some of the static ideas of the agriculturists. Stanley could not add the prestige of his name to a movement which advanced the ideas of the middle class.

Though Stanley spoke at a Protectionist meeting late in December, he still was not hostile towards the Government, and aided Gladstone in his new job whenever he could.[53] In fact at the moment there was no reason to attack the Government, for Peel's intentions were not fully known. Though Stanley feared the worst, he thought Peel might accompany his reduction of the corn duties with tax adjustments in favour of agriculture, for early in December Peel advocated decreasing the tax burdens on land.[54] No one was certain what Peel would do. Croker still put his trust in Peel, and as late as January 6th Wellington had some hope of preserving the Corn Laws.[55] Lord George Bentinck was not even sure that Peel would refer to the Corn Laws in the Speech from the Throne.[56]

Restored to power and freed of opposition in his Cabinet, Peel refused to compromise with the Protectionists. While he advised the Queen to be kind to Stanley at his audience of leave, in order to conciliate the former Colonial Secretary,[57] this was about the only step he took to secure the goodwill of the Protectionists. While he himself was a landowner and not unsympathetic towards the demands of the agriculturists, Peel was unwilling to concede demands which he considered both excessive and unnecessary. 'He would not ask for compensation to the land', he told the Queen on December 25th, 'but whenever he could give it, and at the same time promote the social development, there he would do it, but on that ground.'[58]

The bill he presented to Parliament late in January contained less relief for the agricultural interest than Russell had proposed, and both Whigs and Conservatives were bitterly disappointed.[59] By making obvious concessions to cushion the repeal of the Corn Laws Peel might have retained a very large following within the party, perhaps even the majority, but the stand he took in January brought an end to his leadership. Out of respect for the Duke, who, through a ruse, shut off discussion of the measure at the time in the Lords, Stanley did not immediately voice his views on the subject.

The reaction of the Protectionists against Peel was so strong that Wellington was convinced the Prime Minister was doomed. In the middle of February he suggested that Stanley take over the party leadership in the Lords when the existing administration came to an end.* Stanley replied on February 18th that, as he had feared, Wellington's sacrifice of his own opinion in an effort to keep the party together had failed, and the organization was now shattered. Without a leader in the Commons he saw little chance at the moment of rallying the Conservatives, and he anticipated a long period of opposition to the Whigs before the party could be rebuilt. In his reply Wellington stressed the role of the Conservative Party as the only effective protector of British institutions, and

* This paragraph is based on three letters, two by Wellington and Stanley's reply of February 18th, 1846, found in: Sir Herbert Maxwell, *The Life of Wellington* (London: Edward Arnold, 1913), II, 348-52.

concluded by giving Stanley his blessing: 'But do what you may, it will make no difference to me: you will always find me aiding and co-operating in the road of good order, conservation and government, and doing everything to establish and maintain your influence.'[60] Wellington was fairly consistent in his views. In 1830 he opposed Stanley; in 1846 he tendered him the leadership. That in itself is a short story of Stanley's political evolution into the most Ultra-Conservative period of his life.

As Graham had predicted, Stanley, without effort, became a rallying-point for the Protectionist forces. In a conversation of February 19th with Malmesbury he repeated substantially what he had written the Duke, that the Protectionists lacked a leader in the Commons, and that the party would be formed again only after a period of opposition to the Whigs.[61] All through his career Stanley sought to refer major questions to the electorate. This was as true in 1869, when the electorate was fairly large, as at this time, when it was small and undemocratic. In 1846 he preferred that the Government dissolve, and that the question of the Corn Laws be decided at an election.[62]

Various Protectionists, including Bentinck, began to contact Stanley both in person and by mail. Early in March there was a large meeting of peers at the home of another former member of the Dilly, the Duke of Richmond. Stanley wrote a letter to the group outlining his ideas for opposing the repeal in the Lords, and promising his support against the Government.[63] The Protectionist peers spontaneously acknowledged Stanley's leadership, and sent word that they would do nothing without consulting him. Stanley replied he was 'much pleased and flattered' by their action, and he now found himself leader in the Lords both by Wellington's sanction, and by the election of the peers. His leadership in the Lords was confirmed later in the month.[64]

Meanwhile Peel was anxious to discover just what Stanley's intentions were, and tried to sound Malmesbury on the subject through Sidney Herbert. In April he apparently sent a free-trader named Gardners to seek an interview with Stanley, and in Stanley's reply to Gardners's note, which was sent to Peel, he received the desired information. It was quite definite:[65]

> Entertaining an opinion entirely at variance with that of the Gentlemen whom you represent as to the policy of the measure in question, it is my intention to give them a decided opposition in

> the House of Lords whenever they reach that body; but I have no control whatever over the progress in the House of Commons, or delay of their progress, and this being the case, I trust you will excuse me if I decline giving the Deputation the unnecessary trouble of calling here for the purpose of an interview which can lead to nothing.

Peel thus learned that Stanley's opposition would be confined to the Upper House. The importance of Stanley's translation there was now apparent. As Lord Campbell put it: 'If he had remained in the House of Commons, I think they [the Protectionists] would have won the day.'[66]

In March Stanley presented some petitions in favour of Protection to the Upper House, but staked his hopes of defeating the bill on his own speech against the second reading. On May 25th, 1846, Stanley spoke for more than three hours in the mightiest single effort to save Protection.[67] He traced the institution back to Edward IV, and summoned up the images of Chatham, Pitt, Huskisson, Liverpool, Canning and Grey to support his views. He pointed out the dangers involved in England's becoming dependent upon foreign nations for food, predicted that the bill would ruin both the upper class and the farm labourers, and declared that the economic bonds which united Australia and Canada would be loosened by it. The story of his resignation was told without invective or rancour. He was mildly critical of Peel, but more so of the Anti-Corn-Law League, which he charged stirred up class hatred. He also elucidated his own position regarding Irish relief.* In an impassioned peroration, Stanley called on the Lords to reject the bill. By general agreement, it was one of the great speeches of the era,[68] but the vote went against him. Though a majority of the Lords present voted against the bill, the proxies held by the Duke saved the day for Peel.

Defeated at this time, Stanley did not offer opposition to the third reading of the bill. There was no use stirring up new animosi-

* Stanley said: 'My Lords, I speak of the famine as a vision, an utterly baseless vision, which haunted the imagination, and disturbed the judgment, of the Government. I speak in very different terms, and with very different feelings, of that amount of destitution and individual distress, into which a large body of cottiers in Ireland have been thrown by . . . failure of their potato crop; but . . . this is a kind of distress . . . upon which your repeal of the Corn Law . . . will produce no more effect . . . than if you were to pass a law which should reduce the price of pineapples.' *Hansard* (third series), LXXXVI, 1137. The phrase 'baseless vision' is sometimes taken out of context to discredit Stanley.

ties, and public support for the measure was so widespread now that it was politically unwise to continue the battle. Peel, who had taken a fearful lashing in the Commons at the hands of Disraeli and Bentinck, was impressed by Stanley's moderation, and considered his opposition strictly honourable.[69] Shortly thereafter the Stanleys declined, because of a previous engagement, to visit him, but sought permission to send their elder son, the phlegmatic Edward Stanley, to meet Peel, perhaps to show their refusal was not due to bitterness over the Corn Laws.[70] Apparently Stanley never ceased to have the highest respect for Sir Robert Peel, and the greatest admiration for his ability as a leader, but after the split in the party, it was difficult for him to associate with Peel as he did with Russell after leaving the Whigs, for 'Bentinckism' was a powerful force among the rank and file until Peel died.

It is impossible to overstress the antipathies aroused by the repeal of the Corn Laws. The Duke of Newcastle and his son, Lord Lincoln, remained estranged until the former was on his deathbed. Peel and Croker ended a thirty years' friendship with three bitter letters.[71] When Graham wrote Croker a kindly letter concerning the death of a mutual friend, Croker petulantly reminded him of his apostasy on the Corn Law issue. A duel between Disraeli and Peel's brother, Jonathan, was only avoided because the latter discovered his error.[72] Peel for a time was determined to challenge Bentinck, and was restrained by Lord Lincoln's threat to call in the police.[73] Seldom has the change of one man's opinion had such intense repercussions, breaking friendships of long standing, invading homes and families, and humbling a great Party. Graham sought several times to call on Stanley, but found he was no longer at home to him.[74] The wounds of 1846 were so deep that the Conservative Party could not be effectively reconstructed until many of the statesmen who had fought that year were descended into their graves.

When the Protectionists in the Commons found repeal could not be halted, a large group dedicated themselves to a policy of vengeance.* Stanley at this time had no control of the Commons'

* Bentinck especially was in a fanatical rage against Peel, and, when one of Peel's colleagues became involved in a domestic scandal, wrote: 'This is quite a modern description of profligacy reserved for a Member of Peel's Moral Government. The contagion of its political bad faith spreading into private life.' *Disraeli Papers*, Bentinck XII. (Bentinck to Disraeli, November 9th, 1846). A few saw humour in the

membership, but the political skies brought forth a nova in Lord George Bentinck. Though a member of Parliament for many years, and associated with the Derby Dilly, Bentinck was best known as a sportsman so passionately fond of the Turf that he was often referred to as the 'Jockey', a sobriquet which he himself accepted.[75] 'My sole ambition,' he wrote, 'was to rally the broken and dispirited forces of a betrayed and insulted party, and to avenge the country gentlemen . . . upon a Minister who . . . falsely flattered himself that they could be trampled upon with impunity.'[76]

Lord George's partner in this task was Benjamin Disraeli, and together they were sometimes called 'the Jockey and the Jew'. Both were men of ability, and, when that was not enough to gain their ends, they added to it great energy, daring and vigour. They captured the mood of the bitter Protectionists, and gave voice to the pent-up feelings in many an outraged Tory heart. In April 1846 Bentinck accepted the leadership in the Commons, and though he apparently expected eventually to serve under Stanley, the latter had nothing to do with his elevation. At the moment, however, Stanley was on good terms with the Commons' leader.

Disraeli established his reputation as a debater through his biting, often almost artistic, attacks on Peel. As a final stroke he and Bentinck, during the Whitsun Recess, devised a plot to turn Peel out on his Irish Coercion Bill. Worn out by the abuse he had received, Peel succumbed readily to the plot, and was glad the majority against him demonstrated the impossibility of his continuing in office. Ellenborough suggested that only Peel and Graham resign following the defeat, and that the rest of the Cabinet, uniting with the Protectionists, should continue in office. But Peel rejected the suggestion, and resigned on June 27th.[77] Instead, he promised to co-operate with Lord John Russell, and about the same time Stanley, speaking at a Protectionist rally, declared he would not attack Russell if the Irish Church were left alone.[78] Thus the Whigs won the day by default, and could look forward to retaining office as long as the Conservative Party remained in its ruinous state of division.*

* This writer has no evidence that Stanley was involved in the plot which overturned Peel's Government. Graham, who was not in communication with Stanley at the time, guessed he 'had concurred in much more than he had himself done'.

---

situation. Lady Ashburton noted that a current asseveration was: 'May Peel protect me if . . .' Jennings, *Croker*, II, 276. (Lady Ashburton to Croker, undated).

On the first night of the Russell Government, Stanley was pleased to find that both Peelite and Protectionist peers rallied around him in the Upper House, so that the Opposition benches were badly crowded.[79] In the Commons, however, the situation was quite different, and the split was there quite in evidence. The central problem of the Conservative Party, then, was to reform its Commons forces, but how and under whom could such a reunion take place? Once they had vented their rage on Peel, many Protectionists were ready to replace Bentinck,[80] and there was a rumour that Lord George intended to resign. As almost all the talented and experienced Conservatives had sided with Peel, the problem of replacing Bentinck was not easily solved. No one at the time considered Disraeli, and Gladstone had followed Peel. As one Protectionist put it, if there were a future leader of the Protectionists on the horizon, '. . . I do not see him through my telescope'.[81]

Stanley's programme for the party was fairly definite by late 1846, and he considered it necessary for the well-being of British institutions.[82] Free Trade had to be given a fair trial, and be allowed to discredit itself. Because of the abnormal consumption of grain by the railway builders, the disastrous effects of the policy were not yet felt, but they would be, and thereafter an election would return his group to office. Meanwhile Stanley sought to restrain his followers from attacking the Peelites, and to prevent fresh issues from arising between the two factions.[83] The recent displays of temper in the Commons were in poor taste, and Stanley did his best to remain on friendly terms with his former colleagues.[84]

While this plan was fair and reasonable, the odds were against its success. Though many of the Peelites were conciliatory, and attached to their former party, the two men who led them, Peel and Graham, were not. Peel's feelings had been deeply hurt by the repudiation of his leadership, and Graham once said bluntly: 'My resentment is not against the new government, but against the seventy-three conservative members who displaced the late government by a factious vote . . . with those gentlemen I can never

Morley, *Gladstone*, I, 296. It is also true that Stanley sometimes made suggestions to Bentinck in 1846. *Disraeli Papers*, Bentinck XII. (Bentinck to Disraeli, June 21st, 1846). But it seems that Stanley, if in control, would have chosen an issue other than coercion to overthrow Peel. In his biography of Bentinck, Disraeli does not link Stanley to the plot.

unite.'[85] Graham meant what he said, and Peel, in failing health,* did not anticipate a return to office, certainly not as leader of his old party. Both, in fact, had by this time lost sympathy with the agricultural interest, and leaned towards the middle class. So the Conservatives were doomed, as Stanley put it, to a period of 'downward progress' under his old friend Russell.[86] In fact, when Lord Lyndhurst tried to effect a *rapprochement* between the factions, he met with a brutal rebuff from Bentinck, and the former angrily observed: 'If the councils of the party were to be directed by Lord G. Bentinck, there would soon be an end to the Conservatives.'[87] Stanley thus also faced the task of preparing his followers for a return of the Peelites.

In the autumn of 1846, Stanley received a rather strange letter from Gladstone.† In August Lord George Bentinck had charged Gladstone with 'deliberately affirming, not through any oversight, not through any error of inadvertence or thoughtlessness, but designedly, & of his own malice purposely affirming that which in his heart he knew not to be true'. Gladstone reacted to the charge in his own way, and requested Stanley to study the evidence to determine who was in the wrong. Under similar circumstances, Stanley probably would, in his early career, have challenged anyone who so bluntly called him a liar, but Gladstone's means of settling the issue were quite flattering. As Bentinck had not also requested him to act as arbiter, however, Stanley at first refused Gladstone's request, politely adding that, if he saw a chance to restore good relations between the two men, he would be glad to act. Urged again by Gladstone, Stanley consented to arbitrate, but reserved the right to express or withhold his opinion. Thereafter,

* There were numerous rumours to this effect. In 1848 Goulburn wrote Cardwell: 'I saw Sir Robert who had just returned from Windsor. He was out of spirits about himself. He had had one of those suffusions in the eye coming from a rupture of a blood vessel to which he has been periodically subject and which he had always considered . . . as an indication of fulness of blood in the head and of the weakness of the vessels in the vicinity of the Brain from which he has always been apprehensive of a suffusion affecting a more vital organ than the Eye.' *Cardwell Papers*, PRO 30/48, 50. (Goulburn to Cardwell, October 27th, 1848).

† This account is based on: *Gladstone Papers*, BM 44140. (Gladstone to Stanley, October 12th, 1846). (Stanley to Gladstone, October 16th, 1846). (Gladstone to Stanley, October 19th, 1846). (Stanley to Gladstone, October 22nd, 1846). (Gladstone to Stanley, October 26th, 1846). (Stanley to Bentinck, October 29th, 1846). (Stanley to Gladstone, November 5th, 1846). (Gladstone to Stanley, November 17th, 1846). (Gladstone to Stanley, January 21st, 1847). (Stanley to Gladstone, February 5th, 1847). (Gladstone to Stanley, February 14th, 1847).

he wrote Bentinck, and found that the Protectionist leader would accept mediation only if certain documents in the Colonial Office were presented for study. Gladstone felt that the documents did not pertain to the case, and that he was not justified in producing them. So the matter was dropped, but only after Gladstone wrote Stanley a letter so warm in its tone that the latter had good cause to hope Gladstone might some day become one of his followers.

Lord George Bentinck visited Stanley at Knowsley in November 1846 to formulate 'secret plans' for the coming session,[88] but in so doing he did not mean to place himself under Stanley's orders. Party disorganization was, in fact, in so advanced a state that they could not be sure how many members would co-operate with them in the House of Commons. Stanley came to London several days before the meeting of Parliament in order to help reorganize the party,[89] and, hoping to secure greater unanimity, he gave a party at the Carlton Club. There he tried to set the party line for the coming session, urging moderation, and stressing the necessity of avoiding new quarrels with the Peelites. Bentinck immediately took exception to Stanley's words, convinced that certain of the remarks were directed particularly at him, and he loudly denounced attempts at dictatorship. A hot argument followed. Disraeli intervened, and the two were at length pacified, if not reconciled to each other.* During the session, however, Stanley occasionally made suggestions on tactics to Bentinck.[90] Lord George, at the same time, preserved his independence, and regarded Stanley's conciliatory policy with scorn.†

The session of 1847 could not but have been a let-down after the stormy developments of 1846. Russell carried on the Government in a manner which provided the Protectionists with few opportunities for attack. As Stanley noted at the time, the diminutive Prime Minister, supported by the Radicals, was pursuing a conservative

* The story of this incident is based on: Jennings, *Croker*, II, 305. (Baring to Croker, January 25th, 1847). (Lockhart to Croker, undated). Bentinck's feelings were apparently not healed very quickly. See: S&F, *Greville*, V, 423. (*Diary*, February 21st, 1847). On the other hand, Stanley never had much confidence in Bentinck. During a political crisis in 1852, the Queen asked Stanley what Bentinck, if alive, would do, to which he answered: '. . . he would make the "confusion worse confounded" by his excessive violence'. B&E, *Victoria*, II, 492. (Memorandum by Albert, November 28th, 1852). Stanley said the 'misunderstanding' was entirely removed before Bentinck's death. *Hansard* (third series), CXXIII, 950.

† '*Nine Peelites*,' wrote Bentinck, 'every man voted dead against Stanley in the H. of Lds. yesterday: *not one with him!!!* So much for conciliation.' *Disraeli Papers*, Bentinck XII. (Bentinck to Disraeli, April 24th, 1847).

policy, and courting the alliance of the Established Church even at the expense of the hostility of the Dissenters.[91] Early in the session the Government's Sugar Bill, however, did not meet with Stanley's approval, and he called up his forces for a trial of strength in the Lords. On hearing of his intentions, the Earl of Clarendon, an old Whig, asked Stanley to discuss the bill with a member of the Government to see if his objections could be obviated. After the conference Stanley was satisfied that the measure was innocuous, but, when queried further by Clarendon regarding the division, Stanley replied: 'Oh, yes. I mean to give you a gallop. It is a long time since you have had one and it will do you good. Besides, I have brought my people up, and I must give them something to do now they are come.'[92] While Stanley thoroughly enjoyed his battles in the Lords, some others of his class, such as Clarendon, took the business of government more seriously and could not appreciate his brother aristocrat's attitude. On the other hand, Stanley's motive on such occasions was not mere trifling. Being out of power, the Protectionist members in the Lords were hard to keep on the job, and only an occasional division would stir up their interest in governmental matters. Later in the session he made a more serious attack on the Government for her intervention in Portugal, which violated an article of party faith that was carefully upheld by Stanley; namely that Britain should not meddle in the domestic affairs of other nations. This attack, like the one on the Sugar Bill before it, was successfully beaten down by the Government.[93]

Parliament was dissolved in 1847, and an election was held. During the campaign both Bentinck and Disraeli adopted the policy Stanley had decided upon the year before, that Free Trade had to be given a trial and the opportunity to discredit itself, but neither of them acknowledged his leadership. The only positive part of the Protectionist programme was a guarantee to protect the Established Church, which was, of course, closely associated with Stanley's political fortunes. The results were not very satisfactory either to the Government or the Protectionists. With the aid of the Peelites, the Government had a considerable majority. The Protectionists, however, if they could have secured the unanimous co-operation of the Conservative Free Traders, would have had control. It was obvious that the downward progress under Russell would continue.

By 1847 Stanley was again pessimistic concerning political prospects. Protection, as a battle cry, seemed dead, for the agriculturists seemed lethargic, and most urban citizens, save for those in market towns dependent upon the farmers, seemed satisfied with the change. The air was filled with republican ideas, and Stanley was convinced that a struggle between the forces of monarchy and republic was inevitable. In that crisis he felt that many 'Old Whigs' would furnish more aid in resisting democracy than the followers of Peel. At the moment Stanley believed they were powerless to do anything. The game of Free Trade had to be played out.[94]

The defection of the Peelites, and the apparent hostility of British Radicals towards his class, had alarmed Stanley and driven him further towards static conservatism than ever before. At the same time, as Protectionist leader, he was bound to a considerable extent by the wishes and ideas of an extremely conservative group of Englishmen. On religious subjects the Ultras were much more conservative than Stanley himself. During the Peel Administration he had favoured taking capable Catholics into the Government, and opening unofficial communication with the Pope,[95] but now he had to be very circumspect on such questions. Though he approved of it, Stanley was unable to support a measure for the relief of the Irish Catholic clergy in 1847 because of the sentiments of his followers.[96] Nor could he support aid for Catholic schools, or the use of Catholic Scriptures in them, for these were unacceptable to a large section of the party.[97]

Under these circumstances Stanley, of course, could have resigned his position, but during this period there was no other party for him to join which believed in Protection, stoutly upheld the privileges of the Church, and tended to be isolationist in foreign policy. To secure these, Stanley had to sacrifice his views on some other issues and to support his followers' prejudices. Few parties allowed so little freedom for forward movement as did Stanley's party during the next decade or so.

A religious problem ended Bentinck's tenure of office in the Commons. The question of whether or not the parliamentary oath should be amended by striking out the phrase, 'true faith of a Christian', in order to permit a Jew, Lionel Rothschild, to take his seat became an issue of some concern to the Protectionists. By this time Bentinck was tired of the duties of his office, and disgusted with the lack of real support given to his ideas.* The grand alliance which he hoped to form among the agricultural, shipping and colonial interests had not prospered.[98] While Bentinck had little affection for the Jewish people,† the Rothschild question provided him with a convenient means for relinquishing his leadership.

In November Stanley and some others tried to secure his support against modifying the oath, and a meeting was held at Stanley's in an effort to secure general unanimity.[99] Neither this nor a later meeting moved Bentinck from his position, and he supported Russell's bill to remove the Jewish disability when Parliament met in December. This brought a letter from the Protectionist Whip which indicated that his dismissal from the Commons' leadership might be expected shortly. Without waiting to be 'cashiered', Bentinck resigned.[100] Though Stanley had been warned that a considerable number in the party might withdraw their allegiance if Bentinck continued, he had no hand in forcing the resignation.[101]

The resignation of Bentinck closed an era in the history of the Conservative Party. Whatever were his shortcomings in debate, in political tactics, and of personality, he most truly embodied the feelings of the Protectionists in 1846, and in his battle one might see climactic struggle of agricultural England against the new order. When he departed from the lists, the chances of revival of Protection were virtually ended. Disraeli was a Protectionist only so long as the idea advanced his political career, and Stanley, though he believed in the soundness of the principle, was conciliatory and unwilling to disturb the new system unless it discredited itself. Yet

* For example, Bentinck advocated the repeal of the Bank Charter Act, but received no support. He noted in a letter to Croker: 'Lord Stanley does not profess to understand the subject.' He resented a following which would muster 140 votes against a Jew Bill, but not half that number on economic questions. Jennings, *Croker*, II, 346-7, 354-5. (Bentinck to Croker, November 3rd and December 26th, 1847).

† In spite of Bentinck's close relations with Disraeli, this appears to have been true. On one occasion he expressed concern that Peel's monetary policies were causing the transfer of property into the hands of 'Christian Jews'. Ibid., II, 351. (Bentinck to Croker, November 8th, 1847). In another letter he wrote: '. . . as for the Jews themselves, I don't care two straws about them, and heartily wish they were all back in the Holy Land'. Ibid., p. 360. (Bentinck to Croker, December 28th, 1847). Bentinck apparently did not consider Disraeli a Jew within the meaning of his own definition. Stanley was also to make such an exception later. Bentinck at this time was bitter over Stanley's attitude on the Jew Bill, which was inconsistent with the stands he had taken in 1830, 1833 and 1843. Ibid., p. 360. (Bentinck to Croker, December 28th, 1847).

these two men, for a time at least, had to appear to be staunch advocates of the old system, for among their following were many little Bentincks who were as quick as he was to sense heretical deviations within the upper circle of their leadership.*

NOTES

[1] *PP*, BM 40467. (Stanley to Peel, January 16th, 1841).
[2] *DP*, XVII. Miscellaneous Observations §59.
[3] *PP*, BM 40468. (Stanley to Peel, December 24th, 1844).
[4] Ibid. (Stanley to Peel, September 28th, 1843).
[5] Ibid. (Stanley to Peel, October 20th, 1843).
[6] Parker, *Graham*, II, 352. (Graham to Gladstone, May 27th, 1858).
[7] M&B, *Disraeli*, I, 520.
[8] *PP*, BM 40468. (Stanley to Peel, February 5th and 10th, March 11th, 1844, July 10th and August 18th, 1845). (Peel to Stanley, February 6th, March 12th, 1844, July 10th and August 14th, 1845).
[9] Ibid. (Stanley to Peel, November 17th and 29th, 1844, January 15th, 1845). (Peel to Stanley, November 18th and 30th, 1844).
[10] *GP*, BM 44140. (Stanley to Gladstone, April 20th, 1844).
[11] *PP*, BM 40467. (Stanley to Peel, August 7th, 1841).
[12] *Annual Register* (1842), p. 91; Ibid. (1844), p. 46.
[13] *AP*, BM 43072. (Stanley to Aberdeen, April 4th, 1844).
[14] Morley, *Gladstone*, I, 644.
[15] *RP*, BM 40869. (Stanley to Ripon, September 12th, 1844); *PP*, BM 40468. (Stanley to Peel, July 27th, 1844).
[16] *RP*, BM 40869. (Stanley to Ripon, September 12th, 1844).
[17] *PP*, BM 40468. (Stanley to Peel, July 31st, 1844).
[18] Ibid.
[19] Ibid. (Stanley to Peel, September 28th, 1844).
[20] Morley, *Gladstone*, I, 239.
[21] *Annual Register* (1841), p. 109.
[22] Jennings, *Croker*, II, 314. (Stanley to Croker, June 20th, 1847).
[23] *PP*, BM 40467. (Stanley to Peel, September 21st, 1841).
[24] Jennings, *Croker*, II, 314, 358. (Stanley to Croker, June 20th, 1847). (Bentinck to Croker, October 27th, 1847).
[25] Parker, *Graham*, I, 332. (Graham to Peel, December 30th, 1842).
[26] Morley, *Gladstone*, I, 263.
[27] Ibid.
[28] *Annual Register* (1845), p. 75.
[29] *PP*, BM 40468. (Stanley to Peel, August 12th, November 29th, 1845); Ibid., BM 40451. (Graham to Peel, August 21st, September 6th, 18th, 19th, 25th and 29th, October 6th, 1845).
[30] Ibid., BM 40468. (Stanley to Peel, October 14th, 1845).
[31] Benjamin Disraeli, *Lord George Bentinck* (London: G. Routledge & Co., 1858), pp. 14-15.

* Somewhat later Stanley noted that Bentinck had possessed the 'entire confidence of a large section, and the respect of the whole of our friends'. *Disraeli Papers*, Derby XII. (Stanley to Disraeli, December 21st, 1848).

[32] *PP*, BM 40451. (Peel to Graham, October 13th, 1845).

[33] Ibid. (Graham to Peel, October 15th, 1845); Parker, *Peel*, III, 224. (Graham to Peel, October 17th, 1845).

[34] A. C. Benson and Viscount Esher, *The Letters of Queen Victoria* (New York: Longmans, Green & Co., 1907), II, 78. (Memorandum by Albert, December 25th, 1845). (Hereinafter cited as: 'B&E, *Victoria*').

[35] *PP*, BM 40468. (Stanley to Peel, October 22nd and 24th, 1845).

[36] Ibid. (Stanley to Peel, October 24th, 1845).

[37] Paragraph based on: Parker, *Peel*, III, 280-1. (Peel to Hardinge, December 16th, 1845); Disraeli, *Bentinck*, pp. 16-17; Jennings, *Croker*, II, 315. (Stanley to Croker, June 20th, 1847): B&E, *Victoria*, II, 48. (Memorandum by Albert, December 7th, 1845).

[38] Parker, *Peel*, III, 229.

[39] *PP*, BM 40468. (Stanley to Peel, November 29th, 1845).

[40] Ibid., BM 40452. (Graham to Peel, November 29th, 1845).

[41] Parker, *Peel*, III, 236. (Stanley to Peel, December 1st, 1845).

[42] Jennings, *Croker*, II, 252. (Wellington to Croker, December 29th, 1845).

[43] Parker, *Peel*, III, 238. (Peel to Victoria, December 2nd, 1845).

[44] B&E, *Victoria*, II, 48-51. (Memorandum by Albert, December 7th, 1845).

[45] Ibid., pp. 64-5. (Stanley to Victoria, December 11th, 1845). (Victoria to Stanley, December 12th, 1845).

[46] Ibid., pp. 73-4. (Peel to Victoria, December 21st, 1845).

[47] Ibid.

[48] Lady Dorchester, ed., *Lord Broughton — Recollections of a Long Life* (London: John Murray, 1911), VI, 229. (*Diary*, December 22nd, 1845).

[49] *PP*, BM 40468. (Stanley to Peel, December 22nd, 1845).

[50] Ibid., BM 40452. (Graham to Peel, January 3rd, 1847).

[51] S&F, *Greville*, V, 320. (*Diary*, May 11th, 1846).

[52] Ibid., pp. 294-5. (*Diary*, February 2nd, 1846).

[53] *GP*, BM 44140. (Stanley to Gladstone, January 21st, February 25th, March 15th and 23rd and April 4th, 1846).

[54] B&E, *Victoria*, II, 63. (Peel to Victoria, December 10th, 1845).

[55] Jennings, *Croker*, II, 260. (Wellington to Croker, January 6th, 1846).

[56] M&B, *Disraeli*, I, 758. (Bentinck to Stanley, date not shown).

[57] B&E, *Victoria*, II, 76. (Peel to Victoria, December 23rd, 1845).

[58] Ibid., p. 78. (Memorandum by Albert, December 25th, 1845). This and several subsequent direct quotations from the same work are taken by permission from A. C. Benson and Viscount Esher's *The Letters of Queen Victoria*, published by John Murray.

[59] Malmesbury, *Memoirs*, I, 164-5. (*Diary*, January 27th, 1846); Dorchester, *Broughton*, VI, 163. (*Diary*, January 28th, 1846).

[60] Maxwell, *Wellington*, II, 351. (Wellington to Stanley, February 19th, 1846).

[61] Malmesbury, *Memoirs*, I, 166. (*Diary*, February 19th, 1846).

[62] Ibid., p. 166. (*Diary*, February 18th, 1846).

[63] Ibid., p. 169. (*Diary*, March 9th, 1846).

[64] Ibid., p. 170. (*Diary*, March 21st, 1846).

[65] *PP*, BM 40590. (Stanley to Gardners, April 21st, 1846).

[66] Hardcastle, *Campbell*, II, 264.

[67] *Hansard* (third series), LXXXVI, 1128-76.

[68] Duchess of Argyll, ed., *Duke of Argyll Autobiography and Memoirs* (London: John Murray, 1906), I, 276; Jennings, *Croker*, II, 274. (Ashburton to Croker, May 26th, 1846); Malmesbury, *Memoirs*, I, 172. (*Diary*, May 25th, 1846); Morley, *Gladstone*, I, 296.

[69] A. W. W. Ramsay, *Sir Robert Peel* (London: Constable & Co., 1928), p. 353.
[70] *PP*, BM 40609. (Emma Stanley to Peel, June 8th, 1846).
[71] Jennings, *Croker*, II, 296-7.
[72] S&F, *Greville*, V, 317-18. (*Diary*, April 26th, 1846).
[73] Ramsay, *Peel*, p. 346.
[74] Morley, *Gladstone*, I, 296.
[75] Jennings, *Croker*, II, 328. (Bentinck to Croker, July 10th, 1847).
[76] Ibid., p. 342. (Bentinck to Croker, October 5th, 1847).
[77] B&E, *Victoria*, II, 96. (Memorandum by Albert, June 28th, 1846).
[78] Ibid., p. 99. (Memorandum by Albert, June 30th, 1846).
[79] Jennings, *Croker*, II, 275. (Croker to Hardinge, July 10th, 1846).
[80] Ibid., pp. 283, 284, 291. (Croker to Stanley, August 21st, 1846). (Lyndhurst to Croker, undated). (Lockhart to Croker, December 16th, 1846).
[81] Ibid., p. 281. (Ashburton to Croker, August 20th, 1846).
[82] *Hansard* (third series), LXXXVI, 1131-2.
[83] Jennings, *Croker*, II, 279-80, 290. (Stanley to Croker, August 23rd and October 6th, 1846).
[84] *AP*, BM 43072. (Stanley to Aberdeen, September 2nd, 1846).
[85] Morley, *Gladstone*, I, 296.
[86] Jennings, *Croker*, II, 289. (Stanley to Croker, September 27th, 1846).
[87] Ibid., p. 284. (Lyndhurst to Croker, undated).
[88] *DP*, Bentinck XII. (Bentinck to Disraeli, November 30th, 1846).
[89] *PP*, BM 40452. (Graham to Peel, December 15th, 1846).
[90] *DP*, Bentinck XII. (Bentinck to Disraeli, March 22nd, 1847).
[91] Jennings, *Croker*, II, 308. (Stanley to Croker, June 7th, 1847).
[92] S&F, *Greville*, V, 422-3. (*Diary*, February 21st, 1847).
[93] B&E, *Victoria*, II, 144. (Victoria to King of the Belgians, June 12th, 1847).
[94] Jennings, *Croker*, II, 309, 331-2. (Stanley to Croker, June 7th, 1847). (Stanley to Croker, September 12th, 1847).
[95] *PP*, BM 40467. (Stanley to Peel, August 4th, 1841). Ibid., BM 40492. (Comments on the letters of F. H. Ivers, 1841).
[96] Jennings, *Croker*, II, 306. (Stanley to Croker, February 21st, 1847).
[97] Ibid., pp. 309-10. (Stanley to Croker, June 7th, 1847).
[98] Ibid., p. 343. (Bentinck to Croker, October 5th, 1847).
[99] *DP*, Bentinck XII. (Bentinck to Disraeli, November 3rd, 1847).
[100] Jennings, *Croker*, II, 354-5. (Bentinck to Croker, December 26th, 1847).
[101] *DP*, Manners XIII. (Manners to Disraeli, January 19th, 1848). Jennings, *Croker*, II, 354-5. (Bentinck to Croker, December 26th, 1847).

CHAPTER VI

MID-CENTURY PARTY BATTLES

THE resignation of Bentinck, whom he was never able to control, might have come as a relief to Stanley had the question of his successor not been such a delicate one. Stanley sought two qualities in Bentinck's successor. He must be a man with whole-hearted party support in the Commons, and he must be willing to consult constantly on all issues before the House.[1] Bentinck, for a time, had fulfilled the first qualification, but never tried to satisfy the latter. Stanley himself was unwilling to serve under any statesman, save (under circumstances which could not possibly come about) perhaps Sir Robert Peel, whose ability he was the first to acknowledge.[2] While he desired to remain in the background, and to allow the House of Commons' members freedom in choosing their leader,[3] Stanley's personal choice in January 1848 was Lord Granby, a popular, moderate man, sound on the question of Protection, and one who would meet both of Stanley's requirements admirably. Late in January he wrote to Bentinck, and suggested the Party urge the retiring Granby to accept the position.[4]

Lord George Bentinck, who still planned to be active politically, had already chosen the same individual as his successor. Writing to Disraeli on January 12th, Bentinck described Granby in the most glowing terms, concluding: 'The first wish of my heart is to see Granby installed as Leader of the Party.'[5] Disraeli at the time had apparently suggested that Bentinck might set up an independant faction in the House of Commons, but the former leader desired to unite, rather than to splinter the party further. He urged Disraeli to write Granby and urge him to step forward. Accordingly, early in February the Conservative members of the House of Commons met and elected Granby as their chief, but he modestly declined the honour and during the whole of the 1848 session the Protectionists were without a recognized leader in the House of Commons.[6]

At party discussions the name of Disraeli as a candidate was not even presented for consideration. Bentinck, who fancied that Disraeli was as staunch a Protectionist as himself, felt his friend had been slighted, and blamed Stanley for it. Stanley, at the time, had sufficient reason for overlooking Disraeli. During the recent election, Disraeli had declared his independence of any party leader, and gave promise of being as hard to deal with as Bentinck. Furthermore, how was it possible to accept Disraeli, with his racial background, just after Bentinck had been thrown overboard for merely speaking in favour of the Jews? The Jew Bill was still being projected, and on that issue, had Disraeli been selected, the leaders of the two Houses would have been immediately at odds. There was also the question of social intercourse. While Stanley accepted Bentinck and Granby socially, he still did not look forward to close association with one of Disraeli's background. But perhaps the overriding consideration was the effect Disraeli's appointment would have on the Peelites.* Disraeli had humiliated their leader and hatched the plot to overthrow Peel. To choose Disraeli meant continued alienation from them, for, as a group, they disliked him intensely.

While the Conservative Party had no chief in the Commons during 1848, the party had by this time accepted Stanley's leadership almost unanimously. Late in 1846, Wellington, true to his earlier promise, had advised many of his friends to consult Stanley on matters of party policy.[7] John Wilson Croker, of the Conservative *Quarterly Review*, began a long and intimate correspondence with Stanley at that time, and frequently called attention to Stanley's qualifications in the periodical.[8] An evidence of Stanley's control over the party decisions early in 1848 was the readoption of 'Conservative' as the party name. While Bentinck, Disraeli, Manners and others all disliked the term,† Stanley showed a distinct preference for it because it aptly described the position he desired to occupy. It implied an attachment to the

* This writer has no documentary proof for this interpretation, but Stanley eagerly sought a reunion with the Peelites, and had good reason to hope at this time that Gladstone and Aberdeen would eventually return to the party.

† John Manners wrote: 'Neither you, nor George Bentinck can be more indignant and disgusted than I am at the surreptitious readoption of that hateful word "Conservative". My only consolation is that as I never did call myself anything but "Tory", so I certainly shall not for the future condescend to bear that most miserable of all party names—.' *Disraeli Papers*, Manners XIII. (Manners to Disraeli, February 4th, 1848). For the origins of the term 'Conservative party' see: Myron F. Brightfield, *John Wilson Croker* (Berkeley: University of California Press, 1940), p. 403 (footnote). According to Brightfield Croker was not responsible for introducing the term into British political life. In May 1832 O'Connell called it 'the fashionable term, the new-fangled phrase now used in polite society to designate the Tory ascendency'. *Hansard* (third series), XIII, 150.

past, and a desire to preserve the basic national institutions for the future. Sir Robert Peel had given a moderate and progressive tradition to the name, and it had a better connotation than 'Tory'. Stanley was willing to modify existing institutions for the purposes of strengthening and improving them, but, he would no doubt have agreed with Edmund Burke when he said: 'People will not look forward to posterity who never look backward to their ancestors.'

During the session of 1848 Stanley drew a little closer to Disraeli, and somewhat further away from Bentinck. By spring the latter was disgusted with Stanley's moderation and described him as a 'pusillanimous House of Lords Leader', indicating that he did not acknowledge him as the head of the entire party.[9] Bentinck rather pathetically placed his reliance on Disraeli as the bulwark of Protectionism, and his untimely death spared him the knowledge of his friend's apostasy.

Disraeli thought Stanley acted queerly towards him,[10] and at length resolved to bring about a show-down in their relationship. In July he sent Stanley an invitation to dinner, and, perhaps to make refusal more difficult, gave him a choice of three days. Stanley after some consideration accepted the latest day and the two men, possibly for the first time, met socially.[11] The meeting was satisfactory enough, and Stanley thereafter gave Disraeli an opportunity to distinguish himself. At the end of the session, Stanley asked him, on behalf of the Conservative Party, to sum up the business of the session.[12] Disraeli did so very effectively in a speech which he felt established his position as leader.

The coveted leadership in the Commons, however, was still not offered to Disraeli. Bentinck's death, his own illness, and his difficulties in dealing with the Commons, caused Stanley to consider again the leadership question late in 1848. Lord Granby, he knew, would not accept the position; Disraeli would still not command the confidence of the party in the House. Out of the mediocre body that remained, there was one man of experience, one man who had served officially and had a considerable reputation for financial sagacity – J. C. Herries. In a very long letter to Disraeli in December 1848, Stanley acknowledged Disraeli's great abilities, but described the reasoning behind his choice of Herries. He urged Disraeli to accept temporarily the older man as his leader until such time as he gained the confidence of the party.[13] Disraeli proved disinclined to postpone the moment of his triumph. Couching his refusal in terms which were highly complimentary to Stanley himself, Disraeli expressed his unwillingness to serve under anyone in the Commons, and threatened to assume an independent position.[14] This reaction disturbed Stanley, for Herries was, in turn, unwilling to serve under Disraeli, and it was the opinion both of Granby and the Whip, Newdegate, that the party would not accept Disraeli alone.[15]

Disraeli, while simulating complete indifference towards receiving formal recognition as party leader, now started, together with his friends, an active campaign to achieve that end, and Stanley received letters and petitions from various sources in Disraeli's favour.[16] After studying this material, Stanley, on January 6th, wrote another letter to Disraeli in which he lectured the younger man concerning his obligations to his country, and expressed a readiness to accept any one of three as leader, Granby, Herries or Disraeli.[17] Acting on the suggestion, or hint, made in Disraeli's letter to him, Stanley postponed any decision until they met in town. The exchange had not been wholly unpleasant or unfruitful. Disraeli's letter indicated his willingness to be second in command, and to serve under Stanley. On receipt of the second letter, Disraeli was convinced that his aristocratic superior was 'at his feet', and he seems to have been confident until late January that the leadership would be offered to him.[18] His ambitions, in fact, soared to the point where he could visualize himself as an independent party leader.*

On January 30th Stanley sent a note to Disraeli inviting him to a meeting the following day on the subject of the leadership.[19] To the latter's disgust, instead of being offered the headship, he was required to share it with Granby and Herries. While Disraeli never accepted the proposal, he nevertheless went along with it, and during the session of 1849 the Conservative Party, which had had no leader in the Commons a year before, now had a surfeit of them. Stanley did his best to soften the blow, condescending to

* In a letter to his wife in January, Disraeli observed that 'time will settle' the question of his taking control of the Commons without the sanction of Stanley. *Disraeli Papers*, VII. (Disraeli to Wife, January 23rd, 1849). He probably had mentioned the same possibility to Bentinck in 1848. See: Jennings, *Croker*, II, 362. (Bentinck to Croker, March 2nd, 1848). Self-confident and intensely ambitious, it took Disraeli many years to learn that his future lay in Stanley's hands, and to appreciate the great services the latter rendered to their party.

call on Disraeli the following day just to please him, and frequently thereafter acting as a sort of go-between for Herries and Disraeli.[20] In June of that year, Stanley dined again with Disraeli, and by autumn Disraeli was more content with his lot.[21] Though denied the formal recognition of his leadership, Disraeli carried on much as if he had been elected. By 1850 the tone of Stanley's letters indicated he regarded Disraeli as his second in command, but he endeavoured to keep Disraeli and Herries from falling out and to preserve some semblance of the triumvirate. By early 1851, Granby was thoroughly disgusted with the set-up, and wrote Stanley, urging him to recognize Disraeli – if Disraeli would stand by Protection.[22] It was not until Stanley's abortive attempt to form a government that year, however, that Disraeli's leadership was formally recognized, and by that time the mass of the membership in the House were resigned to Disraeli's command, if not pleased about it. Stanley had given his friendship and confidence but slowly, but once he accepted Disraeli, he stood by his selection under all circumstances, and at the time of his death in 1869, a friend could write Disraeli: 'I fear you will have felt Lord Derby's death much. He was, with all his peculiarities, very true to you.'[23]

Such was the beginning of the combination between the parvenu of Jewish extraction and the aristocratic pillar of the Anglican Church. The benefits of the association were reciprocal, and the relationship was a remarkably stable one, being in danger of breaking up only once or twice during a period of two decades. Disraeli provided the aggressiveness in the Commons, and the driving force which time and again lifted his party, during these very difficult years, from the depths of defeat. On the other hand, Stanley was the great ornament of the party, the symbol of its honour, its stability and its high purpose, the man whom the gentlemen of England were proud to acknowledge as their leader. In Disraeli, Stanley found an associate who was ready and willing to consult with him, in great detail, on all matters before the House of Commons, and their exchange of views was so constant and so all-inclusive that it is impossible, in most cases, to say which man was responsible for any given policy or idea. There was nothing dictatorial in Stanley's direction of the party, and generally he acted as a sort of mediator, a compromiser who tried to reconcile and bring together the ideas of the various factions within the party. Under such circumstances Disraeli could feel he was working with, rather than under, Lord Stanley, but had the latter been less tactful, he would undoubtedly have faced rebellion from his junior officer. Disregarding the differences of their cultural backgrounds, and of some of their ideas, there were a number of similarities between the two leaders. Both were consummate debaters and careful students of the House of Commons. In reaching decisions on minor policies, the primary consideration was always whether or not a certain point of view could be defended before the House, and how the various factions would react to it. Neither was a profound intellectual, but both had the ability to get together the facts on almost any question and to talk convincingly on it at great length. Both also enjoyed party warfare and political battles, and were exhilarated by any victory, however small, over their opponents. On larger issues, however, the two were sometimes at variance, for Disraeli, perhaps because he was a parvenu, did not feel the deep attachment with which Stanley held to certain Conservative principles.

Nevertheless, the strength of the Conservative Party in their time was based on two outstanding men. Less important members were consulted, and their feelings weighed and considered, but party policy was usually set once Stanley and Disraeli reached an understanding. Decisions were thus made quickly and efficiently, and the rank and file, while they sometimes grumbled, generally followed along like well-disciplined British soldiers. During a period when the British party system seemed to be disintegrating, when the traditional parties were in danger of being replaced by petty factions, the Conservative Party stood as an example of disciplined organization, and, in or out of office, had a stabilizing influence on British political life.

During the sessions of 1848-49 the Conservatives clashed with the Government on a number of issues. The Jew Bill came up in 1848, and Stanley defeated it in the Lords on the ground that sitting in Parliament was a privilege, not a right.[24] He was unwilling at the time to allow Jewish citizens to legislate on matters connected with the Established Church.

But the burning question was an economic one. How far would Free Trade be extended, and to what extent would indirect taxation be replaced by the hated income tax? In 1848 the Government brought in a sugar bill. The Conservatives opposed it on the ground that it afforded no preference to British West Indian planters, who were competing with planters who used slave labour. Three prominent Peelites, Goulburn, Gladstone and Cardwell voted with the Conservatives, but the Government won the division. Thereafter the measure faced Stanley's opposition in the Lords, and in June Russell anticipated both defeat and the formation of a Conservative government.[25] But Stanley's effort ended in failure. He did not become Prime Minister in 1848, but it was perhaps some compensation to be solemnly installed as Steward of the Jockey Club that year.[26]

When the session of 1849 opened, the Conservative peers were in a disgruntled and fighting mood, and urged on Stanley the necessity of attacking the Government on behalf of the agricultural interest. While Stanley was lukewarm to the plan,[27] he nevertheless drew up, with the advice of Malmesbury, Richmond and Redesdale, an amendment to the Speech, condemning generally the Government's conduct of foreign and domestic policies, and charging that the agricultural interest was in a progressive depression.[28] This blanket censure of government policy failed in the Lords by only two votes, but the scare it gave the Government was probably not worth the ill-feeling the arguments against Free Trade caused among the Peelite peers.[29]

The great trial of strength in 1849, however, came later when the Government proposed the repeal of the Navigation Acts. Acknowledging Stanley's strength in the Lords and knowing how bitterly he would oppose the bill, Palmerston tried to persuade Russell not to stake the existence of his Government on passing the bill through the Upper House. A defeat would mean an election wherein the Whigs, to win, might have to make new pledges of domestic reform, which Palmerston opposed. Russell, however, rejected his advice, and both parties began to prepare for the fight in the Upper House. The Queen, Prince Albert and the Duke of Wellington were all called upon to stop Stanley, and they responded whole-heartedly.[30] The Conservatives watched closely the divisions on the bill in the Commons, and were encouraged to find that the Peelites split on the measure.[31] At a meeting on May 1st, at Stanley's residence in St. James's Square, the order of speakers was decided upon, and Lord Brougham, who for the time being acted with the Conservatives, was selected to speak first, before Grey spoke for the Government. As Stanley put it:

'Brougham must poke him up, and I will knock him down.'[32]

Their Lordships' House took on new life the night of the debate. Both sides, according to Greville, put on the 'greatest-whip-up . . . that ever was known', and some peers had difficulty in finding seats.[33] They heard Stanley, in his second great defence of Protection, beg the house not to abandon a system which had been the basis of England's greatness for two centuries. But again he failed to stay the advance of Free Trade, and once more proxies made the difference. Stanley continued the fight in committee, but it was a losing battle.

Stanley was hard pressed to revive Protection, both by his own feelings and those of his followers. Agricultural conditions in Ireland were very bad, and his tenants rarely could pay their rents. Hoping to relieve their hopeless condition, Stanley had sent more than three hundred to the colonies to seek a new start in life, but they had hardly vacated their lands when a like number of Irish paupers took their places.[34] He gloomily summarized prospects to Lord Clarendon: '. . . he expected landlords to be bankrupt, tenants to run away, poor rates to be uncollectable; that the Irish who had emigrated were returning, because they found the market overstocked with labourers, and they would return penniless, and would lean on the poor rates, already overburdened.'[35] Many Irish farmers were loud in their demands for a return of Protection. But Free Trade had the backing of the middle class liberals and the Whigs, and there seemed to be no way of stemming its triumphant progress.

During these years the thinking of many British statesmen was deeply influenced by the continental revolutions. Their reactions to the threat, however, differed widely. Some, such as Lord Clarendon, thought a moderate reform programme would forestall a clash between the British classes, and he was convinced that a Conservative government would hasten the destruction of the aristocracy.[36] At the time of the Corn Law crisis Peel stressed to the Court that continued Protection and a Stanley government would create an insurrection, or at least riots among the poor.[37] In 1849 Graham told the Queen a Protectionist government would cause a clash between aristocracy and democracy, with serious consequences to the former,[38] and many shared his opinion. Stanley, of course, differed completely from this view. While never minimizing the threat of republicanism, he desired to meet it another way — by rallying all of the conservative forces of England, whatever their party affiliations, and accepting office. It was up to the Conservatives to prove they were moderate, reasonable and willing to abide by the decisions of the electorate. Out of office they could not do that. They merely filled the office of whipping-boy for the heterogeneous mass of reformers on the other side of the House.

In 1849 the path to power was apparent to all Conservatives, and involved no more than the reunion of the two wings of the party. Bentinck's death helped pave the way for a reconciliation,* and the fact that Stanley had no official leader in the Commons was an invitation to the talented and experienced Peelites not only to return to the party, but to assume a position of importance in its councils. Lord Londonderry early in 1849 attempted to induce Graham to return, presumably to fill the vacant and highly important post, but he met with a refusal.[39] The wounds of 1846 were not yet healed. On at least two occasions Stanley had spoken with Graham,[40] but their old relationship had not been re-established. During the 1849 session Graham attacked Stanley in the Commons, and was answered effectively by Disraeli.

Nevertheless during 1849 there were indications that some Peelites might return to their former connection. Aberdeen disliked Palmerston and his help to democracy abroad, a feeling which was shared by the Queen.[41] In March Stanley received information that the Government had supplied the insurgents in Sicily, and he forced them to admit that such an 'inadvertent' slip had been made.[42] In the Commons Palmerston was able to defend his policy successfully, but in the Lords the peace-loving Aberdeen joined Stanley in an attack which gave the Government some anxious moments.[43] About that time Stanley and Aberdeen resumed their correspondence, and there seemed to be good ground for hoping that this very influential Peelite, and Gladstone in the Commons, would actively join the Conservatives.[44] Disraeli, at the time of the debates on the Navigation Acts, included almost all of the Peelites in a list of the probable members of the next Conservative government.[45]

* Some of the Peelites, however, expected the Protectionists to join their party, rather than conversely. See: *Cardwell Papers*, PRO 30/48 50. (Goulburn to Cardwell, October 1st, 1848).

Other important Peelites gave evidence of wishing to rejoin the Conservative Party. On January 6th Sidney Herbert wrote Malmesbury: 'I wish I could foresee with any confidence when this fiscal question [Free Trade] shall be no bar to our cooperation...'[46] Herbert, however, was under the influence of Lord Lincoln (later Newcastle), who was one of Stanley's most active political enemies,* and this restrained him from promoting a reconciliation. Nevertheless, Stanley felt more confident of his party's future after the 1849 session, and condescended to invite a considerable number of the Commons members to dine with him.[47]

Hoping to avoid another controversy with the Peelites, the Conservatives, in the Stradbroke Amendment to the Address, stressed relief to agriculture through lightening certain local taxes, rather than by reviving Protection. Throughout the debate Stanley was careful not to revive the animosities of 1846.[48] Following their defeat on this amendment, Disraeli, in the Commons, on February 19th moved a proposal to revise the tax system to relieve the agricultural interest of about two million in Poor Law payments. Though a Free Trader, Gladstone immediately supported the plan, pointing out that the rates had been laid when Protection gave land an artificially high value, and now were unjustly high. Again the Government won, but only by twenty-one votes. Stanley now felt that they could, on certain occasions, count on the support of Gladstone and Thesiger, as well as some of the lesser-known Peelites, in the Commons.[49] Late in March Disraeli was convinced that a fusion between 'Lord Aberdeen, Gladstone & Co. with Stanley & Co.' was now a distinct possibility, and the overthrow of the Government would not be difficult.[50] Graham, however, was still obdurate, and rejected another proposal from Lord Londonderry to rejoin the party, and to take the lead in the Commons.[51] But Graham himself was quite worried that Gladstone, Goulburn and Aberdeen would forsake their faction, and go over to Stanley in the formation of a Conservative government.[52]

The session of 1850 brought two questions of very great importance to the Conservative Party, one involving foreign affairs,

* Greville wrote in 1852: 'S[idney] H[erbert] is wedded to Newcastle who equally hates Derby [Stanley] and J. Russell, and dreams of a Newcastle Administration.' Sir Herbert Maxwell, *The Life and Letters of George William Frederick, Fourth Earl of Clarendon* (London: Edward Arnold, 1913), I, 349-50. (Greville to Clarendon, October 1852).

the other, the domestic affairs of Ireland. The first involved the losses of Don Pacifico, suffered during the recent Greek riots. He appealed to the British Government, as a citizen, for aid in recovering damages, and Palmerston, after the Greek Government disallowed the claims, blockaded Piraeus in an effort to force the reimbursement of Don Pacifico. Aberdeen was deeply disturbed at this high-handed action, and Stanley, who usually argued the cases of weak powers effectively, fell in with Aberdeen's scheme to censure the Government on the issue. In March 1850, the French intervened to mediate the question between Britain and Greece, and the opposition postponed their motion pending the outcome of these negotiations. By May it was apparent that the French intervention had resulted only in friction between France and Britain, so on May 13th, Stanley, collaborating with Aberdeen, called for a discussion of Greek affairs.[53] Should the Peelites aid him in censuring and overturning the Government, Stanley felt they would be honour-bound to join him in replacing it.

While the interest of the British statesmen was focused sharply on the coming struggle, Stanley was actually much more concerned over Irish affairs. The Government had carried in the Commons, with some Peelite support, a measure to reduce the Irish qualification for the franchise from £50 annual value to £8. Stanley was in a panic. Writing to Aberdeen in May, he observed:[54]

> If it be carried, I think it impossible that the Protestant Church in Ireland – I doubt whether the Union with Ireland can be maintained: and a body of Representatives will be returned for Ireland of such a description, and under such influence, that I firmly believe the best chance for the preservation of the Monarchy would lie in the Repeal of the Union. And I hardly think you will look on this as an exaggerated view (I state it as my very deliberate opinion and conviction) when you consider what will be the effect on the United Legislature of the whole body of the Irish Representatives returned under the influence of the Roman Catholic Priesthood, acting in conjunction with the large Radical & Republican section already in the House of Commons, first for the extension of a similar franchise to England, and next, through that franchise, for the organic changes which they desire, and we deprecate . . . This is a measure giving the whole preponderance to mere numbers over property, intelligence and independence – to R. Catholic numbers over Protestant property – for however little

I may like to use this argument I cannot overlook it . . . I entreat you to consider whether this be a worthy or even a prudent course for the House of Lords to take, so long as we have a House of Lords, which, if this Bill passed, will not be many years.

A little later in the month, he continued to press Aberdeen for support in rejecting the bill completely:[55]

If this Bill passes, it creates a Constituency for Ireland, which apart from its bearing on England, will render the existence of a Conservative Government thereafter hopeless. Is it wise, in our present position, to embarrass ourselves with a struggle of detail, which may, and I think would, lead to this result. By next year our position must be very different. The question of Protection, which keeps us apart, must by that time have presented itself, one way or the other, in a very altered aspect, which may enable us to deal with it with the aid of another year's experience, but where would we be, if an Election shall have intervened, with the new Irish Constituency? On the other hand, an election with the present Constituency, it is notorious, would add to the strength, I will not say of the Protectionist, but of the Conservative Party: and surely this is a card which is not to be lightly thrown away . . . You see what you have brought on yourself by your frankness and friendliness (twelve and one-half pages of writing) – by your wish that we should be found acting together, and by your admission that my former letter, addressed to the merits of the case, had produced some effect on your mind. I hope that you, and those to whom you have shown my former letter, will give a calm consideration to the additional views I have put forward in this: and great would be my satisfaction if the result should be that, leaving on my shoulders the whole responsibility of active resistance, which I am most ready to take, their abstinence from supporting the measure of the Government should enable us, by rejecting it in the present Session, to gain time and opportunity for maturing, under different circumstances, a safer and a better Bill: and once more consolidate a party, whose power is too essential to the well being of the Country to enable me to contemplate with indifference its continued disruption.

Rarely in his career did Stanley feel so strongly on a subject, being convinced that the adoption of the £8 franchise would not only ruin his party, but eventually subvert the institutions of Britain. Aberdeen suggested they adopt a £12 franchise, but Stanley would not ask his friends to support a second reading of the bill, and urged that they try to defeat it. Late in May, however, Stanley agreed to support a second reading provided the franchise was raised to £15 and the compulsory registration provisions were removed. Though he was himself friendly to these amendments, Aberdeen was unable to assure Stanley of Peelite support for these amendments.[56]

Meanwhile, Stanley was also consulting Aberdeen on the Don Pacifico issue.[57] His feelings on the two matters are indicated in a letter: 'In this matter', he wrote, 'I shall be disposed to act upon your advice and opinion with entire confidence. I wish to God that in this [Irish franchise] I could induce you not only to act, but to influence others to act in accordance with mine!'[58] Though he thought his motion on foreign affairs would have a 'serious effect' on the Government, the attack was marred for Stanley by having the Irish franchise threat still hanging fire.[59]

Excitement was widespread on the night of June 17th, and peers and peeresses flocked to the Lords in almost unprecedented numbers. A minor international incident occurred when testy Lord Brougham asked the corpulent Prussian minister, Bunsen, to leave the ladies' gallery in order to make room for two ladies.[60] Stanley, always an attraction to those who appreciated debate, spoke for three hours, and condemned the Government's '. . . enforcing unjust and exorbitant demands upon a feeble and defenceless ally'.[61] Aberdeen supported him, and they carried Stanley's motion by thirty-seven votes.

Some members of Russell's Government felt he should resign in the face of the censure by the Lords, but the Prime Minister, whose love of office was surpassed only by Disraeli's, found two precedents, one about a century old, to justify his retaining office.[62] Instead of resigning, the Government got Roebuck to sponsor a motion supporting their foreign policy. Stanley doubted Russell's ability to carry the Roebuck motion, and he urged Disraeli to take a leading part in the debate so that, in the Commons as in the Lords, it would have the character of a Conservative rather than a Peelite movement.[63] Despite his urging, Gladstone rather than Disraeli made the most effective speech for the Opposition. All efforts paled, however, in comparison with Lord Palmerston's five hour declamation, the *Civis Romanus sum* speech in which he stressed the obligation of Britain to protect her subjects against injustice anywhere in the world. His sentiments caught the fancy of the age. The Roebuck motion passed, and Palmerston emerged as the most popular statesman of the day.

Meanwhile the Irish bill found its way to the Lords. Stanley proposed and carried an amendment to raise the franchise from £8 to £15, which would cut the number of new voters by fifty per cent. The compulsory registration clause was removed, and with these changes the bill went back to the Commons. Russell rejected the Lords' amendment regarding registration, but compromised the franchise at £12. On August 6th the Lords divided on the question of whether or not to insist on their amendments, and, as Stanley had feared and predicted to Aberdeen two months before,[64] they accepted the compromise. Proxies again spelled defeat for Stanley, and he accepted it disgustedly, noting, because of the Government's proxies '. . . it would be a wanton waste of time to divide again'.[65] What made the loss more maddening was that Stanley felt Russell would have secretly been pleased to have been forced to accept the £15 franchise, but the Peelite Lords had deserted the cause and ruined everything.[66] Describing the Peelites to Croker, Stanley dipped his pen in gall: '. . . the most dangerous men at this moment . . . they are themselves powerless for good . . . never failed to give the Government a helping hand, when, but for them, we could have neutralized, or mitigated, the mischief of their measures'.[67]

Just hours after the Don Pacifico debate, the leader and inspiration of the Peelite Party was fatally injured. The news of the accident reached Stanley in a note from Disraeli's wife, and he inquired concerning Peel's condition in the afternoon.[68] Shortly thereafter the sorrowing Peelites held a meeting to project a memorial to their departed chief, and Aberdeen invited Stanley to attend. Feeling that his acceptance might lead to all sorts of rumours, Stanley declined. 'When the point has been decided', Stanley continued, 'I think that it is perfectly intelligible that differing altogether from his recent course of policy, I may be willing to contribute something towards a Memorial, divested of political meaning, but expressive of respect for the good and great qualities which he undoubtedly possessed, and also of a personal regard which I have never ceased to feel, or hesitated to express, even when most strongly opposed to him.'[69] Then he contacted his friend Russell, urging that they reach an agreement regarding the nature of the tribute to be paid by Parliament to Peel's memory. Many of his party were quite ready to pay respects, but some '. . . might require to be reasoned with privately to induce them to do so, and who, if the matter were brought up suddenly, might raise objections and lead to debates which would naturally impair the value of the vote . . .'[70] No one was more aware than Stanley that Bentinckism survived in his party, and he dreaded, especially on this occasion, to have it flare up.

The death of Peel did not alter the position of the Peelites save, perhaps, to make them hold even more tenaciously to Free Trade. In a conversation with the Queen in 1851, Aberdeen admitted he never understood Free Trade, but it had been first a point of honour with him to uphold it, and, after Peel's death, 'a matter of piety'.[71] In domestic affairs Aberdeen was willing to follow the Whigs, but in foreign affairs he preferred the Conservatives. Goulburn, one of the older members of the clique, hoped to draw enough strength from the Conservatives to form a government.* Gladstone, at this time and for many years to come, was very favourable towards the Conservatives, and only his allegiance to the Peelites and a dislike of Disraeli prevented his joining the Conservatives. Sidney Herbert, while strong for Free Trade, would have been happy otherwise to return to his old party. Some of the lesser Peelites, such as Sir Stafford Northcote, the Earl of Ellenborough and Sir Frederick Thesiger, eventually joined the Conservatives. Newcastle (Lord Lincoln) was always a stumbling-block in the way of reunion, but the strongest opponent was Stanley's old friend, Graham. While Disraeli, Londonderry and Walpole all approached Graham in 1851,† he put them off with the observation that Stanley, a man of honour, would have to try to reimpose Protection, and that he could not join such an administration.[72] The cause of alienation, however, lay much deeper than that. Most of the Peelites considered themselves prophets of a new era of economic and social progress, and they felt, consciously or uncon-

* It is difficult to show clearly what prevented Goulburn's return to the Conservative party. In October 1850 he wrote: 'I fear the growing Radicalism of Whigs on the one side and Protectionists on the other & should desire as far as my wishes go to stem the progress of that march towards Democracy which the Reform Bill originated and which every new political event unless managed with great prudence as well as firmness assists.' *Cardwell Papers*, PRO 30/48 50. (Goulburn to Cardwell, October 5th, 1850).

† Knowing Graham more intimately than the negotiators, Stanley had little hope of securing his former colleague. *Disraeli Papers*, Derby XII. (Stanley to Disraeli, January 23rd, 1851). (Disraeli to Londonderry, January 29th, 1851).

sciously, that a return to the Conservative Party would be a backward step, an associating of themselves with reaction.

Under such circumstances, Aberdeen was discouraged and disappointed. While many of his group hoped to have him effect a reconciliation with the Conservatives, after the session of 1850, he doubted his ability to bring this about.[73] While he remained on good terms with Stanley, the flood of correspondence between the two trickled down to a stream. The great opportunity had come, knocked on the door, and gone away. Stanley was deeply disappointed. It all seemed so hopeless. The men of conservative opinions were apathetic; the country would not awake to its danger; the Free Traders were leading the nation towards republicanism; the Commons would pass any measure, and the Lords feared to oppose them; both the younger men of the Conservative Party and the Court were unwilling to stand by the old order. 'If the country might be roused', Stanley concluded in a letter to Croker, 'it might be well; but we are falling into the fatal sleep which precedes mortification and death.'[74]

The autumn and winter of 1850 were spoiled for Stanley by his own illness and that of two of his children. An attack of gout, which disabled him completely, came on suddenly in December while visiting at his father-in-law's estate, Lathom House, and he was convalescent for a month. The confinement was made more cheerful by the presence of his eldest son, Edward Stanley, who had been touring, and for the first time in four years spent Christmas at the family fireside. His fond mother was in raptures to have him back,[75] and his father was glad to have the opportunity of seeing, and perhaps influencing, him again.

While political discussions were generally taboo in the Stanley household, his father became increasingly convinced that Edward Stanley was drawing away from him ideologically.* Young Edward Stanley was much attached to Disraeli, whom Stanley suspected of being no longer quite sound on Protection,[76] and it seemed possible that the youth might not only be forsaking Protection, but the Irish Church. Such heresy in his household was painful to Stanley, but he was no tyrant, and did not attempt

* Stanley was probably referring to his son when he wrote Croker: '. . . I see few, if any, young men coming forward . . . ready to stand by and with "their order".' Jennings, *Croker*, II, 411. (Stanley to Croker, August 18th, 1850).

to prohibit his son's expressions even when they were embarrassing to him as party leader.

Government finance was still a burning issue. Agricultural depression, fears of the landlords that their tenants might seek lower rents,[77] opposition to the income tax which enabled the Government to get along financially without customs duties,[78] all these things entered into the Conservatives' economic thinking at the time. Before Parliament met, their leaders considered the situation, and finally adopted Disraeli's suggestion to call for an inquiry into the agricultural distress. In 1850 Stanley was still a warm advocate of Protection,[79] but his party now called for a revenue rather than a protective duty.

On the eve of the 1851 Parliament, however, the main problem was not an economic, but a religious one. Late in 1850 the Pope set out to create an organized Catholic hierarchy in England by giving an Englishman the rank of cardinal, and issuing a Bull officially establishing a Catholic organization there. This 'aggression' caused widespread indignation among the Protestants, and Lord John Russell, who was personally more fearful of the Tractarian Movement than Catholicism, found it politically expedient to capitalize upon the indignation of his Low Church and Dissenting followers.[80] Stanley thought the public demanded an extension of the Act of 1829 on the subject of titles, and at length he drew up a resolution denouncing the action of the Pope.* But he did not think there was any real danger to the Church, and decided to '. . . follow the stream, which is running quite strong enough, than attempt to take a lead of our own'.[81]

The situation was fraught with real danger for Russell. While he might please a part of his following by taking strong action against the Catholic Church, he would thereby alienate his Irish and other Catholic adherents as well as many of the Peelites who were liberal in religious matters. But to gloss over the subject might make him generally unpopular. At length he produced a

* Stanley's resolution read in part: 'The existence of a Roman Catholic Hierarchy in a Protestant Country, unrecognized by Law, appointed by a Foreign Potentate, and wholly independent of the Sovereign, is derogatory to the Royal Dignity, tends to an undue interference with the internal administration of the Country, and is injurious to the Civil Liberty of the Subject.' Other sections affirmed the religious freedom of the Catholics, declared that the superintendence of spiritual matters by the Pope was part of that freedom, and called for a committee to study the whole problem. *Disraeli Papers*, Derby XII. (Resolution on Papal Aggression, undated).

measure which forbade the assumption of territorial titles by Roman Catholics in the United Kingdom, but it was too weak to satisfy public opinion, and too strong for his pro-Catholic or liberal followers. With the help of the Conservatives, and the *sub rosa* collaboration with Stanley,* Russell's prospects for passing the unpopular Ecclesiastical Titles Bill seemed good, but his position was by no means secure.

Disraeli hoped to capitalize on the discontent of the Irish members. In February 1851 he moved that a committee inquire into the agricultural distress. Disraeli was pleased when the motion failed by only fourteen votes, but Stanley realized that many who voted with them on the occasion would not support a Conservative government.[82] Nevertheless, in a conversation with Lord Campbell, one of Stanley's friendliest enemies in the Lords, the Conservative leader gave the impression he would be in office soon.[83] Embarrassment followed embarrassment for Russell, as the bonds of unity among his diverse followers dissolved. The *coup de grâce* was given by Locke King, a Radical, who again introduced a motion for the extension of the suffrage. Russell fell in resisting the motion, for the Conservatives stayed away from the division, and he was put in the minority by his own followers. In an audience with the Queen, Russell named Stanley as the logical man to succeed him, and on February 22nd Stanley was summoned to the Palace.

Stanley's favour at Court was none too secure, but his reception was kindly enough.† During the interview Stanley would not acknowledge any responsibility for Russell's defeat, and described his political problems. Though public business would not permit a dissolution at the moment, a dissolution was necessary to secure support for his plan for revenue duties on grain and sugar. He was sure the Peelites would not join him while the tariff question

* This is indicated by an undated letter in the Disraeli collection, with which Stanley forwarded to Disraeli a letter he had received from Russell. Ibid. (Stanley to Disraeli, 11 o'clock). While Stanley apparently wished to avoid making a political question out of the religious issue as such, he was ready to take advantage of any split it created in the Government ranks.

†There was apparently some point of disagreement between Stanley and the Prince in 1845. *Peel Papers*, BM 40468. (Peel to Stanley, March 25th, 1845). (Stanley to Peel, August 18th, 1845). The Queen, however, apparently liked Stanley well enough personally. See: Lady Dorchester, ed., *Lord Broughton, Recollections of a Long Life* (London: John Murray, 1911), V, 251. For a considerable period, however, Stanley was concerned about the attitude of the Court, an important source of patronage.

was pending, and without their aid he could not control the Commons. In view of this Stanley suggested the Queen seek a government composed of the Whigs and Peelites, and that the Conservatives be regarded as a last resort. In making this suggestion, Stanley hoped to force the Peelites to reconsider their position, and, if their pro-Whig faction failed to enlist support for the Whigs, their pro-Conservative wing might then see fit to support a Conservative government.[84]

The Peelite leaders, Graham and Aberdeen, were not prepared to join the Whigs while the papal aggression legislation was pending, and it became clear that the suggested coalition was impossible.[85] The Queen, on February 25th, called in Stanley for a second interview, and this time, though acknowledging his difficulties, he could not refuse. In discussing the composition of his Government with the Queen, he found she would accept Disraeli only if Stanley would be responsible for him. Stanley defended, as well as he could, Disraeli's conduct during the Corn Law debates and was willing to accept the responsibility. Then he outlined a Conservative programme which included a moderate duty on corn, the appointment of a committee to study the position of the Catholic Church in England, and, possibly, a dissolution.[86]

Stanley had in mind a number of possible appointments. His choice for Foreign Secretary was Lord Aberdeen, and, if he proved unavailable, Viscount Canning. Lord Ellenborough was to have the Privy Seal, the Duke of Northumberland the Admiralty, and Gladstone any office, save the Foreign Office, that he might select. After the interview with the Queen, Stanley visited Aberdeen and received a polite refusal from the man who had been so anxious to co-operate with him the year before.[87] Viscount Canning hesitated for a time, then likewise declined.[88] Lord Ellenborough, while trying to induce Goulburn to join the Government, let the latter convince him he should decline.[89] There still remained Gladstone, whose aid would be of immense value and whose presence would give the new Government the appearance of having a wider base. Stanley had tried to contact him as early as February 22nd,[90] but Gladstone, out of town, did not return to London until February 26th. He was met at the station by another note from Stanley asking him to join the Government.* Before seeing Stanley, however, Gladstone con-

* This writer could not locate the second letter in the Gladstone collection.

sulted the Duke of Newcastle, who felt that any Peelite to join Stanley at the moment would be a traitor to their cause.[91] At their interview Stanley offered Gladstone his choice of offices, except the Foreign Office, but did not mention the lead in the Commons.* Gladstone, however, seized on Derby's plan to lay a revenue duty on corn as an excuse for refusing office.[92]

On February 27th Derby called a meeting and surveyed his forces. Among them only one, J. C. Herries, had held office before, and only one inspired fear and respect in the Commons — Disraeli. Nevertheless, Stanley decided to go ahead, only to find that Henley and Herries, who were to receive the Board of Trade and the Exchequer respectively, seemed unwilling to assume these responsibilities. Malmesbury described Herries as looking '. . . like an old doctor who had just killed a patient, and Henley as the undertaker who was to bury him'.[93] Only Disraeli and Beresford seemed determined to go on, but they could not form a government themselves. Stanley had done his best, possibly even having sought some understanding with the Irish Brigade,[94] but, being unable even to carry his own party with him, there was no prospect of forming a stable government. He, therefore, reported to the Queen his inability, without a dissolution, to form a government, and assumed that the Russell Government would continue as if nothing had happened.

The following day in describing his failure to the Lords, Stanley carefully avoided offending the Peelites who had refused to join him.[95] Though snubbed, Stanley was in no position to indulge in recriminations, which might further embitter the Peelites and make even smaller the possibility of help from them in the future. Slender as it was, he had to cling to a hope of reconciliation. Some of the Conservatives were offended, however, by his frank admission that the Conservative Party, as then constituted, lacked men of talent and experience.[96] In compliance with a request made by Prince Albert the preceding day, Stanley explained his party programme in some detail. The income tax, which could not be administered with justice, should be gradually abolished, and a moderate duty would be placed on grain to help make up

* Prince Albert in his memorandum of February 25th quoted Stanley as saying that he hoped to secure Gladstone for the lead in the Commons. The Gladstone memorandum (Morley, *Gladstone*, I, 406) does not mention that the lead was offered, and it seems probable that Disraeli's story (*Disraeli Papers*, XVII, Miscellaneous Observations §24) is correct.

the budget deficit. Attention should also be brought to bear on the plight of the agriculturalists, who were suffering from the drop in corn prices. Papal aggression should be resisted as strongly then as in the time of their forefathers, but he asked for a careful study of the problem and opposed hasty legislation.[97]

Various Conservatives received the news of the failure with widely different feelings. Disraeli was, of course, quite disappointed, and Malmesbury was also discouraged. Some Conservatives, however, agreed wholeheartedly with Stanley's refusal to assume office under such unfavourable circumstances, and their confidence in his leadership increased.[98] Stanley himself thought the incident was mortifying, but that he could have taken no other course.[99] About a month later, he addressed his party at Merchant Taylors' Hall, and helped revive their spirits and self-confidence. Then he went off to Newmarket to enjoy the races. For a time, the Tariff, the Peelites and all the other perennial worries were forgotten. They would return again soon enough.

The abortive attempt to form a government early in 1851 had by no means disheartened Stanley. Early in March he wrote Malmesbury, requesting a list of those he thought qualified for places in the Conservative Government which was certain to be formed before long,[100] and he was even somewhat fearful that the Russell Government would fall apart before the moment was right to replace it. For a time Stanley expected that Russell would be forced out late in the session, after which there would be a dissolution, an election, and a Conservative government with a majority in the Commons for the session of 1852. He hoped, with temper and moderation, to be able to stem '. . . the Democratic tide which has been flowing of late with formidable rapidity. If we fail, we must at all events go through the ordeal of Cobden and Co., if we escape a Republic'.[101] The struggle as he saw it was between the landed proprietors and the manufacturing interests, the former being the proponents of the monarchy, the latter being hostile to it and anxious to get rid of both throne and aristocracy. In his contest with the middle class, Stanley hoped to draw strength from the conservative elements of the counties, and he foresaw that the fear of the Catholic Church might even cause some of the Dissenters, who voted with the Radicals, to seek refuge in the Conservative Party, the bulwark of Protestantism.

Some of the 'Old Whigs' might likewise throw in their lot with the Conservatives because of the religious issue, and because of their secret desire to restore a moderate duty on corn. While Stanley did not expect that the Whigs would join him right away, he meant to encourage such a movement by maintaining a friendly attitude towards them. The experience of February 1851 had demonstrated that, so long as the Protection issue remained unsettled, no aid would be had from the Peelites, but, at the same time, Stanley did not expect them to join the Whig Party. The only Peelite he now thoroughly distrusted was Graham, who, Stanley felt, might even go over to the Radicals. With these things in mind Stanley felt that a slogan, suggested by *The Times* – 'Protestantism, Protection and Down with the Income Tax' –, would be a good one for his party.[102]

The future did not develop quite as he had expected. By May Stanley was forced to conclude that Lord John Russell seemed to be quite popular in the House again. The Conservatives, however, continued to snipe at his Government. In June Disraeli managed to beat the Government on a minor issue, but the division was not important enough to cause a resignation. Later in the month Disraeli attacked once more, but this time was wholly unsuccessful. During June, however, Stanley was again in touch with Aberdeen, and they were trying to concert their activities on financial questions, apart from the Protection issue, as closely as possible.[103] Once again, the conservative Peelites, Aberdeen, Gladstone, Herbert and Goulburn, showed some willingness to co-operate with the Conservatives.

On May 25th, 1851, Stanley received a telegram advising him that his father was very ill, and he immediately went to Knowsley.[104] For a time, the 13th Earl rallied, but on June 28th Stanley received another summons to Knowsley, and his father died four days later. In addition to the Earldom of Derby, his father left Stanley a debt of about half a million pounds,[105] and his huge collection of animal life, the legacy of decades of interest in things zoological. Stanley had never taken much interest in scientific matters, and the museum was given to the City of Liverpool. Stanley, now Derby, though not in good health, could expect to bear the title for many years if he followed the footsteps of his predecessors with regard to longevity. His father was 77 at the time of his death; his grandfather, 73; his great-grandsire, 87.

Derby, however, was not to equal any of them in this respect. In fact, the weight of the past was already beginning to bear down on the new Earl, and there was an air of the past about him. The clothes he wore were generally long out of fashion, and his sartorial symbol was an enormous black satin cravat.[106] His face had long before lost the roundness of youth, and frequent sufferings had sharpened even more his lean, aristocratic features; yet, in spite of this and his whiskers, there was still, at fifty, a certain youthfulness about his appearance.

While the Russell Government had managed to stumble through the session of 1851, it was becoming increasingly obvious that Derby would shortly acquire another title – First Lord of the Treasury. A serious difference of opinion, however, had gradually developed between him and Disraeli on the subject of Protection. To Disraeli the failure of 1851 had shown that, so long as the party clung to the dogma of Protection, they could expect no accessions of strength from statesmen outside their party.[107] He was convinced that Derby had a distorted idea of the feelings of his followers on the subject, gained indirectly from George F. Young, the leader of the Protection Society, through the Party Whip, Beresford, who had the ear of the chief. As the year went by, Disraeli worked increasingly hard to dampen the Protectionist ardour of the membership, and, in August, Malmesbury wrote Derby: '. . . one thing is certain – viz., that he [Disraeli] *wants* to throw over "Protection . . ." '[108] The news came as no shock to Derby, but he was determined that the cause would not be lightly abandoned. Late in October he warned Disraeli that he personally was not prepared to accept a mere reduction of the tax burdens on agriculture as 'a final settlement of accounts'.[109] In January Malmesbury, who by this time had become Derby's *alter ego* and was to remain so, likewise warned Disraeli: '. . . I hold that the nickname of Protectionist is our mainstay & not a clog upon us – if we give it up we would break up into little Dillies – .'[110] The final exposition of Derby upon the subject before taking office, however, was a letter to Disraeli of January 18th, which the latter thought was penned with 'some irritation':[111]

> Now I know that you do not entertain any very strong idea that the approaching election will be such as to render possible the reimposition of even a moderate duty on foreign corn; and I am

ready to say again, as I have said already, that if that should prove to be the case, I was not prepared indefinitely to maintain a hopeless struggle; but until the country shall so have pronounced its opinion, I shall maintain my opinion, that on the grounds both of finance and national interests a reimposition of duties on imports, including corn, is desirable . . .; nor should I think it fair or becoming secretly to instruct our agents in the Press to throw cold water on the prospect of attaining that which our friends are desirous of attaining . . . The time is very critical — the game is, I believe, in our hands; but in order to be played with ultimate success, it must be played honestly and manfully, and to take office with the purpose of throwing over, voluntarily, the main object of those who have raised us to it is to follow too closely an *exemplar vitiis imitabile*, to which I can never submit. . . .

Derby was determined, then, not to give up the idea of Protection until he was convinced it was an unattainable good. Being a careful student of political trends, he was quite aware that his loyalty to the tariff cost him the support of many statesmen, especially the Peelites. Everyone knew that,* and he did not have to be educated by Disraeli on the subject. Yet it was true also that his party was committed to Protection, and he personally was honour-bound to make some attempt to fight its battle. To have been identified with the cause since 1846 and, then, on the eve of office to abandon it in order to secure some support from opponents of Protection, deserting those who had trusted them, this, to Derby, seemed dishonourable. No matter how Disraeli might rationalize the subject, his own career, even more than Derby's, had been founded on Protection, and his readiness to abandon it now was not, for Disraeli himself, politically wise. His attitude tended to make him even more vulnerable to the slurs of his enemies who tried to characterize him as untrustworthy. Too often in his career Disraeli marred his own reputation by seeming unduly clever, and showing openly that he was something of a political weathervane. Without the support of Derby, he would have been repudiated, and Derby, realizing that the party placed its trust in his own name and reputation, rather than that of Disraeli, was determined to keep his own honour bright.

On another subject Derby and Disraeli were somewhat closer together. In 1851 Russell, hoping to bolster his régime, had

* See, for instance, Campbell's observations. Hardcastle, *Campbell*, II, 357-8.

promised to bring in a new measure of Reform, and for the next sixteen years the issue was to be a political football. Derby was annoyed that Russell should reopen the dangerous question, and feared the Radicals might gain new strength for the towns at the expense of the counties. Throughout his career, on this question, it was Derby's contention that voting was not a right, but a privilege granted to those who might be expected to use it for the good of the nation. In 1852, he definitely would not trust the middle class with any more power. But, nevertheless, even at this time he refused to take a stand against all Reform, and the possibility of conservative Reform fascinated him. Writing to Croker, he observed:[112]

> Yet I think we should be cautious of committing ourselves to resist *all* change, even though we might not see its necessity, first, because a change *may* have a really Conservative tendency, but chiefly because an absolute and unflinching adherence to the present system, without listening to what may be said in favour of a change, would, I think, give the Government an advantage which we can ill afford to give them when they start with the prestige of 'enlargement of the franchise' in their favour.

Derby predicted that Russell would find himself in a dilemma, for his Radical supporters would demand a large Reform measure, and any such proposal would alienate the conservative Whigs. But, at the same time, he was both deeply interested in and nervous about the issue, for he was keenly aware of its potential effect on party politics.[113] Disraeli approved of Derby's policy of caution, but began to toy with a plan for colonial representation, a project which Derby himself had investigated thoroughly and found to be impracticable.* Rather strangely, they developed no real plan for dealing with Russell's Reform measure, which was quite a liberal one, and for a time Derby was deeply disturbed about it.[114] As it turned out, however, the Opposition did not have to deal with it at all.

The chain of events which brought about Russell's fall began in France in 1851, when the colourful adventurer, Louis Napoleon, seized power. Palmerston, whose arbitrary ways were unpopular with some of his colleagues, and especially with the Court, chose

* Derby opposed the scheme, partly because of difficulties in administering it, partly because the colonial representatives were likely to add to the strength of the Radicals. *Disraeli Papers*, Derby XII. (Derby to Disraeli, December 11th, 1851).

to extend his personal approval of the *coup* to Napoleon without consulting either his colleagues or the Court. For this act he was summarily dismissed. Palmerston treasured up his grievance against Lord John Russell, and, when the session of Parliament opened, waited for a chance to overturn his former colleagues. His opportunity came on a government measure to strengthen British defences by increasing the militia. Palmerston approved the plan, but demanded that the bill embody the old plan for the regular militia. On a division, Palmerston, supported by the Conservatives, carried his resolution, and when Lord John Russell announced that the resolution expressed a want of confidence in the Government, the Opposition cheered.[115] Lord John ill-humouredly advised the Queen that he had been the victim of a 'pre-arranged determination' between Palmerston and the Protectionists, but he suggested that Derby be requested to form a government.[116] The Queen agreed, and a new era opened for the Conservative Party; not a bright era, but the first steps were to be taken on the road back.

NOTES

[1] *DP*, Derby XII. (Stanley to Disraeli, December 21st, 1848).

[2] Ibid. (Stanley to Disraeli, January 9th, 1849).

[3] Malmesbury, *Memoirs*, I, 205-6. (*Diary*, February 9th, 1848).

[4] *DP*, Bentinck XII. (Bentinck to Disraeli, January 26th, 1848).

[5] Ibid. (Bentinck to Disraeli, January 12th, 1848).

[6] Ibid., Derby XII. (Stanley to Disraeli, December 21st, 1848).

[7] Jennings, *Croker*, II, 279, 283. (Croker to Lockhart, August 19th, 1846). (Croker to Stanley, August 21st, 1846).

[8] See: 'The Close of Sir Robert Peel's Administration', *The Quarterly Review*, LXXVIII (September 1846), p. 579.

[9] *DP*, Bentinck XII. (Bentinck to Disraeli, March 12th, 1848).

[10] Ibid., Manners XIII. (Manners to Disraeli, March 12th, 1848).

[11] Ibid., Derby XII. (Stanley to Disraeli, July 2nd, 1848).

[12] Marchioness of Londonderry, *Letters from Benjamin Disraeli to Frances, Marchioness of Londonderry* (London: The MacMillan Co., 1938), p. 39. (Disraeli to Marchioness of Londonderry, August 7th, 1848).

[13] *DP*, Derby XII. (Stanley to Disraeli, December 21st, 1848).

[14] M&B, *Disraeli*, I, 940-2. (Disraeli to Stanley, December 26th, 1848).

[15] Jennings, *Croker*, II, 395. (Herries to Croker, September 2nd, 1849); M&B, *Disraeli*, I, 942, 951-2.

[16] *DP*. Bentinck XII. (Sutherland to Disraeli, January 10th, 1849); M&B, *Disraeli*, I, 944-54.

[17] *DP*, Derby XII. (Stanley to Disraeli, January 6th, 1849).

[18] M&B, *Disraeli*, I, 948-54.

[19] *DP*, Derby XII. (Stanley to Disraeli, January 30th, 1849).

[20] Ibid. (Stanley to Disraeli, February 1st, 1849). (Stanley to Disraeli, Tuesday, 1849).

[21] *DP*, Derby VII. (Disraeli to Wife, June 5th, 1849). (Disraeli to Wife, November 15th, 1849).

[22] Ibid., Manners XIII. (Granby to Derby, December 1851).

[23] M&B, *Disraeli*, II, 450. (Lennox to Disraeli, date not shown).

[24] *Annual Register* (1848), p. 92.

[25] S&F, *Greville*, VI, 81. (*Diary*, June 24th, 1848).

[26] Ibid., p. 88. (*Diary*, July 5th, 1848).

[27] *DP*, Derby XII. (Stanley to Disraeli, February 1st, 1849).

[28] Malmesbury, *Memoirs*, I, 238. (*Diary*, February 1st, 1849).

[29] Hardcastle, *Campbell*, II, 318.

[30] Ibid., pp. 320-1.

[31] Malmesbury, *Memoirs*, I, 241. (*Diary*, March 13th, 1849).

[32] Ibid., p. 248. (*Diary*, May 2nd, 1849).

[33] S&F, *Greville*, VI, 176. (*Diary*, May 11th, 1849); Malmesbury, *Memoirs*, I, 248. (*Diary*, May 8th, 1849).

[34] *Annual Register* (1849), pp. 96-8.

[35] Parker, *Peel*, III, 517. (Arbuthnot to Peel, October 8th, 1849).

[36] Maxwell, *Clarendon*, I, 326. (Clarendon to Lewis, March 7th, 1851).

[37] B&E, *Victoria*, II, 58-9. (Memorandum by Albert, December 7th, 1845).

[38] S&F, *Greville*, VI, 172. (*Diary*, April 1st, 1849).

[39] Parker, *Graham*, II, 80-1. (Graham to Londonderry, January 20th, 1849).

[40] *PP*, BM 40452. (Graham to Peel, January 3rd, 1847); Hardcastle, *Campbell*, II, 287.

[41] Hardcastle, *Campbell*, II, 324; B&E, *Victoria*, II, 294. (Victoria to Russell, June 21st, 1850).

[42] *Annual Register* (1849), p. 133.

[43] S&F, *Greville*, VI, 180. (*Diary*, July 29th, 1849).

[44] *AP*, BM 43072. (Stanley to Aberdeen, June 18th, 1849).

[45] M&B, *Disraeli*, I, 1022-3.

[46] Malmesbury, *Memoirs*, I, 257. (Herbert to Malmesbury, January 6th, 1850).

[47] *DP*, Derby XII. (Stanley to Disraeli, January 8th, 1850).

[48] S&F, *Greville*, VI, 196. (*Diary*, February 2nd, 1850).

[49] *DP*, Derby XII. (Stanley to Disraeli, March 1st, 1850).

[50] Londonderry, *Letters*, pp. 78-80. (Disraeli to Marchioness of Londonderry, March 21st, 1850).

[51] Parker, *Graham*, II, 95-7. (Londonderry to Graham, February 18th, 1850). (Graham to Londonderry, February 18th, 1850).

[52] S&F, *Greville*, VI, 209. (*Diary*, March 8th, 1850).

[53] *AP*, BM 43072. (Stanley to Aberdeen, May 13th, 1850).

[54] Ibid.

[55] Ibid. (Stanley to Aberdeen, May 21st, 1850).

[56] Ibid. (Stanley to Aberdeen, May 21st and 27th, 1850). (Stanley to Aberdeen, June 5th, 1850).

[57] Ibid.

[58] Ibid. (Stanley to Aberdeen, May 16th, 1850).

[59] Ibid. (Stanley to Aberdeen, May 21st, 1850).

[60] Malmesbury, *Memoirs*, I, 262-3. (*Diary*, June 17th, 1850).

[61] *Hansard* (third series), CXI, 1293-332.

[62] S&F, *Greville*, VI, 228. (*Diary*, June 21st, 1850).

[63] *AP*, BM 43072. (Stanley to Aberdeen, June 20th, 1850); *DP*, Derby XII. (Stanley to Disraeli, June 22nd, 1850).

[64] *AP*, BM 43072. (Stanley to Aberdeen, May 16th, 1850).

[65] *Hansard* (third series), CXIII, 864.

[66] Jennings, *Croker*, II, 411. (Stanley to Coker, August 18th, 1850).
[67] Ibid.
[68] *DP*, Derby XII. (Stanley to Mrs. Disraeli, June 30th, 1850).
[69] *AP*, BM 43072. (Stanley to Aberdeen, Monday, 1850).
[70] G. P. Gooch, *The Later Correspondence of Lord John Russell* (New York: Longmans, Green & Co., 1925), I, 204.
[71] B&E, *Victoria*, II, 356. (Memorandum by Albert, February 23rd, 1851).
[72] S&F., *Greville*, VI, 286. (*Diary*, March 24th, 1851).
[73] Lady Frances Balfour, *The Life of George Fourth Earl of Aberdeen* (London: Hodder & Stoughton, 1922), II, 159. (Aberdeen to Guizot, August 5th, 1850).
[74] Jennings, *Croker*, II, 411. (Stanley to Croker, August 18th, 1850).
[75] M&B, *Disraeli*, I, 1095. (Disraeli to Sarah Disraeli, January 1st, 1851).
[76] *DP*, Derby XII. (Stanley to Disraeli, September 22nd, 1849). (Stanley to Disraeli, October 25th, 1849).
[77] Ibid. Stanley XII. (Edward Stanley to Disraeli, December 31st, 1850).
[78] Ibid., Derby XII. (Stanley to Disraeli, November 15th, 1850).
[79] Ibid. See also: Malmesbury, *Memoirs*, I, 299-300. (Derby to Malmesbury, January 18th, 1852).
[80] B&E, *Victoria*, II, 326-7. (Russell to Victoria, October 25th, 1850); *DP*, Derby XII. (Stanley to Disraeli, November 15th, 1850).
[81] Malmesbury, *Memoirs*, I, 267. (Stanley to Malmesbury, December 2nd, 1850).
[82] Ibid., p. 271. (Stanley to Malmesbury, February 15th, 1851).
[83] Hardcastle, *Campbell*, II, 357.
[84] B&E, *Victoria*, II, 348-9. (Memorandum by Albert, February 22nd, 1851); *DP*, Derby XII. (Stanley Memorandum, undated); *Hansard* (third series), CXIV, 1009-10.
[85] B&E, *Victoria*, II, 359. (Memorandum by Albert, February 24th, 1851).
[86] Ibid., pp. 363-6. (Memorandum by Albert, February 25th, 1851).
[87] Sir Arthur Gordon, *The Earl of Aberdeen* (New York: Harper & Bros., 1893), p. 200.
[88] B&E, *Victoria*, II, 369. (Memorandum by Albert, February 27th, 1851).
[89] Ibid.
[90] *GP*, BM 44140. (Stanley to Gladstone, February 22nd, 1851).
[91] Parker, *Graham*, II, 129. (Newcastle to Graham, February 23rd, 1851).
[92] Morley, *Gladstone*, I, 406-7. (Gladstone Memorandum).
[93] Malmesbury, *Memoirs*, I, 279-80. (*Diary*, March 1st, 1851).
[94] Maxwell, *Clarendon*, I, 324. (Lady Clarendon's Journal, February 22nd, 1851).
[95] *Hansard* (third series), CXIV, 1008-25.
[96] Malmesbury, *Memoirs*, I, 279. (*Diary*, March 1st, 1851).
[97] *Hansard* (third series), CXIV, 1023-5.
[98] A. E. Gathorne-Hardy, ed., *Gathorne Hardy, First Earl of Cranbrook, A Memoir* (London: Longmans, Green & Co., 1910), I, 79. (*Diary*, March 4th, 1851).
[99] *DP*, Derby XII. (Stanley to Disraeli, February 28th, 1851).
[100] Malmesbury, *Memoirs*, I, 281. (*Diary*, March 11th, 1851).
[101] Jennings, *Croker*, II, 421-2. (Stanley to Croker, March 14th, 1851).
[102] Ibid., pp. 426-8. (Stanley to Croker, March 22nd, 1851).
[103] *AP*, BM 43072. (Stanley to Aberdeen, June 14th, 1851).
[104] *DP*, Derby XII. (Stanley to Disraeli, May 25th, 1851). (Stanley to Disraeli, June 28th, 1851).
[105] Ibid., XVII. Miscellaneous Observations §66.
[106] George W. E. Russell, *Prime Ministers and Some Others* (New York: Charles Scribner's Sons, 1919), pp. 32-3.

[107] *DP*, XVII. Miscellaneous Observations §25.
[108] M&B, *Disraeli*, I, 1124. (Malmesbury to Derby, August 19th, 1851).
[109] *DP*, Derby XII. (Derby to Disraeli, October 26th, 1851).
[110] Ibid., Malmesbury XIII. (Malmesbury to Disraeli, January 6th, 1852).
[111] Ibid., XVII. Miscellaneous Observations §25.
[112] Jennings, *Croker*, II, 432. (Derby to Croker, September 22nd, 1851).
[113] *DP*, Derby XII. (Derby to Disraeli, October 26th, 1851).
[114] Malmesbury, *Memoirs*, I, 303. (*Diary*, February 13th, 1852).
[115] B&E, *Victoria*, II, 444. (Russell to Victoria, February 20th, 1852).
[116] Ibid., pp. 445-6. (Memorandum by Albert, February 21st, 1852).

CHAPTER VII

DERBY AGAINST DEMOCRACY

THE news of Russell's defeat reached Derby at Badminton, where he was visiting,* in a triumphant letter from Disraeli on the day following the event. Disraeli strongly urged Derby to try to secure the aid of Palmerston, who, he predicted, would not 'give you trouble about principles, but he may about position', and to facilitate the coalition Disraeli expressed his willingness to serve under Palmerston.[1] A month before, Derby had advised Disraeli carefully to avoid siding with either the Russell or Palmerston faction of the Whigs, and not to consider the possibility of a coalition with the latter faction,[2] but now that Palmerston had engineered the ousting of Russell, the former Foreign Minister seemed bound to act with his successors. A coalition with Palmerston, then, seemed quite possible at the moment. Derby appreciated Disraeli's generous attitude, and wrote him to that effect, but it was obviously impossible to contact Palmerston before going to the Queen, for Her Majesty had only recently dismissed Palmerston, and might object to his return to official life.[3]

At his interview with the Queen, Derby quickly accepted the commission to form a government, even though he had a minority in the Commons, and was not even sure of a majority in the Upper House. Because of these admitted weaknesses, the Queen was not unwilling to allow Palmerston to enter the Government, but she warned the new Prime Minister of his 'dangerous qualities'.[4] Derby had served with Palmerston before, and he felt confident of being able to control him, but, under the circumstances, he decided not to offer Palmerston the Foreign Office.

* All indications are that the charge made by Russell, that the Peelites, Protectionists and Palmerston had a 'pre-arranged determination' to oust him, is baseless. Derby, as noted above, had warned Disraeli not to enter into such an engagement. A rather odd coincidence, however, is to be noted in Malmesbury's *Memoirs*. The day *before* Russell was beaten Lady Derby asked Lady Malmesbury if her husband preferred the Foreign Office to the Colonial Secretaryship. Malmesbury, *Memoirs*, I, 304. (*Diary*, February 19th, 1852). Derby, however, had been working on a list of prospective ministers for some time in anticipation of office, and, according to Lord Campbell, it was completed at least as early as February 15th. Hardcastle, *Campbell*, II, 371.

Constructing a cabinet in 1852 was not characterized by the protracted and futile negotiations of the preceding year. Two months before Derby had broken his silence with a short, non-political letter to Sir James Graham, and his former intimate had replied cordially.* But Derby realized, while the Protection question remained unsettled, negotiations with the Peelites would be futile.[5]

Palmerston's case was altogether different, for he had written Derby on February 21st and offered to open negotiations.[6] The Viscount seemed satisfied with the offer of the lead in the Commons, but he refused to join an administration which would try to impose a fixed duty on corn.[7] Actually, Palmerston did not object to such a duty in principle, though he probably thought it was politically unwise to back it, and possibly reasons of personal ambition loomed large in causing his rejection of the offer. Why should he take a subordinate position when he might, by fishing in the troubled waters of the Opposition, and exploring the fascinating possibilities there, some day become Prime Minister himself? Joining Derby might doom him to indefinite political subordination, and link him to a party which had little popular appeal. Following his refusal, Derby could hope for nothing more than his unofficial co-operation.[8]

Choosing ministers from his inexperienced following was a hit-or-miss proposition. Malmesbury took the Foreign Office reluctantly, for he dreaded its burdens, and perhaps feared the office itself.[9] Disraeli received the most difficult posts – leader in the Commons and the Exchequer. The rest of the appointees were chosen by Derby with the advice of Malmesbury and Disraeli, the first of whom he trusted, and the second he admired.† Some of the men whom Derby had chosen in a list he had drawn up several weeks before, in anticipation of his elevation, would not serve in the capacity he had designated, and there were some last-minute

* Derby's motive here may have been to remove the single exception to his rule that, among gentlemen, political differences should not result in personal grudges. See: Parker, *Graham*, II, 145-6 for excerpts from these letters. A recent biographer of Graham notes that the 'wound' was never healed. Erickson, *Graham*, p. 376.

† Following are the more important officers: Lord Chancellor (Lord St. Leonards); Lord President (Lord Lonsdale); Lord Privy Seal (Lord Salisbury); Home Office (S. H. Walpole); Colonies (Sir John Pakington); Admiralty (Duke of Northumberland); Board of Control (J. C. Herries); Board of Trade (J. W. Henley); Postmaster General (Lord Hardwicke); First Commissioner of Works (Lord John Manners). The Granby protectionist faction remained aloof.

substitutions. But the Government of 1852 was actually formed with a minimum of lost time. Seventeen of his appointees had to be sworn in as Privy Councillors before they could receive their seals of office, an event unprecedented in British history. Later in the Lords Wellington gave the Ministry its nick-name by asking 'Who? Who?' as the names of the men, unknown to the deaf Duke, were announced. The situation was not without some humour. At a dinner at Northumberland House, Lady Clanricarde, poking fun at Derby's appointment of Sir John Pakington to the Colonial Office asked the new Prime Minister: 'Are you sure, Lord Derby, that he is a *real* man?' To which Derby replied, to her consternation: 'Well, I think so – he has been married three times.'[10]

Outside the Conservative Party the reactions to the Government were uniformly bad. Aberdeen thought Derby was throwing away his talents in a hopeless undertaking; Gladstone cryptically observed that the Cabinet was not as good as it 'should have been', and criticized particularly Disraeli at the Exchequer and Henley at the Board of Trade.[11] Clarendon felt Derby must be 'blinded by his Rupertism', and Russell, chagrined by his recent overthrow, thought no worse government could possibly be formed.[12] Campbell anticipated that the Ministry might be 'laughed off the Stage'.[13] The Queen wrote confidentially that she would bear the trial as patiently as she could.[14] Amid the showers of abuse and laughter, however, there stood two rocks – Derby in the Lords and Disraeli in the Commons. The latter faced enormous tasks, and had yet to prove himself in official life. Meanwhile the whole structure rested on Derby. The Queen regarded him as the whole Government,[15] and once, when Derby fell temporarily ill, Disraeli wrote '. . . how things are to go on without him baffles my imagination'.[16] Derby's reputation was so great, and his friendships within his own and the Whig Party were so many, that the Administration virtually rested on the prestige of his name. The nobility of England, regardless of party, were proud of him. Lord Campbell wrote: 'We Peers ought to hold our heads an inch higher at present, as we are for a while to have the Premier amongst us. He is certainly the most stirring orator now in either House. . . .'[17]

Had the Opposition been united the Derby Government would have had no chance of survival, but Derby was aware of their disunity, and, because to have refused office again would have ruined his party, he was prepared to take the gamble that the factions would remain at odds for a time.[18] The Radical Party, which agreed with the Conservatives only on foreign policy, was very hostile. Their leader, Cobden, wanted to 'challenge to instant combat', and try to remove the Conservatives with dispatch lest they gain strength through their control of the Government. Many of his party, however, were so disillusioned with the Whigs that Cobden could not stir them into a fighting mood. In March, Cobden sought an understanding with Russell and Graham to throw out the Government by stopping their supplies. Largely because they felt neither the Peelites nor Palmerston would support them, Graham and Russell were unwilling to join in the attack, and Cobden was disappointed. As the session wore on Cobden lost his fear that the Conservatives would reimpose Protection, but he was still alarmed lest the Conservatives revitalize their party by taking in Palmerston, Gladstone, Goulburn and Herbert.[19]

The Whig Party was divided into its Palmerston and Russell factions, and, at the moment, there was little prospect that the two men would find a *modus vivendi*. Palmerston seemed friendly towards the new Government, and offered advice to Malmesbury at his new post.[20] Realizing his mistake in alienating the powerful Palmerston, Russell, early in March, attempted to lure him to a meeting, but was rebuffed.[21] While Russell, and some of the Ultra-Whigs, such as Lord Grey, were among the most active opponents of the Administration, Derby still hoped some of the 'Old Whigs' might eventually rally to his standard.[22]

From among the Opposition groups, Derby expected the most aid from the Peelites. Late in February he wrote Aberdeen, thanking him for the kindly tone he had adopted towards the Government, and explaining that, after the failure of their *pourparlers* the year before, he had seen no prospect of receiving official aid from the Peelites, and hence had not approached them. But he promised to try to restrain his followers' anti-Peelite utterances.* 'I have every reason to believe,' Aberdeen replied, 'that nothing which can be considered as a factious or obstructive course of proceeding will be attempted.'[23] Derby was thus assured of some help as early as March 1st. Gladstone confirmed the agreement later in the

* On one occasion Beresford exclaimed: 'The Peelites, let them go to hell!' Morley, *Gladstone*, I, 418. Malmesbury described them as: 'Puseyites, Pedants & crotchety, they are what the Cuban Governor said of the American Pirates "without a God, without a law & without a flag".' *Disraeli Papers*, Malmesbury XIII. (Malmesbury to Disraeli, January 6th, 1852).

month, providing there would be a dissolution that summer after necessary business had been transacted.[24]

But the Peelites were divided in their councils. Graham showed very obvious Whig sympathies, and Newcastle wanted to form a new party. Gladstone, Aberdeen and Herbert, perhaps influenced by the majority of their followers, who sought a reconstruction of the Conservative Party once the Protection issue were settled, adopted a 'wait and see' attitude towards the new Government, and were friendly as long as Derby confined himself to measures which were not controversial.

Derby realized that the divisions among the Opposition might keep him in power, but if his party were to grow, it needed some new appeals. Protection was no longer a magnet. Many ardent supporters had already written him, asking him not to sacrifice his Government for the sake of an immediate return to Protection, and Derby realized by March 21st that even a dissolution and election would not give him a mandate to return to it. But he would not abandon Protection until the electorate, at the polls, rejected it. Meanwhile his appeal was to be the preservation of British institutions against the rising tide of democracy. This was more important than a revision of the tariff laws, for it would appeal to conservatives in both the Whig and Peelite Parties.[25] The *Quarterly Review* sounded the theme of the first Derby Administration: 'We humbly but most earnestly desire to submit them [Derby's principles] to all those who . . . may be desirous to avert a democratic and socialist revolution. From this our last chance of escape seems to be in Lord Derby's success.'[26] Fear of a social revolution was present in the minds of many British aristocrats. Shortly before his death, Wellington told Croker: 'But at least, my dear Croker, it is some consolation to us who are near the end of our career that we shall be spared seeing the consummation of the ruin that is gathering around us.'[27] Derby, however, did not plan a frontal attack on the forces he saw working for democracy, but decided rather to show that the Conservative Party could govern England wisely, moderately and well. That was the best antidote for revolutionary maladies.

During February 25th and 26th Derby was busy arranging the Household appointments and some other matters, and the formal change of government took place on February 27th. The outgoing ministers did little to increase the Queen's confidence in her new Government, and were generally critical of their successors. The Conservatives, however, were in high spirits, and, as Malmesbury put it, the Carlton Club had the excited aspect of the Paris Bourse.[28]

The same day Derby faced the task of making a ministerial statement to the House of Lords. Campbell met him in the robing room, and offered congratulations, but Derby replied he was more to be pitied than congratulated. Before their Lordships, however, Campbell noted Derby danced 'his hornpipe among the burning ploughshares with considerable dexterity and felicity'.[29] Asserting that he had achieved now the greatest object of his personal ambition, the new Prime Minister promised to promote peace on earth and goodwill among men. He affirmed again the Conservative policy of non-interference in the domestic affairs of other nations. While calling for increased national defences, and a clean-up of election practices, he refused to unsettle the country by pressing the Reform question. Identifying himself with the rights of the Established Church, he nevertheless demanded religious liberty for all so long as they did not seek to injure that Church. On the issue of Free Trade, the pledged allegiance to what he called the 'American system', which protected both agriculture and industry, but he promised not to try to change present policies without the sanction of an election. While avoiding giving offence to anyone, Derby thus kept the faith, reaffirming his adherence to the principles of the party with which he was identified.[30]

Lord Grey, who hoped to oust the Government within three weeks, immediately pounced on Derby and expressed his consternation that the new Government meant to reimpose the corn tax. Though Derby corrected him by pointing to his promise not to try to change the laws without the sanction of an election, Grey continued to press his point until, with some heat, Derby snapped: '. . . I hope I have satisfied your Lordships the noble Earl misunderstood, and now upon that misunderstanding, so corrected, he is proceeding still to argue.'[31] Grey, no doubt, hurt his own cause by making this precipitous attack. Most of the speakers who followed, however, while tending to agree with Derby on foreign policy, otherwise gave him little support.

Most members were satisfied with Derby's promise of a dissolution, but some, such as the high-minded Lord Shaftesbury, were not,[32] for they felt it was detrimental to the national prosperity to leave the tariff question in abeyance. Fortunately, they were in a minority, and the great majority were content to leave the Government in control until all 'necessary' measures were passed. There was some disagreement both as to the length of the session and the definition of 'necessary measures'. As their election prospects were uncertain, Derby hoped to draw out the session as long as possible.* By mid-March, however, the Opposition became impatient, and Russell in the Commons and Newcastle in the Lords tried to force a more definite statement regarding the time of dissolution. Acting on behalf of the Manchester Commercial Association, Newcastle complained that business was injured by the uncertainty, and called on Derby to clarify his intentions. Carefully avoiding a debate on the Free Trade question, Derby told the House that autumn would find a new parliament in session.[33] Speaking for the majority of the Peelites, who had made a compact with Derby the day before, Aberdeen expressed satisfaction with Derby's promise. Lord Grey, 'looking black as midnight',[34] reluctantly accepted the statement also, and the subject was dropped until March 30th, when Lord Minto re-opened it. A hot argument followed concerning Derby's previous statement, whether he had promised the dissolution in 'April, May or June', or 'May, June or July'. Annoyed, Derby was guilty of a lapse of memory,† and he gave the House little additional information on the subject.[35]

In the other House Disraeli carried on magnificently. Derby was in constant communication with him, giving suggestions as to policy, tactics, and even the content of Disraeli's speeches. But by this time the two were in sharp disagreement on the subject of Protection. Derby refused to desert the cause before the election;[36] Disraeli was convinced that immediate renunciation of it would improve their political position. This difference, actually a question of timing, was never resolved. Disraeli spoke so warmly of Free Trade in his financial statement in April, that Derby sent him a remonstrance. Calling attention to the cheers of the Opposition, and the silence on their own side of the House during the speech,

* Derby wrote: 'I should not deplore a little *factious* delay to our necessary measures which would *unavoidably* carry on Parlmt till June or July.' *Disraeli Papers*, Derby XII. (Derby to Disraeli, March 15th, 1852). He no doubt reasoned that the longer they retained power, the stronger they would be.

† Derby insisted he used the phrase 'May, June or July'. *Hansard* (third series), CXX, 347. Actually he said: 'I will give no pledge, however, that either in the month of April, or May, or of June, that appeal shall be made.' Ibid., CXIX, 1279.

Derby warned him that they might be 'justly stigmatized as impostors who have obtained office under false pretences'.[37] But Disraeli continued to hold his own opinions in spite of Derby's warning.

While Derby danced the hornpipe on the Free Trade issue during the debates regarding dissolution, it arose again in connection with financial matters. In April Derby realized the improbability of their deriving income from a duty on foreign corn, and was ready to ask for an extension of the hated income tax.[38] But he was not ready to announce publicly his lost hopes for Protection. In the Lords, the Opposition were anxious to pry definite statements from him on the subject which might be used during the election. Late in May, during the debates on the property tax, Newcastle delivered a eulogy of Free Trade, and noted that there were even some 'Free-Trade Derbyites' by that time. As no one rose to refute Newcastle, Granville demanded to know on what commercial principles the election was to be fought. Thus forced into the debate, Derby admitted that the election probably would not give him a mandate to reimpose Protection, and also that trade was growing and labour was prosperous. But he insisted that a corn duty was 'desirable' to relieve agricultural distress, and demanded that steps be taken to aid the small farmer.[39] In June he declared that the only way of alleviating the distress of the West Indian planters was to stop the reduction of the differential duties on sugar.[40] With these parliamentary declarations from their leader, the Protectionists had to rest content. It was certainly a bare minimum of satisfaction in return for the support they had given the party for six years. Disraeli, however, would have deprived them of even that. In June, when Derby made some suggestions as to the content of one of Disraeli's speeches, he noted: '. . . it is well to let down the Agricultural body as easily as we can'.[41]

Another difficult issue for Derby was the status of Maynooth. Since the Papal Aggression incident the majority of British people, and especially one wing of the Conservative Party, were deeply suspicious of the Roman Catholics, and they looked askance at the Maynooth grant, which provided funds for Roman Catholic education. Derby believed a committee to study the whole Roman Catholic question would be a useful 'safety valve', for, while the Maynooth College grant had not served, as he had hoped, to create a priesthood more favourably disposed towards England, he was not prepared to associate himself with anti-Catholic reprisals. Derby, on April 20th, tried to sidestep the Maynooth question by refusing to commit himself unless someone moved for a cessation of the grant. Grey interpreted this as an attempt to keep the Government unpledged so that Conservatives could make pro- or anti-Maynooth speeches during the election.[42]

The following month the Marquis of Breadalbane called for the repeal of the Maynooth College Act and forced Derby to take a stand. Irked, Derby said he had no 'present' intention of interfering with Maynooth, and observed there was nothing sinful about granting money to people of a different faith.[43] But in the Commons the Government had sponsored a committee to investigate Maynooth, and Lord Beaumont called attention to this inconsistency. What, then, was the purpose of the committee? '. . . I am not quite so surprised at this as I might have been,' he continued, 'because it is consistent with the only principle which as yet the Government has declared or adopted, namely, that everything in the world is a compromise . . .'[44] It was difficult ground for Derby, for he had no desire to attack the Catholics, yet many of his followers hoped to win the election by a 'No Popery' cry.[45] His only refuge was ambiguity.*

Derby's attitude towards Reform met with considerable approval. Late in May he stressed the theme that political power should not be thrown into the hands of mere numbers at the expense of property and intelligence.[46] Of the three qualifications, he felt that intelligence, which was hardest to determine, might really be the best. His objection to numbers was consistent with his former and later utterances on the subject. The lower class, he feared, was the most 'easily misguided' element in the community, and one could not be sure they would use their voting privilege properly. For this reason he resisted attempts to democratize New Zealand, and the Lower House there was made elective with a franchise based on property, excluding many whites from sharing in the government.[47] During this debate Derby insisted that New Zealand should be British and monarchical, rather than

* As early as 1831 Derby (then Stanley) spoke at some length on Maynooth. He said the institution had been established by Pitt in 1795 so that the Irish priesthood would not have to go to France, where revolutionary ideas were current, for their education. He insisted at that time that Maynooth was a political, not a religious question, and declared it neither promoted the Catholic Church nor injured the interests of the Protestant faith. *Hansard* (third series), VII, 611-14.

American and republican. Before many years, however, responsible government was granted to the colony, and the franchise qualifications were gradually liberalized. Derby, nevertheless, during his term had the satisfaction of replacing the New Zealand Company, dissolved in 1851, with a more efficient type of government.

Another measure before the Lords in June was designed to eliminate corrupt practices at elections. It provided for the trial of delinquent boroughs by special tribunal, replacing the special parliamentary commissions which dealt with such cases. Being interested in preserving the powers of the Lords, Derby insisted on an amendment to allow the Lords to determine in which cases the law would apply, and this touched off a heated debate.[48] Partly because of Derby's desire to uphold the constitution, which, he said, permitted the Lords to share the legislative power equally with the Commons, the problem was not settled satisfactorily at this time, and was the subject of one of Disraeli's measures in 1868.

More important was the Militia Bill, which Derby termed a necessary measure, and which had been drawn up after a plan devised by Prince Albert.[49] The Radicals, especially Cobden, sought to defeat the bill because it placed control of officers' promotions in the hands of the Lord Lieutenants of the shires, and thus fortified the position of the landed aristocracy.[50] Derby defended the measure as being indicative of England's peaceful intentions,[51] and, with Palmerston's support in the Commons, it passed easily.

The Militia Bill quite naturally brought up the larger question of Britain's relations with France, whose government had been taken over by Napoleon III. Many Conservatives distrusted an adventurer so tainted with revolution, who might revive both French jingoism and continental wars. Derby accepted the revolution philosophically. 'France and Frenchmen', he wrote, 'are incapable of rational self-government, and . . . sooner or later they will give themselves a master.'[52] While a revolution might be 'unconstitutional', Derby felt England had no choice but to recognize the governments of other nations, be they any type '. . . from the most absolute despotism down to the most entire red republicanism'.[53] The information furnished him by Malmesbury[54] made Derby fear that some 'unquiet spirits' in

France might seek war with England, and he proposed to meet the threat with his Militia Bill, on the one hand, and a conciliatory recognition of the French Government, on the other. Derby rejected an offensive-defensive alliance with Russia, partly because of its anti-French implications, partly because he did not approve of such entanglements.*

In colonial affairs Derby continued to be anti-imperialistic. He opposed the annexation of Burma, and regarded the annexations in India since 1834 as liabilities forced on Britain by circumstances beyond her control.[55] Derby hoped that the Indian people might some day be trusted with their own affairs, and regarded British occupation as a civilizing stage in Indian development. 'I say that even if the gigantic power of Britain should in the course of years . . . fall to the ground by the operation of our own hands,' he declared, 'it will have been an achievement worthy of a nation like this to have rescued the native population from the state of ignorance, superstition and debasement in which we found a large portion of them sunk . . .'[56] While right in gauging the importance of British rule to India, Derby was wrong in assuming that it would last for centuries, and that the Indian people would look back on the occupation with a deep sense of gratitude.

By and large it was a successful session, and at its close Derby thanked the Lords for their co-operation during this period of the 'interregnum of parties'. For his Government he took credit for having resisted a dissolution, for passing the Militia Bill, law reform, and other legislation, some of it over determined opposition. He boasted that his measures were as important and beneficial as those of any previous Administration, however powerful.[57] Grey immediately arose to declare that the previous Administration had prepared Derby's measures, and, if in opposition, the Prime Minister would have opposed them. Lord Beaumont joined in: 'Aye. You carried out measures which you adopted from recommendations made by Commissions appointed by the late Government. You carried measures which were suggested by your predecessors.'[58] So, in the Lords, the session ended on a sour note. After having failed to convince all their

* According to Disraeli: 'Shortly after the formation of this government, Baron Brunnow, the Russian Ambassador, proposed to Lord Derby an alliance betn. England & Russia, offensive and defensive. Lord Derby at once rejected the proposition. It was never brought before the Cabinet. But it was made.' *Disraeli Papers*, XVII, Miscellaneous Observations §47.

Lordships of the value of his leadership, Derby now faced the electorate for its verdict on his quiet efforts to stem the tide of democracy.

In March 1852 Derby correctly predicted that the election would cause little excitement, and seemed fairly confident that it might bring him a working majority.[59] The idea that a Conservative government would be the signal for a general uprising in England had been disproved. '. . . while a short time ago everybody said a Derby Government was impossible,' Greville wrote in May, 'it now appears to be the only Government which is possible'.[60] Campbell gloomily predicted that Derby would go on till his Government seemed worse than no government at all.[61] Despite their weakness, the Conservatives had shown they could govern the country creditably, and that the mass of British people, imbued with the traditional British sense of 'fair play', were not *ipso facto* hostile towards them.

During the election the Conservative appeal was not clear-cut, and the candidates suited their declarations to their audiences. In some districts they were Protectionists; in others, Free Traders.[62] Disraeli, who favoured abandoning Protection, was dissatisfied with this disorganized state of affairs, and felt it cost the party a number of seats. After declaring that the election was to centre on the trade question, however, Derby could hardly have abandoned Protection completely, and it was a concession to Disraeli's point of view that Derby did not insist on a fixed duty as a party principle.

Protestantism helped the Conservatives considerably. Even the liberal Edward Stanley was forced to admit: 'All the ultra-Protestants voted for me at Lynn.'[63] Perhaps the biggest factor favouring the Conservatives was the new confidence in their moderation, which suited the temper of the prosperous times. The Opposition watched them fearfully. Russell gave them 310-320 members;[64] Greville guessed they would have more than 300 – 'all Derbyites, staunch supporters and moveable like a regiment'.[65] After Parliament met, Derby analysed its membership as 286 Conservatives, 150 Radicals, 120 Whigs, 50 in the Irish Brigade, and 30 Peelites, which was apparently not an exaggerated estimate of a mild Conservative victory.[66] But his party still lacked a majority in the Lower House.

Among Ultra-Conservatives there was a definite lack of confidence in their prospects. Croker thought Derby might avert an immediate revolution, but, if he attempted to retreat or advance, the party would be lost.[67] Lonsdale felt Disraeli 'meant well', but thought too much of winning each night's debate regardless of the cost in principles.[68] To most Conservatives it was apparent that the Government must have outside aid. Stanley and Walpole urged Derby to contact Palmerston, but the Prime Minister was lukewarm towards the idea at the moment.[69] Probably he felt that aid from Palmerston or the Peelites would have to await the opening of Parliament and the official abandonment of Protection.

Derby meanwhile was interested in improving his relations at Court, the source of considerable patronage, which was vital both to his party and his position as leader. Prince Albert had been 'not naturally too well disposed' towards him personally,[70] and Derby seized every opportunity to assist the Prince. Albert, fresh from his Great Exhibition success, had some building projects in mind, and sought financial aid from the Government. He involved himself once in a 'serious scrape' by accepting a large building loan, and Derby had to help him out of it.[71] By August the Prince was more cordial to him than ever before, and his National Gallery project gave the Conservatives a useful topic for discussion at the opening of Parliament. Derby also tried to improve his position with the great humanitarian, Lord Shaftesbury, by helping him complete his laws of lunacy, but failed to enlist him as an ally.

Meanwhile elements in the Opposition were uniting against Derby. Russell was a prime mover, aided by Graham, who by this time could write: 'On every ground, personal and political, I am opposed to the Derby-Disraeli Administration.'[72] They sought a coalition between the Russell Whigs and the Peelites, and a brisk correspondence among Russell, Graham, Aberdeen and Gladstone took place that summer. The last two were partly committed to supporting Derby. Late in February Derby had reopened his correspondence with Aberdeen, who, as noted above, promised to support the general measures of his Government, and his tone was friendly enough to give Derby good reason to hope for his eventual support.[73] Gladstone had likewise promised his support to Derby, and, save on one occasion,* he had given it.

* The disfranchisement of Sudbury and St. Albans question saw Gladstone attack and defeat the Government. Some writers attribute this to a Protectionist speech

Why Gladstone hesitated to join Derby is rather clear – he disliked Disraeli, and would not act as his subordinate in the Commons.[74] Aberdeen's motives have been explained in many places. He criticized Derby for giving up Protection, and disliked the Conservative Party for its association with reaction and religious bigotry. Certainly in the late summer, 1852, if not before,* another motive was added to these. Newcastle wrote him on August 2nd noting that, if Russell formed a government, many of the Peelites would join Derby, but, if Aberdeen became Prime Minister a coalition might be effected between the Peelites and the Whigs.[75] To what extent personal ambition influenced him is uncertain, but about that time Aberdeen concluded, after supporting Derby during the whole session, that the Conservative course was tortuous and shifty. The following month Aberdeen wrote Cardwell: 'I expect to see the Duke of Newcastle before the end of the month, and Graham also talks of coming here. Should they be here together, we shall assuredly give rise to the report of an organized conspiracy.'[76] The plot proceeded apace, and by the time Parliament opened, it apparently had the adhesion of many important Peelites.

A large number of matters occupied Derby's time during the autumn as he visited various places, including Balmoral for a week, and tended his social as well as his political affairs. There was the question of a Chairman of Committees. Derby's choice was an old friend, Wilson Patten, who had associated himself with the Peelite group, but late in August he declined the appointment, and Derby and Disraeli feverishly sought a substitute.[77] After considerable urging from Derby, and a consultation with the Peelite, Sidney Herbert, Patten at length accepted, and Derby

* Aberdeen wrote his son in 1851 that he would have been Prime Minister then were it not for his views on the Ecclesiastical Titles Bill. Sir Arthur Gordon, *The Earl of Aberdeen* (New York: Harper & Bros., 1893), p. 200.

---

made by Lord Derby, but the Gladstone Papers do not seem to make this connection. Derby asked Gladstone's support for the measure as a 'private friend', noting: 'Forgive me if I add, that I should be sorry to see *you* at the head of the first successful move, if you should succeed, against us.' Gladstone replied that the measure violated their agreement not to introduce controversial legislation during that session, and, because of this, he would have to oppose it. But he noted that his opposition indicated no change of feeling towards the Government. *Gladstone Papers*, BM 44140. (Derby to Gladstone, May 9th, 1852). (Gladstone to Derby, May 10th, 1852).

took this as a sign of Peelite favour.[78] Patronage likewise presented some problems. Two posts, the Receivership of Crown Rents and a Treasurership, were open. Disraeli's request that his brother receive the former was refused on grounds of qualification, but Derby was happy to be able to offer the second to the brother of his Commons chief.[79] The Duke of Wellington died at this time, and there were the details of his funeral to be arranged.[80] These matters, and many others, prevented Derby from having the uninterrupted rest at Knowsley that he had hoped for. But during his stay at Balmoral he was pleased to find his position with respect to the Royal Family greatly improved, and he analysed the domestic situation at the Palace very practically. 'The Queen & Prince are both very friendly and communicative', he wrote Disraeli. 'We must keep *him* with us, which I think may be managed. His influence is boundless.'[81]

When Parliament opened on November 11th, the Conservative position, though Derby was apparently unaware of the plot, was not encouraging. The pact made with the Peelites no longer obtained; most of the Whigs and all the Radicals were hostile, and the Conservatives could be put in the minority at any time. The announcement the political world awaited was soon forthcoming. Speaking in the Lords, Derby admitted that a very large majority of British people, including many from agricultural districts, no longer sought a reimposition of the Corn Laws, and that he himself saw there might be advantages to the nation as a whole in retaining Free Trade. Derby added: 'On the part, then, of myself and my colleagues, I bow to the decision of the country.'[82] No yells of triumph came from the Free Traders, nor moans of despair from the beaten Protectionists – the announcement was received in silence by both sides of the House.[83] However, the bitter Protection controversy was now finally ended for Derby's time and several decades beyond. The only balm that Derby could offer to his party was a promise to try to help those who suffered from Free Trade.

If he expected that the way was now clear for the Free Trade Conservatives to bury the hatchet, Derby was disappointed. Such a clear-cut victory did not satisfy the Free Traders. Like a high priest, Cobden declared: 'They must profess adhesion to that policy and recant their own errors; they must promise to promote and to extend these principles . . .'[84] Though Derby asked the Opposition to postpone its attacks until they saw the budget, a hostile move was launched almost immediately by Charles Villiers, who professed dissatisfaction at the Free Trade declaration in the Speech, and gave notice that he would introduce his own on November 22nd.[85] His resolution was designed to satisfy Cobden, and contained such objectionable references to the past that Derby wrote Disraeli: 'I own I do not see how we can swallow Villiers' motion, which I have just seen.'[86] Meanwhile, the Peelites, working with Russell, had drawn up their own resolution, which called for the prudent extension of Free Trade, but made no references to the past.[87] Either this resolution was given to Palmerston, or he drew up one very similar himself.*

Though about seventy last-ditch Protectionists were unwilling to support any resolution at all, the Conservatives at a meeting gave Derby a free hand to deal with the crisis.[88] It was finally decided that Disraeli should offer an unobjectionable resolution as an amendment to that of Villiers, and, as it was drawn up, it was necessarily weak, so much so that Gladstone was prepared to vote with Villiers.[89]

Villiers introduced his resolution into the Commons, tracing British prosperity to the 'wise, just and beneficial' Act of 1846, and Disraeli introduced his amendment. In so doing Disraeli tried to justify his own conduct by saying he rejected Free Trade in 1846 for fear of its effects on labour,[90] but his prospects, both of carrying his amendment, and of convincing the House he had always favoured Free Trade, were poor indeed.

Palmerston saved the Government from ruin.[91] On November 21st, the eve of the struggle, he dispatched two letters, one to Villiers, and the other to Gladstone, together with his own resolution, asking: 'What do you think of such an amendment as is attached on the accompanying paper as a Middle Term between the Resolution of Villiers and the amendment of Disraeli?'[92] Villiers, however, rejected Palmerston's compromise. The follow-

* Parker, in his life of Graham, states that Gladstone and Herbert furnished Palmerston with a copy of Graham's resolution. (Parker, *Graham*, II, 187). However, Palmerston sent one to Gladstone on November 21st which he said was 'compiled from the Queen's Speech, and the Resolution & Amendment', and Gladstone said he would accept 'your draft'. This evidence indicates that Palmerston himself drew up the amendment. *Gladstone Papers*, BM 44271. (Palmerston to Gladstone, November 21st, 1852). (Gladstone to Palmerston, November 21st, 1852).

ing day Palmerston sent the same resolution to Disraeli, stating that he did not want to see a great principle become the plaything of a party struggle, and suggesting that Disraeli accept it.[93] Disraeli thereupon withdrew his amendment and called on his party to support the Palmerston resolution. But a mighty debate took place in the Commons, and all the pent-up feelings of six years of political wrangling flooded across the floor of the House. The emotional climax was reached in a speech by Sidney Herbert, who, after a eulogy of Peel, pointed to the Treasury Bench, and shouted: '— if a man wants to see humiliation — which, God knows, is always a painful sight — he need but look there'.* But, in spite of the invective they poured on Disraeli, the Villiers resolution was defeated by a comfortable margin when the Peelites supported Palmerston's compromise. A reprieve was thus granted to the Government.

Derby was a 'good deal galled' by the tone of the debate in the Commons,[94] and was more annoyed when the same project was mooted in the Lords. Early in the discussion there, Derby called it 'unpleasant and mortifying' to admit his sentiments on the commercial question had not been in accord with those of the nation, but he promised to carry out the Free Trade policy in good faith. Lord Wodehouse gathered from the statement that Derby still believed in Protection, and suggested that the honourable course would be to base his government on it. To this Derby replied cuttingly: 'The noble Baron may be a competent judge of what is due to his own personal honour; I claim to be the best judge of what is due to mine; and I want no advice from him as to the mode in which I should maintain it.'[95] Wodehouse apologized, and Derby accepted. Later Derby agreed to accept a resolution provided it made no reference to the past, and Lord Clanricarde introduced one on December 2nd. After a spirited debate, during which the Free Traders, in a gentlemanly way, attacked '. . . the head and chief and the mainstay, as well as the ornament of the great party who had been identified with the principle of protection',[96] a resolution was passed which was agreeable to all. Derby defended both his party and himself ably,

* *Hansard* (third series), CXXIII, 613. Derby, who still had hopes of Peelite support, told Gladstone that he felt Herbert had said more than he had really intended to say. Morley, *Gladstone*, I, 435. (*Diary*, November 27th, 1852).

and soothed the feelings of his followers who still, in some cases, believed in Protection.*

This rude reception by Parliament turned the minds of Derby and Disraeli more determinedly to the problem of strengthening their position. Palmerston appeared quite friendly, and the night of November 24th found Disraeli trying to win him over. Palmerston, however, would not reveal his intentions, and refused to commit himself to future co-operation.[97] Shortly thereafter Gladstone attended a party at Derby's, and the latter took him aside to explore the possibilities of arriving at an understanding. Speaking for Herbert, Goulburn and himself, Gladstone averred that their position had not changed since last spring, and they waited for the Budget before determining their course.[98] The impression left with Derby was that a dislike of Disraeli prevented collaboration with Gladstone and perhaps some others. The Prince Consort likewise distrusted Disraeli. On November 26th the Prince wrote the Prime Minister, criticizing Palmerston and Disraeli for their lack of principles, and suggesting that, in any reconstruction, Gladstone be made leader in the Commons.[99]

A number of factors stood in the way of securing either Palmerston or the Peelites. The Queen would not accept Palmerston as leader in the Commons,[100] but Derby knew from his interview with Gladstone, and from information provided by another source,† that the Peelites would possibly serve under Palmerston, but not under Disraeli. During an interview of November 27th with the Queen, Derby would not consider Gladstone as an alternative Commons' leader because he lacked boldness and decision. Disraeli, he informed them, had no intention of giving up the lead. Attempts to strengthen thus reached an impasse. Derby was unwilling to sacrifice Disraeli to gain the support of the Peelites, and, even with such a concession, they might not have joined him. He felt that Palmerston, alone, would not help him very much.[101] Because of their conflicting attitudes on foreign affairs, an alliance between Palmerston and Derby would have no doubt led to embarrassing

* Derby also defended his dealing with Peel: '. . . I defy — I do not use the word offensively — the warmest friends of the late Sir Robert Peel to find in any speech or writing of mine a single expression derogatory to his character, or affecting the integrity or the motives of that statesman.' *Hansard* (third series), CXXIII, 950.

† Derby said that he had received a letter report from one who had contacted the Peelites, but did not identify the sender. B&E, *Victoria*, II, 491-2. (Memorandum by Albert, November 28th, 1852).

situations, and probably would not have been long-lived. The Government was thus thrown back on their own resources and faced the supreme test of passing a budget through a hostile House.

The construction of a budget, which at once adopted the principle of Free Trade and provided relief to the agricultural interest, was a difficult task; and the matter was further complicated by the threatening foreign situation, which seemed to justify further armament outlays. Derby tried to keep the demands of the armed forces at a minimum, and the Queen was critical towards him for not being 'alarmed enough' over foreign affairs,[102] but he finally consented to an increase of 5000 seamen and 1500 marines.[103] During November Disraeli, aided by Derby, slowly pieced together a budget, but prospects were so slim of their being able to satisfy everyone that the resourceful Disraeli was in despair. Derby urged unconvincingly: 'Put a good face upon it, and we shall pull through.'[104] Disraeli, under the circumstances, relied more upon behind-the-scenes agreements than his speaking, and he apparently made an effort about this time to solicit the votes of the Irish Brigade, which could have spelled the margin of victory.[105] The details of the negotiation are not clear, but apparently either the repudiation of such a bargain by Derby, or the sure knowledge of Disraeli that Derby would not sell out the landed interest of Ireland in return for the assistance of the Irish Brigade, prevented any deal being made.*

On December 3rd Disraeli introduced his Budget in one of his mighty five-hour marathons. The Budget attempted to aid the West Indies sugar-producers by allowing them to refine sugar in bond for home consumption; to provide relief for agriculture by halving the malt tax; and to eliminate passing tolls and to cut down the light-dues for the benefit of the shipping interest. As a boon to the general public, the tea tax was to be gradually reduced,

* The story of this negotiation is told in Greville's diary under the date of January 29th, 1853. According to it Disraeli toyed with the idea of adopting the projects of the Tenant Right League, whose proposals were inimical to the interests of the Irish landed aristocracy. Greville added that Derby rejected the idea with considerable heat. However, on January 30th, 1853, Derby wrote Disraeli concerning an offer he had heard had been made by Disraeli to an Irish leader, and added: 'I am perfectly satisfied that no *offer* could have been made to him without my sanction or knowledge . . .' If this letter refers to Disraeli's negotiation with the Tenant Right League, it appears that Derby had no knowledge of it at the time. *Disraeli Papers*, Derby XII. (Derby to Disraeli, January 30th, 1853).

and beer was to be cheapened by halving the hop tax. To make up these losses in revenue, the House Tax was to be increased, and, in general, the amount and area of direct taxation.[106] Derby was present for almost the whole speech, and immediately dispatched a letter to his second in command, warmly congratulating him, and adding: '. . . I think you have weathered the really dangerous point, and that the Ship is now in comparatively smooth waters.'[107] While Derby did not like to trust in first impressions, he foresaw there was now some chance of success. At the Lord Mayor's dinner shortly thereafter the two were so favourably received that Greville was forced to admit: '. . . I believe, if the Country were polled, they would as soon have these people for Ministers as any others.'[108]

The story of the battle of the Budget belongs to Disraeli. Immediately the brains and talent on the other side of the House fell on the Budget and began to tear it to pieces, each having his individual objections to it, and all opposing the idea of receiving a Free Trade Budget from the hands of Disraeli. Little or no support came from the Conservative side, for the simple reason that they had no speakers up to the task. Disraeli sensed defeat, and, under such conditions, his every instinct told him to fight with whatever weapons might be handy. So, on an off night during the debate, Disraeli sent a note to the Radical, John Bright, asking him to call. The interview brought no alliance, for Disraeli could have offered none, but the Chancellor of the Exchequer even pictured the eventual formation of a government which would contain Cobden and Bright.[109] Bright, however, was unimpressed, though perhaps somewhat mystified.

The same evening Derby, who had discussed the situation earlier with Disraeli, wrote his Chancellor of the Exchequer a long letter in which he discoursed at length on politics and honour. As they could not carry the reduction of the malt tax, or provide any other relief to agriculture, they would put themselves in a false position if they abandoned their supporters in order to secure a short-lived existence. They owed their position to the agriculturists, and were as much committed to aiding them now as previously they had been pledged to Protection. They had staked their existence on the Budget as a whole. '. . . I own', he continued, 'that if you are only to escape defeat tomorrow by a virtual surrender of your Budget, at least of so much of it as promises *any* relief to our own friends . . . I think the temporary respite will be dearly bought; and that you had better be defeated honestly in a fairly fought field, than escape under a cloud, to encounter aggravated defeat with alienated friends & sneering opponents.'[110] With all the concessions they had made and could honourably make if the House still were hostile to them, then it was time that another government be formed to replace them. To be beaten fairly was not to be discredited, and they might look forward to a return to power, when and if their opponents tried to carry on and failed. These were his own sentiments, Derby wrote, but he was willing to listen to everyone in the Cabinet before revealing his ideas to their colleagues. Disraeli replied and agreed with Derby, adding: '. . . I would prefer being your colleague in opposition to being the colleague of any other man as a Minister.'[111] It must have been abundantly clear to both by this time that they were being attacked by a well-organized coalition.

The night of December 16th-17th, Gladstone wrote, was the most exciting in his parliamentary career.[112] Derby sat beside Lord Campbell during the debate, and kept up his hopes by describing the impossibility of anyone forming the diverse elements of the Opposition into a stable government without creating a Cabinet of at least thirty-two men. Campbell smilingly asked if Derby included Cobden and Bright in his total, to which Derby retorted that they would make thirty-four.[113] He saw his Chancellor of the Exchequer arise at ten o'clock, a solitary figure, a man who had stood up gallantly against tremendous odds for the past nine months, now at bay, to defend a budget that all of the great political minds of Britain had cut to shreds. He heard Disraeli refuse, as he, Derby, had suggested, to amend his Budget to suit his opponents, and saw him turn on his harassers with the bludgeons of brilliantly chosen phrases. It was one o'clock when Disraeli finished the defence of his Budget, his party and himself. Then Gladstone arose to show the Conservatives how Disraeli was 'hoodwinking and bewildering them',[114] but Derby found the reply quite dull. At four in the morning the division was taken, amid the violence of the thunderstorm outside, but the loudest crash was that of the Derby Government as it went down under the combined weight of the Whigs, Peelites, Radicals and Irish. Derby turned to Campbell: 'Now we are properly smashed', he said, 'I must prepare for my journey to Osborne to resign.'[115] But he was satisfied that they had been beaten, not discredited. Regretfully, early in the morning, Derby wrote Her Majesty and informed her of the result of that night's work.[116]

Few governments in British history had to face such a consistently hostile Press as the Derby Ministry of 1852. Periodicals and newspapers abounded with all sorts of allegations against them. *Fraser's* wrote:[117]

> Their three most conspicuous articles of faith — Protection, Protestantism and resistance to democracy — have been abandoned in a moment of power . . . Their financial policy is a delusion; they have deceived the farmers, and forsaken the shipping interest; they have fraternized with the French revolutionists, and not only suffered the Roman Catholics to violate the law with impunity, but crowned their impunity with triumphs . . . Where they did not actually deceive their Party, they disappointed them.

Some years later the *Edinburgh Review* still recited such charges:[118]

> From the moment they took office, their sole desire seemed to be to induce the public to forget . . . all their former professions and principles, and from that time forward there has been no Conservative Party . . . the Derby Government of 1852 was the first administration in this country which reduced inconsistency to a system, and want of principles to a principle.

The powerful *Times* added its influential voice to the damnation of the Conservatives.[119] Adjectives, such as 'degraded', 'disgraceful' and 'dishonourable', appeared among the pages of the almost universally hostile Press, chiefly from writers who considered themselves to be the high priests of liberalism. Malmesbury was hurt particularly to discover that some of the attacks made on him personally were penned by Herbert, who, two years before, had wished so fervently for a reconstruction of the Conservative Party.[120]

Criticism of the Derby Government, however, was not limited to Opposition circles. It was perhaps inevitable that the more reactionary elements of the Conservative Party should also be dissatisfied. After the fall of the Ministry, the *Quarterly Review* still called Derby the 'sheet anchor' against the storm of revolution, but criticized the record of his Government, whose poor showing it traced to inferior discipline, tactics and general influence.[121] Croker thought Derby provided poor leadership, and called Disraeli 'worse than nothing' in the Commons.[122] His intimate correspondence with Derby now ceased, and the old Tory made up his quarrel with Graham.

If the Ultra-Conservatives were angry that Derby did not fight harder for Protection and Protestantism, so were the Opposition. The former were so out-of-tune with the times that they would have been satisfied with nothing less than a return to 1845, or earlier, and the latter, in some cases, were disappointed that the Conservatives did not associate themselves irrevocably with reaction and thus discredit themselves. One group identified Conservatism with reaction; the other with political immobility. Derby did not remain still, or go backward, so both were disappointed.

Nevertheless the Conservative record was not a bad one. They established a militia, created a government for New Zealand, and passed some Chancery reforms. They dealt effectively enough with some minor problems, and had on hand some constructive Irish legislation. In foreign affairs Malmesbury surpassed expectations,[123] and Derby warmly praised his friend's efforts in a speech Malmesbury proudly reproduced in his *Memoirs*.[124] But, working within the Peel-Aberdeen tradition of peace and conciliation, Malmesbury achieved no flashy successes. The new tie of friendship with France was to be utilized shortly in the Crimean War. Several years later Cobden wrote: 'I look back with regret on the vote which changed Lord Derby's Government; I regret the result of that motion, for it cost the country a hundred millions of treasure and between thirty and forty thousand good lives.'[125] Derby's group were thus established as the peace party.

Lord Derby's own record of keeping the faith with his party was a good one. His was a double responsibility — to carry out the wishes of his supporters, and to improve the position of his party in Parliament and the country. The two were difficult to reconcile, and the only possibility of accomplishing both was through compromise. He clung to Protection beyond the time it was politically wise to do so, and gave it up only when most thoughtful men in his party were convinced it was a dead issue or an unattainable good. When Protection was given up, he turned to compensation, and insisted on retaining that element in Disraeli's Budget. As his Government fell because of its unwillingness to amend the Budget, the supreme sacrifice was thus made to the wishes of its supporters.

Regarding resistance to democracy, it should be noted that the Reform Bill was dropped, and that the recognition of France was a peace measure, not a condoning of revolution. Croker thought Derby should have fallen in the cause of extreme Protestantism,[126] but it is to Derby's credit both from the standpoint of character and of political sagacity that he did not do so. Many Catholics were highly conservative, and perhaps represented a potential element of strength for the Conservatives – if the party as a whole could have been brought to share Derby's own views. When compromises were made they did not infringe on the principles of conservatism as Derby saw them, but gave his administration a conciliatory tone. A definite step on the road back had been taken, for the electorate had shown it was mildly sympathetic towards Derby's efforts. Under these circumstances, it was to be expected that some day they would have another chance.

NOTES

[1] M&B, *Disraeli*, I, 1158. (Disraeli to Derby, Friday night, 1852).

[2] *DP*, Derby XII. (Derby to Disraeli, January 7th, 1852).

[3] Ibid. (Derby to Disraeli, February 22nd, 1852).

[4] B&E, *Victoria*, II, 447-8. (Memorandum by Albert, February 22nd, 1852).

[5] *AP*, BM 43072. (Derby to Aberdeen, February 29th, 1852).

[6] Malmesbury, *Memoirs*, I, 305. (*Diary*, February 22nd, 1852).

[7] B&E, *Victoria*, II, 448. (Derby to Victoria, February 22nd, 1852).

[8] Ibid.

[9] Malmesbury, *Memoirs*, I, 305. (*Diary*, February 21st, 1852).

[10] Ibid., pp. 312-13. (*Diary*, March 6th, 1852).

[11] Morley, *Gladstone*, I, 417. (Gladstone to Wife, February 23rd, 1852).

[12] Gooch, *Later Correspondence*, II, 100. (Clarendon to Russell, February 3rd, 1852); Ibid., I, cxxxvii.

[13] Hardcastle, *Campbell*, II, 372.

[14] B&E, *Victoria*, II, 450. (Victoria to King of the Belgians, February 24th, 1852).

[15] Ibid., pp. 466-7. (Victoria to King of the Belgians, March 23rd, 1852).

[16] M&B, *Disraeli*, I, 1184. (Disraeli to Sarah Disraeli, May 14th, 1852).

[17] Hardcastle, *Campbell*, II, 372.

[18] Jennings, *Croker*, II, 421. (Stanley to Croker, March 14th, 1851).

[19] John Morley, *The Life of Richard Cobden* (1881), pp. 385-8. (Cobden to Wilson, February 28th, 1852). (Cobden to Sturge, March 11th, 1852). (Cobden to Wilson, March 20th and 23rd, 1852).

[20] Malmesbury, *Memoirs*, I, 308. (Palmerston to Malmesbury, February 24th, 1852).

[21] B&E, *Victoria*, II, 458-9. (Phipps to Victoria, March 10th, 1852).

[22] Ibid., p. 465. (Memorandum by Albert, March 22nd, 1852).

[23] *AP*, BM 43072. (Aberdeen to Derby, March 1st, 1852).
[24] *DP*, Derby XII. (Derby to Disraeli, March 18th, 1852).
[25] B&E, *Victoria*, II, 465. (Memorandum by Albert, March 22nd, 1852).
[26] 'The Old and New Ministers'. *The Quarterly Review*, XC (March 1852), pp. 567-92.
[27] Jennings, *Croker*, II, 542. (Croker to Palmerston, April 25th, 1852).
[28] Malmesbury, *Memoirs*, I, 307. (*Diary*, February 23rd, 1852).
[29] Hardcastle, *Campbell*, II, 373.
[30] *Hansard* (third series), CXIX, 889-905.
[31] Ibid., p. 906.
[32] Edwin Hodder, *The Life and Work of the Seventh Earl of Shaftesbury* (New York: Cassell & Co., 1887), II, 379. (*Diary*, February 23rd, 1852).
[33] *Hansard* (third series), CXIX, 1279-80.
[34] *DP*, Derby XII. (Derby to Disraeli, March 19th, 1852).
[35] *Hansard* (third series), CXX, 345-7.
[36] B&E, *Victoria*, II, 465. (Memorandum by Albert, March 22nd, 1852).
[37] *DP*, Derby XII. (Derby to Disraeli, April 30th, 1852).
[38] Ibid. (Derby to Disraeli, April 25th, 1852).
[39] *Hansard* (third series), CXXI, 1014-47.
[40] Ibid., CXXII, 383.
[41] *DP*, Derby XII. (Derby to Disraeli, June 3rd, 1852).
[42] *Hansard* (third series), CXX, 874-85.
[43] Ibid., CXXI, 876.
[44] Ibid., pp. 876-9.
[45] Ibid., p. 880.
[46] Ibid., pp. 1188-92.
[47] Ibid., CXXII, 1287-8.
[48] Ibid., pp. 565-89.
[49] B&E, *Victoria*, II, 452-3. (Memorandum by Victoria, February 26th, 1852).
[50] Morley, *Cobden*, pp. 390-1.
[51] *Hansard* (third series), CXXII, 706-13.
[52] Jennings, *Croker*, II, 439-40. (Derby to Croker, December 22nd, 1851).
[53] *Hansard* (third series), CXIX, 21.
[54] Malmesbury, *Memoirs*, I, 292-3. (Derby to Malmesbury, December 5th, 1851).
[55] *Hansard* (third seres), CXX, 556.
[56] Ibid., p. 558.
[57] Ibid., CXXII, 1404-9.
[58] Ibid., p. 1411.
[59] B&E, *Victoria*, II, 465-6. (Memorandum by Albert, March 22nd, 1852).
[60] S&F, *Greville*, VI, 340. (*Diary*, May 12th, 1852).
[61] Hardcastle, *Campbell*, II, 378.
[62] *The Times* (London), January 10th, 1854.
[63] *DP*, Stanley XII. (Edward Stanley to Disraeli, July 19th, 1852).
[64] Walpole, *Russell*, III, 154-5. (Russell to Aberdeen, July 21st, 1852).
[65] S&F, *Greville*, VI, 345-6. (*Diary*, July 23rd, 1852).
[66] B&E, *Victoria*, II, 501. (Memorandum by Albert, December 18th, 1852).
[67] Jennings, *Croker*, II, 446. (Croker to Derby, August 11th, 1852).
[68] Ibid. (Lonsdale to Croker, August 22nd, 1852).
[69] *DP*, Stanley XII. (Edward Stanley to Disraeli, July 22nd, 1852).
[70] Ibid., Derby XII. (Derby to Disraeli, August 3rd, 1852).
[71] Ibid. (Derby to Disraeli, June 1st (?), 1852).
[72] Parker, *Graham*, II, 180. (Graham to Aberdeen, September 29th, 1852).

[73] *AP*, BM 43072. (Derby to Aberdeen, March 22nd, 1852). (Derby to Aberdeen, May 14th, 1852). (Derby to Aberdeen, Monday, 1852).

[74] Morley, *Gladstone*, I, 428-9. (Gladstone to Aberdeen, July 30th, 1852). (Gladstone to Aberdeen, August 5th, 1852).

[75] *AP*, BM 43197. (Newcastle to Aberdeen, August 2nd, 1852).

[76] *CP*, PRO 30/48 48. (Aberdeen to Cardwell, September 14th, 1852).

[77] *DP*, Derby XII. (Derby to Disraeli, August 28th, 1852). (Derby to Disraeli, September 3rd, 1852).

[78] Ibid. (Derby to Disraeli, September 28th, 1852).

[79] Ibid. (Derby to Disraeli, September 23rd, 1852).

[80] Ibid. (Derby to Disraeli, September 18th, 1852).

[81] Ibid. (Derby to Disraeli, September 12th, 1852).

[82] *Hansard* (third series), CXXIII, 53-4.

[83] S&F, *Greville*, VI, 369. (*Diary*, November 12th, 1852).

[84] Morley, *Cobden*, p. 391. (Cobden to Wilson, October 4th, 1852).

[85] *Hansard* (third series), CXXIII, 74.

[86] *DP*, Derby XII. (Derby to Disraeli, November 17th, 1852).

[87] Parker, *Graham*, II, 185. (Graham to Russell, date not shown).

[88] S&F, *Greville*, VI, 370-1. (*Diary*, November 21st, 1852); Malmesbury, *Memoirs*, I, 367. (*Diary*, November 21st, 1852).

[89] *GP*, BM 44271. (Gladstone to Palmerston, November 21st, 1852).

[90] *Hansard* (third series), CXXIII, 382.

[91] *GP*, BM 44271. (Gladstone to Palmerston, November 21st, 1852).

[92] Ibid. (Palmerston to Gladstone, November 21st, 1852).

[93] M&B, *Disraeli*, I, 1227-8. (Palmerston to Disraeli, November 22nd, 1852).

[94] B&E, *Victoria*, II, 491. (Memorandum by Albert, November 28th, 1852).

[95] *Hansard* (third series), CXXIII, 282-92.

[96] Ibid., p. 926.

[97] B&E, *Victoria*, II, 488-90. (Derby to Victoria, November 25th, 1852).

[98] Morley, *Gladstone*, I, 435. (*Diary*, November 27th, 1852).

[99] M&B, *Disraeli*, I, 1239-40. (Albert to Derby, November 26th, 1852).

[100] B&E, *Victoria*, II, 491-2. (Memorandum by Albert, November 28th, 1852).

[101] Malmesbury, *Memoirs*, I, 369. (*Diary*, November 28th, 1852).

[102] B&E, *Victoria*, II, 487. (Victoria to King of the Belgians, November 23rd, 1852).

[103] *DP*, Derby XII. (Derby to Disraeli, undated). (Derby to Disraeli, November 30th, 1852).

[104] Ibid. (Derby to Disraeli, November 30th, 1852).

[105] S&F, *Greville*, VI, 394-5. (*Diary*, January 29th, 1853).

[106] *Hansard* (third series), CXXIII, 838-901.

[107] *DP*, Derby XII. (Derby to Disraeli, December 4th, 1852).

[108] S&F, *Greville*, VI, 376-7. (*Diary*, December 9th, 1852).

[109] R. A. J. Walling, ed., *The Diaries of John Bright* (New York: William Morrow & Co., 1931), pp. 128-30. (*Diary*, December 15th, 1852).

[110] *DP*, Derby XII. (Derby to Disraeli, December 15th, 1852).

[111] M&B, *Disraeli*, I, 1257-8. (Disraeli to Derby, December 16th, 1852).

[112] Morley, *Gladstone*, I, 438. (*Diary*, December 18th, 1852).

[113] Hardcastle, *Campbell*, II, 381.

[114] Morley, *Gladstone*, I, 438. (*Diary*, December 18th, 1852).

[115] Hardcastle, *Campbell*, II, 381-2.

[116] B&E, *Victoria*, II, 499-500. (Derby to Victoria, December 17th, 1852).

[117] 'The Government and the Country', *Fraser's Magazine*, XLVII (1853), 235-44.

[118] 'The Late Ministry and the State of Europe', *Edinburgh Review*, CX (1859), 133-9.

[119] *The Times* (London), January 3rd and 10th, 1854.
[120] Malmesbury, *Memoirs*, I, 316-17. (*Diary*, March 11th, 1852).
[121] 'The Budget', *The Quarterly Review*, XCII (1852), 236-74.
[122] Jennings, *Croker*, II, 449. (Croker to Hardwicke, December 31st, 1852).
[123] S&F, *Greville*, VI, 358-9. (*Diary*, August 28th, 1852).
[124] Malmesbury, *Memoirs*, I, 376-7. (*Diary*, December 22nd, 1852).
[125] Morley, *Cobden*, p. 411.
[126] Jennings, *Croker*, II, 449. (Croker to Hardwicke, December 31st, 1852).

CHAPTER VIII

THEIR LORDSHIPS' HOUSE

THE defeat of his Government posed a difficult problem for Derby. As some Tories pointed out,[1] the Ministers had not fallen in the defence of any principle which might serve as a rallying-point for their 300 odd members* during the coming bleak period of Opposition. Protection was no longer a bond of union – what might replace it? Derby could excogitate nothing beyond resistance to democracy, but this cry would probably attract few new adherents. By this time, in fact, fear of Radicalism had died down considerably, and many people considered the Whigs as safe a bulwark against excesses as the Derby Conservatives.† At the moment the only real bond was the party itself. Disraeli had shown the way in his Budget speech when he charged the Government was ill-used by a factious coalition. Partisan resentment might be a bond.

The preceding autumn, in a moment of annoyance, Derby had declared he would retire if defeated on the Budget.‡ His harassing experiences as a minority Prime Minister, the failure of his class to respond to his warnings, and growing uncertainty regarding his health had combined to make him toy with the idea of retiring, but the cavalier treatment of his party by the Opposition and his own love of politics made him reconsider. When he tendered his resignation to the Queen on December 17th, therefore, Derby tried to induce her not to publicize the fact that he had suggested Aberdeen as his successor.[2] Some of his party, he feared, might

* Not even its leaders were sure of the party's strength. Derby variously estimated it at 310 (*Hansard*, third series, CXXIII, 1699), 300 (Ibid., CXXXVI, 1338), and 286 (B&E, *Victoria*, II, 501. Memorandum by Albert, December 18th, 1852). Some members who usually voted with the Opposition supported Derby while in office, then deserted him. See: G. P. Gooch, ed., *The Later Correspondence of Lord John Russell* (New York: Longmans, Green & Co., 1925), II, 121. (Russell to Murray, February 9th, 1853).

† See: Jennings, *Croker*, III, 259. (Hardwicke to Croker, December 30th, 1852). This writer is indebted to Mr. M. G. Brock for this interpretation.

‡ Even Disraeli feared Derby might retire. See: W. F. Monypenny and G. E. Buckle, *The Life of Benjamin Disraeli* (London: John Murray, 1929), I, 1257-8. (Disraeli to Derby, December 16th, 1852). (Hereinafter cited as 'M&B, *Disraeli*').

join Aberdeen if they heard of it. Being unsuccessful in this effort, Derby hastily called a meeting at his residence and assured the party he would continue to lead them.[3] This was still not enough. What his followers needed was a fighting speech to stir up partisan spirit. After rehearsing his oration at a rally, Derby on December 20th attacked Aberdeen in the Lords, and blamed the fall of his Government on a factious coalition.[4] As Aberdeen's Government was not yet formed, many, including the Queen, thought the speech was ill-timed, and on December 21st Derby received a letter of protest from his Sovereign. Replying, Derby showed some bitterness towards the Peelites, but promised not to try to overthrow Aberdeen. 'It is his determination', he wrote, 'honestly to undertake the task, difficult as it must be, of keeping together a powerful Party, without the excitement of opposition to a government by which their own leaders have been superseded, and of some members of which they think they have reason to complain.'[5]

At his audience of leave, Derby explained further that he had to make clear that his fall resulted not from an accident, but from a hostile coalition.[6] Perhaps seeking to regain the favour of the Queen, Derby had his wife write the Marchioness of Ely, a confidante of the Monarch. Together with the usual flattery was a statement certain to make an impression. 'He [Derby] is also very grateful to the Prince for whose abilities he has the highest admiration, often speaking of his wonderful cleverness.'[7]

The attack on Aberdeen and his party speeches completed Derby's condemnation of enemy tactics. Aberdeen was offended,* and showed his disapproval of Derby's activities at the opening of Parliament by refusing to answer his questions.[8] The prospect of reunion with the Peelites now seemed far away, for Aberdeen, Gladstone and Herbert were all members of the new Government. Palmerston, too, after momentarily considering a junction with the Conservatives,† joined the new Ministry, which contained most

* Derby had occasion to write Aberdeen shortly after the incident. The old salutation 'Dear Aberdeen' was changed to 'Dear Lord Aberdeen'. Aberdeen likewise changed his salutation in reply. *Aberdeen Papers*, BM 43072. (Derby to Aberdeen, January 2nd, 1853). (Aberdeen to Derby, January 3rd, 1853).

† 'If I had been a reckless adventurer,' Palmerston wrote, '. . . I might have become a factious Conservative . . . I might possibly . . . have put the present Government in a minority & have brought Derby in again & have become the Leader . . . in the House of Commons. What would the great Liberal Party . . . have

of the outstanding administrators of the day. In spite of this glittering array of talent, there were fundamental weaknesses in the new Government, for its majority in the Commons depended on the co-operation of the Whigs, Peelites, Radicals and Irish, each of whom might become dissatisfied with some policy which suited the others. There was already some dissatisfaction with the composition of the Cabinet, which included many Peelites at the expense of the Ultra-Whigs of Lord Grey, the Irish and the Radicals. Derby summed up the situation late in January: 'We shall have a difficult game to play, but we must exercise . . . great patience & forbearance, if we do not wish, by an active and bitter opposition on our part, to consolidate the present combination between those who have no real bond or union, and who must, I think, fall to pieces before long. . . .'[9]

The Derbyites were generally bitter towards the new Government,[10] and, when the seals were surrendered, the old officials took a railway to the Palace other than the one used by the new Ministers, to avoid meeting them.[11] Derby was not there at the time, for he had taken his leave previously, and had returned to Lancashire as 'a free man'.[12] For once he was unable to divorce politics from sport, however, and, as he shot, Derby singled out certain rabbits and named them for his various opponents.[13] The noble Earl was more than usually accurate that day, and imaginary corpses of Whigs and Peelites lay in heaps in Bickerstaffe Woods.

With an ineffective minority in the Commons, the task of opposing undesirable legislation fell to Derby in the Lords. Matters concerning religion were always of interest to him, and he rarely missed an opportunity to influence measures on the subject. A sincere Protestant, Derby once stated that the Reformation was among the greatest blessings ever bestowed on England,[14] and at the prayer services held in his private chapel at Knowsley he is said to have read 'most impressively'.[15] He tended to be neutral in the Tractarian controversy, though, from his attitude in the St. George's-in-the-East affair, it seems he favoured sim-

said of such a course: nay . . .what would that party at Tiverton by whom I have so long been returned have said, & how should I have been sure of not having to go a-begging like Graham from one place to another?' Mabell, Countess of Airlie, *Lady Palmerston and Her Times* (London: Hodder & Stoughton, Ltd., 1922), II, 151-3. (Palmerston to Sullivan, December 31st, 1852).

plicity in church services.* Apart from frowning on the elaborate Catholic ritual and distrusting the Jesuits, Derby had no antipathy against the Roman Catholic or any other faith, but stressed the common bases of Christian groups rather than their differences.[16] But he considered the Anglican Church to be a vital part of the British way of life. Unlike Nonconformist ministers or Roman Catholic priests, Anglican clergymen were not dependent upon their congregations for their livelihood, and hence did not have to consider as much their political attitudes. This left them free to preserve the *status quo*. How far such practical considerations influenced Derby's attitude towards the Church, however, is uncertain.

A problem of Church rights involved the Clergy Reserves in Canada. In 1775 one-seventh of the Crown land in Quebec was set aside as an endowment for Protestant clergy, and the Church's title to these lands had subsequently been confirmed. But by 1853 Canadian opinion opposed the Clergy Reserves, and the Canadian Legislature sought control of them, supposedly to divide them among the various churches on a fair basis. Aberdeen was favourable towards the request, and the bill passed the Commons rather easily. In his youth, Derby himself had been unfavourable to the Reserves, but in 1853 he defended them strongly. Speaking on February 28th, Derby called the government bill a serious violation of property rights, and asserted the Canadians planned both to secularize the church revenues and establish 'the republican principle of voluntaryism adopted in the United States'.[17] Church property in the colonies must be maintained, he insisted, even as they would defend the rights of the Church of Scotland or Ireland.

Though he carried on the fight by speeches and amendments, Derby was chagrined to find he could not even count on the support of the Lords Ecclesiastical. During the debates the Bishop of Oxford made a statement which offended Derby, but

* *Hansard* (third series), CLVI, 566-73. The introduction of elaborate ritual at St. George's resulted Sunday after Sunday in services being interrupted '. . . by singing, by banging of doors, by loud coughing, by catcalls . . .' One clergyman complained to Derby that he had been struck by a peashooter, but the Earl had little sympathy for Anglican clergymen who introduced 'novelties' into their services. Regarding Catholic services he noted '. . . the spiritual character of religion is overloaded with that which is merely external and apparent to the senses'. Ibid., CLXXI, 504.

later apologized, noting that he had smiled while saying it. Derby sarcastically replied that, while not meaning to apply the phrase to the Bishop '. . . A man may smile and smile, and be a villain.'[18] Clarendon arose angrily and shouted: 'We are not accustomed to hear such expressions. We are not accustomed even in the language of poetry to hear such a word as "villain" applied to any noble Lord in this House.'[19] After some repartee, Clarendon and Derby closed the matter by drinking each others' healths in water across the table.[20] Derby's statements, however, were in vain, and the Clergy Reserves Bill opened the way for the disendowment of the Protestant Church in Canada. Two years later, when the Bishop of Oxford complained of the difficulties of the Church there, Derby reminded him of his vote on the Clergy Reserves Bill, and expressed his own satisfaction at having opposed the separation of Church and State in Canada.[21]

The following year the Government's Canadian legislation again offended Derby. This time they presented a bill conceding Canada the right to elect her Second Chamber rather than having it appointed by Britain. Derby seized this opportunity to attack democracy in general. 'The spirit of democratic encroachment is the same throughout the world', he exclaimed. 'Give it the means of obtaining power, and it will not hesitate to stretch out its hand to grasp more and more.'[22] Rather than have Canada develop along American lines, he suggested that she be governed by viceroys or independent sovereigns allied to the British Royal Family. Their lordships, however, did not take fright at Derby's assertion that the bill would cause an early separation of Canada from Britain, and the former Premier was beaten by twenty-four votes in a small house.

Closer to home, Aberdeen's proposal in 1853 for a succession tax on real property also stimulated Derby's eloquent opposition. His move to sidetrack the bill by referring it to a select committee was beaten by only thirteen votes, and the Government became so alarmed at their prospects for carrying a second reading that they brought back their ministers from Paris and Brussels, as well as the Lord Lieutenant of Ireland, to vote with them.[23] Aberdeen defended the measure on the ground that it would relieve industry of its financial burdens, and aid the Government in dispensing with the income tax. Pointing out that securities and bonds were subject to a 10 per cent inheritance tax, he suggested that it was only fair that real property should pay a like amount.[24] On the other side, Derby contended that real property paid poor rates and county rates, from which personal property was exempt. Insisting that the bill would affect all settlements of property '. . . for the miserable purpose of getting rid of the soap duty, and diminishing tea duties', he pictured the hardships it would create by recounting the pathetic story of three 'elderly maiden ladies' who had nothing but their real property inheritance and no way to pay the tax upon it. Though the tax would undoubtedly hurt his own class, Derby insisted it would weigh most heavily on the poor.[25] His eloquence, however, did not save him from defeat. When a member of the Government asked whether or not he would oppose the third reading, Derby exclaimed in disgust: 'The bill may go to the devil for all I care; I shall take no further trouble about it.'[26] In the Lords he more decorously stated his hope that the tax would not become a permanent part of the revenue of the nation. Though beaten, Derby had shown his willingness to lead their Lordships in an attack on money bills, and a number of years later he was to do so more successfully.

In changing England, the status of the Universities also came up for comment and criticism. Derby had a special interest in this subject, for in October 1852 he had been inaugurated Chancellor of Oxford, and the following June was installed in the position. Going through the ceremony with 'great dignity and grace', Derby rose to the occasion by making a Latin oration so perfectly that the most learned critics could find only two minor errors in it.[27] It was his fate, however, to be installed at a time when the Universities were under fire. Speaking at the opening of the 1854 session, Derby promised that the Universities would modernize their curriculums, and make other necessary changes without the help of a parliamentary commission.[28] The Government, however, announced a bill to reform Oxford, and Derby was unsuccessful in having it sent to the Hebdomadal Council at the University before being presented to Parliament.[29] During the second reading in July, Derby called it a violation of the rights of self-government granted by the Crown to the University, and later confirmed by Parliament. But, on the vital point regarding the admission of Dissenters, he agreed, so long as the teaching were not altered to suit their religious views. 'I will never', he declared, 'sacrifice the inestimable advantage of having the two Universities of Oxford and Cambridge as nurseries for the Church of England.'[30]

While Derby supported the second reading of the bill, in committee he objected strongly to the opening of residences as private halls for the reception of students. Though these might interfere with discipline and become private halls for the rich, his main objection was that such halls would become centres of Dissent in the heart of the University.[31] Once more Derby was beaten, and again found he could not depend on the support of the Bishops. Annoyed, Derby announced that, as the Government was set against any amendment of their bill, he opposed the removal of the Thirty-Nine Articles oath.[32] Both the Bishop of Oxford and the Bishop of St. Asaph spoke against Derby, and the clause was carried against him without a division. Thus, one of the more important church preserves was thrown open to Dissenters, over whose activities the University could exercise little control. Derby had tried to compromise, and, in so doing, had been completely defeated.

These years were marked by repeated defeats in the Lords, but Derby lost no opportunity to serve the cause of his class whenever possible. His speeches continued to be vigorous, beautifully constructed, and generally entertaining. On one occasion *The Times* saw fit to pay Derby one of its left-handed compliments. 'Last night the House of Lords heard . . . with considerable pleasure one of those ingenious and even impassioned orations which Lord Derby is able to . . . deliver on almost any subject, and perhaps we might add, on almost any side.'[33] As Derby affected a complete indifference to the 'scribblings' of the Press, his notices were rarely of a complimentary kind, and often quite unfair. Save for some minor inconsistencies, it is clear that Derby did not talk on both sides of the question, and that his main purpose during those years was to maintain whenever possible the rights and privileges of the aristocracy. Even he realized, however, that this approach could not be maintained indefinitely, especially if those whom he chose to defend were indifferent towards his efforts. The 'Old Whigs' somehow simply would not let him be their champion!

Following the collapse of his Government, Derby faced considerable dissatisfaction in the party ranks. Being a veteran of the Commons, Derby realized that by forming a coalition with one or another of the disappointed factions among the Opposition, he could probably put the Aberdeen Government in a minority on some question; but such a move would not strengthen the Conservatives, or give them the strength to carry on a government.[34] Until some question arose which would unite some Opposition faction ideologically to the Conservative Party, and operate to make the union at least reasonably permanent, there was no point in winning a single division for the mere purpose of disconcerting the group in power.

Disraeli, a younger man and in the prime of life, viewed the prospect of continued opposition with alarm, and being an opportunist, sought to mend the situation as best he could. Supporting him was Edward Stanley, and, to some extent, the Earl of Malmesbury. There seemed to be three possible ways of securing added strength for their party, namely, by making an alliance with the Ultra-Whigs of Lord Grey, by forming an alliance with the Irish Brigade, or by suggesting a measure of Reform which would attract Radical support. The fact that Derby had been at odds with Grey during his whole term of office, that the Conservative Party stood for Protestantism and a cautious policy on the suffrage, did not deter Disraeli in his projects. The Irish alliance, however, was too much for Edward Stanley, who wrote: 'Irish votes count for as much as any others; but the less we say about an alliance with the Brigade the better.'[35] Nevertheless, Disraeli continued to court Irish support during the session.[36]

The other two ideas found more favour with both Malmesbury and Stanley. Disraeli's Reform project was apparently, for the time, a radical one, involving the reduction of the franchise qualification in the boroughs to £5. While Disraeli was merely vote-seeking, Malmesbury was apparently the first in the party to realize the possibility of a Conservative democracy! Writing in January 1853, Stanley said he had talked with Malmesbury '... and find him very liberal personally, but he is nervous about the possibility of defections from our party to the Govt. if we make any move in advance. On the Reform question he contends that the five-pounders are democratic, the labourers Conservative: therefore if we must go as low as £5 he would rather go on to universal suffrage'.[37] None of the three, not even Malmesbury, however, had the nerve to suggest the project to Derby, who had a slight attack of gout, and, as Stanley explained, was not inclined to receive new ideas favourably.[38] The Reform project remained therefore in the talking stage. Stanley, however, brought up the alliance with Lord Grey, and received a definite reply. 'Grey', Derby observed, 'is more than a Whig – there is scarcely a single point on which we agree – we could not act together without loss of character.'[39] Chagrined at his failure, Stanley wrote Disraeli that his father did not seek office, but merely wanted to impede progress.[40]

Late in January 1853 Derby sent a remonstrance to Disraeli, noting: 'You must not build upon a possible union between me and the Ultra Whigs, such as Lord Grey, or the Manchester School. Such an union is simply impossible; and I name it only because I infer from Edward's language that such an idea had passed through your mind. I hardly think it could long dwell there.'[41] Disraeli's activities would have seemed to confirm Aberdeen's low opinion of Disraeli's political morality, an opinion which, Derby felt, had kept Aberdeen from joining his party.[42] But once he had accepted Disraeli, Derby was intensely loyal to him, even during his periods of restlessness. The following month, George Tomline, Disraeli's fellow-member from Shrewsbury, told Greville that Disraeli '. . . dislikes and despises Derby, thinks him a good "Saxon" speaker and nothing more . . .'[43] Whatever his private opinions, Disraeli was always careful to accord his superior the highest respect, and to defer both to his political and social rank. Perhaps as a conciliatory gesture, Derby listed Disraeli among those to receive honorary degrees at the time of his installation as Chancellor of Oxford.[44]

Disraeli's and Stanley's activities alienated many members of the Conservative Party that session. On one occasion, Thomas Baring, of the powerful Baring financial establishment, told Greville that the Government could have Disraeli 'with pleasure'.[45] Malmesbury noted in June that the party was angry with Disraeli – 'which is constantly the case' – and that they were displeased with Edward Stanley also.[46] A number of incidents gave rise to a suspicion that Disraeli and Stanley were co-operating with the Manchester School. Disraeli was absent from the divisions and discussions on the Succession Tax, which Derby had fought so hard in the Lords, and he also walked out before the division on the ballot. The final act of treason, according to the Ultra-Conservatives, was the support given by Disraeli and Stanley to the Radical attacks on the East India Company, which many Conservatives thought was a 'good Tory group'.[47] When the Government brought in a bill for the permanent maintenance of the Company, Stanley, backed by Disraeli, attempted to delay its passage.

The Stanley motion to reconsider the problem brought a letter of protest from Derby to Disraeli. 'I should not do my duty by you and by the party,' he wrote, 'if I did not frankly express to you my opinion that a considerable portion of the dissatisfaction which has shown itself is attributable to an uneasy feeling among our Conservative friends as to a supposed understanding, and, to a certain extent, combination, between yourself and the Manchester School.'[48] He went on to protest against Disraeli's seeking alliances in quarters where the Conservatives had no bond of union, and warned Disraeli that his tactics might lead to a disruption of the Conservative Party in the Commons. Deeply disturbed by the activities of his chief lieutenant and his son, Derby said that he would be personally indifferent to such a disruption, but felt it would be unfortunate for England.[49] Ignoring the protest, Disraeli would not change his course or ideas regarding the government of India.

The activities of his independent son were a source of much embarrassment to Derby. Of Edward, Bright once said: 'I think I know what a Radical is, but I have never seen such a one as young Stanley.'[50] Full of the vigour of youth, and impatient of the ideas of the older Conservatives, Stanley had more in common with the Manchester School than with the Ultra-Tory element of his own party. A handsome young man, with an open, frank face, there was a suggestion around his jaw of the stubbornness with which he held his opinions. The single bond which tied him to the Conservative Party at this time was a deep devotion to and sense of duty towards his father. During 1853 and thereafter, however, father and son were rarely in agreement in political matters, and young Stanley was actually more difficult for Derby to handle than Disraeli.

Suddenly, on October 17th, the attack of gout which had threatened the preceding winter struck Derby. These illnesses were characterized by very great pain, so intense that the Earl would be scarcely able to turn over in bed, to be followed by a period of extreme debility, which might last for days or weeks.

Derby's illness of 1853 was the worst siege he had had since 1850, and he was not yet fully recovered by late November.[51] During such periods, realizing his inability to participate in that exhausting game effectively, Derby's mind turned from politics to his other loves, and during the early winter of 1853 he passed the time by translating parts of the *Iliad*, and a number of other poems in various languages, copies of which he distributed among his intimate friends.[52]

The winter months, however, brought some encouragement to Derby. Disraeli and Malmesbury visited Knowsley in December, and while Derby showed a disinclination to discuss politics, Disraeli apparently promised to mend his ways and not to flirt with the Manchester School.[53] Apart from the dispirited state of their party, now numbering but two hundred and sixty, which Derby felt might be improved by establishing confidence in Disraeli among the rank and file,[54] there were several subjects which occupied Derby's attention. The impending war with Russia Derby blamed on the weak and vacillating course pursued by Aberdeen, which tended to encourage the aggressive spirit of Russia.[55] Even more important was the projected Government Reform Bill, for it seemed quite possible that the Government would be broken up if it tried to deal with Reform.[56] Still another topic of the season was the strikes in various branches of industry. Derby believed capital to be much too strong for labour, and expected the industrial unrest to solve itself without the need of legislation on the subject. In holding this view, Derby noted that, for almost the first time in his life, he agreed with Cobden.* The war, the Reform question, and the strikes seemed to make the future of the Aberdeen coalition quite uncertain, and the Conservatives gradually recovered their spirits. Pakington wrote Disraeli in December that a large majority of their party still regarded Derby as the 'greatest & safest statesman of the present day', and that they would also rally around Disraeli in the Commons.[57]

* *Disraeli Papers*, Derby XII. (Derby to Disraeli, November 14th, 1853). The year before Cobden had attacked Derby in the Commons for having once said he would supervise the voting of his tenants. The reference he made was quoted differently in *Hansard* and the *Mirror of Parliament*, and the meaning was changed completely. Derby wrote Cobden that he hoped no one could rightfully charge him with being an oppressive landlord, and Cobden subsequently apologized. *Hansard* (third series), CXX, 583-7. Derby took pride in his reputation as a just and kind landlord.

Encouraging also were reports of dissensions within the Ministry. Palmerston, according to rumour, was disaffected, and Derby thought the loss of Palmerston would end the coalition.[58] Lord Lansdowne, a powerful Whig leader, opposed the introduction of a Reform measure, and his attitude further weakened the coalition, for Lord Russell, spurred on by his wife and others, was determined, in spite of the foreign situation, to go ahead with a bill on the subject.[59] To the satisfaction of Joliffe, the Party Whip, Derby consented to give three House of Commons dinners that year, an unusual concession, but one dictated by the state of the party.[60] Disraeli, who had a real grievance against Derby for his reluctance to meet the party members socially, felt there should have been at least nine. Had Derby chosen to unbend more often, and to rub elbows with his followers, the morale of the party would undoubtedly have been higher.

With the opening of Parliament, Derby was prepared to assume the offensive, and on January 31st he launched a powerful attack on Aberdeen's foreign policy. At this time, and when war was declared in March, Derby voiced his views on the conflict with Russia. He charged that Aberdeen had entered into a 'gentleman's agreement' with Russia in 1844, which led her to believe that he would not interfere with a settlement of the Eastern Question. When he came to power, Aberdeen increased this belief in Russian circles by adopting a vacillating attitude towards Russian operations in the Balkans. Firmness, Derby contended, would have prevented the war from breaking out, and it had come as a result of the Government's policy of 'fusion and confusion', which had prevented decisive action.* Nevertheless, Derby did not seek to undermine British confidence in the necessity of the war, nor to sow the seeds of defeatism; but he was attacked by the hostile *Times* for attempting to whitewash Russia for alleged partisan purposes.[61]

The other topic to which Derby alluded at length in his speech of January 31st, and again in February, was Reform. Being unable to excogitate any such measure which would have a conservative

* See: *Hansard* (third series), CXXX, 70-80; CXXXII, 153-69. Here, again, Derby apparently got much of his material from Malmesbury. See: Malmesbury, *Memoirs*, I, 402-3. (*Diary*, June 3rd, 1853). Derby took the occasion to attack Aberdeen for releasing secret information to *The Times*, and the latter, for printing it. *Hansard* (third series), CXXXI, 621-38, 879-83. See also: Ibid., CXXX, 95-107 for another Derby squabble with *The Times*.

influence, he was reluctant to see the subject reopened. The war provided a logical excuse for postponing action, and many in the Government were agreeable to it. But Derby did not commit himself against all Reform. He merely declared that wartime was no time to take up such questions, and, while opposed to increasing the borough representation at the expense of the counties, he promised respectful consideration to any measure the Government might introduce.[62] Under pressure from almost all sides, Russell at first consented to a postponement of his measure, and later he withdrew it altogether, promising to try again at a more propitious time.

The Aberdeen Government was able to weather both its foreign and domestic difficulties. In February Derby stated that, while lacking confidence in the Government, he did not desire to replace it during the emergency.[63] Gradually, most factions rallied around Aberdeen, and Disraeli's winter hopes suffered a spring freeze. In April, Derby's health again failed him, and he was once more bedridden, though this time he did not suffer the excruciating pain of the last attack. His physician, Dr. Ferguson, diagnosed his ailment as 'rheumatic neuralgic gout', and from the illness both his physical and spiritual recovery was slow.[64] Malmesbury in May found Derby 'low and weak', sitting in a back room of his mansion all day, and never leaving save for his visits to the Lords. The leaves were already turning before Derby was well again.

When Malmesbury stayed at Knowsley in November he found Derby recovered and ready for work. His chief concern at the moment was Gladstone's 'crotchet' of paying for the war with a fifteen per cent income tax levy. But he planned no amendment to the Address, merely criticism of the Government's want of foresight, which made every step, in the phrase he later made famous, a 'leap in the dark'.[65] That summer Disraeli had again been critical of his chief, and mentioned the possibility of heading the next Tory government himself,[66] but in December he found Derby full of his 'ancient spirit' and Disraeli was ready to assume his normal place in the relationship.[67]

Disraeli and Walpole were invited to dine with Derby, to discuss the Speech, and to make plans for a cordial support of the war effort, and to offer an 'unsparing criticism' of the Government's tactics. Their conference was satisfactory, but neither leader foresaw the dramatic events which were shortly to be upon them. In January, in returning to Knowsley from Manchester, Derby learned from Joliffe, the Whip, that Disraeli and many of the party were anxious to give notice regarding the Government's conduct of the war on the first day of the session. Derby wrote Disraeli on January 18th that he doubted the 'policy' of such a step, and suggested that they discuss the matter before anything was decided upon.[68] This conference gave Derby the impression that Disraeli was not anxious to attack the Government, and he wrote Malmesbury on January 23rd: 'Disraeli agrees with me as to the patience policy — indeed he even wishes to carry it further than I do. Our people, however, will be very hard to hold.'[69] The very same day, however, Disraeli wrote a friend that the Aberdeen Government probably would not last more than ten days.[70]

There were ample grounds for Disraeli's opinion. Reports had been coming back from the Crimea that winter telling of incredible mismanagement of supply, underfed soldiers, disease and general hardship. The Government's popularity was further blighted by its plan to enlist 15,000 foreign troops, which seemed to call Britain's ability to fight the war into question. Derby and Newcastle wrangled over the measure in the Lords, and the former gave his vote to it only because he had privately agreed to do so.* After the Christmas recess the reports from the front were even more alarming. Because he could see no way to form a government with a majority in the Commons, however, Derby was reluctant to attack Aberdeen.

Some on the government side were not so circumspect. A disaffected Radical, Roebuck, gave notice of a motion to inquire into the conduct of the war. Lord John Russell, perhaps hoping to succeed Aberdeen, decided to resign from the Government rather than to resist the motion. His resignation, which in itself seemed to condemn the conduct of the Government, came on January 23rd, but neither Derby nor Disraeli apparently knew of it when they wrote their letters of that date.

Derby had a slight attack of gout as the crisis grew, but it did not return him to bed.[71] Learning of Roebuck's motion he decided the Conservatives must support the inquiry, but he did not antici-

* Derby objected to the foreign enlistment because it might give Russia the impression that England was exhausted and ready to quit the war. *Hansard* (third series), CXXXVI, 265-7. The Prince favoured the scheme and was offended by Derby's opposition to it. Later the two discussed the bill privately at some length. B&E, *Victoria*, III, 107. (Memorandum by Albert, February 1st, 1855).

pate success and believed that the Government would emerge stronger than before.[72] The Government was at first badly shaken by Russell's resignation, but they recovered quickly for the trial. As the Conservatives were silent during the opening round of the debate, Aberdeen concluded they were reluctant to attack his Government,[73] but the issue assumed such national importance that Derby, on January 29th, finally urged Disraeli to speak. The information supplied by Joliffe indicated that the division would be very close.[74] Disraeli's oratory, reserved for the end of the debate, probably had little influence on the outcome. The Government fell through the defection of its own supporters, the Radicals and the Whigs, who followed Russell. The factions, then, who joined the Conservatives on this crucial division would definitely not provide support for a Conservative government.

In this crisis, any one of three men could have been called in to form an administration, Derby, Russell or Palmerston. The first two were convinced that Palmerston would be unable to form a government, and the choice thus seemed to be narrowed down to Derby or Russell.[75] In discussing the matter with Clarendon before his resignation, Aberdeen thought he should advise the Queen to summon Derby because he was the only man who had a party. Clarendon, however, rightly urged that Lansdowne and Palmerston be consulted first so that, if Derby were called in, it would be apparent to all that he was a necessity, and a last resort.[76] Such a course would have improved Derby's position immeasurably, but Aberdeen did not recommend it to the Queen. Though he correctly predicted that Derby would meet with great difficulties unless he secured men from other parties, Aberdeen advised that Derby be summoned first.[77] Though he convinced the Queen that he would behave more generously towards Derby than the latter had done towards him in 1852, she could not secure Aberdeen's promise to support a Derby government.

About ten in the evening of January 30th Derby received a summons to appear at Buckingham Palace the following morning.[78] Disraeli again agreed to step down in favour of Palmerston, and Derby went to the Queen armed with this information.[79] In his interview Derby refused to accept responsibility for Aberdeen's defeat, and explained that Russell's resignation had forced the Conservatives to back the motion for an inquiry. Admitting he controlled two hundred and eighty members in the Commons,

Derby insisted that he had no man capable of governing the House. He explained:*

> . . . he should not be able to present an Administration that would be accepted by the country unless it was strengthened by other combinations; he knew that the whole country cried out for Lord Palmerston as the only man fit for carrying on the war with success, and he owned the necessity of having him in the Government.

Palmerston's advanced age, Derby admitted, rendered him unfit to be Prime Minister in spite of what the 'ignorant public' might think; but, at the moment, his need of the colourful Whig was very apparent. In addition, he wanted help from the Peelites, especially Gladstone and Herbert, and also the aid of Grey or Ellenborough at the War Department.

Shortly after leaving the Palace Derby visited Palmerston, who expressed his willingness to join the Government, but not alone.[80] The lead in the Commons was satisfactory to Palmerston, but he urged that Clarendon be retained at the Foreign Office, and that Gladstone and Herbert, whose aid he would personally solicit, should form part of the coalition. Derby was surprised and rather dissatisfied with Palmerston's demands,[81] as well he might be, for it was obviously impossible to secure the services of Clarendon. In fact, after the interview with Palmerston, Derby assured Malmesbury that he would again be Foreign Secretary.[82] While Derby seemed 'in high spirits and confident of success', Malmesbury was not too 'keen' to undertake the demanding work of the Foreign Office at such a time.[83] After his interview with Palmerston, there was little for Derby to do but await the responses to his overtures.

Palmerston, meanwhile, visited Herbert and found his friend 'disinclined' to join the Derby Government. Gladstone was likewise unwilling to accept the offer unless Aberdeen gave his approval. In neither case did Palmerston press for an acceptance of Derby's proposals; instead, he explained to Gladstone that he did not himself refuse immediately for fear the public might feel personal ambition had dictated his course. After a discussion, Gladstone left to talk with Aberdeen, and Palmerston went to see Clarendon.†

* The story of this interview and the quotation are found in: B&E, *Victoria*, III, 102-4. (Memorandum by Victoria, January 31st, 1855).

† The story of Palmerston's negotiation with the Peelites is found in: Morley, *Gladstone*, I, 525-7. (*Diary*, January 31st, 1855).

Both sought a reasonable excuse to leave Derby in the lurch, and they were equally successful. Clarendon, of course, refused to join the new Administration because of his distrust of Derby, and this left Palmerston free to refuse also.[84] Shortly thereafter he informed Gladstone of his decision, and Gladstone and Herbert immediately sat down to write their refusals. After a 'merry party' at Grillions, the two visited Aberdeen and Graham to show them for their approval the letters they had written.[85]

Derby received Palmerston's reply about 9.30 p.m., the evening of January 31st. It was short and uninformative, stating briefly that he thought his presence would not give strength to the Administration, but promising an out-of-office support if Derby followed a satisfactory foreign policy. The last paragraph hinted that Gladstone and Herbert would likewise refuse. Gladstone's letter arrived at 12.30 a.m., and that of Herbert later in the morning.[86] Both promised out-of-office support, except where their opinions left them no choice but to oppose the new Government.[87] All three promises Derby correctly diagnosed as worthless, coming as they did from men who held strong opinions both on foreign and financial affairs, and who would be unwilling to yield on these points for the sake of supporting the Government. Derby had opposed Palmerston consistently on foreign affairs for many years — what hope, then, was there that Palmerston would support Malmesbury? Gladstone had been one of the major opponents of Disraeli's Budget in 1852 — what hope, then, was there that he would accept the next one they devised? There was, indeed, one hope. If the Conservatives chose to take their orders on these important subjects from Palmerston and Gladstone, they could have their support; but, if Palmerston and the Peelites determined the measures of the new Government, Derby and Disraeli would be mere figureheads, clinging to office for the sake of office itself. Derby discussed his position with his son, Edward, who was satisfied that his father, under the circumstances, should refuse. There was still a ray of hope that Palmerston and Russell would be unable to form a government, and that the Conservatives would then come to power as the only government possible at the time.[88]

The morning of February 1st Derby advised Disraeli of the fruitlessness of his negotiations, and promised to call on him before going to the Palace.[89] Just what passed between the two leaders during that interview is not known, for Disraeli left no memorandum of this important crisis. Whatever Disraeli said, however, did not alter Derby's determination to refuse the commission. In his audience with the Queen, Derby explained his unwillingness to form a government without outside aid, or with the undependable support offered him. In refusing the appointment, Derby requested that the Queen withhold the story of his failure, but Her Majesty would not co-operate.[90] The following day Derby wrote Aberdeen, hinting very strongly his hope that Aberdeen would make no reference to his own activities in Aberdeen's speech that evening.*

Lord John Russell next tried unsuccessfully to form an Administration, and finally Palmerston was called to power. Avoiding a repetition of 1852, Derby refused to reveal the details of his abortive efforts until after the new government had been formed, and it was February 8th before he laid his case before their Lordships. In a lucid speech he first explained that, because his party had furnished the votes which overthrew Aberdeen, he would usually have felt duty-bound to replace him. Then he continued:[91]

> On the other hand, to hold that high and responsible situation dependent for support from day to day upon precarious and uncertain majorities, compelled to cut down this measure, and to pare off that — to consider with regard to each measure not what was for the real welfare of the country, but what would conciliate some half-dozen men here, or obviate the objections of some half-dozen there — to regard it as a great triumph of Parliamentary skill and Ministerial strength to scramble through the Session of Parliament and boast of having met with few and insignificant defeats — I say this is a state of things which cannot be satisfactory to any Minister, and which cannot be of advantage to the Crown, or to the people of the country . . . to carry on with a minority is an intolerable and galling servitude as no man of honour or character would expose himself to.

In 1852 he had had some three hundred followers; in 1855, between 270 and 280. How, then, could he expect to carry on? After outlining his unsuccessful efforts to secure added strength, Derby expressed hope that his party would understand the reasons for his refusal to take office at that time.

* *Aberdeen Papers*, BM 43072. (Derby to Aberdeen, February 1st, 1855). It seems probable that Derby believed the crisis would be protracted, and there was still a possibility of his being called in a second time. He wished, therefore, to conceal his failure.

Some members of the party were deeply disappointed and angry with Derby. The case of Disraeli is particularly interesting. About sixteen months before, Disraeli had written: '. . . a mere reproduction of the late Government is impossible, nor was it ever contemplated'.[92] But when, in 1855, Derby refused office with a 'mere reproduction' of the 1852 Government, Disraeli was 'in a state of disgust beyond all control'.[93] It took him about a year to recover from the blow, and during that time his discontent spread among a section of the Conservatives. A decade later, Disraeli recalled that there was a movement afoot in 1855 to dislodge Derby from the leadership, and at this later date he took credit for helping to stop it.[94] Undoubtedly the idea was never widespread, and was limited to Disraeli's personal following, for many of the rank and file agreed with Derby's course in 1855. Stanley, for one, supported his father. Pakington commented: 'I think Lord D. was, on the whole, right in his late difficult decision – but I feel the force of what you said about the probable effects upon our own party.'[95] The Whip, Joliffe, did not lose confidence in Derby and minimized the effects of the incident on the party: 'No doubt we must expect some trouble with a few of our Party . . . We must trust to Gladstone being Chancellor of the Exchequer and our Captain being able to hold out hope and consolation . . . to get us on our legs again.'[96] Disraeli's friend Bulwer wrote: 'Pardon me, my dear Diz, if I cannot attach the weight you seem . . . to do – to the suggestion that the party you so gallantly led against all pacific waverers last session shrunk or is supposed to have shrunk from the responsibility of conducting the Wars! Certainly I never so considered it – & certainly after Lord Derby's refusal to form a Govt. that was not the line we took . . .'[97] Disraeli's correspondence suggests that much of the discontent and the criticism of Derby did not arise spontaneously, but was incited by Disraeli himself.

Joliffe's hopes were not disappointed when Derby faced some two hundred and thirty of his followers late in February, for the Earl had one of the outstanding qualities of leadership – that of being able to face his followers, and to cheer and inspire them. Disraeli was still unconvinced, but admitted that it was a fine speech, and several days later wrote that time alone would prove whether or not Derby was justified in declining to form a government.[98] After listening to his explanation, the party registered a vote of confidence in Derby and went away satisfied.[99]

There can be no simple explanation of Derby's conduct in 1855, for it was inspired by a variety of motives. Having once been Prime Minister, and satisfied his personal ambition, Derby was not anxious to take office again unless he could be First Minister in fact as well as in name. Above all, he did not want to force himself upon both an unwilling Commons and an unwilling nation. He was the first to admit that the nation as a whole wanted Palmerston,[100] and in wartime especially the voice of the people had to be respected. Had Palmerston been unable to form a government, the nation would have been reconciled to a second choice, and the Commons, whether they liked it or not, would have been forced to pass the measures he suggested. How different were the positions of the two men! Could Derby ever have written as did Palmerston: 'I think our Government will do very well. I am backed by the general opinion of the whole country.'[101] Derby could only have done so if Palmerston had failed, and the latter, of course, succeeded.

The criticism of Derby's decision is based largely on supposition. It is supposed that because of the war crisis, the general public, indifferent towards the Conservatives for many years, would suddenly have backed them unanimously; it is supposed that the Whigs' factions, the Peelites, Radicals and Irish, who for many seasons past had distinguished themselves by their independent action and their united opposition to the Conservatives, would change their ways overnight and accept Disraeli's proposals with sound majorities. All this lies in the land of make-believe, but some, who do not take into account the personalities and the following of the two men, feel that because Palmerston built his career on the war, Derby, the isolationist and pacifist, could have done so also. Quite as likely the Conservatives would have been overthrown on the first *conservative* measure they introduced into Parliament, and would have been remembered as those who, even in wartime, were unable to command the confidence of the Lower House.

Derby, however, was willing to form a government, even under these uninviting circumstances if he were first strengthened by Palmerston's failure. Disraeli himself, after he had cooled down, was convinced that Derby's refusal had not resulted from timidity, but from a gamble that Palmerston could not form a government.*

* Disraeli wrote as follows: 'In 1855 after the breakup of Lord Aberdeen's

Derby's difficulties at this time are indicated by the attitude of his party towards two possible leaders in the Commons, Disraeli and Gladstone. The more conservative elements in the party distrusted Disraeli, and the Peelites would not accept the lead of the 'Peel-Smasher'. But the party was also hostile towards Gladstone. At a party rally in February 1855 Derby was greeted by cries of 'No Puseyites — No Papists', and one member told him, had Gladstone joined the Government, a hundred Conservative members would have withdrawn.[102] The Conservative Party, then, was a most difficult one to strengthen.

Moderation, caution and willingness to wait were characteristics of Derby. Opportunity would come again, and he hoped on the next occasion, time and new developments would considerably strengthen his party in the Lower House, and makes possible a truly Conservative government rather than a repetition of 1852.

Derby had refused the Government because he had no majority in the Commons. It was likewise true that he had no dependable majority in the Upper House either. The Lower House, however, had become so all-important that Disraeli could say he did not care a fig for the Lords, and Shaftesbury, a decade later, could wail: 'It is allowed to debate, transact private business, and reject a few unimportant Bills; but its vital powers are gone, and never will it dare to resist the House of Commons for two years on any point . . .'[103] While both statesmen correctly noted the decline of the Lords' importance, they were guilty of exaggeration. For the Lords in Derby's time were still a body to be reckoned with, and there the noble Earl held sway.

Their Lordships came to look to Derby, just as they had

Government, Ld. John Russell & Ld. Derby, who both made great mistakes in the course they took, the latter almost a ruinous one, both said & acted on the belief that "Ld. Palmerston could not form a government". Yet Ld. Russell & Ld. Derby were two of the most experienced men in our public life then existing.' *Disraeli Papers*, XVII, Miscellaneous Observations §43. See also: Malmesbury, *Memoirs*, II, 8. (*Diary*, February 9th, 1855). Writing many years later Gladstone called Derby's failure to form an administration at this time an error 'palpable and even gross', and noted that 'strong parliamentary courage' was not characteristic of Derby. The first charge is a matter of opinion; the second, in view of the fact that Derby three times took office with a minority in the Commons, and throughout his career was the spokesman for unpopular causes, seems rather unfair. It is interesting to note that Cobden, writing shortly after the event, observed: 'Lord D[erby] seems to me to have played a clever game for the future . . .' Morley, *Cobden*, p. 424. (Cobden to Bright, February 11th, 1855).

previously to Wellington, for leadership, but they by no means always supported him, and Derby's control of the Upper House has sometimes been exaggerated. The divisions recorded in *Hansard* between 1846 and 1867 show Derby on the winning side 116 times, and a loser on 64 occasions.* But 24 of his victories found him voting with the Government, and hence they were not victories for him. Apart from the Jew Bills, which he helped to throw out every session, Derby almost always lost important divisions on which he opposed the Government. His censures of government foreign policy in 1850 and 1864, and his victory on the second reading of the Paper Duty Bill in 1860 were unusual exceptions. When he was Prime Minister he could count on their Lordships' support, but the rest of the time the 'professed neutrals' and the Peelites, who held the balance of power in the Lords, would not support him against the Government.[104] In fact, though Derby was the acknowledged champion of the Church, he could not even depend upon the Archbishops and Bishops. While the Ecclesiastical Lords usually did not vote as a unit, their influence was generally exercised against the Conservative Party.†

Another weakness of Derby in the Lords were the proxies held by Whig magnates. More often than not, proxies helped turn the tide against the Conservatives. In 1850 Russell feared Derby might seek to throw out the proxy system in an effort to increase his power in the Lords.‡ Following a defeat in 1855, Derby noted that the custom of calling for proxies was dying out, and he was glad of it.[105] After 1858 one rarely finds proxy lists given in *Hansard* and apparently the trend observed by Derby three years before set in about that time.

Handicapped by the neutrals, churchmen and proxies, all of which Derby had to count against his cause, the Earl was by no

* This writer counted 180 divisions during the above period the lists of which show Derby's name, and it is absolutely certain how he voted. There were, of course, many more divisions during the period.

† This is a rather interesting fact. In the divisions studied, the majority of the bishops voted with Derby on sixty-seven occasions, and against him seventy-one times. However, on thirty-five of the occasions when the majority of the bishops supported Derby, the interests of the Church were involved, and they voted not with Derby, but to protect themselves. Sometimes, even on questions involving the Church, Derby was unable to secure their united support.

‡ Dorchester, *Broughton*, VI, 262-4. Russell charged that Derby controlled the Scotch and the Irish representative peerage, and seventeen years later Granville made a similar observation. *Hansard* (third series), CLXXXVIII, 1861-2. This was apparently one source of Derby's power in the Lords.

means a despot in the Lords in the sense that he determined its decisions. But he was the watchdog of the ancient practices and customs there. He would call members to order for commenting on statements made in the Commons,[106] and was once indignant when the Lord Chancellor read the remarks of the Lord Advocate, thus, in effect, allowing him to speak in the Lords.[107] He insisted that an official peer be in attendance throughout the session,[108] and was distressed that the poor turn-out in the Lords seemed to indicate that they took their duties lightly.[109] Himself a master of the English language, Derby sometimes corrected his fellow members in a superior manner.*

The function of the Upper House, Derby felt, should be to revise and correct the 'rough work' sent to them from the Commons. While he thought nineteen out of twenty bills should originate in the Commons, because they were better adapted to discussing measures in the first instance, Derby disliked the custom of the Lords in giving all bills an automatic first reading without discussion.[110] The most serious flaw in the whole system, however, arose from the fact that the Commons rarely expedited their business, and many important bills were not passed till August. This meant that the Lords twiddled their thumbs during most of the session and then were so flooded with work towards the end of the session that they had little opportunity to correct the errors of the other house. While Derby advanced various plans for obviating the difficulty,[111] they still were forced to deal with minor matters until the Commons saw fit to send some business their way.†

Much of Derby's prestige in the Lords rose from the fact that the members, regardless of party connections, regarded him as the champion of their class. For Derby was quick to defend the privileges of the nobility, and in many cases he did so effectively. On

* Disraeli wrote: 'Ld. D. would insolently correct Lord Granville across the House of Lords. Ld. Granville always said "wropped up". "Wrapped" Ld. Derby wd. say in a tone clear to the Reporters. As he wd. sometimes say to me "If we look to what Lord Granville calls the 'arithmettic' of the question".' *Disraeli Papers*, XVII, Miscellaneous Observations §45. According to the same source, Edward Stanley spoke with a 'Lancashire patois'. This trait obviously did not increase Derby's popularity. He sometimes poked fun at Aberdeen in much the same way. See: *Aberdeen Papers*, BM 43072. (Stanley to Aberdeen, September 2nd, 1846).

† Derby still was pondering this problem during his last year in Parliament. *Hansard* (third series), CXCIV, 1309.

June 11th, 1855, Derby called the attention of the House to the question of the Barony of Fermoy. This barony dated back to 1491, and was in existence until the family holding the title was outlawed by Cromwell in 1652; and, though some descendants tried to claim the title thereafter, it was not recognized. In 1855 the Government decided to revive the title and give it to Edmund Burke Roche of Trabolgen, who was a descendant of the Roche family who originally held it. Derby had a twofold interest in challenging the action of the Government, first, because he held the Government's course was illegal, and secondly, because Roche was a steady supporter of the Government and an enemy of the Irish Church. Derby pointed out that a clause of the Act of Union was intended to reduce the number of Irish peerages to one hundred, and that the Crown was permitted to create only one Irish peer for every three which became vacant in Ireland. It was a serious question whether that 'old ghost of a peerage' might be used as one of three vacant peerages for the purpose of making Roche a peer. Following a discussion, Derby requested a committee of privileges to consider the matter, but it was allowed to rest until 1856. By then the problem solved itself, for another Irish peerage became extinct, and it was used to create the Baron of Fermoy.[112]

Of greater importance than the 'barren honours of an Irish peerage', to use Derby's phrase, was the question of the legality of life peerages, and the privileges attached to them. Back in 1850 following his censure by the Lords, Russell had toyed with the idea of making enough life peers to assure his majority in the Upper House, but he was unable to secure the support of his Cabinet.[113] In 1855 Palmerston, for reasons not entirely clear,* decided to create Sir James Parke, an eminent lawyer, a peer for life. The Lord Chancellor considered the creation legal, and the patent of Parke, Lord Wensleydale, passed the law officers and the Heralds' College without objection. Before the session of Parliament opened, however, Lord Wensleydale, in the best tradition of the circle he had entered, had an outbreak of gout and was absent at the opening.[114]

* See: Herbert C. F. Bell, *Lord Palmerston* (New York: Longmans, Green & Co., 1936), II, 158; also Argyll, *Duke of Argyll*, II, 10-11; and Edmond Fitzmaurice, *The Life of Granville, George Leveson Gower, Second Earl Granville* (New York: Longmans, Green & Co., 1899), I, 157-8. Palmerston had been much opposed to 'packing' the Lords in 1832. In this case he may have preferred to make deserving legal authorities life, rather than hereditary, peers.

As life peerages might be used for the purpose Russell contemplated in 1850, Derby took fright, and planned to challenge the legality of such creations before the Speech was read.[115] Lord St. Leonards met with Derby to consider the subject. Owing to Wensleydale's illness, however, Derby did not demand the production of the letters patent at the first meeting of Parliament, but he announced his intention of questioning the practice, which had been in a state of desuetude for four centuries.[116]

On February 7th Derby kept his promise. Pointing out that the prerogative was now actually in the hands of the Ministers rather than the Crown, he affirmed it was the duty of the Lords to guard against its being stretched to unconstitutional lengths. Demanding that the customs since 1688 be used as their guide, Derby showed the danger of life peerages, which might be dangled as bait from father to son to keep a family loyal to a government. He predicted that life peerages would doom the Lords, and leave the Throne isolated, to be overthrown whenever it so pleased the public.[117] Lord Lyndhurst likewise energetically opposed the creation, and his motion to refer the case to a Committee of Privileges passed by a comfortable majority.

According to Greville, no one at the time talked of anything but the war and Lord Wensleydale,[118] and there was considerable popular support for this 'manly and dignified resistance of the Lords'.[119] Those involved had various motives prompting them. Most of the peers agreed with Derby, and opposed cheapening their position by the creation of life peers. Some feared that the Prince Consort might distribute lavishly such peerages among his literary and scientific friends, which would have been a far cry from Stuart times, when monarchs granted such titles to women of questionable reputations, and perhaps this indicates the changing nature of the Monarchy.[120] The Law Lords and prominent barristers opposed the plan for fear that thereafter their class might be unable to receive hereditary peerages.[121] On the other hand, some liberals saw in the project the only means of breaking down the innate conservatism of the Lords, and they could show that, as then constituted, the Lords did not fulfil their function as highest court efficiently.

Lord Glenelg, on February 22nd, made a motion that the matter be referred to the Judges to determine whether or not the Crown had the power to create life peers. Fearing that the Judges would decide in favour of the Crown, Derby opposed the motion, and defeated it handsomely.[122] Lord Lyndhurst then moved that precedent did not entitle a life peer to sit in the Lords, and this was carried by a wide margin.[123] Defeated, the Government sought a face-saving compromise, which would allow them to create a limited number of such peers.[124] Shortly afterwards, Derby dined with the Queen and the Prince, and found that, far from being angry at the Lords' action, the Queen would not have granted the peerage had she anticipated the furore it would create.[125]

The Prince Consort acted as intermediary between the Government and the Opposition, and, as a result of his conferences with Derby, the appellate jurisdiction of the Lords was discussed on February 28th. Derby pointed out weaknesses in the system, that most of the Lords merely assented to the decisions of the Lord Chancellor, and few listened to cases, and that an individual sometimes referred a question from himself in one capacity to himself in another. His motion that an investigating committee be set up was carried.[126]

Derby worked in harmony with Granville during the investigation, and a compromise was worked out. Confirming the appellate jurisdiction of the Lords, it was decided to strengthen their court by adding two life peers, who would be paid to assist the Lord Chancellor. These life peers would receive their writs of summons by authority of Parliament, and the Lords would thus retain control of such members.[127] Though Lord Clanricarde pointed out this introduced the principle of paying members of Parliament, the Lords accepted the compromise.[128] Derby was disappointed, however, to have it rejected by the Commons on the ground that it restricted the prerogative of the Crown.

In June Wensleydale received an hereditary peerage and took his seat in their Lordships' House.[129] In the later stages of the struggle Derby had apparently enjoyed himself. Granville wrote a friend that Derby and Lyndhurst, in committee, amused everyone by imitating the Law Lords, and at a dinner at Derby's residence, Granville was amused at the chaffing between Derby and a friend.[130] The one who enjoyed the incident least was Lord Wensleydale. That eminent barrister, who had perhaps presented many test cases during his law career, did not enjoy being one himself, and told a friend: 'I have plenty to forget.'[131]

The Conservative Party was slow to recover from its disappointment of 1855. In May, to inspire his followers a little, Derby attacked the Government, but the assault was listless and unsuccessful.[132] In July Lord John Russell unwisely admitted that his views on Russia differed from those of his colleagues, and Disraeli quickly pointed out that the nation could not trust a government divided on this important issue. Bulwer Lytton gave notice of a censure of Russell's conduct, and the Government's position became so critical that Derby wrote Disraeli: '. . . I am living almost in dread of a telegraphic message.'[133] Derby, however, did not want to press the issue to a showdown,[134] and Russell aided his colleagues by tendering his resignation. The incident merely sowed more seeds of discontent among the Conservatives, who criticized Derby for allowing Disraeli to attack the Government without previously consulting others in the party.[135]

Having failed to capitalize on the war, the restless Disraeli cautiously explored the political possibilities of a peace movement. While he did not publicly identify himself with the movement, Disraeli's activities brought a remonstrance from Derby:[136]

> . . . we cannot with honour, or even with regard to party interests, constitute ourselves a peace Opposition, merely because we have a War Ministry, and I will never consent to weaken an Administration to which I am opposed, by increasing their difficulties in carrying the country through what has become an inevitable war . . . If the Conservative party cannot be kept together on any other grounds, it is time that it should fall to pieces. . . .

Others also disapproved Disraeli's tactics. Wrote Bulwer Lytton: '*The Country will never take peace from a peace party.* It will take peace only from those whom it feels to have been thoroughly in earnest when the business was fighting.'[137] Disraeli sent Derby a chilly reply, refusing to argue the matter, and about that time wrote Malmesbury that their party was 'off the rail of politics' for the duration.[138] He continued to brood over what he considered to be Derby's errors of leadership.

Derby himself was certain that there was no prospect of a return to power before the war ended.[139] When peace came, he conferred with Malmesbury and Disraeli to form a policy regarding it,[140] but his speech on the subject was mediocre.[141] But in

May he strongly opposed the Declaration of International Maritime Law of the Treaty of Paris on the ground that England was weakening her naval power by renouncing the right to seize enemy goods under a neutral flag as a lawful prize of war.[142] This was not a mere partisan attack, for Derby sought to make a strong navy one of his party principles, but he was unable to secure the backing of the Lords.[143] Shortly after the defeat Derby went to York to see one of his horses run, had an attack of gout, and was *hors de combat* the rest of the year.[144]

The disorganization of the Conservative Party in 1856 caused some worry even among its opponents. Granville thought it might shortly break up, and observed: 'I look upon this as anything but an advantage for us or for the country.'[145] Even Cobden had lost some of his antipathy for the Conservatives, and, knowing they would make concessions to keep it, saw some advantages in returning them to power.[146] Derby's prestige still acted to hold it together, but the pro-Disraeli faction added to the disorganization. Malmesbury wrote in April 1856:*

> I can see that many believe Disraeli would like to place himself at the head of the Conservative Party, to the exclusion of Lord Derby. These suspicions are strengthened by the tone of his paper, 'The Press', which avoids ever mentioning the name of Lord Derby, or of anyone except Disraeli himself, whom it praises in the most fulsome manner. I have also myself been sounded on the subject of making Disraeli or Lord Stanley our leader, but I do not think that the person to whom I allude will ever do so again.

Another wing of the party was disgusted with Disraeli. In December Malmesbury wrote Derby that Disraeli's unpopularity, and the impression that he, Derby, did not want to return to power, were the reasons for the despondency of the party. Derby replied he saw and regretted Disraeli's unpopularity, and the fact that Disraeli did not see more of the party in private, but he

* Malmesbury, *Memoirs*, II, 45-6. (*Diary*, April 26th, 1856). Derby was on bad terms with Disraeli's paper, and for that matter almost all others. Fitzmaurice, *Granville*, I, 146. (Granville to Canning, January 30th, 1856). But see: M&B, *Disraeli*, I, 1321. Disraeli evidently did not control *The Press* to any great extent after February 1856. Derby was an opponent of the press from early times, and O'Connell observed in 1834 that there had been more prosecutions during Derby's (then Stanley) administration in Ireland than in any preceding one. *Hansard* (third series), XXI, 801. He no doubt thought it presumptuous of editors to take men of his social standing to task.

considered him indispensable to the party. 'For myself', he added, 'I *never* was *ambitious* of office, and am not likely to become more so as I get older; but I am now, as I have been, ready to accept the responsibility for it if I see a chance, not only of taking, but of keeping it.'[147] At this time particularly Disraeli undoubtedly had solid grievances against Derby for his tendency to isolate himself socially from the party, and the smallness of his donations to it.*

The party was also badly divided in its ideas at this time. Pakington wrote Disraeli: 'I suspect that you & Ld. Ellenborough & Stanley & I have little in common with the party behind us, & that the party know it – & I suspect that we four have little in common with Ld. Derby & Walpole & John Manners & Henley.'[148] This was so noticeable that Palmerston actually offered Stanley the Colonial Office. It is said he hurried home to consult with his father, who greeted him: 'What the devil brings you here, Edward? Are you going to be married or has Disraeli cut his throat?'[149] Stanley at length rejected the offer, and later explained his motive to Disraeli: 'I need not tell you that both from personal feelings and from considerations of what a family owes itself, I shall never during my Father's public life, connect myself with a party opposed to his.'†

The admiration and love Stanley felt for his father were constant as the years went by, and one occasionally finds him imitating Derby's distinctive style of writing.[150] But he realized in 1857 that, with his ideas, he had no business sitting on the front Conservative benches, and so Stanley retired to the rear. Since 1852 he had differed from the great majority of the party on church rates, religious tests in Parliament, religious tests for the Universities, the repeal of the newspaper stamp, the constitution of the Army, the constitution of the Civil Service, Irish and English education.[151] No one was more aware of their differences than Derby himself, but he never was quite able to understand his son's thinking, especially on Church matters.

* Lord Redesdale criticized not only Derby, but Malmesbury and Disraeli also, for their unapproachability, which contrasted with the attitude of the great Whig leaders. Redesdale, *Memories*, II, 534.

† *Disraeli Papers*, Stanley XII. (Edward Stanley to Disraeli, January 27th, 1857). His mother may have made him aware of the obligations referred to in the letter. Fitzmaurice, *Granville*, I, 131. (Granville to Canning, December 15th, 1855).

During the early winter, Derby pursued his usual pastimes with zest,* but the attitude of his son, and his obvious discontent, caused Derby also to consider seriously the problems of his party. He subscribed a considerable sum to the party,[152] began to lend money to the *Herald*,[153] and once again sought means of strengthening his party numerically. Writing to Joliffe, whose earnest representations had helped to stir him to action, Derby assured the Whip that he would do his best to keep the party together, though he realized it would be difficult to satisfy them.[154] To strengthen the party, one had to bring them to power; to bring them to power, one needed aid in the Commons; to secure such aid, there was still only one place to go — the Peelites.

In 1856 Derby felt that there was an excellent feeling springing up again between the Peelites and Conservatives.[155] During the spring of 1856 Derby again sounded Gladstone concerning his views and those of the Peelite Party, not directly, but through Sir William Heathcote. Gladstone replied that his ideas were much like those of Derby, in so far as a desire for co-operation were concerned, and that he and the Peelites acted together merely as a result of general agreement and personal friendship. When he made known to his friends, particularly Graham, the fact that Derby was again sounding him, the old obstacle of Disraeli's leadership of the Commons, which Gladstone regarded with 'doubt and dread', again arose, to prevent the success of the negotiation.[156] Gladstone, however, was obviously weakening. In November, in a letter to Graham, he described himself as a man '. . . who thinks Lord Palmerston is a bad Minister for this country, and who thinks Lord Derby would be a better'.[157]

In December, a friend of Gladstone's named Elwin, who was personally unknown to Derby, began negotiations anew by suggesting that Gladstone co-operate with the Conservative Party.[158] The same gentleman then wrote several letters to Derby stating that Gladstone was ready to discuss public affairs in confidence with Derby. On January 25th, 1857, Derby wrote direct to Gladstone, suggesting that they have a personal interview regarding plans for the coming session.[159] Derby received a

* Lennox, who often wrote critically of Derby, described his activities in a letter to Disraeli: 'As a leader of a party, he is more hopeless than ever — devoted to whist, billiards, racing, betting . . .' M&B, *Disraeli*, I, 1459. (Lennox to Disraeli, date not shown).

friendly, but cautious, reply,* proposing that they postpone their talk until after the Address, and Derby quickly agreed to do so.[160] On February 4th Gladstone called and had a four-hour conversation with his former colleague, which Derby described as 'very satisfactory', but Gladstone did not commit himself concerning what would follow a successful attack on Palmerston.[161] While both Conservatives and Peelites disagreed with Palmerston on financial matters, and on foreign policy, their points of disagreement were not held in common. On February 10th Gladstone left four resolutions on finance with Derby, and, upon examination, the latter could agree with only two of the four. Derby's chief objection was that the wording of Gladstone's resolutions might aid in making the income tax, which his party was anxious to do away with by 1860, a permanent feature of the Budget.[162] Gladstone, however, after some alterations of the Conservative resolution, agreed to support it, and by February 15th the attack on Palmerston's Budget had been agreed upon by both parties.[163] Even this united force failed to shake the Palmerston Government, and, supported by some of the independent Conservatives, he won the division by 80 votes.

Derby, however, was quite as interested in another attack he was preparing, for it involved a fundamental difference between Palmerston's foreign policy and his own. Late in January he wrote Disraeli that the Government had been wrong in their dealings with China, and the great majority of his party tended to agree with him.[164] Britain had, in fact, been guilty of demanding excessive satisfaction from China over a minor incident, and, when an apology had been refused, she had bombarded Canton. Such a case was made to order for Derby, and on February 24th, he made a slashing attack on Palmerston's policy:[165]

> . . . I appear as an advocate: but an advocate from a conviction of the justice in my case: but an advocate disinterested, and most certainly, unpaid. I am an advocate in a cause which I believe to be that of policy, of justice and humanity. I am an advocate for weakness against power, for perplexed and bewildered barbarism against the arrogant demands of overweening, self-styled civili-

* The sequence of letters here is confused. Gladstone's letter of January 26th suggested an interview after the Address, and Derby thought it a reply to his letter of January 25th. But it was actually written before he heard from Derby. *Gladstone Papers*, BM 44140. (Derby to Gladstone, January 25th and 31st, 1857). (Gladstone to Derby, January 26th, 1857).

> zation. I am an advocate for the feeble defencelessness of China against the overpowering might of Great Britain.

He pointed out that such high-handed actions might discredit Christianity in China. Though eloquent, the plea failed to bring a censure of Palmerston's policy, and, aided by proxies, the Government won.* But in the Lower House Palmerston was defeated on the issue, and, rather than resign, he took his case to the country.

Derby did what he could to win over the Peelites, and to help bring victory at the polls. Ordinarily a patient man who considered the prejudices of his followers, Derby sought at this time to override their opposition to the Peelites. At a party rally he declared that '. . . should any member of the Conservative connection attempt to dictate to him the course he should pursue with regard to any political personages whatever, he would regard it as an insult, and no longer recognize that member as attached to his party'.[166] Following this declaration, the party again expressed complete confidence in his leadership, but there were still some ideological and personal obstacles preventing a reunion with the Peelites.[167]

Realizing that the China question would not be a vote-getter, Derby on March 16th sought, during the Income Tax debate, to broaden the issues of the election. His reference to Palmerston is an oratorical classic:[168]

> . . . the noble Viscount is at the present moment playing half-a-dozen parts at the same time. He is not content with being the Janus Biceps, he is a Janus Septiceps — a political chameleon which offers a different hue and colour to the spectator according to the side from which he gazes. I defy any man, even the most ardent of his supporters, to say, when he professes confidence in the noble Viscount, what upon any great domestic question of the day is the policy to which he pledges himself.

This attack was directed towards Palmerston's most vulnerable spot. Basically a conservative, the Viscount drew his support

* *Hansard* (third series), CXLIV, 1385-8. Shaftesbury did not do Derby justice at this time when he wrote: 'Does anyone believe that if J. Russell had been in the government, he would not have said the very reverse of what he did say last night. Does anyone doubt the same of Derby?' Edwin Hodder, *The Life and Work of the Seventh Earl of Shaftesbury* (New York: Cassell & Co., 1887), III, 39-40. (*Diary*, February 27th, 1857).

from the liberal side of the house. The Earl then described his own convictions:[169]

> My notions may perhaps be old-fashioned and contrary to the enlightenment of the day, but they are the opinions to which I have steadfastly adhered through no inconsiderable period of my life, and I cannot change them now . . . I intend to maintain inviolate the great institutions of the country: I intend to support as far as my feeble voice can go, the prerogatives of the Crown, the independence and hereditary character of your Lordships' House and the rights of the people. I intend to support the doctrines and rights of property of that Established Church of which I have always been an attached member: I desire to see her weak places strengthened and her defects repaired – I desire to see her taking a firmer hold on the affections of the people . . . no one can say of me during my life, nor, I hope, will any man be able to say, with truth to my memory, that I have ever shrunk from the avowal of my political opinions – that I ever sunk a principle for the purpose of obtaining an advantage, or that I have ever betrayed the trust reposed in me by those friends who have honoured me with their political confidence.

While not yet sixty, Derby's speeches at this time were already beginning to echo his years and illnesses.

During the election the Peelites went their separate ways, and refused to co-operate with the Conservatives.[170] The public, wearied of their distracting influence, practically obliterated the Peelite Party at the polls. The Conservatives,. while they lost 20 members, returned 260 men on whom Disraeli felt he could count, and he was therefore more satisfied with them than with the old group of 280, which had contained 60 unreliables.[171] Derby thought his party had entered a state of 'suspended animation', but felt that it could be restored to life rather easily.[172] The victory went to Palmerston, who was now closely identified with national feeling, and who was probably the only genuinely popular leader in the country. Some of the Conservatives had not yet forgiven Derby for abandoning Protection.*

* One of the members of the time reported the feelings of his own constituency: 'Taking the feelings of the Constituency as to ''leaders'', I may put them: ''Palmerston'', ''Derby'' (not popular), ''D'Israeli'' (unpopular), ''Lord John'' (very unpopular), ''Gladstone'' (extremely unpopular). Lord Palmerston *very popular because* he carried out the Russian War – Lord Derby unpopular *because* he did not carry out the Russian War & because the *farmers* think he *dropped them* in /52 . . .' *Disraeli Papers*, Taylor XIII. (Stanhope to Taylor, April 19th, 1857).

Derby outlined the party's course in a letter of April 24th. The Whigs, he thought, were becoming fearful of the Radicals, but Russell, ousted from the leadership of the party by Palmerston, now would turn to the latter for support. Derby therefore proposed to let Palmerston lean on Conservative support to resist the Radicals.[173] This was the beginning of the quasi-coalition with Palmerston, which was to last, on and off, until the Viscount's death. By May 1857 Derby was in communication with him, but there was no real meeting of minds at that time.

Spring brought another attack of gout, and Derby expected that every joint of his body would have its turn before the attack passed.[174] Malmesbury replaced him temporarily as the spokesman for their party in the Lords, but was warned by Derby not to commit his party on the question of Reform.[175] In the middle of May he returned to his accustomed place in the House, and confided to a friend: 'Palmerston says I am dying, but I'll show him I'm alive.'[176] In spite of this show of pugnacity, Derby was not very active that session, and when Malmesbury visited him in the autumn he found his friend without his 'usual *entrain*'.[177] Derby, indeed, was not dying, but during those days he seriously considered how a man in such uncertain health might expect to be an effective Prime Minister, and he rather envied Palmerston, his senior, who carried on year after year like a hardy perennial. As leader of a party which was divided, disappointed, discouraged, he had to fight for power in order to hold the party together. But what could he do with it, if it came to him? He shuddered at the thought of another minority ministry, and, since the collapse of the Peelites that spring, there was now no one to turn to, and Palmerston was more solidly ensconced than ever before. The coming year seemed to promise nothing more than new defeats and the further disintegration of his party. The night, however, was now at its blackest, before the dawn.

NOTES

[1] Jennings, *Croker*, II, 449, 454-5. (Croker to Hardwicke, December 31st, 1852). (Lonsdale to Croker, May 22nd, 1853).

[2] B&E, *Victoria*, II, 500-1. (Memorandum by Albert, December 18th, 1852).

[3] Malmesbury, *Memoirs*, I, 376. (*Diary*, December 20th, 1852).

[4] S&F, *Greville*, VI, 383. (*Diary*, December 23rd, 1852).

[5] B&E, *Victoria*, II, 509-10. (Derby to Victoria, December 22nd, 1852).

[6] Ibid., pp. 517-18. (Memorandum by Albert, December 27th, 1852).

[7] Ibid., p. 518. (Emma Derby to Marchioness of Ely, December 27th, 1852).

[8] *Hansard* (third series), CXXIV, 16-17.

[9] *DP*, Derby XII. (Derby to Disraeli, January 30th, 1853).
[10] M&B, *Disraeli*, I, 1292. (Disraeli to Londonderry, December 31st, 1852).
[11] S&F, *Greville*, VI, 388. (*Diary*, December 28th, 1852).
[12] *DP*, Derby XII. (Derby to Disraeli, December 26th, 1852).
[13] Kebbel, *Derby*, p. 101.
[14] *Hansard* (third series), CLXI, 1289.
[15] C. Kinloch Cooke, *A Memoir of Her Royal Highness Princess Mary Adelaide, Duchess of Teck* (London: John Murray, 1900), I, 298. (*Diary*, October 11th, 1852).
[16] *Hansard* (third series), CLXXI, 502-5.
[17] Ibid., CXXIV, 707.
[18] Ibid., CXXVI, 449.
[19] Ibid.
[20] S&F, *Greville*, VI, 421. (*Diary*, May 3rd, 1853).
[21] *Hansard* (third series), CXXXVIII, 1092.
[22] Ibid. CXXXIV, 843.
[23] S&F, *Greville*, VI, 436. (*Diary*, July 31st, 1853).
[24] *Hansard* (third series), CXXIX, 587-90.
[25] Ibid., pp. 593-612.
[26] S&F, *Greville*, VI, 436. (*Diary*, July 31st, 1853).
[27] Malmesbury, *Memoirs*, I, 403-4. (*Diary*, June 9th, 1853).
[28] *Hansard* (third series), CXXX, 66.
[29] Ibid., pp. 1132-3.
[30] Ibid., CXXXIV, 1237-8.
[31] Ibid., p. 1347.
[32] Ibid., pp. 1360-1.
[33] *The Times* (London), June 30th, 1854.
[34] *DP*, Derby XII. (Derby to Disraeli, June 20th, 1853).
[35] Ibid., Stanley XII. (Edward Stanley to Disraeli, January 28th, 1853).
[36] Ibid. (Tennent to Disraeli, January 31st, 1853). (Duffy to Tennent, January 10th, 1853).
[37] Ibid. (Edward Stanley to Disraeli, January 28th, 1853).
[38] Ibid. (Edward Stanley to Disraeli, January 27th, 1853).
[39] Ibid. (Edward Stanley to Disraeli, January 20th, 1853).
[40] Ibid.
[41] Ibid., Derby XII. (Derby to Disraeli, January 30th, 1853).
[42] M&B, *Disraeli*, I, 1291-2. (Derby to Londonderry, December 21st, 1852).
[43] S&F, *Greville*, VI, 405. (*Diary*, February 25th, 1853).
[44] *DP*, Derby XII. (Derby to Disraeli, April 27th, 1853).
[45] S&F, *Greville*, VI, 404. (*Diary*, February 20th, 1853).
[46] Malmesbury, *Memoirs*, I, 404. (*Diary*, June 25th, 1853).
[47] *DP*, Derby XII. (Derby to Disraeli, March 27th, 1853).
[48] Ibid. (Derby to Disraeli, June 20th, 1853).
[49] Ibid.
[50] S&F, *Greville*, VI, 443. (*Diary*, September 2nd, 1853).
[51] *DP*, Stanley XII. (Edward Stanley to Disraeli, November 28th, 1853).
[52] Malmesbury, *Memoirs*, I, 414. (*Diary*, December 3rd, 1853).
[53] Ibid., pp. 414-15. (*Diary*, December 9th-12th, 1853). Jennings, *Croker*, II, 485. (Lonsdale to Croker, December 16th, 1853).
[54] Jennings, *Croker*, II, 455. (Lonsdale to Croker, December 22nd, 1853); *DP*, Derby XII. (Derby to Disraeli, November 14th 1853).
[55] *DP*, Derby XII. (Derby to Disraeli, November 14th, 1853).
[56] Ibid.
[57] Ibid., Pakington XIII. (Pakington to Disraeli, December 16th, 1853).

[58] Ibid., Derby XII. (Derby to Disraeli, December 15th, 1853).
[59] S&F, *Greville*, VII, 23. (*Diary*, March 6th, 1854).
[60] *DP*, Joliffe XIII. (Joliffe to Disraeli, January 10th, 1854).
[61] *The Times* (London), April 3rd, 1854.
[62] *Hansard* (third series), CXXX, 396-8.
[63] Ibid.
[64] *DP*, Derby XII. (Emma Derby to Disraeli, April 18th, 1854).
[65] Ibid. (Derby to Disraeli, November 28th, 1854).
[66] Londonderry, *Letters*, pp. 130-2. (Disraeli to Marchioness of Londonderry, August 7th, 1854).
[67] M&B, *Disraeli*, I, 1366. (Disraeli to Lennox, December 2nd, 1854).
[68] *DP*, Derby XII. (Derby to Disraeli, January 18th, 1855).
[69] Malmesbury, *Memoirs*, II, 2. (Derby to Malmesbury, January 23rd, 1855).
[70] M&B, *Disraeli*, I, 1372. (Disraeli to Marchioness of Londonderry, January 23rd, 1855).
[71] *DP*, Derby XII. (Derby to Disraeli, January 23rd, 1855).
[72] Ibid.
[73] B&E, *Victoria*, III, 97-8. (Aberdeen to Victoria, January 27th, 1855).
[74] *DP*, Derby XII. (Derby to Disraeli, January 29th, 1855).
[75] *DP*, XVII. Miscellaneous Observations §43.
[76] Maxwell, *Clarendon*, II, 56-7. (Clarendon to Lewis, January 30th, 1855).
[77] B&E, *Victoria*, III, 100-1. (Memorandum by Victoria, January 30th, 1855).
[78] *DP*, Stanley XII. (Edward Stanley to Disraeli, January 30th, 1855).
[79] M&B, *Disraeli*, I, 1375.
[80] *Hansard* (third series), CXXXVI, 1345-6.
[81] B&E, *Victoria*, III, 104. (Memorandum by Victoria, January 31st, 1855).
[82] Malmesbury, *Memoirs*, II, 5. (*Diary*, February 2nd, 1855).
[83] Ibid., pp. 6-7. (*Diary*, February 6th, 1855).
[84] Maxwell, *Clarendon*, II, 57.
[85] Morley, *Gladstone*, I, 525-7. (*Diary*, January 31st, 1855).
[86] *DP*, Stanley XII. (Edward Stanley to Disraeli, January 31st, 1855); Ibid.. Derby XII. (Derby to Disraeli, February 1st, 1855).
[87] *GP*, BM 44140. (Gladstone to Derby, January 31st, 1855).
[88] *DP*, Stanley XII. (Edward Stanley to Disraeli, January 31st, 1855).
[89] Ibid., Derby XII. (Derby to Disraeli, February 1st, 1855).
[90] B&E, *Victoria*, III, 106-7. (Memorandum by Albert, February 1st, 1855).
[91] *Hansard* (third series), CXXXVI, 1333-49.
[92] M&B, *Disraeli*, I, 1339-40. (Disraeli to Londonderry, September 26th, 1853).
[93] Malmesbury, *Memoirs*, II, 7-8. (*Diary*, February 9th, 1855).
[94] M&B, *Disraeli*, II, 150. (Disraeli to Derby, August 6th, 1865).
[95] *DP*, Pakington XIII. (Pakington to Disraeli, February 9th, 1855).
[96] Ibid., Joliffe XIII. (Joliffe to Disraeli, February 15th, 1855).
[97] Ibid., Bulwer XIII. (Bulwer to Disraeli, November 12th, 1855).
[98] M&B, *Disraeli*, I, 1386. (Disraeli to Mrs. Willyams, February 25th, 1855).
[99] Malmesbury, *Memoirs*, II, 9-10. (*Diary*, February 21st, 1855).
[100] *Hansard* (third series), CXXXVI, 1339-41; B&E, *Victoria*, III, 102-4. (Memorandum by Victoria, January 31st, 1855).
[101] Ashley, *Palmerston*, II, 306. (Palmerston to Temple, February 15th, 1855).
[102] Morley, *Gladstone*, I, 536.
[103] Hodder, *Shaftesbury*, III, 201-2.
[104] Jennings, *Croker*, II, 411. (Stanley to Croker, August 15th, 1850).
[105] *Hansard* (third series), CXXXVIII. 587.
[106] Ibid., CLXX, 1511.

[107] Ibid., CLIX, 2016.

[108] Lord Edmond Fitzmaurice, *The Life of Granville, George Leveson Gower, Second Earl Granville* (New York: Longmans, Green & Co., 1899), I, 240.

[109] *Hansard* (third series), CXLIV, 1243.

[110] Ibid., CLIX, 2130-1.

[111] Ibid., pp. 2131-42; Ibid., CLXI, 182-3.

[112] Ibid., CXXXVIII, 1761-5; Ibid., CXL, 448, 699, 705. See also: 'The Peerage of Ireland and the Title of Fermoy', *The Gentleman's Magazine*, XLIV (July 1855), 43-7.

[113] Dorchester, *Broughton*, VI, 262-4.

[114] Argyll, *Duke of Argyll*, II, 10-11; Roundell Palmer, *Earl of Selborne, Memorials Part II Personal and Political* (London: Macmillan & Co., 1898), p. 35.

[115] Malmesbury, *Memoirs*, II, 41. (Derby to Malmesbury, January 19th, 1856).

[116] *Hansard* (third series), CXL, 38.

[117] Ibid., pp. 364-74.

[118] S&F, *Greville*, VII, 203. (*Diary*, February 21st, 1856).

[119] 'The Declining Efficiency of Parliament', *The Quarterly Review*, XCIX (1856), 539.

[120] Fitzmaurice, *Granville*, I, 159.

[121] Argyll, *Duke of Argyll*, II, 14.

[122] *Hansard* (third series), CXL, 1149.

[123] Ibid., pp. 1216-17, 1289.

[124] Fitzmaurice, *Granville*, I, 167. (Granville to Canning, February 23rd, 1856).

[125] Malmesbury, *Memoirs*, II, 43. (*Diary*, February 27th, 1856).

[126] *Hansard* (third series), CXL, 1449-78.

[127] Ibid., CXLII, 1071-6.

[128] Ibid., p. 1076.

[129] S&F, *Greville*, VII, 234. (*Diary*, July 27th, 1856).

[130] Fitzmaurice, *Granville*, I, 171, 177. (Granville to Canning, March 7th, 1856). (Granville to Canning, April 26th, 1856).

[131] Ibid., p. 220. (Granville to Canning, December 2nd, 1856).

[132] Malmesbury, *Memoirs*, II, 21-3. (*Diary*, May 6th, 1856). *Hansard* (third series), CXXXVIII, 518-31.

[133] *DP*, Derby XII. (Derby to Disraeli, Wednesday, 1855).

[134] Ibid. (Derby to Disraeli, July 16th, 1855).

[135] Malmesbury, *Memoirs*, II, 30. (*Diary*, July 12th, 1855).

[136] *DP*, Derby XII. (Derby to Disraeli, October 25th, 1855).

[137] Ibid., Bulwer XIII. (Bulwer to Disraeli, November 12th (?), 1855).

[138] Malmesbury, *Memoirs*, II, 37. (Disraeli to Malmesbury, November 30th, 1855).

[139] *DP*, Derby XII. (Derby to Disraeli, October 25th, 1855).

[140] Ibid. (Derby to Disraeli, April 1st, 1856).

[141] *Hansard* (third series), CXLI, 2002.

[142] Ibid., CXLII, 522-35.

[143] Argyll, *Duke of Argyll*, II, 50-1.

[144] Malmesbury, *Memoirs*, II, 50-1. (Derby to Malmesbury, August 25th, 1856).

[145] Fitzmaurice, *Granville*, I, 146. (Granville to Canning, January 30th, 1856).

[146] Morley, *Cobden*, p. 435. (Cobden to Parkes, December 11th, 1856).

[147] Malmesbury, *Memoirs*, II, 53-5. (Derby to Malmesbury, December 15th, 1856).

[148] *DP*, Pakington XIII. (Pakington to Disraeli, October 8th, 1857).

[149] Viscountess Enfield, ed., *Leaves from the Diary of Henry Greville* (London: Smith, Elder & Co., 1884), II, 262-3. (*Diary*, November 5th, 1855).

[150] *DP*, Stanley XII. (Edward Stanley to Disraeli, September 5th, 1859).

[151] Ibid. (Edward Stanley to Disraeli, January 27th, 1857).
[152] M&B, *Disraeli*, I, 1459. (Joliffe to Disraeli, December 27th, 1856).
[153] *DP*, Joliffe XIII. (Joliffe to Disraeli, November 17th, 1857).
[154] Ibid. (Joliffe to Disraeli, January 19th, 1857).
[155] Andrew Lang, *Life, Letters and Diaries of Sir Stafford Northcote* (Edinburgh: William Blackwood & Sons, 1899), pp. 88-9. (Northcote to Lady Northcote, undated).
[156] Morley, *Gladstone*, I, 551-2.
[157] Parker, *Graham*, II, 291. (Gladstone to Graham, November 29th, 1856).
[158] *GP*, BM 44140. (Derby to Gladstone, January 25th, 1857).
[159] Ibid.
[160] Ibid. (Gladstone to Derby, January 26th, 1857). (Derby to Gladstone, January 31st, 1857).
[161] Morley, *Gladstone*, I, 558-61; *DP*, Derby XII. (Derby to Disraeli, February 4th, 1857).
[162] *GP*, BM 44140. (Derby to Gladstone, February 11th, 1857); *DP*, Derby XII. (Derby to Disraeli, February 11th, 1857).
[163] *DP*, Derby XII. (Derby to Disraeli, February 14th (?), 1857). (Gladstone to Derby, February 15th, 1857).
[164] Ibid. (Derby to Disraeli, January 23rd, 1857). (Derby to Disraeli, February 11th, 1857).
[165] *Hansard* (third series), CXLIV, 1155.
[166] Malmesbury, *Memoirs*, II, 62. (*Diary*, February 28th, 1857).
[167] *DP*, Manners XIII. (Manners to Disraeli, March 10th, 1857).
[168] *Hansard* (third series), CXLIV, 2337.
[169] Ibid.
[170] Malmesbury, *Memoirs*, II, 63-4. (*Diary*, March 6th, 1857).
[171] M&B, *Disraeli*, I, 1476. (Disraeli to Mrs. Willyams, April 13th, 1857).
[172] *DP*, Derby XII. (Derby to Disraeli, April 24th, 1857).
[173] Ibid.
[174] Malmesbury, *Memoirs*, II, 68-9. (*Diary*, May 1st, 1857).
[175] Ibid., pp. 67-8. (Derby to Malmesbury, April 30th, 1857).
[176] Ibid., pp. 71-2. (*Diary*, May 16th, 1857).
[177] Ibid., p. 79. (*Diary*, September 9th, 1857).

CHAPTER IX

DERBY ATTENDS DEMOCRACY

WHEN the session opened in December 1857, Lord Derby did not expect that foreign affairs, the field which Palmerston had dominated for several decades, would provide the incident which would dislodge the popular Viscount from his post at the Treasury. No one, indeed, could have predicted it, even had he been privy to the plot being hatched by certain Italian refugees to violently remind Napoleon III of his broken promise to aid Italian unification by making an attempt on his life. For one might confidently expect that Palmerston would be careful under any circumstances to uphold British international prestige, for this was the field in which his talents found their most striking expression. Yet in this familiar field the noble Viscount made a false step, and he was overthrown.

In January 1858 an unsuccessful attempt was made on the life of the French Emperor. As Malmesbury put it, Napoleon did not 'stand being shot at as well as he used to',[1] and he was angry with Great Britain, the nation from whence both the plotters and the bombs had come. Walewski, the French Minister, demanded that Britain take steps to prevent political refugees from hatching such plots in the future. Derby took the occasion to orate on the subject of England as an asylum for all who did not break her laws,[2] but there was little opportunity at the moment to make political capital from the incident. Complying with French demands, Palmerston on February 8th introduced his Conspiracy Bill, and ordinarily the measure would have caused little comment, but the hostile and arrogant attitude adopted by France towards Britain served to stiffen British public opinion against concessions. However, with Conservative support, the Premier carried the first reading of his measure on February 9th.

While neither Derby nor Disraeli apparently realized the potentialities of the situation, some of Palmerston's alienated allies were quick to do so. Milner Gibson, a Radical, sensed that public opinion would back a censure of Palmerston for bringing in the Conspiracy Bill before answering an intemperate dispatch from Walewski, for, to all appearances, the Conspiracy Bill had been forced upon him by the French. Gibson, apparently supported by Russell, Graham and Bright,[3] gave notice of his proposed censure on February 16th. Success or failure depended, of course, upon the attitude of the Conservatives towards the attack.

Derby realized immediately that Palmerston might be overthrown, and wrote Disraeli 'C'est le commencement de la Fin' immediately upon learning of Gibson's notice.[4] Victory on such a question, however, would not give the Conservative Party those additions of strength necessary to form a stable government, and Derby sought more time, perhaps by an understanding with Palmerston to postpone the debate, to analyse the political situation. But he called in Disraeli to confer and they apparently decided to support the censure, though Derby was not sure that such a step would necessarily depose Palmerston. Disraeli, of course, was eager for office.

The debate on the censure took place on February 19th, and resulted in the defeat of the Government by 19 votes. In describing his defeat to the Queen, Palmerston traced the plot to Lord Derby,* trying to make it appear that the Conservatives had used the dissident Liberals to serve their own political ends. Derby later gave the Queen a different account, and correctly traced the conspiracy to Russell and Graham.[5] Because they had furnished the votes necessary to oust Palmerston, however, the Conservatives, to Derby's way of thinking, were morally bound to accept office if it were offered. At the same time, he also thought that those of the Opposition who had aided in upsetting Palmerston were likewise obliged to aid the Government which their votes had created.

Early on the evening of February 20th, Derby, in response to a

* B&E, *Victoria*, III, 337. (Palmerston to Victoria, February 19th, 1858). Chagrined by his defeat, Palmerston apparently was loath to admit that his fall was due to the political chicanery of men who usually supported him. A rather curious story, however, is told by one of Palmerston's biographers. According to this account, Derby watched the debate while sitting under the gallery of the House of Commons and, sensing that the tide was turning against the Government, sent word to Disraeli to support the censure. Ashley, *Palmerston*, II, 355-6. See also: Fitzmaurice, *Granville*, I, 293. (Granville to Canning, February 24th, 1858). It seems more probable that this decision was made at their conference on February 17th, and Disraeli was quite prepared to take part in the debate.

summons, appeared at the Palace. When the Queen advised him of Palmerston's resignation and asked him to form an Administration, Derby requested that the offer should not be made to him until she was fully aware of his political prospects. With a two-to-one majority against him in the Commons, little prospect of securing aid outside his party, and a threatening foreign situation, the future of a Conservative government was hopeless, unless it was made clear to the Commons that it was the only government possible at the time. Acting on Derby's suggestion, the Queen agreed to defer her offer on condition that, if called in again, Derby would accept immediately.[6]

Derby left the Queen with mixed feelings. He even suspected that Palmerston might have intentionally created a crisis hoping that it would increase his power.[7] In fact, at the moment, he expected that the Queen would recall Palmerston.[8] But one thing was clear: absolutely to refuse office again would mean the disruption of the Conservative Party, and that must be avoided at all costs. Immediately on arriving home he wrote to a man who, in a crisis, offered both intelligent suggestions and good cheer. He reported the interview to Disraeli, expressed complete uncertainty as to future developments, and cautioned him to keep the affair a secret, lest a rumour go out that he had declined office again.[9]

On February 21st the Queen received Derby again with a definite offer, and this time Derby accepted without further hesitation.[10] He felt his tactic had strengthened his position at Court, but the failure of the Queen to offer the Government to other party or factional leaders had not improved his chances to secure outside aid. Disraeli was informed immediately of the development and called to a conference.[11] They apparently decided to seek the services of Gladstone, who had taken a leading part in the assault on Palmerston's Government, and Lord Grey, who had been rather friendly towards the Conservatives during recent years. The impression was strong among some members of the Conservative Party that Gladstone was ready to return to his old allegiance,[12] but Derby no doubt wrote him more with hope than expectation of success.

Writing Gladstone on February 21st, Derby merely promised that, if Gladstone accepted, his wishes in so far as possible would be consulted in distributing offices, but he did not offer him any specific position. Anticipating that Gladstone would prefer an offer which included others of the Peelite group, Derby explained that he would have contacted Sidney Herbert, but felt that Herbert was now too closely associated with Lord John Russell to entertain a proposition.[13] No doubt this tie also influenced Derby's thinking with regard to Graham, who now was also a Russellite. Gladstone's reply was polite, even warm in some places, but he again found reasons for declining, including an assertion that alone he could render Derby little service, and would, in fact, be a source of weakness to him because of the anti-Gladstone faction within the Conservative Party.[14] His reply had the approval of Aberdeen, Herbert and Graham[15] and they may have been responsible for the deletion in the final draft of a lead which could have led to further and perhaps even successful negotiations. 'Should I have failed to state it [his sentiment on the subject] clearly, and you wish to see me upon it, I will readily wait upon you', wrote Gladstone, but then he crossed it out.[16] This closed the door to further negotiations. About the same time, however, the Radicals were opening theirs to Gladstone.*

Grey's reply was more brief, and even more definite in its refusal. As his political friends would be in opposition to Derby's Government, Grey decided that it would not be useful or honourable for him to join.[17] Later Grey is quoted as stating, had it not been for Disraeli, he would have accepted, and that Gladstone, too, would have joined, had he been offered the lead in the Commons.[18] This was, no doubt, an over-simplification of their motives, but at the same time indicates that neither refused because of a dislike for the Conservative Party leader.

By Sunday night Derby was discouraged. Gladstone and Grey had declined. There were objections to Ellenborough at the War Office, and he was advised by the Queen to apply to the Duke of Richmond. St. Leonards, because of his advanced age, had declined the Chancellorship, and Derby was about to contact Pemberton Leigh, a 'true friend' who had refused before, but

* John Bright wrote as follows: 'If you join Lord Derby, you link your fortunes with a constant minority, & with a party in the Country which is every day lessening in numbers & in power. If you remain on our side of the House, you are with the majority, & no Government can be formed without you . . . and I know nothing that can prevent your being Prime Minister before you approach the age of every other member of the House who has or can have any claim to that high office.' *Gladstone Papers*, BM 44112. (Bright to Gladstone, February 21st, 1858). In his reply to Bright, Gladstone was careful to note that he had reached a decision *before* receiving Bright's letter.

might now accept 'if he thinks we are not likely to be long lived, then he will have his peerage for nothing'.[19] Stanley, who thought they should not have accepted office without outside aid, was disinclined to join the Government. Informing Disraeli of these developments, Derby added he must report 'progress, no progress or retrograde' to the Queen the following afternoon, and asked his lieutenant to call the next morning.

At such moments Disraeli revealed the strength of his own character, and his own determination was communicated through his letters. 'I have just heard that *The Times* has decided to support you. So much for public opinion. Delane says we "shall do much better without Gladstone". Assuming that General Peel does not join, I have drawn up a complete scheme with the resources at our command. It will obtain public respect. There is really only one sorrow in all this: it draws tears from my eyes, and from your heart, I am sure, drops of blood. What mortifies me most is that I feel he [Stanley] is making a great mistake.'[20]

Very slowly the Cabinet took form. St. Leonards refused to reconsider, and the Lord Chancellorship, after likewise being rejected by Pemberton Leigh, was given to Sir Frederic Thesiger, who became Lord Chelmsford. While not considered outstanding, Thesiger was popular with members of his profession, and his elevation was viewed with satisfaction.[21] Stanley, who had achieved such eminence that Graham expected him eventually to lead the Whig Party, was put under great pressure by Malmesbury, Disraeli and probably his family, and finally accepted the Colonial Office.[22] General Peel received the War Secretaryship. Of him, Derby wrote: 'Of J. Peel I know little: and what little I know I do not admire, but he is an able man, though unpopular.'[23] But the Conservatives were glad to secure him, for the acceptance of office by Peel's younger brother seemed to symbolize the end of the Conservative split.

Another Peelite, Newcastle, probably for motives of personal ambition, would not comply with the Queen's request to lend his services to Derby.[24] Malmesbury at the Foreign Office, S. H. Walpole as Home Secretary, Henley at the Board of Trade, Lord John Manners as First Commissioner of Works were, apart from Derby and Disraeli, the only Cabinet officers holding the same positions as in 1852. The Marquis of Salisbury became Lord President, the Earl of Hardwicke Lord Privy Seal, Sir John

Pakington First Lord of the Admiralty, and the Earl of Ellenborough President of the Board of Control. Among the disappointed office seekers was Bulwer Lytton, who desired a peerage and wanted thus to avoid an election campaign. Derby, however, felt that he could only help them in the Commons, and refused to secure his elevation.[25] Eventually Lytton joined the Government as Colonial Secretary, but he was a source of concern again later. Young Robert Cecil applied for a minor position, but Derby was unable to accommodate him.[26]

The Derby Government of 1858 was stronger than that of 1852 not because it contained more prominent new men, but mainly because the Ministers were older, more experienced, and more respected in the Commons. Even Granville admitted that it was 'respectable enough'.[27] But it was again a minority government, holding office on sufferance, and dependent on the divisions of the Opposition. The Whigs, of course, were split into the Palmerston and Russell factions, and the Radicals were temporarily alienated from Palmerston because of his aggressive foreign policy and lack of interest in reform at home.[28] No doubt the Radicals also correctly reasoned that the Conservatives, hoping to strengthen their party by a long term of leadership, would pass many reforms that, in Opposition, they would oppose. The Peelites were hopelessly split. In the Lords, Newcastle was consistently hostile towards the Government, and Aberdeen was generally neutral. In the Commons, Cardwell and Herbert opposed the Government, while Graham and Gladstone supported it. By this time Cardwell had identified himself with Palmerston,[29] and Graham, in the twilight of his career, was a rather unenthusiastic follower of Russell.* Derby realized that this condition existed, and was aware that he might even expect support from the Radicals.[30]

Within his own party there were also divisions. Stanley, Ellenborough, Pakington and Lytton were quite as liberal as many of the Whigs and Peelites; but Walpole, Manners, Henley, Beresford, Newdegate and many others were highly conservative. The former group was more influential in Parliament; the latter

* Graham wrote in 1859: 'Friends drop so fast around me, that I am almost tempted sometimes to say, "I'd join the Party, who repose without." It is better far than any Party, which I see surviving.' *Cardwell Papers*, PRO 30/48 47. (Graham to Cardwell, January 16th, 1859). His attitude towards Derby and the Conservatives was still unfavourable. Ibid. (Graham to Cardwell, January 21st, 22nd, 1858).

more accurately reflected the sentiments of the Conservative voters as a whole. During the 1858-59 Administration, Derby and Disraeli had to walk a tight-rope between these two divisions, and at the same time they had to consider the ideas and wishes of the factions within the heterogeneous Opposition, and the sentiments of their relatively few Scotch and Irish supporters. Disraeli by this time was conservative in his thinking, but he was not hampered by being so closely identified with the party's principles as was Derby, and was constantly alive to tactical possibilities which Derby might overlook. His function was to observe, to study and to make suggestions. It fell to Derby to find means of reconciling these ideas with the party's principles, for, in his time, Derby was the arbiter of conservatism, and many in the rank and file would accept his definition of it.

It was up to these men to fashion a new conservatism, and, in a sense, to direct it along the path pointed out by Sir Robert Peel, but which, because of Peel's precipitancy and failure to compromise, had been obscured for twelve years. Some Liberals hoped to see 'the Conservative Ministers sitting night after night to be macadamized under the hammers of a Liberal majority',[31] and, on accepting office, Derby realized they had to take that chance. If he followed his 1852 programme and sought to rally the anti-democratic forces of England, it was bound to occur. His experiences of 1852, indeed, had made a profound impression on him. In spite of his efforts the 'Old Whigs' had failed to rally behind him, and he had gone down without the thanks or well wishes of many of his own class. Since that time, and because of this experience, Derby's ideas had been gradually changing. His fear of the lower classes in 1858 was not nearly as deep as it had been during the revolutionary period a decade before, and he now admitted that the 'considerable democratic element' in Parliament had shielded Britain from the revolutions that had disturbed the continental nations.[32] He did not, and never would, idealize democracy, but, being a practical man, Derby would not hide his head in the sand and pretend that the movement was not a growing factor in political life. In such a situation, he could resist it, but that would lead to a repetition of 1852; or he could seek to promote it, but that might lead to a disruption of his party. So he decided to do neither, but to seek a middle way. This time he would attend democracy for one mile, if not for the second. This decision, which had the cordial support of Disraeli, was of major importance in the history of the Conservative Party, and set the tone for his difficult second Administration.

On March 1st Derby appeared before the Lords to explain the events which had brought him to power, and to furnish them the outlines of governmental policy. Their lordships heard a man who, from time and illness, had aged considerably since 1852, whose voice had lost some of its compelling qualities, and who, as he had seldom done before, used notes as a crutch for his memory.[33] But he told the story of his efforts to secure aid in forming his Government with all of his old frankness, and once more enunciated his intention to refrain from interference in the internal affairs of any nation, while, on the positive side, he declared his intention to improve relations with France.

Going on to domestic issues, Derby described beautifully and tellingly the philosophy of his new Government:[34]

> My Lords, there can be no greater mistake than to suppose that a Conservative Ministry necessarily means a stationary Ministry. We live in an age of constant progress, moral, social and political ... Our constitution itself is the result of a series of perpetual changes. Like the venerable old country houses of England, it has been framed from time to time by successive occupants, with no great regard for architectural uniformity or regularity of outline, but adding a window here, throwing out a gable there, and making some fresh accommodation in another place, as might appear to suit, not the beauty of the external structure, but the convenience and comfort of the inhabitants. My Lords, in politics, as in everything else, the same course must be pursued — constant progress, improving upon the old system, adapting our institutions to the altered purposes they are intended to serve, and by judicious changes meeting the demands of society.

In keeping with these sentiments, Derby promised, when time would permit, to study the problem of Reform, and to bring in a measure which would be acceptable to all 'moderate, impartial and well-educated men'.[35]

This promise of a major change in Conservative policy alarmed rather than satisfied the Liberals, who would have much preferred to deal with a stand-pat administration that might be thrown out at any time. 'Our fear', wrote the *Edinburgh Review*, 'is rather that, like other new converts, they may caricature the doctrines of the party to which they apostatize . . . they may propose wild and fantastic measures intended to captivate the tastes of the uneducated classes, and though Conservatives in name, they become destructive in reality.'[36] The old Peelite, Herbert, expressed much the same fear when he noted: 'If Derby goes for universal suffrage, Palmerston and Johnny will produce the women and children.'[37] The idea current in 1852 that the Conservatives would attempt a reaction which inevitably would be followed by a republican revolution was long since laid to rest. Nevertheless, the reception of Derby's speech was fairly good, and a few of his old opponents stood ready to co-operate with him.*

Of more importance than Derby's speech, however, was a telling victory in the field of foreign affairs. Malmesbury and Derby discussed the Walewski dispatch with the excitable French minister, de Persigny, and arrived at a solution which allowed both sides to retreat with dignity. Though Clarendon had warned Derby that the feeling in France was hostile towards England, Malmesbury diagnosed the situation more correctly when he observed that Napoleon III was 'pretending to be more angry than he really is' to please his countrymen. The Foreign Secretary, after the consultation with de Persigny, sent a dignified, but conciliatory answer to the Walewski dispatch, and the French Government, in turn, wrote a wholly satisfactory reply to Malmesbury. The latter arrived just before Disraeli was to meet the Commons, and the Commons' leader almost knocked over a messenger in his haste to receive it.[38] Though a victory for the Government, the Opposition did not acknowledge it as such, and the absolute silence that greeted Disraeli when he announced it almost 'daunted' him.[39]

Another major problem inherited from the Palmerston régime was the reorganization of the government of India. Palmerston had introduced a bill to transfer the Indian government from the East India Company to the Crown, but he had been defeated before it passed. Lord Ellenborough, the President of the Board of Control, drew up his own measure, creating a governmental council which was partly elective and partly appointive, and which

* Greville wrote: 'It is curious that I should be acting a friendly part towards Derby's Government, he being of all men the one to whom I have felt the greatest political and personal repugnance.' S&F, *Greville*, VI, 348. (*Diary*, March 2nd, 1858). This should be borne in mind when evaluating Greville's observations on Derby's character.

is best remembered for having almost overthrown the Government. On March 28th Granville wrote that the plan was regarded with universal reprobation, and the only question was whether Palmerston or Russell would replace Derby.[40] Palmerston held a political meeting on March 29th to determine the best way to defeat the measure, and he had reason to think that Russell was ready to attack it also.[41]

But Russell hesitated. Though Palmerston was a fellow Whig, his principles were similar to Derby's on domestic issues,[42] and, as Russell saw no means by which he could again become Prime Minister, there seemed to be little point in aiding Palmerston. So he penned a letter to Derby suggesting that the groundwork for an India Bill be laid through resolutions debated by a committee of the whole House, and he cited a similar tactic used by Liverpool in 1813 as a precedent. He warned, however, that he would not guarantee his course if Derby persisted with the Ellenborough bill.[43] But he did not send the letter;* and instead explained the plan to a friend, who conveyed it to Disraeli, who communicated it to Derby on April 2nd.[44] Speaking on April 5th at the Mansion House, Derby indicated his acceptance of the plan by requesting the co-operation of Parliament and the country in constructing the new government, and at a Cabinet meeting of about April 8th, the Conservatives agreed to the course.[45]

While he gratefully accepted Russell's aid, Derby nevertheless wanted an India Bill designed by his Government. The Cabinet drew up the substance and phraseology of the resolutions, but, to Derby's consternation, Disraeli arbitrarily introduced some changes in them,[46] and the House as a whole had a hand in constructing the measure. Derby later expressed pleasure at the final form of the bill, and also at the conciliatory manner in which discussions on it had taken place in the Commons,[47] but he wrote to Disraeli in May: 'I think you will be attacked for having taken too much credit for ourselves in the India question.'[48] Nevertheless, the India Bill, which ended the East India Company's rule in British India and transferred control of the sub-continent to the Crown, was a landmark in Derby's second Administration.

* As Russell's draft letter is undated, the sequence of events is not clear. In his letter to Derby, Disraeli suggested that the plan outlined to him by an unidentified liberal had probably been originated by Russell. M&B, *Disraeli*, I, 1529-30. (Disraeli to Derby, April 2nd, 1858). It seems probable that Russell adopted the indirect means after deciding not to contact Derby personally.

As Derby had anticipated, the lot of a minority Prime Minister was not an enviable one, and his nerves were frayed by minor dissensions which arose with disturbing frequency. 'These eternal changes are very annoying', he wrote Disraeli when a minor incident arose in March. 'What do you say to this letter? Let me know your opinion and I will act on it.'[49] Disraeli's Budget, however, passed easily even though Disraeli proclaimed his hope that the income tax would eventually be abolished. Derby immediately sent his Chancellor of the Exchequer a note of congratulation and encouragement.[50]

Such encouragement was abundantly necessary, for the Conservatives had hardly surmounted the obstacles of the government of India and the Budget when an even more serious threat appeared. The Sepoy Rebellion left the Derby Administration with the problem of punishing those who had taken up arms against the British in India. Oudh had been the centre of the revolt, and, when the fall of its capitol at Lucknow was imminent, Canning, the Governor-General, issued a proclamation declaring the property within the province forfeit to the Crown. These severe terms were challenged by Sir James Outram, the Chief Commissioner of Oudh, and it was finally decided that confiscations should be made only in exceptional cases. The original proclamation, however, unamended, had already been sent to the Home Government along with a covering letter wherein Canning stated he could not find time just then to explain the reasons for his severity. The proclamation and covering letter both reached England while Palmerston was still in power, and, according to Derby, Palmerston turned over the proclamation, but intentionally neglected to give the covering letter to Ellenborough.[51] Lord Ellenborough, then, could not take Canning's explanation into consideration.

Ellenborough, after reading the proclamation, wrote a dispatch roundly condemning the programme of confiscations contemplated by Canning. Derby and Disraeli, before coming to power, were known to be critical of Canning, and the Governor-General had stayed on rather unwillingly when they took office.[52] Ellenborough's dispatch, then, appeared to be an outgrowth of this hostility, for Derby and Disraeli had both seen it in April shortly after it was written, and had approved of its contents.[53] Proud of the humanitarian sentiments contained in his work, Ellenborough made a grave error by sending copies of the document to Granville and Bright. The news of it got out, and the full text of the Ellenborough dispatch was laid on the table of the House of Commons on May 7th. In that way, the public learned of the censure of Canning before the Governor-General himself received it, or had had a chance to defend himself. 'Nothing could be worse,' Malmesbury wrote on May 8th, 'and it may lead to the resignation of the Government, or, at all events to a dissolution.'[54]

Public opinion was strong against the Conservatives for their quick censure of a man working at a most difficult task, and the move was regarded by some as a crude attempt by the Government to discredit Canning. The Queen was somewhat nettled also, in her case because the dispatch was sent without her having seen and approved it.[55] Derby hastened to the Palace to smooth things over, but, on leaving after his audience, he remarked gloomily: 'We have been beaten horse and foot.'[56] In these difficult circumstances, with the error of the Government so apparent to all, there was little that could be done immediately. On May 10th Malmesbury hastily sent an apology to Canning, but this did nothing to absolve the Government of its error. Palmerston, of course, could not let such an opportunity slip by. Originally it was planned that Palmerston in the Commons and Granville in the Lords would call for censure of the Government, but later it was decided to assign the task to Cardwell and Lord Shaftesbury.

Ellenborough, now 'miserably crestfallen', did what he could to extricate his colleagues from the situation, first by tendering his resignation to the Queen while still pledging out-of-office support to the Government, and then by rising in the Lords and, in an excellent speech, accepting full personal responsibility for the error.[57] Derby hoped that this act of his former colleague would lead to a withdrawal of the motions of censure,[58] but, if the Opposition persisted in its attack, he had one more card to play—dissolution. Many members of the 'Palmerston Parliament' were none too sure of re-election, and would be anxious to avoid both the expense and uncertainty of standing again so soon.[59] Derby could not be sure, however, but that the Queen might refuse a dissolution and merely try a new combination if his Government were defeated. When, after Ellenborough's resignation, the Opposition gave no sign of calling off its attack, the dissolution question became a pressing one.

To use dissolution as a threat, Derby had to be absolutely sure that the Queen, upon request, would grant it, or run the risk of spreading a false rumour. Visiting the Palace on May 11th, he asked for a definite promise that a dissolution would be granted if the Government were censured. While the Queen said that he might 'take the benefit of the doubt' in talking to others on the subject, she refused to commit herself in advance and dwelled upon the inconvenience of so frequent dissolutions. Derby was 'very much disappointed and mortified' by her attitude, and left the Palace fearing that the Queen might refuse a dissolution.[60] Because of this uncertainty, it was impossible to try to use dissolution as a weapon.

Derby's request disturbed the Queen, who was none too certain as to her prerogatives in such a situation, and she contacted a man whom she trusted implicitly – Lord Aberdeen. Aberdeen agreed that the Queen was not warranted in promising a dissolution in advance, but he pointed out that, if a Prime Minister requested a dissolution, the Crown was bound to grant it. Theoretically, the Crown could refuse, but Aberdeen could think of no precedent for such a refusal for it would automatically dismiss the Prime Minister who made the request. He advised, therefore, that the Queen comply with the request, if Derby asked for a dissolution. When asked who might replace Derby if he resigned, Aberdeen opined that Palmerston would have to be recalled.[61] This last point indicates perhaps the Queen's trend of thought. As Derby's Government was obviously weak, she would probably have preferred its replacement by a stronger one, but not if Palmerston, whom she disliked, headed it.

Aberdeen's attitude was of great consequence in this crisis.* While his former intimacy with Derby had not been resumed after 1852, he still preferred the Conservative moderate foreign policy to the jingoism of Palmerston. Consequently, when the debate on the censure came up in the Lords on May 14th, he refrained from attacking Derby, and abstained from the division altogether. While Ellenborough made another great speech, Aberdeen's attitude was the decisive factor in the situation, and even the weight of their proxies could not bring victory to the Opposition.[62]

* Granville said Aberdeen was under the influence of a more powerful and youthful mind, probably referring to Gladstone. Fitzmaurice, *Granville*, I, 307. (Granville to Canning, May 17th, 1858).

But the victory by merely nine votes in the Lords, where the Conservatives were usually strong, seemed to presage a disaster when the matter came to a division in the Commons.

Palmerston meanwhile was spreading a rumour that the Queen had refused dissolution. Writing to Derby on May 16th, two days after the debate had begun, Disraeli painted a rather dreary picture of their prospects.[63] All of the Peelites, save Gladstone, were hostile, or indifferent, and many other members were swinging to Palmerston because of the dissolution situation. Everything depended on the attitude of the Queen, and to a lesser extent on Aberdeen, whom Derby and Disraeli were at this time trying to enlist in their cause. That same day, however, Derby won a major victory. In an interview with the Queen, Derby bluntly declared that, unless he received assurance of a dissolution, his Government would be beaten by anywhere from 15 to 35 votes. Rather than bear the return of Palmerston, the Queen assured him that, if necessary, a dissolution would be granted, but she trusted he would not use this information dishonourably. Greatly relieved, Derby observed that, had he been forced out, he would have retired from public life, and the Conservative Party would have been for ever broken up. A dissolution, however, would probably bring the party a 'large gain'.[64]

Once Derby had received this assurance, the game was won. Some of the Peelites, Gladstone, Graham and probably Aberdeen, now worked to prevent a disruption of the Government. Graham's attitude was for a time so helpful that Derby offered him a seat in the Cabinet, but his old friend refused, noting that he was too old and broken in health, and that his sympathies were with Russell.[65] The support of the fading Peelites was of great consequence, and the Conservative Party was transformed from a beaten party into an aggressive one.[66] The threat of dissolution worked like magic. At the last moment about one hundred Radicals agreed to do anything to prevent such an occurrence. Certain of defeat, Cardwell, after a consultation with Palmerston, withdrew his motion, and the end result of the attack was aptly expressed by Granville when he observed: 'We cut rather a foolish figure.'[67]

To Derby this parliamentary victory brought some satisfaction, if only because he gained a tactical victory over Palmerston. Yet such a feeling was only momentary. Victory meant a return to the 'galling servitude' of a minority Prime Minister, with all its scrambling for votes, coddling of independent members, incessant compromises, and constant insecurity. The brunt of the weight fell, of course, on his Chancellor of the Exchequer, who daily fought for the party in a hostile house. If Disraeli could stand it, Derby felt that he could also. Disraeli survived on his nerve; Derby, on his prestige. Together they would get on somehow.

Cobden was right in his prediction that the Conservatives once in office would make concessions to the reform spirit, and it was to the credit of the second Derby Administration that Jewish parliamentary disabilities were removed. A clause in the parliamentary oath pledging the 'true faith of a Christian' rendered it impossible for anyone of the Jewish persuasion to be seated. The Commons had generally been in favour of altering the oath in the case of Jewish members, and year after year bills for this purpose had been brought in and passed, only to be rejected by the Lords. When, in 1854, the Commons themselves rejected such a bill, *The Times* had observed sarcastically: '. . . instead of the Jews falling into the hands of the Norman barons, they have met their fate from the Saxon churls of the Lower House . . . We are concerned for the Lords. What will they do without their annual pastime?'[68] The statement indicates the perennial nature of the bill.

The admission of Jews into Parliament involved a number of questions, such as the prayers offered daily in Christian form, the possibility thereafter of creating Jewish peers to sit in the Lords, and whether or not those of the Jewish faith should be allowed to legislate in matters affecting the Established Church. Add to these religious bigotry, not uncommon in any country during the nineteenth century, and the reasons for the continual rejection of the bill become clear. Which of these considerations weighed most heavily on Derby's mind is not certain. He had no prejudices against the Jews as a race, but he apparently did not trust them as a religious group. This is indicated by his observation that he would not feel comfortable with a Jew as Chancellor of the Exchequer,[69] a position which he pressed on the Christianized Jew, Disraeli. Derby considered the Jews to be alien in culture, and, as he regarded membership of Parliament as a privilege rather than a right, it seemed logical to exclude them.[70]

Perhaps, however, his chief objection was to non-Anglicans legislating on Church matters.

The Conservative Party, as well as most of his class regardless of party, opposed an alteration of the oath in favour of the Jews. In the Lords, therefore, the amendment of the oath had to be introduced as part of a reform which all had to agree was badly needed. The parliamentary oath contained a number of obviously archaic elements. There were, for instance, clauses abjuring the doctrine that any excommunicated prince might be murdered, denying to any foreign potentate or prelate temporal or spiritual power in the realm, abjuring allegiance to the descendants of James II, whose line had died out. Session after session bills had been introduced ostensibly for the purpose of disposing of these inapplicable elements, but really to remove the 'true faith of a Christian' clause. In 1856 Derby had introduced a bill to delete the out-of-date portions of the oaths, but, when he received no support for the measure, he withdrew it.[71]

By 1858 Derby was obviously weakening in his opposition to the exclusion of the Jews. Reasons were piling up to cause this. In the first place, both Disraeli and Stanley consistently supported removal of this Jewish disability, and there was an obvious conflict within the leadership of the Conservative Party. Secondly, the Commons asserted the right to determine their own membership, and it seemed unwise to continue the running battle with them. Sometime that spring, Derby talked over the possibility of a compromise with Disraeli, but he was extremely wary of pushing the matter too fast. When Disraeli discovered this change of attitude, he contacted John Russell on the subject of compromise, and Derby, learning of this, remonstrated with him for rushing the matter.* Meanwhile, Lord Lyndhurst had introduced an Oaths Bill designed to serve the dual purpose of admitting Jews and striking out the archaic references. Speaking against the measure in April, Derby admitted the inconvenience of differing with his colleagues in the other house, but insisted on retaining the 'true faith' clause, and, in committee, he was successful in so doing.[72] Late in May, however, the Prime

* Derby's letter on the subject is unfortunately undated, and the '*possible* solution' he had in mind is not explained therein. Just what part Derby played in the eventual compromise, then, is rather uncertain. *Disraeli Papers*, Derby XII. (Derby to Disraeli, Sunday).

Minister suggested a compromise whereby a Jewish member might declare that the 'true faith' clause was not binding on his conscience.[73] This was a rather typical Derby expedient, which would secure the end in view without forcing the Lords seriously to modify their previous stand. This compromise, probably the one he had discussed earlier with Disraeli, was not accepted.

A delay, due to Derby's illness, prevented immediate action on a compromise plan. On July 1st, however, Derby supported a proposal offered by the Earl of Lucan, and appealed to his followers on the ground that a continued resistance to the Commons would be dangerous.[74] Lucan's bill simply allowed the Commons, if they chose, to pass a resolution admitting Jews. In Committee Derby tried to sugar-coat the measure for his followers by pointing out that it did not give the Jews an absolute right to sit in Parliament, and that the procedure outlined in the bill placed a moral restraint upon the Crown not to create a Jewish peer.[75] A little later, Derby was successful in securing the agreement of the Lords to the following statement:[76]

> Because, without imputing any disloyalty or disaffection to Her Majesty's Subjects of the Jewish Persuasion, the Lords consider that the Denial and Rejection of that Saviour, in whose Name each House of Parliament daily offers up its collective Prayers for the Divine Blessing on its Councils, constitutes a moral unfitness to take part in the Legislation of a professedly Christian Community.

The intent of this statement was probably to warn the Crown against the creation of a Jewish peer.

In retrospect, the conduct of Derby during the incident might be criticized if viewed in the light of twentieth-century idealism. According to Greville, Derby supported the compromise 'sulkily and reluctantly', and resorted to 'all sorts of paltry shifts and pretences to make up a show of consistency, and to make the sacrifice of their old prejudices somewhat palatable, or rather less painful and mortifying to his Party'.[77] Yet, Derby should not be judged outside of his century and the situation in which he found himself. While Derby supported the compromise, most of his followers refused to go along with him, and many expressed great fear that the peerage might now have been opened to Jews.[78] But he carried enough of his party with him, and enough proxies were obtained to secure passage of the measure, and, in the final analysis, that is what counted. Had he not swung his great prestige, reluctantly or otherwise, behind the measure, the reform might conceivably have been postponed for many years.

Apart from the India Bill and the Jewish question, there were few matters that session which primarily concerned Derby. Irish education was discussed briefly in March 1858, and, though Derby said united education had not realized his fondest hopes, he thought it should continue.[79] He agreed that opportunity for public service should be given to qualified members of the middle class, and in June he cautiously supported civil service examinations of a competitive type.[80] Derby also supported the abolition of the property qualification restriction for membership in the Commons, noting that the qualification included personal as well as landed property, and did not guarantee the independence of the individual members.[81]

Part of Derby's time, however, was spent in resisting legislation. He successfully opposed the appointment of a royal committee to study the liturgy because this might indicate they were considering the merits and demerits of the liturgy as such.[82] Still fighting a rear-guard action to maintain the Church's influence in educational matters, Derby disposed of a proposal to open the trusteeship of schools to Dissenters in all cases wherein they were not specifically excluded in the deed.[83] In July the introduction by the Duke of Somerset of a bill to abolish church rates gave Derby his opportunity to defend the property rights of the Church, and to call for a large majority against the measure.[84] He was never, of course, more effective than when he defended this dogma of conservatism.

While the legislation of the session was not discreditable, the Conservatives might have done better if their time had not been divided between trying to govern and warding off hostile attacks. Following Ellenborough's resignation there was a Cabinet opening which Derby hoped, but probably did not expect, could be used to strengthen his Government. On May 22nd Derby offered Gladstone his choice of the Board of Control or the Colonial Office, and Disraeli, who the week before had unsuccessfully tried to surrender the lead to Graham, wrote Gladstone urging strongly to accept. Once again Gladstone consulted his friends, and this time Graham encouraged him to join Derby, but he hesitated until Derby, who had to settle the matter as soon as possible, wrote him a brief letter of inquiry on May 26th.[85] Gladstone's reply came the same day, and once again he insisted that, alone, he could not help strengthen the Government; but he kept the door open slightly by suggesting that Derby should sound Aberdeen with a view to a coalition.[86] Derby took this to be a refusal, but Disraeli and Stanley still had hopes,[87] and on May 28th Stanley was sent to consult with Aberdeen. The interview proved the impossibility of a coalition, and the Conservatives had to reshuffle their own men, Stanley taking the Board of Control, and Lytton, according to Derby's directions, going to the Colonial Office.[88]

Disraeli about this time made a rather intemperate speech at Slough in which he praised the accomplishments of the Government and declared a 'cabal' existed for the purpose of overthrowing them. Derby thought the speech read well, but was 'not light on my friend L. Shaftesbury'.* Early in June, Derby in the Lords and Disraeli in the Commons were called upon to defend the speech at Slough. The Old Whig, Clarendon, attacked the speech, and Derby defended it, crediting his Government with successful financial and foreign policies, and darkly alluding to the party intrigues which had been designed to scuttle the Budget.[89] Derby could well understand a speech such as Disraeli made at Slough, for, over his long career, he made a number of them himself.

The session of Parliament closed in August 1858, and the country had an opportunity to evaluate the merits and prospects of the Conservative Government. While opinions varied, and there was much disagreement concerning the ideals of the Government, conspicuously absent among the charges brought against it was that of reaction. The Old Whigs, whose refusal to support the Conservatives had given such power to the liberal forces in England, were especially fearful. Lord Campbell observed:[90]

> He [Derby] has been saved by dissensions of the Liberals, by truckling to Bright, and by courting the Radicals. I prophesied many years ago that in England the Whigs would be (as in America they are) the only true Conservatives. The Tories as a body are

* *Disraeli Papers*, Derby XII. (Derby to Disraeli, May 27th, 1858). Disraeli had called Shaftesbury 'Gamaliel himself, with the broad phylacteries of faction on his forehead'. Though Shaftesbury asserted his political neutrality, he was hostile towards the Conservative Government.

> still staunch and sincere, but the Tory leaders are ready to sacrifice the monarchy that they may keep their places. Democracy has made more progress in England during the last three months than during twenty years of Whig rule.

And the observations of Shaftesbury were even more caustic:[91]

> How are they [Derby's Government] in any sense, Conservative? They accept every proposition and make every concession. They refuse no committees and grant all inquiries. They yielded the county franchise, the property qualification; they are prepared to surrender the church rates. Their Law Officer gave an opinion which rendered further resistance to the Oaths Bill absurd. They introduced an India Bill so ultra-democratical that it was repudiated by Bright, and they pledged themselves to Reform. In what sense, and of what are they Conservatives?

Prince Albert was apparently convinced that the 'weak and incapable Tory Government' had entered into a secret bargain with the Radicals.[92] These statements indicate how successfully, by 1858, the Conservatives had sloughed off the vestments of reaction which the Whigs had pinned on them a decade before.

Among the Opposition opinion varied as to the probable life span of the Conservative Government. The Duke of Argyll, an influential Whig and friend of Gladstone's, was pleased with the session and professed his readiness to aid Derby rather than the liberals who so frequently sacrificed their principles for Radical support.[93] Lord John Russell gave the Government until the following February, but when Derby sold his stud that summer, he was worried lest this indicate the Prime Minister expected to be in power for years rather than months. Granville gloomily predicted that the Conservatives were good for two or three years, after which they would lose out through their accumulated mistakes. Herbert thought the Government would continue into 1861, and Lyndhurst felt that 'only a chapter of incidents' would turn them out. At the moment, the key to the situation was the continued estrangement between Russell and Palmerston, but, in Conservative circles, there was some hope of converting their minority into a majority. A proper Reform Bill might create an enlarged group of voters in their favour, but just who these new voters were to be was a topic of controversy which lasted throughout the summer.

The problem of Reform had always fascinated Derby, along with most statesmen of his age, because therein lay such tremendous possibilities for the building up of a party. Over a period of years, his thinking on the subject went through a slow evolutionary process, which can be traced only imperfectly. When the subject arose back in 1851, he wrote Croker in September of that year that they must not resist all change, for that would give the Opposition too great a political advantage.[94] Writing Disraeli the following month, he decided that they should not pledge themselves against Reform but merely try to prevent any 'extensive alteration' as being uncalled for.[95] Coming to power in 1852, however, he refused to legislate on Reform because there was no real demand for it. Late in 1853 he was fearful that Aberdeen meant to make the county and borough franchises identical, and abolish a distinction which Derby felt it was important to maintain; viz., the county franchise which was based on permanence and property ownership, and the borough franchise which was based on mere evidence of occupation. To eliminate the distinction, he felt, would be eventually to abolish the property qualification in favour of personal qualification.[96] At this time he also opposed the ballot, and thought any intellectual or educational franchise would be impracticable and probably unpopular. Speaking in Parliament in January 1854, he suggested that action on Reform be postponed, and declared against attempts to increase the borough representation as against that of the counties.[97] The following month, however, he promised respectful consideration to any measure of Reform which might be introduced by the Government. Derby, then, up to this time was not pledged against all Reform, but was committed to a conservative approach to it. For a time the Crimean War and other matters postponed the Reform agitation.

In April 1857 Derby again, by letter, took up the Reform question with Disraeli, anticipating that the Government would probably, under the urging of Russell, bring forth a bill. Derby concluded that, as Conservatives, they should declare they had been willing to allow the settlement of 1832 to go unaltered, but, since the subject had come up, they were ready to remove the 'inequalities and defects' of the system.* Again he advised that

* Here, as always, Derby had to consider fully the wishes of his party. He advised Disraeli against bringing up the subject of Reform, if it did not appear in the Speech,

the distinction between the county and borough franchises be maintained, but this left unsolved the question of the £10 householders who lived in the counties. To add them to the county voters would have undermined the county representation, so Derby proposed a scheme which had suggested itself to him in 1854; viz., to allow such householders to vote in the boroughs. Concluding his observations, Derby added: 'We ought to resist lowering the franchise, abolition of Rate-paying Clauses, and the Ballot . . .'[98] His thinking up to this point, then, is quite clear. While willing to make adjustments in the settlement of 1832, Derby was not ready to democratize the legislature.

Speaking in December 1857 Derby admitted that the present Reform Act was not perfect, and expressed a willingness to consider any changes offered by Palmerston.[99] As, at the time, he had no intimation that he would shortly be in power, this statement cleared the way for him to take up the problem when in office. There was not, however, much popular demand for Reform until the following summer, when the Radicals began a campaign for a new measure. On their part, the various Conservatives set out to meet the demand.

During the early stages of collecting facts and figures, Philip Rose, an influential party worker, did considerable work, and he came to favour an experimental adoption of the ballot, and a lowering of the borough qualification to £6.[100] Stanley and Disraeli, meeting in August 1858 decided on a four-point programme which included a lowering of the qualification in the counties to make it identical with the borough franchise, possibly some new type franchises based on personal property, an optional ballot, and the disfranchisement of from sixty to ninety seats.[101] Derby remained undecided and open to suggestion through the summer and early autumn, but he was inclined to oppose any lowering of the borough franchise, especially to the level of £6, and to reduce the county franchise no lower than £25, while making only a limited disfranchisement.[102] The 'keystone' of Derby's programme was to make the freeholders in the boroughs voters in the boroughs rather than in the counties as they were at present.[103] Disraeli did not consult Derby immediately on the question and

adding: 'We must, after all, look to our own adherents; and I do not think it would please them to see us apparently anxious to take up the Question . . .' *Disraeli Papers*, Derby XII. (Derby to Disraeli, April 24th, 1857).

in September Derby was again stricken with gout and in bed. The attack was kept secret until Derby had recovered, but it discouraged Disraeli, who noted: 'Nothing disheartens a party as much as an invalid chief, and they are always afraid he is going to die and break up the Ministry.'[104] This is the first appearance of the term 'invalid' in describing Derby, and it was probably an exaggeration, for, on October 23rd, Malmesbury found him 'in great force'.[105]

Derby was in the best of spirits at the first Cabinet council on November 3rd, and the situation he entered certainly wanted a man of both mental and physical endurance. He did not attempt to dictate his own ideas to the Cabinet. On the various aspects of the Reform plan votes were taken and each member's vote was weighted equally. On one unidentified point on December 3rd, Derby was badly beaten. He, Malmesbury and Manners at this time seem to have been in a centre position between the highly conservative wing, which included Chelmsford, Walpole, Henley, Hardwicke and Peel, and the liberal wing composed of Disraeli, Stanley, Pakington, Salisbury and Lytton. Disraeli, however, always considered Derby's feelings and views, and often acted as a mediator.[106] On November 26th Derby drew up a draft programme, the points of which had been adopted by large majorities in the Cabinet.

It was generally agreed that the Reform would apply to England only, with Scotland to be left for later consideration, and Ireland to go unchanged. As opinions on the borough suffrage ranged all the way from manhood suffrage to little or no change, it was decided not to reduce the borough qualification, but to cause the freeholders and leaseholders in the boroughs to vote in the boroughs rather than the counties. A lodger franchise based on £20 and a year's residence was tentatively agreed upon. The county occupation franchise was to be reduced to the borough figure of £10. This large added group of county voters made it possible for them to propose an increase in the county representation. Boroughs of less than 5000 population were to lose their seats, and those between 5000 and 15,000 were to be partly disfranchised. These sources provided 73 seats for distribution, and of these 52 would go to the counties, 18 would be distributed among under-represented boroughs, and 3 would be given to the Universities or Scotland. The ballot, in any form, was to be resisted.[107]

In this form, the proposed bill was conservative. It would have added the well-to-do lodgers, who were moderates, given a large block of seats to the counties, which were made free of the leasehold and freehold voters, and would have continued to exclude the unpredictable lower classes of the city. But the draft report represented only a stage in the evolution of the Reform Bill, and not the final programme. By early December the Cabinet was so divided that Malmesbury predicted they would not produce a Reform measure which would satisfy either themselves or the general public.[108] Peel, Henley and Walpole all made difficulties. Walpole objected to the assimilation of the borough and county franchises at any total, and wanted only slight disfranchisement. Henley accepted considerable disfranchisement, but was against the transfer of the borough freehold voters to the borough and the assimilation of the county and borough franchises. Peel, Pakington and Salisbury were likewise against the transfer.[109] Derby himself was rather fearful of reducing the county franchise to £10, and rather reluctantly consented to it on the basis of evidence presented by Joliffe.[110] After studying Rose's statistics, he felt that the transfer principle, which was objected to by the others, was actually the most conservative portion of the bill. Early in January, after reading Walpole's voluminous notes on the subject of Reform, Derby sought to reason with him. Noting that Walpole admitted the necessity of a Reform bill, Derby pointed out that it logically followed that the bill must have some chance of being passed, and that it must be extensive enough to put an end to demands for further Reform. In dealing with Walpole's objection to the assimilation of the two franchises, Derby reasoned that, once they admitted that personal property created the right to vote both in borough and county, it was impossible to maintain the distinction which he, Derby, had previously thought so important to uphold. Agreeing that the £10 county franchise was controversial, Derby urged that it be considered calmly, and warned Walpole of the seriousness of the defections at that time.*

January was a wearing, dragging, unruly month. Six months before Malmesbury had confidently observed to Disraeli '. . . you will find that in the pinch you command a Party better disciplined

* *Disraeli Papers*, Derby XII. (Derby to Walpole, January 6th, 1859). Walpole's notes were so bulky and complicated that Derby dubbed them the 'Chancery Brief'.

than any I ever recollect even in Peel's time'.[111] However, in the pinch it proved to be otherwise. The basic difficulty was determining which specific proposals were conservative, and which were dangerously radical. Stanley, for instance, felt that the ballot had a conservative tendency, though no one agreed with him.[112] Another vital consideration was to produce a bill that might be passed by Parliament, though Derby realized more fully the dangerous consequences of failure than did Disraeli.[113] Success in Parliament involved not only attracting liberal support for the measure, but also keeping in line the dissident members of the Conservative Party. To satisfy Walpole, and the rank and file of the party, Derby considered for a time reducing the county franchise to £16 rating,[114] but found his son strongly protested, not only on personal grounds, but because such a measure could not be passed.[115] Early in February the Duke of Montrose demanded that they consider Scotland in the Reform Bill, and thus beclouded one of the few issues on which the Cabinet had reached some unanimity.[116]

The Government, in fact, seemed on the point of disintegrating. Late in January Walpole and Henley resigned from the Cabinet, but they continued to attend Cabinet meetings until the bill was introduced in order to keep the schism a secret. Early in February Stanley talked of resigning, and sent his father a formal protest concerning a recent decision on disfranchisement. Lord Hardwicke and Peel felt that the bill was much too democratic, and the latter also talked of leaving the Cabinet. Malmesbury, discouraged at these internecine struggles, observed: 'It may possibly end in Lord Derby's resigning.'[117] Even Malmesbury and Disraeli added to Derby's burdens. Early in January the two became involved in a tiff regarding whether or not Disraeli had the right to make suggestions on foreign affairs, and the controversy ended with Disraeli's losing all confidence in his colleague's ability as Foreign Secretary.[118]

To further embarrass Derby, relations with the Court became rather touchy. The basic problem concerned the reorganization of the government of India, and the extent to which the Crown would control political, military and patronage matters there. Stanley favoured a maximum of parliamentary jurisdiction; the Court, of course, sought to preserve its influence. A series of unpleasantries followed. The Queen, in July 1858, objected to losing her prerogative with regard to peace and war in India, and the establishment of civil service examinations under the control of Parliament. Then there followed a controversy regarding the wording of the Royal Proclamation which was to announce the change of government. Stanley sought to minimize the religious references in this document, and the Queen finally turned the job over to Derby, to be done in his 'excellent' style. Then, there was the question of the control of the Indian army.* Early in February 1859 Derby received a protest from the Queen on the subject of the Indian army, and Derby, on February 6th, strongly hinted at resigning if the Queen persisted in her opposition to the Government reorganization plan.[119] On all of the questions involved, Derby sought to conciliate the Queen on the one hand, and his son, who favoured a minimum of Royal control, on the other. Edward Stanley apparently felt, for a time at least, that his father too often sided with the Queen; and the Queen occasionally accused Derby of not upholding her prerogatives. By spring 1859 most of the difficulties had been smoothed over.

While the Conservatives were engaged in exhausting internal struggles, the Opposition was watching them hostilely. They were interested in the Reform Bill, of course, but of it, owing to the policy of secrecy adopted by the Conservatives, they knew but little. In the autumn Derby had told Clarendon '. . . no one wanted a measure of Reform, yet that a measure there must be, and that it must not be a sham one, which would only irritate and lead to extensive demands'.[120] Palmerston thought Derby would bring in a moderate bill, but that Disraeli would probably attach some 'absurd' provisions to it. Argyll reported nervously to Aberdeen in December that Derby might even allow the ballot to become optional.[121]

Russell's attitude was, of course, of great importance to the Conservatives, for his aid during the session had saved them from disaster. That autumn Russell visited Knowsley, and assured Derby that he would support a 'good' Conservative Bill just as if it were his own.[122] This visit caused some speculation as to a possible merger between the two old friends.[123] In writing to a friend late in November, however, Russell's discussion

* The Commander-in-Chief, the Duke of Cambridge, sought to control the discipline of the Indian army, and to give instructions direct to the Indian commander. Stanley wrote: 'It is scarcely necessary to say that the Premier is on the side of the D. of C., though he has used his influence in moderating the demands of the Court.' *Disraeli Papers*, Stanley XII. (Edward Stanley to Disraeli, October 5th, 1858).

of the Conservative Reform Bill had a slight note of hostility in it. 'When we have seen his scheme, we can nurse it or strangle it, as the majority think proper.'[124]

Between his autumn visit to Derby, and January 1859 Russell's attitude changed completely. He ceased to be tolerant of the Conservative Government, and, weeks before he knew the provisions of their Reform Bill, Russell was in a state of 'feverish excitement', laying plans for overthrowing the Conservatives.[125] Part of this hostility may have sprung from dislike of what he considered the pro-Austrian position of the Government in the Italian question; part, perhaps, from his ambition to return to office. This change of front doomed the Conservative Government, and Derby evidently felt it was inconsistent with the promises Russell had made at Knowsley. But no formal agreement was reached between Russell and Palmerston at this time, and the Government was allowed a few months more of life.

After long hours of conference and compromise, the Government constructed a Reform Bill. Derby thought it was both conservative and extensive, and it represented a compromise with his own views. The county occupation franchise was reduced to £10. Derby also gave up his objections, based largely on administrative considerations, to 'fancy franchises', and the vote was given to owners of a certain amount of personal property, to university graduates, ministers, lawyers, doctors and schoolteachers. On the other hand, there was no change in the borough franchise, and this was undoubtedly agreeable to Derby, as was the transfer of the urban freeholders from the counties to the boroughs. The disfranchising provisions were modest, a member was taken from each two-member borough with a population of less than 6000, and the seats distributed to certain counties and unrepresented towns. As Derby had predicted, it was not such as 'to excite any popular enthusiasm in its, or our, favour',[126] but it did give the vote to some obviously deserving people, and corrected some faults of the old system.

Disraeli introduced the bill into the Commons the last day of February. As Henley and Walpole did not attend, it was apparent to all that they had resigned. It was then a question whether the Conservatives could keep their ranks closed, or whether the Ultra-Conservative wing would join the revolt. The following day some 211 members meeting at Derby's residence expressed satisfaction with the bill, and shortly thereafter the Conservative peers, at a special meeting, likewise gave support to the measure.[127] But the ex-ministers, Henley and Walpole, who had promised to promote 'union', became the storm centres of rebellion and were joined by forty Conservative dissentients.[128] In mid-March there was a meeting of some House of Commons members, and, while they pledged allegiance to the Government, eight of them, including Beresford and Newdegate, decided to vote against the Reform Bill on its second reading.[129] However, they dispatched a delegation to Lord Derby asking him not to resign if beaten on the Reform Bill, but to demand a vote of confidence.[130] Derby's patience with his own party was by this time wearing thin. Shortly before, he had written Disraeli, '. . . I cannot submit to be dictated to where no real objection exists', and, on this occasion, he confided: 'We must command this Parliament, and throw the die for the next, and let our friends know that it is the last card.'[131] He was somewhat embarrassed also by Stanley's attitude. While his son spoke ineffectively in favour of the measure, in conversation with Bright he gave the Radical leader the impression of not really favouring the bill.[132]

On the other side of the House the situation was even more grim. Bright and the Radicals were, of course, hostile towards the measure because it was too moderate, and their opposition was to be expected. Russell had long since decided to oust the Government on the issue, and planned to attack by means of a critical resolution. For a time, at least, the Conservatives hoped to receive help from Palmerston, for the former Prime Minister had occasionally expressed a desire to have the Conservatives solve the problem in a moderate way. At this time, however, Palmerston was unwilling to risk having the Conservatives acquire new strength and perhaps lessen his own chances for office, and he likewise opposed the bill. Some years later, Clarendon looked back with regret at the activities of the Whigs at this time, and admitted they had behaved with 'shameful factiousness'.[133]

The debate in the Commons centred around a resolution by Russell condemning the change of the freehold franchise, and the failure to extend the borough franchise.* Derby decided to meet

* This objection would have been impossible had the Cabinet adopted Derby's suggestion that they recommend the Irish franchise of £12 and £8 for England. *Disraeli Papers*, Derby XII. (Derby to Disraeli, January 19th, 1860).

this threat by intimating that a defeat of the Government would mean dissolution, and he decided it was better to meet defeat on the Russell resolution, which would be regarded as a purely factious move, than to be beaten on a specific part of the bill which might not command support in a general election.[134] Disraeli defended the measure as best he could, and later in the debate still appeared rather confident of beating Russell.[135] This time, however, the Opposition managed to overcome the general fear of a dissolution, and in a House which Graham said was the fullest he had seen since 1835, the Russell resolution was carried by thirty-nine votes.

The defeat did not catch the Conservatives unprepared. On March 25th Derby advised Disraeli that the Queen had sanctioned the whole 'batch' of peers and baronets that he had recommended, but wanted a clearer view of their prospects of gain before promising a dissolution.[136] On March 30th Derby decided to advise the Queen that, if beaten, they would ask for an early, if not an immediate, dissolution.[137] A few days later the Queen wrote Derby and asked what was going on in the 'enemy's camp'.[138] On April 1st a party meeting was held, and the two leaders consulted as to the substance of their announcement of the dissolution. By this time Derby was greatly fatigued by the exertions and responsibilities of his position, and he predicted to Disraeli that he would not be able to carry off his part very well. While announcing the dissolution on April 4th, Derby's doubts were confirmed, for his speech was long and not well delivered.[139] But the speech was not without interesting passages. Its theme was the decline of the two-party system in Britain, and the factious state of the Opposition. It was on that issue, the disorganized state of the Commons, that they planned to appeal to the country. On various occasions in the past Derby had singled out a particular statesman for his verbal abuse – Aberdeen, Palmerston and Graham, as well as many others, had had their turns. But he never reviewed a man's career as he did Russell's. Noting that Lord John had helped overthrow more governments than any other statesman, Derby began in 1834, when Russell's 'imprudent statement' caused secessions from the Grey Government, and traced his career up to 1858, when Russell had been one of the 'principal executioners' of the Palmerston Government. Then he discussed the existing situation, and accused Russell of condemning a bill which added more voters to the electorate than Russell's own bill simply because he had not introduced it himself.[140] Perhaps it was not one of Derby's better speeches, but it revealed the resentment engendered by the cavalier treatment of his moderate bill. His faith in some of the 'Old Whigs' was considerably shaken, and to 'dish' them became an object much to be desired.

All the party leaders went before their constituents with slightly damaged reputations that spring. The Conservatives had alienated some of their supporters by their liberalism;* Palmerston's arrogance had offended some of his followers, and Russell's Radical leanings made him politically suspect. All were subject to attacks and smears in the press, and all were to some extent, at least, vulnerable.

While Derby had hoped the election would be held on the issue of the disorganized state of the Commons, foreign affairs crept in to play a major role. On the foreign scene the war of France and Sardinia against Austria occupied general attention, and among the British people sympathy generally lay with little Sardinia. In a speech early that year Derby predicted that Italy, because of her many conflicting interests, could not be united.[141] He also treated the Italian ambassador so coldly that he seldom spoke with Derby for fear of starting an argument. This lack of sympathy for Italian aspirations was, in fact, the main reason for his new-found popularity at Court, for the Queen and the Prince were quite partial to Austria.† If at all, Derby was only mildly pro-Austrian, but he had an isolationist's disgust with the troubles of other nations. While he frequently praised the French emperor because he wished to maintain friendly relations with France,

* The following letter from a Conservative member to Joliffe illustrates this point: 'Lord Derby and Mr. Disraeli have led the Conservative party to adopt every measure they opposed as Radical ten years ago. They have made that party the tool of their own ambition, & sacrificed everybody, private & public interest, beginning with Walpole. I do not think it creditable to the intelligence or to the honour of the Country Gentlemen of England to vote black to be white, or white to be black at their bidding.' *Disraeli Papers*, Joliffe XIII. (Henry Drummond to Joliffe, June 15th, 1859).

† Graham observed: 'It would be the first time in the Queen's reign when she placed herself in conflict with a majority of the House of Commons. She identifies her prerogative with the fate and fortunes of a falling Ministry. She marks a deeper sense of foreign relations than of domestic policy. She declares that Lord Derby and Lord Malmesbury alone are trustworthy in the management of foreign affairs.' Parker, *Graham*, II, 376. (*Graham Journal*, April 3rd, 1859).

Derby looked upon him as an impulsive and rather overbearing man.* At the same time, however, he felt that the Austrians were obstinate and gave considerable unnecessary offence and provocation. Early in 1859, when the tension began to grow in central Europe, Malmesbury had informed Apponyi, the Austrian ambassador, that England would furnish no aid in putting down an Italian insurrection.[142] The Conservatives maintained a wholly correct attitude towards all of the nations involved in the struggle, but the liberals, especially Palmerston, made political capital by supporting Italian independence warmly.

During the election, the French minister, Persigny, according to Malmesbury, helped to subsidize the Palmerston candidates in order to beat the Conservatives.[143] The Conservative coffers, however, were quite full, and Derby contributed perhaps £20,000 to the campaign fund.[144] The rumour of Derby's donation brought charges of bribery, and the Prime Minister later explained to the Lords that all parties customarily defrayed the expenses of candidates who were financially unable to bear them.[145]

Derby, of course, did not allow the contest to influence his social relationships. On May 13th at a concert at the Palace Derby was observed 'in the highest spirits, chaffing Lord Palmerston, Lord Clarendon and a number of other Whigs into the midst of which he had got and who were all roaring at his jokes'.[146] At the time of this incident Palmerston had already tentatively selected a government to replace Derby, and the latter was aware of it.[147] Shortly before, at the Royal Academy dinner, Derby had joked with Lord Campbell over their parliamentary battles in the Lords.[148]

Disraeli carried on the campaign in deadly earnest. It was apparent by April 30th, however, that the Conservatives would not secure a majority,[149] and early the following month he unsuccessfully sought to secure Lord Palmerston. Next, on May 8th, he asked Derby once again to contact Gladstone. There seemed to be a slim chance of success, for Gladstone had, the year before, accepted a governmental mission to go to the Ionian Islands, and he had also supported the Conservative Reform Bill. Derby, however, was not sanguine, and wrestled with his pride for more

* The Emperor reciprocated the feeling. Granville wrote: 'He [Napoleon] detests the Derby Government, and pines for Palmerston and Clarendon.' Fitzmaurice, *Granville*, I, 324. (Granville to Canning, February 9th, 1859).

than a week before writing his former colleague. It was hardly a hopeful letter:[150]

> Finding that you are returned to Town, having seen you pass at the Drawing room today, I should be obliged by your informing me whether you would object to have some private conversation with me on the present state of public affairs and political parties ... If, however, you feel any difficulty as to putting me fully in possession of your views and feelings, I shall not be the least affronted by your declining to call.

To this Gladstone replied: 'It is fair I should say that I am not an approver of the Dissolution, and that I am not able to flatter myself that in the present position of affairs I can make any useful suggestion.'[151] He agreed, however, to visit Derby if, after reading his note, the Prime Minister still desired to see him. On May 20th, Derby brought to an end the decade of attempts to bring Gladstone back to his party. 'I cannot conceal from myself that the general tenor of your note is not such as to lead to the hope of any satisfactory result of the conversation I had proposed; and I will not therefore give you the unnecessary trouble of calling here at 12 o'Clock.'[152] Then, to Disraeli: 'I think you will agree with me that it would have been useless to waste time by unmeaning conversation, leading to nothing – I own, I hardly regret it.'[153] Later that month Gladstone was so pleased with one of Palmerston's Italian speeches that he decided to join the man whose foreign policy he had always deplored. So Disraeli's negotiations had no positive results.

Some help came from an unexpected quarter. According to one source the Pope ordered the Roman Catholics to support the Derby Government, whose Italian policy he approved.[154] At the opening of Parliament, Derby acknowledged Catholic support, but he hastened to deny his Government had entered into a bargain with them, or promised them anything which might injure the Established Church.[155] The Conservatives thus faced the new Parliament with about twenty-five new seats gained in the election, some small support from the independent liberal groups, the support of the Roman Catholics and the cordial best wishes of the Throne.

As late as May 20th Derby did not expect that the Whigs would attack them on the Address,[156] and he probably relied on the continued alienation between Palmerston and Russell to prevent it.

On May 29th, however, Palmerston made an indirect overture to Russell, suggesting, through Granville, that they simply agree to serve in the same Cabinet if the Government were overturned, leaving the problem of who should be the Prime Minister in abeyance.[157] Russell demurred at this suggestion, but at a meeting at Willis's rooms early in June, the Whig Party largely accepted Palmerston's suggestion.[158] So, while the Whig ranks were still not entirely closed, and their means of forming a government were not too clear, they were all decided on one point — that Derby must go.

Two almost evenly matched political groups were committed to action on June 7th. The Opposition plan was not to attack a specific measure of the Government, but to offer a no-confidence amendment to the Address. On the first night 17 Opposition members had not yet taken their seats, and Disraeli unsuccessfully sought to force an immediate division.[159] Night by night, almost hour by hour, as the debate continued, the reports from the House of Commons became ever more hopeless, and it became obvious to Derby and Disraeli that their patient, the Second Derby Ministry, was dying. On June 10th Derby advised the Queen that the situation was critical,[160] and the same day Disraeli, like a physician driven to his last resort, proposed a heroic remedy. Both he and Derby should resign, leaving Stanley to form a coalition and become the next Prime Minister.[161] Derby rejected the suggestion, knowing, no doubt, that his son could not command the support of the Conservative Party. The plan, no doubt, merely reflected Disraeli's desperation. The following day the amendment was carried against the Government by 13 votes. The margin this time was even smaller than in 1852, when they had been beaten by 19 votes. While it was maddeningly close, they could not have continued for long even if they had, for the moment, gained a slight majority.

Such a majority could probably have been obtained had it not been for a tactical mistake on Disraeli's part. Malmesbury attributed the defeat to his colleague's failure to lay the Blue Book containing the Italian and French correspondence on the table of the Commons, for the book would have shown that Britain had tried to prevent the outbreak of the war in central Europe, and had pursued a neutral and unbiased course. The Foreign Minister noted that twelve to fourteen individuals, including Cobden, who voted against them, later told him they would have supported the

Government if Disraeli had produced the Blue Book.[162] Malmesbury undoubtedly realized the importance of these papers at the time, for he wrote Disraeli on June 7th: 'In the event of an *adverse* division how are the Italian papers to be presented at all? We cannot do so after we have tendered our resignation.'[163] Later he wrote: 'Could you best present the papers before you adjourn after the division? You are, however the best judge . . .'[164] Disraeli's biographers have been unable to account for this error in judgment, but, in Derby's case, the motive for not producing them is quite clear. Malmesbury explained: ' . . . he wished to resign, worn out by repeated attacks of gout and the toil of office, and was indifferent to continuing the struggle'.[165] Derby's failing energies are attested to by some letters written at the time.*

After the defeat in the Commons, on June 11th, Derby presented his resignation to the Queen, and was highly pleased to receive the Garter in recognition of his services.[166] This recognition was the more significant because he was made an extra knight, which was '. . . hardly ever done, except for Royalties'.[167] Malmesbury's services were likewise recognized with the Grand Cross of the Bath. Nor was Disraeli left to go empty-handed. Derby had already secured an important job for his Chancellor's brother,[168] and on June 12th he reported to Disraeli: 'The Queen has signed the warrant for your pension.'[169] As Derby had already secured what he described as a 'whole batch' of peerages and baronetcies for his followers, it seems clear that the faithful members of his party did not go unrewarded. Over his long career Derby managed to build up within the party a loyal personal following through the astute use of patronage.

On retiring, the Conservatives left behind them a record which tended to buttress some of the fundamental ideas of their party. They still styled themselves as the protectors of the Church, though

* Lytton, who felt that his health would not permit him to continue in office, tried for many months to resign, but the Government could not spare him. When he appealed to Derby, in April, for a release, Derby sent the letter to Disraeli with the expostulation: 'What on earth is to be done with this fellow?' Another letter, undated, perhaps reveals even better Derby's unsettled state: 'I find I have written nonsense. I read your note all wrong. I do not think *A* would go even to Vienna, but the case is very different. Pray excuse my stupid misapprehension. I was confused with the multitude of papers all pressing at once.' *Disraeli Papers*, Derby XII. (Derby to Disraeli, April 6th, 1859). (Derby to Disraeli, undated). These letters, and the fact that his speaking was at times, though certainly not always, ineffective, seem to confirm Malmesbury's interpretation.

since the passing of the Jew Bill, they had rid themselves of some of the intolerance which the protectorate implied. In domestic affairs they had shown that their party was both moderate and progressive, and not opposed to Reform. In financial matters they still stood for economy in government and the abolition of the income tax, but Derby had insisted on certain expenditures for defence. About a year before, Derby had warned Disraeli: 'We have, on several occasions, urged so strongly the embodying a large force of militia, that it would be difficult to account for a sudden change of purpose, on financial considerations only.'[170] Even more important to Derby was the Navy, and he showed considerable insight in demanding that the Navy be converted from sailing ships to screw steamers, which he hoped might be armoured. On this point he enjoined Disraeli: 'We *must* have a naval preponderance over France, however inconvenient the outlay must be, and however unreasonable the system on her part which forces on us corresponding efforts.'[171] Both of these programmes were undoubtedly defensive, and coupled with a conciliatory and isolationist foreign policy, they could be interpreted in no other way. These ideas and interests, together with a general defence of the British constitution, formed the stock-in-trade of the Conservative Party during Derby's time.

For a while after his resignation Derby contemplated an attack on the new government for not having their Cabinet ready before dislodging his government, and especially on Lord Granville for communicating some confidential information to *The Times*. Stanley was strongly against the move, and sought Disraeli's aid in restraining his sire's belligerency. 'I think,' he wrote, 'that any attack at present (and a speech from my Father will be an attack, whether he intends it or not) is ill-timed and undignified . . .'[172] No doubt the urgings of Stanley and Disraeli caused Derby to change his mind, for his 'valedictory harangue' was a small pop rather than an atomic explosion. Granville was singled out for some polite criticism, but Derby promised to give the new government an 'independent and generous support'.[173] Thereafter, as Lord Campbell put it, Derby and Malmesbury absconded, and the affairs in the Lords became quite dull, without mighty divisions and interesting 'party logomachy'.[174] For the moment, however, Derby was content to seek other pastimes outside the exhausting political arena.

NOTES

[1] Malmesbury, *Memoirs*, II, 102-3. (*Diary*, March 6th, 1858).
[2] *Hansard* (third series), CXLVIII, 693-6.
[3] Walling, *Bright*, p. 233. (*Diary*, January 16th, 1858).
[4] *DP*, Derby XII. (Derby to Disraeli, February 17th (?), 1858).
[5] B&E, *Victoria*, III, 338. (Memorandum by Albert, February 21st, 1858).
[6] Ibid., pp. 338-40.
[7] Ibid., p. 339.
[8] Fitzmaurice, *Granville*, I, 293. (Granville to Canning, February 24th, 1858).
[9] *DP*, Derby XII. (Derby to Disraeli, February 20th, 1858).
[10] B&E, *Victoria*, III, 340-1. (Victoria to Derby, February 21st, 1858). (Derby to Victoria, February 21st, 1858).
[11] *DP*, Derby XII. (Derby to Disraeli, February 21st, 1858).
[12] *GP*, BM 44112. (Bright to Gladstone, February 21st, 1858).
[13] Ibid. (Derby to Gladstone, February 21st, 1858).
[14] Ibid. (Gladstone to Derby, February 21st, 1858).
[15] Ibid. See also: Morley, *Gladstone*, I, 577. (*Diary*, February 21st, 1858).
[16] *GP*, BM 44112. (Gladstone to Derby, February 21st, 1858).
[17] B&E, *Victoria*, III, 342. (Grey to Derby, February 21st, 1858).
[18] Malmesbury, *Memoirs*, II, 99. (*Diary*, March 2nd, 1858).
[19] *DP*, Derby XII. (Derby to Disraeli, February 21st, 1858).
[20] M&B, *Disraeli*, I, 1517-18. (Disraeli to Derby, February 22nd and 25th, 1858).
[21] Hardcastle, *Campbell*, II, 428.
[22] Malmesbury, *Memoirs*, II, 98. (*Diary*, February 26th, 1858); B&E, *Victoria*, III, 344-5. (Derby to Victoria, February 25th, 1858).
[23] *DP*, Derby XII. (Derby to Disraeli, Sunday, 1858).
[24] Parker, *Graham*, II, 346. (Graham to Gladstone, May 25th, 1858); B&E, *Victoria*, III, 344. (Victoria to Derby, February 22nd, 1858).
[25] *DP*, Derby XII. (Derby to Disraeli, February 25th, 1858). (Joliffe to Disraeli, February 23rd, 1858).
[26] Lady Gwendolen Cecil, *Life of Robert Marquis of Salisbury* (London: Hodder & Stoughton, 1926), I, 65.
[27] Fitzmaurice, *Granville*, I, 293. (Granville to Canning, February 24th, 1858).
[28] B&E, *Victoria*, III, 366. (Memorandum by Phipps, May 1858).
[29] Parker, *Graham*, II, 346. (Graham to Gladstone, May 25th, 1858).
[30] B&E, *Victoria*, III, 368. (Memorandum by Albert, May 16th, 1858).
[31] 'The Second Derby Ministry', *The Edinburgh Review*, CVII (1858), 298.
[32] *Hansard* (third series), CXLVIII, 25.
[33] S&F, *Greville*, VI, 346. (*Diary*, March 2nd, 1858).
[34] *Hansard* (third series), CXLIX, 41.
[35] Ibid., p. 43.
[36] 'The Second Derby Ministry', *The Edinburgh Review*, CVII (1858), 298.
[37] Argyll, *Duke of Argyll*, II, 121. (Herbert to Argyll, March 15th, 1858).
[38] Malmesbury, *Memoirs*, II, 100-4. (Malmesbury to Cowley, March 2nd, 1858). (*Diary*, March 6th and 12th, 1858).
[39] B&E, *Victoria*, III, 347-8. (Disraeli to Victoria, March 12th, 1858).
[40] Argyll, *Duke of Argyll*, II, 112. (Granville to Argyll, March 28th, 1858).
[41] Ibid., pp. 113-14. (Palmerston to Argyll, March 31st, 1858).
[42] Walpole, *Russell*, III, 295-6.
[43] Ibid., pp. 297-8. (Russell to Derby, undated).
[44] M&B, *Disraeli*, I, 1529-30. (Disraeli to Derby, April 2nd, 1858).
[45] *DP*, Derby XII. (Derby to Disraeli, April 8th (?), 1858).

[46] Ibid. (Derby to Disraeli, April 30th, 1858).
[47] *Hansard* (third series), CLI, 1449-52.
[48] *DP*, Derby XII. (Derby to Disraeli, May 27th, 1858).
[49] Ibid. (Derby to Disraeli, March (?), 1858).
[50] Ibid. (Derby to Disraeli, April 20th, 1858).
[51] B&E, *Victoria*, III, 370. (Derby to Victoria, May 23rd, 1858).
[52] Fitzmaurice, *Granville*, I, 293-4. (Granville to Canning, February 24th, 1858).
[53] M&B, *Disraeli*, I, 1541. (Ellenborough to Derby, May 13th, 1858).
[54] Malmesbury, *Memoirs*, II, 117. (*Diary*, May 8th, 1858).
[55] B&E, *Victoria*, III, 358. (Victoria to Derby, May 9th, 1858).
[56] Fitzmaurice, *Granville*, I, 305-6. (Granville to Canning, May 10th, 1858)
[57] Ibid. See also: B&E, *Victoria*, III, 358. (Ellenborough to Victoria, May 10th. 1858); Malmesbury, *Memoirs*, II, 118. (*Diary*, May 11th, 1858).
[58] B&E, *Victoria*, III, 361-2. (Derby to Victoria, May 11th, 1858).
[59] Fitzmaurice, *Granville*, I, 308-9.
[60] B&E, *Victoria*, III, 359-60. (Memorandum by Albert, May 11th, 1858).
[61] Ibid., pp. 363-6. (Memorandum by Phipps, undated).
[62] Fitzmaurice, *Granville*, I, 307-8. (Granville to Canning, May 17th, 1858).
[63] M&B, *Disraeli*, I, 1543-4. (Disraeli to Derby, May 16th, 1858).
[64] B&E, *Victoria*, III, 367-8. (Memorandum by Albert, May 16th, 1858).
[65] Malmesbury, *Memoirs*, II, 120. (*Diary*, May 17th, 1858).
[66] Ibid., pp. 120-1. (*Diary*, May 18th, 1858).
[67] Fitzmaurice, *Granville*, I, 308-9. (Granville to Canning, May 24th, 1858).
[68] *The Times* (London), May 26th, 1854.
[69] *Hansard* (third series), CXLVI, 1227.
[70] Ibid., pp. 1220-36.
[71] Ibid., CXLIII, 4-5.
[72] Ibid., CXLIX, 1477-80.
[73] Ibid., CL, 1167-8.
[74] Ibid., CLI, 696-7.
[75] Ibid., pp. 925-7.
[76] Ibid., pp. 1255-6.
[77] S&F, *Greville*, VII, 374. (*Diary*, June 22nd, 1858).
[78] *Hansard* (third series), CLI, 1259-66.
[79] Ibid., CXLIX, 403-4.
[80] Ibid., CL, 1693-6.
[81] Ibid., pp. 1840-2.
[82] Ibid., pp. 173-7.
[83] Ibid., CLI, 1667.
[84] Ibid., pp. 825-36.
[85] *GP*, BM 44140. (Derby to Gladstone, May 26th, 1858).
[86] Ibid. (Gladstone to Derby, May 26th, 1858).
[87] *DP*, Derby XII. (Derby to Disraeli, May 27th, 1858).
[88] Ibid.
[89] *Hansard* (third series), CL, 1287-97.
[90] Hardcastle, *Campbell*, II, 430.
[91] Hodder, *Shaftesbury*, III, 68. (*Diary*, May 15th, 1858).
[92] B&E, *Victoria*, III, 381-2. (Memorandum by Albert, September 4th, 1858).
[93] Argyll, *Duke of Argyll*, II, 123. (Argyll to Aberdeen, August 19th, 1858).
[94] Jennings, *Croker*, II, 432. (Derby to Croker, September 22nd, 1851).
[95] *DP*, Derby XII. (Derby to Disraeli, October 26th, 1851).
[96] Ibid. (Derby to Disraeli, November 14th, 1853).
[97] *Hansard* (third series), CXXX, 81-2.

[98] *DP*, Derby XII. (Derby to Disraeli, April 24th, 1857).
[99] *Hansard* (third series), CXLVIII, 54.
[100] *DP*, Stanley XII. (Edward Stanley to Disraeli, June 3rd, 1858), Ibid., Derby XII. (Derby to Disraeli, August 25th, 1858).
[101] Ibid., Stanley XII. (Edward Stanley to Derby, February 8th, 1859).
[102] Ibid. (Edward Stanley to Disraeli, October 16th, 1858).
[103] Ibid., Derby XII. (Derby to Disraeli, August 25th, 1858).
[104] M&B, *Disraeli*, I, 1586. (Disraeli to Mrs. Willyams, October 11th, 1858).
[105] Malmesbury, *Memoirs*, II, 140. (*Diary*, October 23rd, 1858).
[106] Ibid., pp. 142, 145, 156. (*Diary*, November 3rd, December 3rd, 1858, February 9th, 1859).
[107] *DP*, Derby XII. (Draft Report, November 26th, 1858).
[108] Malmesbury, *Memoirs*, II, 145. (*Diary*, December 3rd, 1858).
[109] *DP*, Derby XII. (Derby to Disraeli, January 2nd, 1859); Malmesbury, *Memoirs*, II, 152-3. (*Diary*, January 28th, 1859).
[110] *DP*, Derby XII. (Derby to Disraeli, December 21st, 1858). (Derby to Walpole, January 6th, 1859). (Derby to Disraeli, January 8th, 1859).
[111] *DP*, Malmesbury XIII. (Malmesbury to Disraeli, July 6th, 1858).
[112] Ibid., Stanley XII. (Edward Stanley to Derby, February 8th, 1859).
[113] Ibid., Derby XII. (Derby to Disraeli, December 30th, 1858).
[114] Ibid. (Derby to Disraeli, January 8th, 1859).
[115] M&B, *Disraeli*, I, 1595.
[116] *DP*, Derby XII. (Montrose to Derby, February 10th, 1859). (Derby to Disraeli, February 10th, 1859).
[117] Malmesbury, *Memoirs*, II, 152-3, 156. (*Diary*, January 28th, February 9th, 1859).
[118] *DP*, Derby XII. (Derby to Disraeli, January 8th, 1859).
[119] Ibid., Stanley XII. (Edward Stanley to Disraeli, October 5th, 1858); B&E, *Victoria*, III, 375-7, 404-9. (Victoria to Derby, July 8th and 29th, 1858). (Victoria to Derby, August 15th, 1858). (Victoria to Derby, February 5th, 7th and 9th, 1859). (Derby to Victoria, February 6th and 7th, 1859).
[120] Argyll, *Duke of Argyll*, II, 129. (Clarendon to Argyll, November 27th, 1858).
[121] Ibid., p. 133. (Argyll to Aberdeen, December 29th, 1858); Maxwell, *Clarendon*, II, 173. (Palmerston to Clarendon, November 27th, 1858).
[122] Walpole, *Russell*, III, 300-1.
[123] Argyll, *Duke of Argyll*, II, 124. (Argyll to Aberdeen, October 12th, 1858).
[124] Ibid., p. 131. (Russell to Argyll, November 24th, 1858).
[125] Maxwell, *Clarendon*, II, 176. (Clarendon to Lady Theresa Lewis, January 13th, 1859).
[126] *DP*, Derby XII. (Derby to Disraeli, December 30th, 1858).
[127] Malmesbury, *Memoirs*, II, 158. (*Diary*, March 1st, 1859); *DP*, Derby XII. (Derby to Disraeli, March 5th, 1859).
[128] Gathorne-Hardy, *Cranbrook*, I, 128. (*Diary*, March 2nd, 1859); Malmesbury, *Memoirs*, II, 161. (*Diary*, March 13th, 1859).
[129] *DP*, Derby XII. (McPalmer to Derby, March 16th (?), 1859). (Derby to Disraeli, March 16th, 1859).
[130] Ibid. (Derby to Disraeli, March 16th, 1859).
[131] Ibid. (Derby to Disraeli, March (?), 1859). (Derby to Disraeli, March 16th, 1859).
[132] Walling, *Bright*, p. 236. (*Diary*, March 21st, 1859).
[133] Maxwell, *Clarendon*, II, 310. (Clarendon to Lady Salisbury, March 17th, 1866).
[134] *DP*, Derby XII. (Derby to Disraeli, March 20th (?), 1859).

[135] M&B, *Disraeli*, I, 1608. (Disraeli to Derby, date not shown).
[136] *DP*, Derby XII. (Derby to Disraeli, March 25th (?), 1859.
[137] Ibid. (Derby to Disraeli, March 30th (?), 1859).
[138] Ibid. (Derby to Disraeli, April 3rd (?), 1859).
[139] Ibid. (Derby to Disraeli, April 5th, 1859).
[140] *Hansard* (third series), CLIII, 1267-91.
[141] Ibid., CLII, 43.
[142] *DP*, Derby XII. (Derby to Disraeli, January 8th, 1859).
[143] Lady Burghclere, *A Great Lady's Friendships, Letters to Mary, Marchioness of Salisbury, Countess of Derby* (London: Macmillan & Co., 1933), pp. 21-2.
[144] S&F, *Greville*, VII, 412. (*Diary*, April 15th, 1859); *Hansard* (third series), CLIV, 84.
[145] *Hansard* (third series), CLIV, 85.
[146] Arthur Ponsonby, *Henry Ponsonby* (New York: The MacMillan Co., 1943), I, 27. (Ponsonby to Lady Ponsonby, May 14th, 1859).
[147] Malmesbury, *Memoirs*, II, 178-9. (*Diary*, May 8th, 1859).
[148] Hardcastle, *Campbell*, II, 435-6.
[149] Malmesbury, *Memoirs*, II, 175-6. (*Diary*, April 30th, 1859).
[150] *GP*, BM 44140. (Derby to Gladstone, May 19th, 1859).
[151] Ibid. (Gladstone to Derby, May 19th, 1859).
[152] Ibid. (Derby to Gladstone, May 20th, 1859).
[153] *DP*, Derby XII. (Derby to Disraeli, May 20th, 1859).
[154] S&F, *Greville*, VII, 418. (*Diary*, May 27th (?), 1859).
[155] *Hansard* (third series), CLIV, 82-3.
[156] *DP*, Derby XII. (Derby to Disraeli, May 20th, 1859).
[157] Fitzmaurice, *Granville*, I, 330. (Palmerston to Granville, May 29th, 1859).
[158] Ibid., pp. 331-2.
[159] S&F, *Greville*, VII, 423. (*Diary*, June 9th, 1859).
[160] B&E, *Victoria*, III, 436. (Derby to Victoria, June 10th, 1859).
[161] M&B, *Disraeli*, I, 1659-60. (Disraeli to Derby, June 10th, 1859).
[162] Malmesbury, *Memoirs*, II, 188-9. (Undated entry).
[163] *DP*, Malmesbury XIII. (Malmesbury to Disraeli, June 17th, 1859).
[164] Ibid. (Malmesbury to Disraeli, undated).
[165] Malmesbury, *Memoirs*, II, 189. (Undated entry).
[166] B&E, *Victoria*, III, 437. (Derby to Victoria, June 11th, 1859).
[167] Malmesbury, *Memoirs*, II, 188. (*Diary*, June 11th, 1859).
[168] *DP*, Derby XII. (Derby to Disraeli, August 12th and 25th, 1858).
[169] Ibid. (Derby to Disraeli, June 12th, 1859).
[170] Ibid. (Derby to Disraeli, March 14th, 1858).
[171] Ibid. (Derby to Disraeli, October 12th, 1858).
[172] Ibid., Stanley XII. (Edward Stanley to Disraeli, June 14th, 1859).
[173] *Hansard* (third series), CLIV, 424-6.
[174] Hardcastle, *Campbell*, II, 446.

CHAPTER X

GOVERNMENT OUT OF OFFICE

BACK at Knowsley Derby rapidly recovered his spirits and his health. In August he was grouse-shooting, and the autumn gave prospects of early cover-shooting.[1] But in September came an invitation from the Conservatives of Liverpool who planned a banquet for him, and his attention was once again turned to politics.[2] While he laboured to give the opposite impression, politics was in his blood, and all other sport was secondary. After a rest, and with the return of his energy, Derby was ready again to enter the lists, and the party always hailed his return.

There was considerable work to be done. Palmerston's Government held some attractions for the more opportunist Conservatives, and there was always a danger that many would desert to his camp if their own party became inactive.[3] Derby knew of this and, before leaving for Knowsley, had held a large meeting of his party to encourage the younger men, and to speak in praise of Disraeli, with whom some of the party were again dissatisfied.* Derby's ability to inspire his party followers at these meetings was remarkable. The year before, when Indian affairs had threatened his government, one of the members recorded: '. . . then to Lord Derby's. A good muster and a stirring speech seemed to set the party on its legs again'.[4] The rank and file eagerly seized every opportunity for associating with him, and on those occasions, unfortunately rare, when they would be called to meet at his home, they felt highly honoured.† While an astute politician in most ways, Derby missed the opportunity of advancing his own cause by

* In some cases Disraeli gave cause for complaint within the party. In the autumn of 1859, Stanley, writing in his father's style, remonstrated: 'My reason for writing at this moment is to beg you earnestly . . . not for the sake of the Irish alliance, to give any countenance, direct or indirect, to the move of the R.C. bishops against the National System . . . It will not do to have a No-Popery cry raised against us . . .' *Disraeli Papers*, Stanley XII. (Edward Stanley to Disraeli, September 5th, 1859). In some cases, however, the Ultras attacked Disraeli, simply because they hesitated to blame Derby for the liberalizing of the party.

† 'All here', wrote Joliffe on one occasion, 'are of opinion that a meeting at Ld. Derby's will be very desirable . . . they will like to go there better than to any other place.' *Disraeli Papers*, Joliffe XIII. (Joliffe to Disraeli, December 29th, 1857).

failing to associate with his supporters, and also with the gentlemen of the press. But, in so doing, he marked himself as a sort of transitional type between the old-style and new-style politician.

The programme which Derby mapped for his party for 1860 consisted of 'masterly inactivity', but, in spite of this, the session saw some interesting developments. Early in January the Government secretly contacted Disraeli to seek support for a Reform Bill. Before this Derby had already learned from Newcastle that the Government planned a mild bill which would be acceptable to the Conservatives, and the former Prime Minister was inclined to concert a measure with their opponents.[5] *Sub rosa* negotiations continued throughout the month, and on January 19th Derby wrote that he would support a £10 franchise for the counties, and an £8 franchise for the boroughs, or even, if necessary to prevent a collision between the two Houses, a £7 borough franchise.[6] He would resist a £6 borough franchise, however, as very dangerous. While no formal arrangement was reached before the opening of Parliament, when Derby spoke on the Address on January 24th, he encouraged the Government to bring forward a Reform Bill and promised co-operation in solving the problem.

Derby's support, however, was limited to a moderate Reform measure, and his fear that Palmerston had 'knocked under' to Russell and the Radicals on Reform was confirmed when Russell introduced his bill on March 1st. The bill called for a £10 county franchise, and one of £6 in the boroughs, as well as a modest redistribution programme. Derby genuinely feared the £6 franchise, and wrote Disraeli on March 13th: '. . . if the new Elections under the Government Bill would be disastrous to the Tory party, they would be, to the Whigs, political annihilation.'[7] In their dilemma, the Whigs turned to Derby for aid, and Derby, who had decided the best policy was to keep the conservative Palmerston in office, was disposed to help them. Replying to a plea from Lord Grey, however, he demanded that the Whigs themselves speak out against the bill, so that the onus for its rejection would not be placed exclusively on the Conservative Party.[8] In his conversations with Clarendon on the subject, he pledged the co-operation of his party only if a score or so liberals would lead the attack.[9]

As many of the government side opposed the bill, its course through the Commons was noticeably slow. By late May Derby felt the Government must give it up, but Russell persisted, doggedly, and many of the Conservatives began to show signs of uneasiness, and to put pressure on their leaders to secure the withdrawal of the measure.[10] Derby had already, on April 19th, sharply attacked the bill in the Lords and termed it the most unstatesmanlike, unconstitutional and inconclusive that had ever been presented,[11] but this did not serve to scuttle it. Early in June, therefore, he sent Malmesbury to see Lady Palmerston and give assurance that the Conservatives would support her husband's government against the Radicals, which would allow Palmerston to risk offending them by throwing out the bill. At a later interview with the Prime Minister himself, Malmesbury found him to be as anxious as the Conservatives to shelve the measure.[12] Thereafter, the resistance within the Government became so strong that Russell, in disgust, withdrew his bill. Thus, the Whig-Conservative combination sidetracked Reform, and it was laid to rest for a number of years.

Derby never became very excited over Russell's bill, for his interest was riveted on important constitutional problems which arose that session. Early in February he met Gladstone at a dinner given by Russell, and found that the new Chancellor of the Exchequer was anxious to secure approval of his Budget as soon as possible. At the time, however, Gladstone did not mention to Derby that one feature of the Budget was a repeal of the paper duties to be accompanied by an extension of direct taxation. As early as February 7th Palmerston was lukewarm towards the plan and did his best to discourage Gladstone, but the latter, like Russell, persisted in his course.[13] In April Derby learned some of the details of the Budget, and correctly predicted that Palmerston would tend to oppose it.[14] To him, it was obnoxious on two grounds, first, because it meant an extension of direct taxation, and secondly, because it would aid the penny press, with whom Derby was usually on bad terms.*

Confident that Palmerston, Clarendon and others in the Government would be sympathetic, Derby studied the history of the powers of the two Houses with a view towards defeating the repeal in the Lords. Besides getting rid of an obnoxious financial measure, he

* Malmesbury wrote: 'Lord Derby has never been able to realize the sudden growth and power of the Political Press, for which he has no partiality, which feeling is reciprocated by its members . . . Lord Derby is too proud a man to flatter anybody, even his greatest friends and equals, much less those of whom he knows nothing.' Malmesbury, *Memoirs*, II, 73. (*Diary*, June 29th, 1857).

probably hoped also to strengthen the Lords by extending their control over money bills. After some study, he concluded that, while the Lords could not introduce a money bill, they had the power to reject or to alter one, the only restriction on the latter power being a unilateral resolution of the Commons dating to 1671, which was not binding on the Lords.[15] In May Derby, speaking on the Customs Bill, warned that he would oppose the abolition of the paper duties when the opportunity presented itself.[16] Three days later, he sent Malmesbury to visit Lady Palmerston, and he found that the official household shared the hostility towards repeal.[17]

On May 21st the debate in the Lords came on, and the overflow crowd in attendance witnessed the rather curious spectacle of Lady Palmerston openly telling people in the gallery she hoped that Derby would win.[18] It was almost midnight when Derby rose to speak. His attack centred on the Manchester School principle of taxation, which sought to replace all indirect taxation with grinding direct taxes, and he went on to show how this would weaken the Government. He also called attention to the fact that the so-called Liberal Government repealed wine duties for the benefit of the wealthy, but kept the tea and sugar duties which injured the lower classes. He made clear, however, that he had no intention of overthrowing the Government.[19] Following his speech, their Lordships threw out the bill by almost 90 votes.

The repeal of the paper duty was not a popular measure, and Derby certainly considered this before campaigning against it. The Queen supported the Lords, and Palmerston gave Gladstone little sympathy. 'Of course,' he said, 'you are mortified and disappointed, but your disappointment is nothing to mine, who had a horse with whom I hoped to win the Derby, and he went amiss at the last moment.'[20] As he had repeatedly advised against the measure, Palmerston showed little inclination to join in any hostile action against the Lords. Some of his party, however, contended that the rejection of the repeal by the Lords was the equivalent of an unconstitutional reimposition of the duty. So Palmerston reluctantly agreed to appoint a special committee to consider the constitutional aspects of the case.[21]

Derby followed the deliberations of the Commons with deep interest. According to his view, the Lords had been guilty of no usurpation whatsoever, and Derby asked Disraeli to keep their friends from compromising constitutional principles for the sake of harmony in the Commons.[22] At length three resolutions were produced in which the Commons restated their power over money bills, but they were quite innocuous and the Conservatives supported Palmerston in resisting amendments to them. So vague were they, in fact, that Derby could write Disraeli: 'I have no objection to offer to the first two, nor indeed any that I think it essential to press to the third . . .'[23] In them, he saw no additional power which the Commons had acquired for the future '. . . except the adoption of a system of Annual votes for all the services of the Country'.[24] The following year, however, Gladstone presented an omnibus bill containing the paper duties repeal in addition to his other financial measures. While Derby at this time reaffirmed the right of the Lords to alter such bills, and declared that any resolutions adopted by the Commons in no way affected that right, he did not, because of the threatening foreign situation, press for a division.[25] Hoping, perhaps, to strengthen his point of view, Derby also voiced the same opinion the following year when discussing finance.[26] Derby had, indeed, established a precedent, but it was of rather doubtful value to the Lords, for the circumstances of 1860, when the Prime Minister co-operated with the Opposition against his own Chancellor of the Exchequer, were not likely to be repeated.

The co-operation between Derby and Palmerston continued through the session of 1860. In August of that year Derby subtly arranged to keep his men away from a division on one of Palmerston's bills in order to assure its passage. Advising Gladstone of the manœuvre, Palmerston added: '. . . he said to keep this to ourselves lest there should be mutiny in Derby's Camp if it was proclaimed that he had come to a private understanding with us'.[27] Sometime thereafter Derby had a sharp attack of gout, which weakened him considerably and caused mental depression, and his recovery occupied the autumn and early winter.[28] While the family sought to keep his condition a secret, a rumour got out, and immediately caused speculation concerning the realignment of parties if Derby retired.[29] By December 1860 he was well enough to write, and at that time, Derby set the stage for the next session in a letter to Disraeli, which advocated 'keeping the present men in, and resisting all temptations to avail ourselves of a casual majority'.[30]

In December 1860 Derby, pleased with the last session, wrote Malmesbury and authorized him to enter into negotiations with the Prime Minister for the following session.[31] Malmesbury contacted Palmerston with the information that he had been 'deputed by Ld. Derby to hold language also analagous to my former assurances . . .'[32] The ageing Viscount eagerly seized on the offer, and invited Malmesbury to visit him, but the latter felt it best to have a shorter interview in London later.[33] At this interview the Conservatives were committed to support his government in anything but a war with Austria, if he would guarantee to stop Gladstone's attempts to democratize the Budget.[34] Just how much Palmerston promised is not certain, but events showed that the co-operation in 1861 was quite as cordial as the year before.*

Had they chosen to be opportunists, the Conservatives could have returned to power in 1861. Bright and Cobden were convinced by this time that no domestic reform could be expected from Palmerston, and during the autumn had contacted the Conservatives with a definite proposition. The Radicals pledged their support in ousting Palmerston, and in establishing a Conservative government for two years. After that period, the Conservatives were to pass a good Reform Bill.[35] This offer was apparently never seriously entertained, though the Conservative leaders might conceivably have entered into such a bargain without the rank and file of their party knowing about it. Derby probably rejected the offer for reasons of principle. He was satisfied to exercise considerable influence through his *sub rosa* alliance with the Old Whigs, who usually followed the domestic policies of the Conservative Party.

During 1861 Gladstone did not offer any new financial proposals which the Conservatives thought it worth while to resist, but he carried his repeal of the paper duties. Derby would have liked to prevent Gladstone from putting all his financial measures into a single bill, which made it difficult for the Lords to influence money matters, but many in his party, such as Stanley,[36] would not

* Two undated letters in the Disraeli collection were probably written about this time. In one of them Derby mentioned receiving a communication from Palmerston through Granville, which made it important that he see Disraeli the following day. The other read: 'Here is Palmerston's letter, received last night. I have told him he has my good wishes, and I hope he may persuade the House to take his course. I will write to old Henley. You must keep Pakington straight.' *Disraeli Papers*, Derby XII. (Derby to Disraeli, Thursday). (Derby to Disraeli, Sunday).

support him on it. On one occasion Derby complained to Gladstone that one of his speeches violated an agreement he, Derby, had made with Granville,[37] the government leader in the Lords, but otherwise the session went along smoothly.[38] The lethargic attitude adopted by his colleagues to any suggested measures of reform caused Gladstone to observe: 'We live in anti-reforming times. All improvements have to be urged in apologetic, almost supplicatory tones.'[39] This was the fruit of the informal coalition.

The years 1860 and 1861 brought a few important events in Derby's personal life. In October 1860 his daughter, Emma, married W. P. M. Chetwynd Talbot, a brother of the Earl of Shrewsbury. Talbot had been Derby's private secretary, and his only failing was a lack of financial means. For two years Derby refused to allow either Lady Derby or his daughter to speak of such a match, but at length the former said the Clarendons had expressed their willingness to have their daughter marry a 'poor curate', if it would make her happy. This seems to have satisfied Derby that members of his social world would not blame him for allowing his daughter to make a financially poor match, and he at length consented.[40] On her birthday in 1862 the new Lady Talbot came down to breakfast to find a cheque for the sum of £5000 under her napkin, which helped, no doubt, to solve their financial problems at the time and gave hope for continued indulgence in the future.[41] To complete the tale, the aristocratic Clarendons, who would have married their daughter to a poor curate, instead bestowed her a few years later on Derby's second son, Frederick Arthur Stanley.

As the younger generation set out on their own, the older began to falter. In his uncertain health, these were years of foreboding events for Derby. In 1860 Lord Aberdeen, a man whom Derby never ceased to respect deeply, and who was associated with so many political incidents of the past, died. In October 1861 the statesman with whom Derby had once been on closer terms of friendship than any other, Sir James Graham, passed away, and what memories must have gone with him! Shortly thereafter, another of the prominent Peelites, Sidney Herbert, later Lord Herbert of Lea, also died. The climax, however, was reached with the death of the Prince Consort late in 1861. Russell wrote his old colleague informing him of the Queen's reaction to her loss, and Derby replied with a friendly letter.[42] When Derby was appointed to a committee to erect a memorial to the Prince, he was able to observe the Monarch's feelings first hand. She talked freely on the subject. He *would* die, she said, for he seemed not to care to live. 'He died from want of what is called pluck.'[43]

During 1862 Derby's health took a turn for the worse. Both family and party policy were to keep secret the periodic attacks which struck him down, and just what happened that year is not very clear. Ralph Earle, writing to Disraeli late in October, passed on a rumour: 'What, however, really is interesting & perhaps new, even to you, is that Lord Derby's health is more than ever precarious. As far as I could follow the mysterious communication, some new symptom has shown itself, of an alarming character. The fact is kept very secret & is supposed to have been divulged to three persons only.'[44] Shortly thereafter, in November, Derby wrote one of his usual letters to Disraeli in which he admitted weakness in wrists and ankles, but hoped to be in force for the next session. The impression Derby gave to Disraeli was merely that he had another attack of gout, but probably there were added complications.* During 1863 Derby continued to be in uncertain health, and in the autumn of that year he could not participate actively in the hunt. In the summer of 1864 there was another prolonged attack of gout, and then, for the first time, Derby realized that he could not expect many more years of life.[45] In November he was in bed, this time with 'ulcerated sore throat'.[46] His illness of 1864, by chance, could not be concealed from the public. The Prince of Wales had planned to visit Liverpool, and, when his plans were cancelled, the Derbys had to make clear to the disappointed people that they had good reason to ask for a postponement. Stanley admitted that his father's condition had alarmed the family, for 'the gout would not come out' for a time, but the crisis was past in about twenty-four hours. All these fragments add up to a man in rapidly declining health, who was so often ill that he must be classified as an invalid, and whose body, if not his mind, was seriously affected by his malady. It seems quite possible that later in life the acute pain also brought mental

* A note by Disraeli which tells of a 'paroxysmal affection' may or may not refer to Derby. *Disraeli Papers*, VII. (Disraeli to Wife, January 26th, 1863). After his long illness of 1863, Derby evidently had trouble with his hearing. *Hansard* (third series), CLXXIII, 22.

distress, perhaps even moments of derangement, but this is not too clear.

Under such circumstances, retirement would have seemed to have been strongly indicated, but Derby never seriously considered it until he was no longer able to meet Parliament. So long as he could be in London for the pre-opening meetings, and give aid and guidance during the early rounds, he felt justified in hanging on to his position. According to Disraeli, he also had another motive – that he would not retire so long as his party were in a minority.[47] Perhaps, however, the overriding consideration was the question of his successor. Both Disraeli and Stanley had the talents, prestige and experience to succeed him, but each had certain counts against him. Even at this late date Disraeli was not accepted whole-heartedly by the rank and file of the party, and, as one writer put it, he was merely tolerated as Derby's foreman.[48] Malmesbury was thoroughly alienated and wrote late in 1862: 'We shall never get on till we get rid of Disraeli.'[49] In that year, Disraeli returned to his habit of factionalizing, and a hint of his thought might be gleaned from a sentence written to him by Earle: 'Peacocke returned. His tone is all right & as regards us, I think fair, but he is very anti-Derby, which is perhaps as well. . . .'*

Because Disraeli lacked the confidence of the party, he was for the time unfitted to head it. Stanley might have been accepted more readily, and would have won over a number of Whigs, but the rank and file correctly judged him to be unrepresentative of their ideas. Of the two, Derby preferred to work with the opportunist Disraeli, rather than his son, whose tenaciously-held ideas were often in opposition to his own and those of the party majority. 'Stanley is going, or gone, down to Lynn,' Derby wrote Disraeli in 1863. 'I am always rather apprehensive as to what he might say on those occasions . . .'[50] On the whole, in spite of his minor intrigues, Derby was well pleased with Disraeli, and came to lean on the younger man more and more. Disraeli's cooperation, in fact, made it possible for Derby to head the party long after his health would naturally have caused him to seek retirement.

In spite of poor health and being out of power, Derby continued

* *Disraeli Papers*, Earle XII. (Earle to Disraeli, October 27th, 1862). Earle reported that Malmesbury and Clarendon were 'caballing' at Knowsley, and Disraeli perhaps feared he might be eased out. This writer has no evidence that Derby ever contemplated such a thing.

to exercise considerable influence over legislation in the Lords. Into that House, in July 1862, came an old friend and rival, Lord John Russell, and Derby is said to have met him at the door with the remark: 'What fun we will have, now you have come!'[51] Neither was the speaker he had been twenty or thirty years before, and Clarendon feared Russell might 'not have the temper for the pokes that Derby will delight in giving him'.[52] However, if neither could carry on in the style of yesteryear, they maintained inviolate their opposition to each other, and took opposite sides on almost every question that came before the House.

While Derby continued to be conciliatory towards general reforms, he still was reluctant to compromise on matters affecting the Church. Lord Lyveden, taking heart by the recent decision in favour of the Jews, in 1860 introduced a bill calling for the abolition of the church rates.[53] Derby was aware of the weaknesses of the law on the subject, which was practically unenforceable, and he was ready to compromise if it meant the Church would receive a greater actual income.[54] But, as those who favoured abolition would offer no compromise, Derby called for and received a large majority against Lyveden's bill.* Disraeli made something of an issue of the subject, and defeated a similar measure in the Commons. While this action satisfied their High Church supporters, it tended to alienate the non-Anglican groups.

A question which arose annually concerned an oath not to injure the Established Church which was taken by persons holding positions of trust in the corporations. The tactics used to promote the abolition of this oath were similar to those used in connection with the Jew Bills. One such measure appeared in the Lords in 1859, but did not come to a vote.† In 1860, Derby claimed that its promoters were seeking to establish equality for the dissenting sects, and he secured a two-to-one division against the measure.[55] When it came up from the Commons for the fifth time, Derby was weakening a bit, but contended that the oath had been accepted

* The compulsory church rates were abolished in 1868, but Derby never was reconciled to the change. As he was no longer the party leader then, however, he did not call for a division. *Disraeli Papers*, Derby XII. (Derby to Disraeli, April 20th, 1868).

† The clause objected to read in part: 'I do solemnly . . . profess, testify and declare . . . that I will never exercise any . . . authority . . . which I may possess by the virtue of the office of ——, to injure or weaken the Protestant Church as it is by law established in England . . .' *Hansard* (third series), CLXX, 658.

by the Dissenters when the Test and Corporation Acts were repealed, and it should stand.[56] Though victorious again, he did not eliminate the measure, and it returned again in 1865, when, in a reflective mood, Derby recalled how his friend, Lord John Russell, back in 1828, had thought the oath quite unobjectionable.[57] Once again it was turned down. About this time, however, the Catholics projected a measure to remove their special parliamentary oath, established in 1829, by which they, 'without mental reservations', pledged themselves not to weaken or disturb the Protestant religion or Protestant government in England. Many Catholics felt the special oath was a standing reproach to them.

In 1865 the Roman Catholic vote, which had aided them in 1859, was being eagerly sought by the Conservative Party, and this tended to complicate the issue. Derby conferred with Disraeli, and they evidently decided to compromise. Unfortunately, in calling for a compromise solution in the Lords, Derby used the expression 'unmuzzle the Catholics', which he picked up from a speaker in the Commons.* Derby used the phrase, which he called 'more forcible than elegant', a number of times, much to the dissatisfaction of the Catholics, and secured a majority against the bill in the form then advanced.[58] Early in 1866, however, he compromised by helping create a uniform oath for all members of Parliament regardless of religion. Derby concerted with Disraeli while the bill went through the Commons,[59] and on April 14th wrote Russell: '. . . so far as I am aware, there is not likely to be an opposition, certainly no organized opposition to the 2nd Reading of your Bill'.[60] When the compromise bill came up to the Lords, Derby and Chelmsford amended the act with a pronouncement that the repeal in no way affected the laws upholding the supremacy of the Crown in all civil and ecclesiastical matters.[61] Russell agreed readily, and the new oath was finally constructed. The abolition of the Catholic parliamentary oath was followed quickly by the repeal of the corporations oath. Derby now consented, reasoning that since the members of Parliament had been relieved of the special oath, there was no point in forcing municipal officials to take it.[62] Lord Derby, then, was instrumental in bringing about reasonable compromises on both of these touchy, if not highly important, issues.

In the Derby of the 1860s, in fact, there were flashes of the

* Kennedy, who favoured repeal of the oath, declared that it 'muzzled the representatives of six millions of population'. *Hansard*, CLXXX, 473.

Stanley of so many years before. His speeches more than once echoed his early reforming zeal. Particularly effective were his speeches in behalf of the poor who were being displaced through the construction of metropolitan railways. Picturing for their Lordships the unbelievable crowding in certain districts of London, the drunkenness and improvidence which arose out of slum conditions, he went on to declare:[63]

> . . . when 8000 or 9000 persons are simultaneously turned out by the passing of a particular measure, it is no longer a case of individual hardship, but becomes a social grievance and of political importance . . . I ask whether the displacement of such a large number of houses is not a fit subject to be considered in Committee, and whether the removal of such a large number of persons may not counterbalance the advantage to the gentlemen on the north side of London of being brought in ten minutes' time to the Bank of England.

Whatever sympathy his words may have created among the members was quickly overborne by the feeling that nothing should be done to hurt the commercial enterprise of the country. Derby was successful in securing a committee to study the problem of these displaced persons, but little was done to meet the problem. Nevertheless, as Derby pointed out, he represented a group who, because of their poverty, were unable to seek redress of their grievances against the railway magnates.[64]

Consciously or unconsciously, Derby during these years set out to show that the Lord of the manor was the real friend of the lower classes, and he shortly engaged in a humanitarian work which called forth the approbation of friend and foe alike.[65] The Civil War in America had cut off the supply of cotton to the British textile factories, many of which were located in Derby's home county of Lancashire, and hence the problem of the unemployed was dropped at his front door. Sufficient supplies were on hand for 1861, but during the following year the pinch began to be felt. Responding to the calamity, some one hundred and forty-three committees were set up to collect clothing and donations for the unemployed, and these were put under a Central Relief Fund, of which Derby became chairman of the Central Executive Committee. On December 2nd, 1862, Derby, at a rally in Manchester, praised the 'noble manner, a manner beyond all praise in which this destitution has been borne by the population of this great county'.[66]

In dealing with the distress, Derby followed a number of principles, notably that relief should be furnished from private rather than public funds.[67] In adopting this principle, he did so with deference to the feelings of the workers, who, he thought, abhorred the idea of receiving public charity. An attempt was made also to distinguish between the honest and industrious and the 'idle and profligate', in other words, the unemployed should be separated from the paupers. In judging cases, however, he enjoined the committee to err on the side of liberality rather than stricture.[68] The work continued through 1865. By January 1863, there were almost a half million receiving one form of relief or another. The year following, this had decreased to 203,352, and by January 1865 the number had sunk to about 126,000.[69] While Stanley tended to minimize the suffering,[70] almost all other observers, including his father, were deeply impressed by the manner in which the people bore their hardships.

Derby devoted some of his time, at least a day each week,[71] to the relief work, presiding over committees, and influencing the wealthy to contribute to the fund. He himself contributed £12,000,[72] and on one occasion gave £5000, which was said to have been the largest single subscription, up to that time, made by a single Englishman to a public fund for a single purpose at a single time.[73] In view of his income, which by this time, owing to his good management, was in a very healthy state, the amount of his donation does not seem excessively large,* but at the time his donations were very favourably regarded. Disraeli observed: 'His [Derby's] subscription of many thousands was munificent, but his administrative talent in managing the vast sums entrusted to the Central Committee by the nation not less admirable.'[74]

Derby no doubt had various motives in devoting time and money to the cause. He had often, perhaps as *noblesse oblige*, taken the lead in starting subscriptions for various worthy causes. He was also quick to respond emotionally to the distress of the poor. Also perhaps, he feared what might happen if relief were not provided in the distressed area. Writing to Malmesbury in 1862, he said:

* Some writers have criticized Derby for not subscribing a larger sum. This might easily have laid him open to charges of buying votes, and have given his efforts too definite a political colouring.

'... it is impossible to say what continued and aggravated suffering may lead them [the people] to'.[75] Gladstone, about the same time, expressed similar anxiety to Palmerston. 'The population of Lancashire', he wrote, 'have borne their suffering with a fortitude exceeding all example ... But if in any *one* of the great towns, resignation should, even for a single day, give place to excitement, and an outbreak should occur ...'[76] The rest of Gladstone's letter is irrelevant to the subject, but this portion indicates he entertained the possibility of rioting. So, in aiding the people, Derby could feel he was keeping the peace. At the same time, he could not have been blind to the political implications of his work. Speaking of the distress in 1863 Derby observed: 'It has led the rich to think of the duties they owe the poor, and it has shown the poor that the rich are not unmindful of them.'[77] While carefully avoiding any mention of party, Derby knew he had shown the working classes of Britain that the Conservatives had a deep interest in the welfare of the poor. This could hardly hurt his party.

In various small ways Derby sought to bring his party closer to the people. He was careful not to support the cause of the South in the American Civil War, for the working classes favoured the North.* The Austrian connection, real or imagined, had cost his party votes in 1859, so Derby set himself 'right' on the Italian issue. In 1864 he attended a banquet, and rubbed elbows with Garibaldi, a gesture which so shocked some of his followers that two threatened to stay away from an important division.[78] And after the election of 1865 Derby wrote Disraeli: 'There was indeed one R.C. Lady who would not allow her Servants to vote for us, *because I had met Garibaldi at dinner*!'[79] These gusts of wind of the 1860s gathered momentum, to become the gale of 1867.

Derby had few intimate friends, only acquaintances who joined him in hunting or at other amusements. As his physical state increasingly prevented outdoor pastimes, he turned again during the 1860s to literary pursuits.[80] Lacking creative originality, the most he could do along poetic lines was to translate the works of others, and this had been a lifelong interest.[81] In 1842, at Wellington's request, he translated Lord Wellesley's Latin lines for an

* For a discussion of Conservative policy during the war see: Wilbur Devereux Jones, 'The British Conservatives and the American Civil War', *The American Historical Review* (April 1953), LVIII, pp. 527-43.

inscription at Eton.[82] A decade later he turned to translating parts of the *Iliad*, which he showed to various friends.[83] In later years, as his outside interests lessened, Derby began to devote more time to this type of work, and in 1862 he printed privately his *Translations of Poems, Ancient and Modern*, which contained the first book of the *Iliad*. The reception of the work was encouraging, and during 1863 he continued his translation.

In 1864 the Derby translation of the *Iliad* was published. In the preface he expressed regret that interest in the classics was dying out, and predicted that his work would not rival the polished version by Pope.[84] At home this prediction proved accurate, for the copy he gave Edward Stanley remained uncut so long that Derby opined he would have to have it bound like a Blue Book in order to get him to read it. However, the general public was more receptive. *The Times* published a very favourable review (a 'puff' Derby termed it),[85] and the first edition was sold out in a week. Thereafter his work went through nine British and five American editions.

Estimates of the work, in Derby's time, were generally favourable. *The Times* was impressed by the clearness and precision of the translation.[86] Bulwer Lytton observed to a friend: 'I have just read Lord Derby's *Homer*. I admire it intensely. In fact it amazed me.'[87] Gladstone, who was also a devotee of the classics, wrote Derby that his work had won universal acclaim,[88] but later in life he regarded it less favourably.[89] Even the hostile *Edinburgh Review* had high praise for Derby's accomplishment.[90]

Derby never indulged in self-delusion. He considered that the greatest virtue of the work was its literalness of translation, but he realized it was not 'spirited'.[91] This was the conclusion of the reviewer in *Fraser's Magazine*, who concluded that, though full of simple force and effort, it lacked passion.[92] Perhaps, then, it reflected the personality its author usually presented to the public, and since then its appeal has been greatest among kindred spirits. While his translation did not place Derby in the ranks of the great Victorian poets, it was evidence of the remarkable versatility of a man whose name had become prominent in many other, and quite alien, fields.

Because of Palmerston's conservatism at home, the Opposition during these years centred on his foreign policies. Traditionally Derby supported the tie with France which his government created in 1852, though he had little confidence in the French people. Acting together, Derby thought, England and France could have 'dictated terms to Europe, and preserved the peace of the world'.[93]

France's support of the Italian cause against Austria in 1859 muddled the diplomatic picture considerably. Derby had a rather negative attitude towards the Italians, and looked upon the Austrians as inept diplomats.[94] Probably hoping to preserve his popularity with the pro-Austrian Court, Derby in 1859 opposed Shaftesbury's attempt to have the Lords express sympathy for the Italians.[95] By late 1860, however, he concluded that the British people backed Russell's policy of Italian independence, and, without adopting an anti-Austrian line, he declared for a free and united Italy completely independent of any foreign power.[96] While he dubbed the Garibaldi expedition, and the Sardinian support thereof, a violation of international law, he characterized the Italian patriot as a great soldier and an honest politician. During these years he gradually lost confidence in the motives of the French Emperor.[97]

If Derby was guilty of various inconsistencies in matters of detail, the ends he had in view remained constant. Peace and freedom from the taxation which accompanied war, or war readiness, were ideas predominant in his thinking. Among the armed forces, only the Navy received his constant support, and a strong Navy became a definite part of the Conservative programme.

At the same time, Derby sometimes made political capital out of foreign affairs. Lord John Russell, as Foreign Secretary, was a favourite target for criticism. For a time the proposed cession of the Ionian Islands to Greece caused Derby some discontent. Greek politics had been very unstable, but Palmerston, bowing to the desire of the Ionian Islanders, was ready to cede the islands to Greece once she set up a monarchy and reorganized her government. Though Edward Stanley was considered as a possible candidate for the Greek throne,[98] Derby still opposed the cession, which he felt might weaken the British naval position in the Mediterranean, and spoke against it twice in 1863.[99]

For a time the Government's blundering in foreign affairs in 1863 made it seem that they might be overthrown. '. . . but how far are we prepared to take the responsibility of the consequences of success?' Derby asked Disraeli late that year. 'I wish I saw my way more clearly, and were better prepared to meet a *danger* which appears growing more imminent.'[100] The by-elections of this period did not strengthen the party, and the means of forming a government were not apparent. Nevertheless, Derby and Malmesbury in January 1864 were considering who should be Foreign Secretary in their new government, and the reason for their sudden interest was the question of Denmark.[101]

Late in 1863 the Palmerston Government announced that Britain would not stand idly by if Denmark were partitioned, and seemed to commit Britain to war if Prussia and Austria seized Schleswig-Holstein. These provinces were largely German in nationality, but had been the property of the King of Denmark. In March 1863 the King of Denmark had broken a settlement of 1852 by annexing Schleswig to his kingdom, and this gave the Germanic powers a cause to intervene on behalf of the German minorities in those states. When they went to war with Denmark in February 1864, it remained to be seen how far the Palmerston Government would stand by its promise to prevent the partition. Public opinion in England sympathized with little Denmark, and the Government meditated how best to intervene on her behalf.

On January 28th Derby visited the Queen. Her Majesty, he found, opposed Britain's single-handed intervention to aid the Danes, and she sought Derby's advice concerning his party's attitude on the question. Derby himself was inclined to be pro-Danish,[102] but hesitated to take up their cause in the face of opposition both by the Court and many members of his party. So he pointed out that, because both sides were divided in their sympathies, the issue probably would not become a party question.[103] The Queen was very cordial during the interview, and the rumour went out that she wanted him to form a government.[104] Derby, both for personal and party reasons, therefore, had to tread lightly on the issue, but he could hardly afford to ignore it altogether.

When Parliament met, Derby, though weak from illness, castigated Russell, whose policy of 'meddle and muddle' was characterized by 'lecturing, scolding, blustering and retreating'.[105] The criticism was well-earned, for by this time the Government was so completely divided on the question that they were incapable of dealing with the situation. Had the Conservatives chosen to do so, they might have gained ephemeral popularity by strongly espousing the Danish cause, but, being divided themselves, this would have been difficult. Disraeli apparently feared that a defeat of the Germanic powers would too greatly strengthen France; Derby was motivated largely by pacifist feelings. During the critical month of May, while the British conferred with Austria and Prussia, Derby refrained from partisan hostilities. He refused to let his ideas be made known to the negotiators, and would not discuss any of the issues before the conference. On one occasion, he warned Disraeli about being 'rather less guarded than is your wont'.[106] Though he now thought the loss of the provinces would not be of great consequence to Denmark, he fully appreciated the embarrassing position of a government which was pledged to defend them.[107]

In the unravelling of this tangled diplomatic skein, and in making political capital from it, Derby was unable to play a major part. Once it were clear that England could not prevent the partition of Denmark, the Government was clearly open to a severe censure for diplomatic bungling. But the summer of 1864 found Derby ill again, and, according to Malmesbury, 'in dreadful pain'.[108] It fell, then, to Malmesbury to introduce the censure in the Lords, and he was successful in carrying it. In the Commons, however, Disraeli failed by eighteen votes, and the Government chose to ignore the action of the Upper House. With this failure the climax of Conservative attacks on the conduct of foreign affairs was reached, and, if the affair proved anything, it was that conspicuous errors in that field alone were not sufficient to oust the Palmerston Government. 'Old Pam', Derby had written some months before, 'appears as young and as popular as ever.'[109] And even the Danish blunder did not change that!

His inability to take part in the censure discouraged Derby, but he was still alive to political developments. Writing to Disraeli in October he correctly predicted that the Government would hold an election soon while Palmerston was still around to bring them victory. 'I need say nothing to *you*,' Derby added, 'of the vital importance of the next Election. It will decide the fate of parties, at all events, for my time.'[110] For the coming session, however, he had no positive programme to offer. Before the session, in fact, he had a relapse, and for a time was in 'great danger',[111] but he was once again able to appear at the opening of Parliament in

1865, and to speak vigorously and rather humorously. Following him, Granville described Derby as hoping 'to lie in wait for a few months, tranquilly expecting that the next Parliament will see him wafted into office, and enjoying the sweets which come with office'.[112] To Derby, at the moment, these sweets seemed like a far-off illusion of youth, which, in his present condition, he could not hope to taste.

As Derby expected, there was an election that year. Some Conservatives allowed their hopes to soar, and predicted it would bring them from fifteen to thirty new seats.[113] Derby's healthy respect for Palmerston's popularity prevented his falling into such an error. On July 24th he predicted that, though all their important men would be returned, their ultimate loss would be twenty-five seats.[114] In Scotland especially the Conservative cause had a severe set-back. To Derby, this defeat seemed final. '. . . a purely Conservative Government', he wrote Disraeli, 'is all but hopeless, until, upon Palmerston's death (for he will never resign), Gladstone tries his hand with a Radical Government and alarms the middle classes. Then there *may* come a reaction: but it will probably be too late for *my* time . . .'[115] Derby admitted that his use of Kennedy's 'unmuzzling' metaphor might have lost some of the Catholic vote, but he minimized this cause, pointing out that the Conservatives had done well in his own county, which was a Roman Catholic stronghold. Derby was inclined to blame the defeat on 'over-confidence and want of exertion'.[116]

Whatever were the causes of the loss, a sizeable movement to reorganize the Conservative Party began to take shape. Disraeli, quite discouraged, was among the first to suggest such a course to Derby. Writing on August 6th, he concluded that their cause was hopeless, and suggested that he retire from the lead in the Commons, leaving Derby free to form an anti-revolutionary government by a coalition with his Whig friends.[117] In his reply, Derby presented the highest compliments to Disraeli, and refused to consider anyone else as his leader in the Commons.[118] As Derby pointed out, a coalition might lead to the installation of a Commons leader who would act independently, and he refused to be the mere nominal head of a coalition government. These letters indicate the strength of the bond between the two men, a tie based both on the expediency of their political positions, and the compatability of their ideas and views. Two things were certain.

Disraeli would not serve under anyone else in the Commons, and Derby would not take a secondary position in any government. Disraeli wrote that he was 'disinclined, in the decline of life, to serve under anybody in that assembly', and Derby felt it was a 'great mistake for anyone who has been at the head to take a subordinate post'.[119] Thus, with the two top posts occupied, a strengthening of the party by coalition with some faction was impossible. For himself, Derby expressed a desire to 'make no greater show in public affairs than that which may attach to any personal influence which I may exercise'.[120] But, in spite of this and the poverty of their prospects, Derby urged that they try to keep the party together. Derby indicated that his refusal of Disraeli's suggestion was final by observing that his letter required no answer. While the leaders, then, could find no way to strengthen the party, the undercurrents against their combined leadership waxed and waned. The election of 1865 seemed to doom the Conservatives to an indefinite period of opposition. Then, in October, Lord Palmerston died.

Palmerston's death, an event which, as Derby put it, everyone expected, but no one prepared for, caused some major political readjustments. As was expected, Lord John Russell came to power, with Gladstone as his first lieutenant. An attempt was made to strengthen the Government by offering Edward Stanley two seats in the Cabinet, but once again he was true to his House, if not to his own political beliefs, and refused. After studying the composition of the new Government, Derby concluded it would be moderate, but the appointment of an advanced Radical and a supporter of Catholic Ireland to important positions indicated that Russell expected to collaborate with those groups.[121]

The creation of a more liberal government gave impetus to the reorganization sentiment within the Conservative Party. Joliffe had called after the election, and told Derby there was a group of thirty or forty men who might join a government headed by Stanley but they would not become Derbyites. He suggested that a party meeting be called to consider the situation. To this Derby replied that neither he nor Disraeli would stand in the way of any feasible arrangement, but he objected to a meeting lest it expose their weakness.[122] Somewhat later Derby wrote Malmesbury that, if opportunity arose for a substantially Conservative government to be formed, he would not stand in the way.* However, the idea of Stanley taking over, which found favour with some Whigs, was rejected by many Conservatives, such as Peel, who said, in such a case, he would retire. But Disraeli considered the idea carefully, and spoke with Stanley regarding the possibility of his becoming both Prime Minister and leader in the Commons, only to find that Stanley was wholly unprepared to accept such responsibilities.[123] The heir to the Earldom of Derby, however, continued to receive support for the leadership from one section of the party.

Just how strong were the currents against Derby at this time is not certain. As Derby was to observe in 1866, the old Ultra-Tories had almost vanished.[124] There were younger men rising, some perhaps impatient with Derby's cautious leadership. They were to play a large part in the Reform drama of 1867. But at the moment, they wanted power, and the continued Derby-Disraeli reign seemed to block the avenues to office. According to Malmesbury, a 'small and unimportant' group wanted to replace Derby with Stanley or Disraeli. Faithful Malmesbury, when approached on the subject, asked: 'Where is the rank and file?' and turned his back on the unidentified individuals who made the suggestion.[125] Various plans, however, were put forth. One would have made the Duke of Devonshire the Prime Minister, with Disraeli as the leader in the Commons.[126] Another would have given the post of Prime Minister to Lord Lansdowne, a peerage to Disraeli, placed Stanley as leader in the Commons, and relied on Derby for out-of-office support.[127] Disraeli meanwhile strove to better relations with the anti-Reform Whigs, led by Lord Grey in the Lords, and Lowe in the Commons, as well as others of doubtful allegiance, most of whom were traditionally anti-Derby, and he tried to reassure them that his superior would do 'nearly as he is told'.[128] His influence was apparently in Derby's favour, and Disraeli sought to retain power for the man who had given him his opportunity for distinction.

The visit and frank explanation by Joliffe, as well as the persistent rumours of combinations, must have disturbed Derby considerably. His was a long record of service to the party, and he had seen it through the worst and most trying period in its modern history. But he was not one to sympathize with himself. Instead, he worked to vindicate his leadership, and no doubt

* Malmesbury, *Memoirs*, II, 342-3. (Derby to Malmesbury, November 6th, 1865). One receives the impression, however, that Derby did not want to retire.

these attacks on him, together with the implication or assertion that his ideas were old-fashioned or out-of-date, strengthened his desire to adapt himself to the new conditions and factors of the era, and made him more receptive to new ideas. In this mood, the following year, he was to advance the plan which opened a new phase of Conservative history.

Russell had always been associated with Reform, and his elevation immediately caused the question to be mooted once again. So far, however, was Derby in November 1865 from his position of two years later, that he wrote: 'The country is not for extreme measures on that head [Reform]', and hardly expected Russell to bring up the subject.[129] But Lord John Russell had decided there must be a Reform Bill and he faced a problem quite similar to Derby's in 1858 – how a bill could be fashioned to suit both Conservatives and Reformers, the Whigs and Radicals of his own group.

Derby decided that his support for a Reform Bill would be highly conditional. Speaking on February 6th he called to mind the ignoble treatment of his own bill of 1859, and warned that support of his party depended on the nature of the new measure. He went on to outline almost impossible conditions:[130]

> . . . if we disapprove of it and think it is imperfect, inadequate, or dangerous, and above all, if we think it one leading to future agitations within a brief period of a perilous character, then with whatever means we may possess we shall do our best to throw it out by fair debate and honourable opposition.

If Russell produced a mild measure, the Conservatives were likely to dub it as not likely to prevent future agitations; if it were radical, it would be thrown out on the ground that it was dangerous.

Drawing up the bill, however, was Gladstone's task. Aware of the hostility of the Conservatives, and of the Whigs in his own party, he became irresolute and indecisive. His personal desire was to produce a bill which appeared to be liberal, but at the same time not radical. On February 10th Bright wrote him in disgust:[131]

> You have had three months in which to frame a Bill, which any man knowing anything on the subject could have done in a week – & the Bill is not only not drawn, but its very purpose & extent are not yet determined. You have been hunting for figures from Parish

> offices to prove how many working men are now electors . . . as if a few thousands of Electors more or less were of the smallest consequence. I venture to predict injury to the cause & a wreck of the Administration if this miserable indecision is continued . . . This is friendly criticism, if not pleasant. I think you are digging our own political graves — *& I lament it bitterly*. . . .

At the same time, even before the introduction of the bill, Lord Grosvenor and some other Whigs were stirring up opposition to it, and Disraeli was making some overtures to help them defeat it. Being less conciliatory than Derby and Disraeli, Gladstone squirmed uneasily in his position between the two wings of his party.

Illness again prevented Derby from being present on a major occasion,* this one on March 12th when Gladstone finally presented his bill. He proposed to lower the county franchise to £14, higher than in the 1859 measure, and to lower the borough franchise to £7, a figure which Derby had been prepared to accept, rather reluctantly, for some time. None of its provisions was of a sensational nature. Its reception by the Conservatives followed that accorded their own bill by Russell in 1859. Derby, still quite ill, was unable to meet his party at their rally four days later, but he advised Disraeli '. . . you will clearly explain to them that we cannot accept, and intend to resist to the uttermost, the Government Bill — reserving only for consideration the best mode of doing so effectively'.[132] Disraeli faithfully repeated these instructions almost verbatim to the party following.

The question rapidly developed into a three-way battle. The Conservative opposition was joined by the anti-Reform Whigs, dubbed the 'Adullamites' by Bright, to block the measure. The Commons, of course, was the scene of the struggle, and there Gladstone spoke for his measure under attacks by Robert Lowe, speaking for the Adullamites, and Disraeli. During all the stages of the battle Disraeli was in touch with the Adullamites through Lord Elcho, while Derby was in communication with Lords Grosvenor and Clanricarde. The bill was brought in for a second reading on April 12th and an extended battle followed. Writing Malmesbury on April 22nd, Derby was not confident of

* Lady Derby was ill at the same time, and it was feared she might be dying. Derby, bedridden, could not even visit his wife, but sent her a message of farewell. Lady Derby, however, recovered and outlived her husband. Malmesbury, *Memoirs*, II, 350. (*Diary*, March 22nd, 1866).

the outcome, and correctly predicted that even a successful opposition would not bring the Adullamites to support the Conservatives in office.[133] A mere margin of five votes spelled success for the Government on the second reading. Thereafter Derby's chief interest was to keep the bill out of committee, for, though he had an assurance that Grosvenor would oppose the bill at every step there, he feared that the Government might in the end be successful.[134] During May the Conservatives gave the Government some close calls, but failed to force a withdrawal of the bill. The incessant attacks, however, were cumulatively becoming so effective that, on May 29th, the Queen wrote Derby as a loyal friend and asked him, because of the state of foreign affairs and her own health, not to make a party issue of the bill.[135] Much as he respected the wishes of his sovereign, Derby gave her no hope in his reply. To save himself, Russell would have to withdraw the measure.[136] The Government was by this time so committed to it that compliance with Derby's terms was impossible.

The outcome was still in doubt in early June. On June 10th the Conservatives prepared their forces in the Lords, should they be unsuccessful in stopping the measure in the Commons. In this House also the Whigs prepared to desert Russell, and Derby carefully listed those whom he might expect to aid in defeating the bill. These deserters, however, did not mean to turn out the Government.[137] What might follow a Conservative victory was still in doubt, and Derby reasoned that Russell might successfully call for a vote of confidence and win an extension of office.[138] At length, however, the oppositionists in the Commons hit upon a device which would attract enough support to scuttle the bill. Lord Dunkellin submitted an amendment to change the franchise in the borough from £7 rent paying, to £7 rate paying, thus rendering it considerably more conservative. On this amendment on June 18th the Government was beaten by eleven votes, and the struggle was over. Dunkellin was a Whig. The votes which provided the majority were Whig votes. After thirty years, then, the Whigs parted company with their allies and threw out a Whig Government, bringing in the Conservatives to defend them against the evils of Reform. But they opened the door to a party starved for office, with the memories of years of weary opposition behind them, and whose leaders were determined to find some way to rule as well as reign.

NOTES

[1] *DP*, Stanley XII. (Edward Stanley to Disraeli, August 16th and September 29th, 1859).
[2] Ibid., Derby XII. (Derby to Disraeli, September 6th, 1859).
[3] 'The New Administration', *Fraser's Magazine*, LX (July 1859), 122-6.
[4] Gathorne-Hardy, *Cranbrook*, I, 117. (*Diary*, May 1st, 1858).
[5] *DP*, Derby XII. (Derby to Disraeli, January 5th and 19th, 1860).
[6] Ibid. (Derby to Disraeli, January 19th, 1860).
[7] Ibid. (Derby to Disraeli, March 13th, 1860).
[8] Ibid.
[9] S&F, *Greville*, VII, 466. (*Diary*, March 27th, 1860).
[10] *DP*, Derby XII. (Derby to Disraeli, May 28th, 1860).
[11] *Hansard* (third series), CLVII, 1953-65.
[12] Malmesbury, *Memoirs*, II, 228-9. (*Diary*, June 2nd, 1860).
[13] *GP*, BM 44271. (Palmerston to Gladstone, February 7th, 1860). (Gladstone to Palmerston, February 8th, 1860). (Palmerston to Gladstone, April 20th and 24th, 1860).
[14] *DP*, Derby XII. (Derby to Disraeli, April 14th, 1860).
[15] *Hansard* (third series), CLXIII, 719-20.
[16] Ibid., CLVIII, 1003-4.
[17] Malmesbury, *Memoirs*, II, 227. (*Diary*, May 13th, 1860).
[18] S&F, *Greville*, VII, 478. (*Diary*, May 28th, 1860).
[19] *Hansard* (third series), CLVIII, 1528-43.
[20] S&F, *Greville*, VII, 478. (*Diary*, May 28th, 1860).
[21] B&E, *Victoria*, III, 510-11. (Palmerston to Victoria, May 22nd, 1860).
[22] *DP*, Derby XII. (Derby to Disraeli, June 27th, 1860).
[23] Ibid. (Derby to Disraeli, July 5th, 1860).
[24] Ibid.
[25] *Hansard* (third series), CLXIII, 719-24.
[26] Ibid., CLXVII, 180.
[27] *GP*, BM 44271. (Palmerston to Gladstone, August 16th, 1860).
[28] *DP*, Stanley XII. (Edward Stanley to Disraeli, October 13th, 1860).
[29] Ibid., Malmesbury XIII. (Malmesbury to Disraeli, November 20th, 1860).
[30] Ibid., Derby XII. (Derby to Disraeli, December 12th, 1860).
[31] Malmesbury, *Memoirs*, II, 242-4. (Derby to Malmesbury, December 4th and 26th, 1860).
[32] *DP*, Malmesbury XIII. (Malmesbury to Disraeli, January 2nd, 1861).
[33] Ibid.
[34] B&E, *Victoria*, II, 547-8. (Palmerston to Victoria, January 27th, 1861).
[35] Ibid.
[36] *DP*, Derby XII. (Derby to Disraeli, May 2nd, 1861).
[37] *GP*, BM 44140. (Derby to Gladstone, July 22nd, 1861).
[38] *DP*, Derby XII. (Derby to Disraeli, April 12th, 1860). (Derby to Disraeli, November 12th, 1861).
[39] Morley, *Gladstone*, II, 37. (Gladstone to Graham, November 27th, 1860).
[40] Maxwell, *Clarendon*, II, 222-3. (Emily Eden to Clarendon, date not shown).
[41] *DP*, XVII. Miscellaneous Observations §46.
[42] *RUSP*, PRO 30/22 29. (Derby to Russell, December 18th, 1861).
[43] *DP*, XVII. Miscellaneous Observations §43.
[44] Ibid. Earle XII. (Earle to Disraeli, October 27th, 1862).
[45] Ibid., Derby XII. (Derby to Disraeli, October 15th, 1864).
[46] Ibid., Lennox XIII. (Lennox to Disraeli, November 11th, 1864).

[47] M&B, *Disraeli*, I, 1635-7. (Disraeli to Palmerston, May 3rd (?), 1859).

[48] Maxwell, *Clarendon*, II, 237. (Lady Theresa Lewis to Clarendon, February 13th, 1861).

[49] *DP*, Earle XII. (Earle to Disraeli, October 27th, 1862).

[50] Ibid., Derby XII. (Derby to Disraeli, November 19th, 1863).

[51] Ethel Peel, ed., *Recollections of Lady Georgiana Peel* (New York: John Lane Co., 1920), p. 172.

[52] Maxwell, *Clarendon*, II, 228. (Clarendon to Lewis, October 10th, 1860).

[53] *Hansard* (third series), CLIX, 618-29.

[54] *DP*, Derby XII. (Derby to Disraeli, December 12th, 1860).

[55] *Hansard* (third series), CLVII, 1014-15.

[56] Ibid., CLXX, 662-4.

[57] Ibid., CLXXVIII, 1232-5.

[58] Ibid., CLXXX, 789-90.

[59] *DP*, Derby XII. (Derby to Disraeli, March 1st, 1866).

[60] *RUSP*, PRO 30/22 16. (Derby to Russell, April 14th, 1866).

[61] *Hansard* (third series), CLXXXII, 1329-36.

[62] Ibid., pp. 1983-4.

[63] Ibid., CLXI, 1699.

[64] Ibid.

[65] Ibid., pp. 1064-9, 1695-9, 1710. Ibid., CLXIX, 623-7, 1917.

[66] *Distress in Lancashire*, Speech of the Rt. Hon. Earl of Derby at the County Meeting held in Town Hall, Manchester, December 2nd, 1862. (Manchester: Thomas Sowler & Sons, 1862).

[67] *Hansard* (third series), CLXVI, 1539-41.

[68] *The Times* (London), January 22nd, 1863. (Derby's Minute to the Executive Committee, January 19th, 1863).

[69] *Report of the Central Executive Committee to the General Committee*, Fund for the Relief of Distress in the Manufacturing Districts. (British Museum).

[70] *DP*, Stanley XII. (Edward Stanley to Disraeli, September 4th, 1862). (Edward Stanley to Disraeli, October 31st, 1863).

[71] Ibid. (Edward Stanley to Disraeli, October 31st, 1863).

[72] T. E. Kebbel, *A History of Toryism* (London: W. H. Allen & Co., 1886).

[73] George Saintsbury, *The Earl of Derby* (New York: Harper & Bros., 1892), p. 146.

[74] M&B, *Disraeli*, II, 65-6. (Disraeli to Mrs. Brydges Williams, February 7th, 1863).

[75] Malmesbury, *Memoirs*, II, 285. (Derby to Malmesbury, October 31st, 1862).

[76] *GP*, BM 44272. (Gladstone to Palmerston, September 25th, 1862).

[77] *Hansard* (third series), CLXIX, 27.

[78] *DP*, Earle XII. (Earle to Disraeli, (?) 1864).

[79] Ibid., Derby XII. (Derby to Disraeli, August 4th, 1865).

[80] *DP*, XVII. Miscellaneous Observations §67.

[81] Earl of Derby, *The Iliad of Homer* (Philadelphia: Henry T. Coates & Co.), pp. v-vi.

[82] Philip Henry, Fifth Earl Stanhope, *Notes of Conversations with the Duke of Wellington* (London: John Murray, 1889), p. 286.

[83] Malmesbury, *Memoirs*, I, 414. (*Diary*, December 3rd, 1853).

[84] Derby, *Iliad*, pp. xxi-xxii.

[85] Malmesbury, *Memoirs*, II, 332. (Derby to Malmesbury, December 9th, 1864).

[86] *The Times* (London), December 3rd, 1864.

[87] Burghclere, *A Great Lady's Friendships*, p. 61. (Lytton to Lady Salisbury, January 11th, 1865).

[88] *GP*, BM 44140. (Gladstone to Derby, December 3rd, 1864); Morley, *Gladstone*, II, 193. (Gladstone to Duchess of Sutherland, December 28th, 1864).

[89] Horace G. Hutchinson, *Private Diaries of Sir Algernon West* (London: John Murray, 1922), p. 15.

[90] 'The Iliad of Homer', *The Edinburgh Review*, CXXI (1865), 70-8.

[91] *GP*, BM 44140. (Derby to Gladstone, May 17th, 1863).

[92] 'Translations of the Iliad', *Fraser's Magazine*, LXXVIII (1868), 518-31.

[93] *DP*, Derby XII. (Derby to Disraeli, December 12th, 1860).

[94] Ibid. (Derby to Disraeli, Tuesday, 1859).

[95] Ibid. (Derby to Disraeli, (?) 1859).

[96] Ibid. (Derby to Disraeli, December 12th, 1860); *Hansard* (third series), CLXI, 23.

[97] *Hansard* (third series), CLXI, 30.

[98] M&B, *Disraeli*, II, 65. (Disraeli to Mrs. Brydges Williams, December 9th, 1862).

[99] *Hansard* (third series), CLXX, 187-91. Ibid., CLXXI, 1720.

[100] *DP*, Derby XII. (Derby to Disraeli, November 5th, 1863).

[101] Malmesbury, *Memoirs*, II, 309-10. (*Diary*, January 9th, 1864). (Derby to Malmesbury, January 10th, 1864).

[102] Ibid., p. 314. (*Diary*, January 24th, 1864); Argyll, *Duke of Argyll*, II, 223.

[103] *DP*, Derby XII. (Derby to Disraeli, January 29th, 1864).

[104] Lang, *Northcote*, p. 125. (Northcote to Lady Northcote, February 3rd, 1864).

[105] *Hansard* (third series), CLXXIII, 22-41.

[106] *DP*, Derby XII. (Derby to Disraeli, May 12th, 1864).

[107] Ibid. (Derby to Disraeli, May 29th, 1864).

[108] Malmesbury, *Memoirs*, II, 327-8. (*Diary*, July 3rd and 8th, 1864).

[109] *DP*, Derby XII. (Derby to Disraeli, January 29th, 1863).

[110] Ibid. (Derby to Disraeli, October 15th, 1864).

[111] Malmesbury, *Memoirs*, II, 334. (*Diary*, February 9th, 1865).

[112] *Hansard* (third series), CLXXVII, 30.

[113] Malmesbury, *Memoirs*, II, 340. (*Diary*, July 11th, 1865).

[114] *DP*, Derby XII. (Derby to Disraeli, July 24th, 1865).

[115] Ibid. (Derby to Disraeli, August 4th, 1865).

[116] Ibid. (Derby to Disraeli, July 24th, 1865).

[117] M&B, *Disraeli*, II, 150-1. (Disraeli to Derby, August 6th, 1865).

[118] *DP*, Derby XII. (Derby to Disraeli, August 12th, 1865).

[119] M&B, *Disraeli*, II, 150-1. (Disraeli to Derby, August 6th, 1865); *DP*, Derby XII. (Derby to Disraeli, August 4th, 1865).

[120] *DP*, Derby XII. (Derby to Disraeli, August 12th, 1865)

[121] Ibid. (Derby to Disraeli, November 21st, 1865); Ibid. Stanley XII. (Edward Stanley to Disraeli, November 4th, 1865).

[122] Lang, *Northcote*, p. 147. (*Diary*, February 22nd, 1866).

[123] Ibid., pp. 140-1. (*Diary*, February 4th, 1866).

[124] *Hansard* (third series), CLXXXIV, 730.

[125] Malmesbury, *Memoirs*, II, 348. (*Diary*, February 18th, 1866).

[126] Lang, *Northcote*, p. 157. (*Diary*, March 25th, 1866).

[127] Gathorne-Hardy, *Cranbrook*, I, 187. (*Diary*, May 20th, 1866).

[128] Lang, *Northcote*, p. 153.

[129] *DP*, Derby XII. (Derby to Disraeli, November 21st, 1865).

[130] *Hansard* (third series), CLXXXI, 101.

[131] *GP*, BM 44112. (Bright to Gladstone, February 10th, 1866).

[132] *DP*, Derby XII. (Derby to Disraeli, March 16th, 1866).

[133] Malmesbury, *Memoirs*, II, 351-2. (Derby to Malmesbury, April 22nd, 1866).

[134] *DP*, Derby XII. (Derby to Taylor, May 15th (?), 1866). (Derby to Disraeli, May 26th (?), 1866).

[135] George Earle Buckle, ed., *The Letters of Queen Victoria* (London: John Murray, 1926), I, 330. (Victoria to Derby, May 29th, 1866). (Hereinafter cited as 'Buckle, *Victoria*').

[136] Ibid., p. 331.

[137] *DP*, Derby XII. (Derby to Disraeli, June 10th, 1866).

[138] Ibid. (Derby to Disraeli, June 11th (?), 1866).

CHAPTER XI

DERBY EXTENDS DEMOCRACY

On June 19th Lord John Russell announced to the Lords that, in consequence of the vote in the Commons the night previous, Parliament would adjourn till the following Monday. It was June 26th before he tendered his resignation to the Queen and provided Derby with the opportunity of becoming the first British statesman to hold the part of Prime Minister on three different occasions.

Though on April 22nd he had written Malmesbury that he would not again become a minister on sufferance, and had announced substantially the same thing at a party meeting of May 9th,[1] Derby showed less indecision at this time about taking office than he did in 1852 or 1858. Possibly he was influenced by Disraeli's plea that the honour of the Derby House demanded it, but more probably it was Disraeli's observation that, if Derby refused, the more conservative members of the outgoing government might be joined by a considerable section of the Conservative Party in forming a new government, which caused Derby to accept with alacrity.[2] It is possible that Derby had decided that Russell's stumbling-block, Reform, might be utilized to change the balance of power in the Commons.*

Because of the recent opposition to his leadership within the party, Derby considered it necessary to receive a vote of confidence from the membership. At the moment his son, Edward, was his main rival for the leadership of the party, not because he desired to be, but because he was the only man able to command support from factions outside the Conservative Party. On June 22nd Malmesbury learned on good authority that the Adullamites, the 'Forty Thieves' as Bright called them,[3] thought joining Derby

* Just when Derby decided to legislate on the subject is uncertain. In 1865 he did not think there was a real demand for Reform, and his letter to Disraeli of September 16th, 1866, is the first real evidence of such a decision. It is possible that he toyed with the idea earlier, as he stated in his famous speech of July 22nd, 1867, but, if he did, he apparently did not have in mind the extensive Reform measure which he eventually passed.

would be 'ratting', but they were willing to support Stanley as Prime Minister.[4] Probably reluctantly, Malmesbury advised his old friend that all forty of the dissident liberals would follow Stanley, but only a dozen would support a Derby government.[5] Just how Stanley felt about this boom in his behalf is uncertain. Certainly he would not take the leadership — assuming that he wanted it — without the blessing of his father, and this apparently was not given. The question was still undecided, when, on June 27th, Derby received a summons from the Queen. He immediately contacted Disraeli, and the audience was postponed for twenty-four hours while Derby consulted his friends.[6]

The two leaders arranged a meeting at Lord Derby's for the following morning, and twenty-two of the more important members arrived. Given the opportunity to express their opinions, only Lord Bath spoke out for Stanley and against a purely Conservative government. Disraeli was quick to take the force out of his arguments by declaring that the chances for coalition under Derby were not unpromising. So the meeting adjourned after giving Derby a vote of confidence to form a government, preferably with outside aid, but from his own forces if necessary.[7] Derby, on receiving these assurances from his party, immediately accepted the Queen's commission to form a government.

The position of the Conservatives, with a minority in the Commons, was similar to that occupied on the two previous occasions. So it behoved Derby once again to seek outside aid. After leaving the Queen, he wrote to a perennial political opponent, but one brought recently closer to him by the marriage of their children, and asked him to remain at the Foreign Office. In this epistle he did not neglect to mention that Clarendon's daughter was greatly excited over the prospect of their being colleagues.[8] Clarendon, however, refused. While admitting they had no important differences in foreign policy, he added quite frankly: 'I cannot quit my party, because allegiance to party is the only strong political feeling I have.'* The answer did not surprise

* Maxwell, *Clarendon*, II, 319-20. (Clarendon to Derby, June 28th, 1866). Clarendon's biographer indicates that the refusal was dictated by his distrust of Derby. Ibid., p. 317. The explanation given by Clarendon himself seems to be both frank and logical. Apparently there were also some differences between Clarendon and Disraeli. George Earle Buckle, ed., *The Letters of Queen Victoria* (London: John Murray, 1928), I, 345. (Memorandum by Victoria, June 28th, 1866). (Hereinafter cited as 'Buckle, *Victoria*').

Derby,[9] but it complicated his forming a government, for Disraeli was immovably against Malmesbury again being Foreign Secretary.

If Derby expected no aid from Clarendon, he was quite as certain that the Adullamites would not join him. About June 23rd he received news of a decision reached at a meeting of the 'Forty Thieves'— Clarendon should form a government and Stanley should lead in the Commons, thus excluding the two men who had fought the party's battles for twenty years.[10] A conversation with Elcho later confirmed Derby's suspicion that the Adullamites were unwilling to form a coalition save on their own exorbitant terms.[11] As these reports reached Derby before he received his commission to form a government, it is clear he did not expect much outside assistance. Nevertheless, Derby called in the powerful Lord Lansdowne on June 29th for an interview. Speaking with Lansdowne, Derby was much more insistent than usual and refused to be put off with a vague promise of out-of-office support. 'I entirely dissented with this view', wrote Derby, 'and argued that although I knew I could rely on his good intentions . . . the effect in the public mind of seeing him occupying a high post in the Cabinet would be very different from that produced by his non-official support . . .'[12] Lansdowne promised to consult Lord Grosvenor, another leading Adullamite, and the latter made two visits to St. James's Square. At the first meeting, only generalities were discussed, but at the second the proposals were more definite. Derby advised Grosvenor that he hoped especially to secure Lansdowne, Gregory and himself, but that his offer was not necessarily limited to those three. That evening the Adullamites considered Derby's offer, but decided to give only independent support to the new Government. Derby concluded his memorandum by remarking: 'As this answer appeared to be conclusive, I did not enter into any details, but contented myself with expressing my great regret at the decision.'[13] This action by the Whigs was decisive. They had thrown away the last chance to put a purely Conservative government in power. They forced Derby once more to face the hazards of a minority ministry, and lived, perhaps, to regret it.

Derby still hoped to secure one other statesman, who, because of his influence with the working classes, was of considerable importance. Lord Shaftesbury, the great humanitarian, was offered the Duchy of Lancaster, and, according to his own account, the proposition caused him 'much anxiety', but failed to enlist him.[14] Nor did a later offer of the choice between the Home Office and the Presidency of the Council win him over, but these offers indicate the trend of Derby's thinking. Almost as important as the confidence of the Commons was that of the British masses, and, failing everywhere else, Derby hoped for their intangible support. According to his own statement, Shaftesbury 'laboured much' to set Derby right with the masses, but was not too successful.[15]

These days during which a government was being hammered into form were always trying. This time the Foreign Office caused difficulties, for Malmesbury did not want it.[16] Stanley, a possible candidate, did not have the confidence of the Queen, and many others did not trust him. 'I own', wrote Lord John Russell, 'I should dread Stanley at the Foreign Office if Derby were not over him to keep up the traditional policy of England.'[17] The Queen's objections were overcome by Clarendon's offer to help Stanley, and by the fact that Derby could not find a more suitable man.[18] Large numbers of major and minor positions had to be filled carefully if ruffled feelings, or, worse, defections, were to be avoided.* In some cases Derby simply accepted Disraeli's recommendations.

In time the Cabinet was placed in order, and it was a rather talented one. Derby, Disraeli, Walpole, Chelmsford, General Peel, Pakington and Manners were repeaters, as First Lord of the Treasury, Chancellor of the Exchequer, Home Secretary, Lord Chancellor, War Secretary, First Lord of the Admiralty and First Commissioner of Works respectively. But some new and able men were added. Carnarvon, a scholarly man, was Colonial Secretary; Cranborne, later to be Prime Minister, was the Secretary for India; Sir Stafford Northcote, formerly a Peelite, became President of the Board of Trade. Disraeli, no doubt, deserved some credit for attracting new blood into the party and the Cabinet, and some of the younger men were not the staunch Derbyites

* Derby could usually view these political claims with good humour. He wrote Disraeli: 'Stanhope is very angry at being passed over: his Son is a sure and steady vote; and if Sir E. K. should not approve of the selection, the knowledge by Stanhope (or rather, the Stanhopes, for she is as angry as he) might serve to put them on terms of Christian charity with me – which at present they are not.' *Disraeli Papers*, Derby XII. (Derby to Disraeli, July 14th, 1866).

that had once characterized the rank and file. Gathorne-Hardy liked Derby and respected his leadership, but had little confidence in the 'old Derby team' which had governed before.[19] Carnarvon and Northcote had both been interested in reforming the leadership of the Conservative Party the previous spring.[20] Cranborne, a most difficult individual to deal with, wrote the following year: 'My connection with the Conservative party has been purely one of principle – for, as you know, I have no feelings of attachment to either of the leaders.'[21] While the Cabinet of 1866, then, was perhaps the most able of the three constructed by Derby, it was perhaps the least attached to him personally. This made it the more remarkable that, in the crises to come, he and Disraeli could hold the Government together as well as they did.

On July 9th Lord Derby made his ministerial statement before a crowded House. It provided a frank and interesting account of the current condition of parties, and contained some of those nostalgic elements which so frequently creep into the utterances of those who are consciously ageing. The old Tories, such as he and Russell had known so well, were now practically gone, Derby said, and the various factions blended into one another without sharp dividing lines between them. They were Conservatives, Liberal Conservatives, Conservative Liberals, Whigs, Liberals, Advanced Liberals and Radicals, and the problem was how to form a government out of these factions. After describing his unsuccessful efforts at coalition, he declared that his own acceptance of this 'onerous post' was dictated by fear that the Conservative Party, a material element of strength in the Empire, might be disrupted if he refused. Noting that he had been in public life too long to have to profess his political beliefs, he observed that the Conservatives, having the largest stake in the country, were the most interested in maintaining peace and prosperity. In line with this, he extended the olive branch to all nations, and stressed particularly the ties which bound England with America. Finally he took up the question of Reform,* and his remarks on the subject, though brief, were full of meaning. Desiring to remain free and unpledged, Derby at the same time

* *Hansard* (third series), CLXXXIV, 739-40. Derby asserted that the problem should be solved by an understanding between the two parties – the means unsuccessfully adopted the following February. Of some significance was his remark: 'Nothing, certainly, would give me greater pleasure than to see a very considerable portion of the class now excluded admitted to the franchise.' Ibid., p. 740.

pointed out he would not introduce a measure unless there was a fair chance of carrying it, and also that a moderate measure might not stop agitation. In closing he described the British constitutional system as '... a monarchy limited, an aristocracy tempered, a House of Commons not altogether democratic'.[22] The speech represented a great change from his position in 1852, when he was primarily interested in resisting the rising tide of democracy. But Derby, too, had changed. He was pale and nervous, his delivery was enfeebled by illness, and only at moments did he reach the old heights of eloquence. And so were many of his listeners changed. Lords Russell and Brougham, colleagues of another day, both looked 'very old and broken'.[23] The speech was well received, but Conservatives both in and out of the party were somewhat nervous about prospects,* as well they might be, for once again the Conservatives were in a desperate minority.

The session was well started when Derby took office, and any serious legislation had to be postponed until the year following. Meanwhile, the debates on Gladstone's bill, which had been received apathetically, had stimulated a new interest in Reform, which gradually spread throughout the country. This feeling, while not nearly so widespread and dangerous as in 1832, culminated in the riots at Hyde Park. Walpole, as Home Secretary, had forbidden a demonstration to be held there, but a mob of about three thousand men broke down the park fence and held their meeting. During the riots, which lasted for three days, several people were injured and one was killed. Derby at first regarded these demonstrations as a crude attempt to overawe the legislature, and to give a false impression of the depth of public feeling on Reform.[24] More orderly meetings on the subject continued to be held.

From Knowsley on September 16th Derby wrote Disraeli as follows:[25]

> I am coming reluctantly to the conclusion that we shall have to deal with the question of Reform. I send a memorandum, which

* Clarendon was rather gloomy. 'It *may* go well,' he wrote, 'but if Bright is not in office before a twelvemonth I shall be most agreeably mistaken.' Maxwell, *Clarendon*, II, 324. (Clarendon to Lady Salisbury, July 5th, 1866). The conservative *Quarterly Review* warned prophetically: 'The Conservatives would forfeit every shred of a title to the name which they assume, if they tampered one moment with democracy.' 'The Coming Session', *The Quarterly Review*, CXIX-CXX (1866), 145.

> I will thank you to return, containing a sketch of a Reform Bill drawn up by R. D. Baxter, who has the whole question at his fingers' ends. Some of his suggestions are very good. But I wish you would consider whether, after all the failures which have taken place, we might not deal with the question in the shape of Resolutions, to form the basis of a future Bill. We *need* not make the adoption of any of the Resolutions a vital question; while, if we should be beaten on some great leading principle, we should have a definite issue on which to go to the country. . . .

Three days later he left Knowsley to visit the Queen for ten days at Balmoral, while his colleague pondered the whole problem. As his biographers carefully point out,[26] Disraeli was opposed to bringing up the subject of Reform and continued lukewarm towards it for the rest of the year. One can understand that, after having witnessed Gladstone's discomfiture only recently, Disraeli had good reason to hesitate, but the reasons for his hesitation are not so important as the mere fact that he did so. This seems to indicate that he did not share Derby's conclusion 'we shall have to deal with the question of Reform', but felt that public opinion might be diverted from the subject. In his letter to Derby of September 24th he stated he saw no necessity of bringing up the subject.[27]

Derby found that the Queen was anxious to lend her support in solving the question, so, on September 27th, he again pressed the matter on Disraeli:[28]

> I agree with you that the Reform question requires very mature consideration. There is considerable difference of opinion among our own friends upon the policy: but I think the general feeling is that we cannot escape doing something. The Queen spoke to me about it the other day. She said she is very anxious to see it settled, and that if she could do anything personally to bring opinions together, she would most readily do it. On the other hand the violence of Bright's language is, I think, in our favour: not in favour of resisting all Reform, for which I believe there is a genuine demand *now*, however it may have been excited, but in favour of the acceptance of a moderate & Conservative measure. But I think that Resolutions, on which the sense of the House might be taken separately, and on which defeat on one or two might not be fatal, afford many advantages. I wish you would consider the Question seriously before we meet.

From the content of these two letters one might, perhaps, speculate upon Derby's general view of the situation. Because there was a genuine public demand, which he thought had not been present previously, the Government would have to deal with Reform. He apparently hoped that 'Bright's language' would cause the moderates of all parties to seek a conservative solution to the Reform question, and that they would co-operate with the Government, as they had on the India question, in its plan to introduce resolutions. Certainly Derby at this time did not contemplate a radical measure of Reform. On the other hand, being a politician of long experience, he could not have been unaware that there were dangers in bringing up the subject at all, and that the Government might be led into a situation which would prove highly embarrassing, or even fatal to it.*

Disraeli replied that they might inquire into certain aspects of the question, but he did not encourage Derby to any extent. On October 9th Derby wrote again to inform Disraeli that the Reform question would be taken up at the Cabinet meeting of November 1st. He explained that their resolutions would end the cry that they were 'opponents of all Reform', and suggested that many members would probably compromise to avoid a dissolution and general election.[29] He thought that the creation of a parliamentary commission with definite plans for study would also be useful. Possibly he thought that the discussions on the resolutions would bring the moderates on both sides of the House together, and end with the strengthening of the Conservative Party.

Late in October the Queen offered to contact Russell and Gladstone regarding the possibility of a private understanding on the subject, but the Conservatives did not accept.[30] Disraeli described the royal project as a 'mere phantom', and probably he was right, for about this time Gladstone wrote a friend: 'I do not envy Lord Derby and his friends their reflections this autumn on the course they have pursued. Meanwhile I wish our

* Recognizing the difficulties of dealing with Reform, the *Review* noted: '. . . to bring forward any measure affecting the representation of the people in the presence of adverse forces strong enough to engraft democratic amendments on it, would be to throw away all the advantages which the labours of this session have secured.' 'The Coming Session', *The Quarterly Review*, CXIX-CXX (1866), 147-9. While Derby at this time did not plan a bill, he did recognize the possibility of defeat on the resolutions, and a dissolution. As noted in his letter of September 16th, however, they might, in falling, identify themselves with 'some great leading principle' which would unite conservatives of all parties. Thus democratic amendments might be avoided, and the Conservative Party greatly strengthened.

press . . . will write on this text: that a bill from them, to be accepted by the people, must be larger, and not smaller, than would have been, or even would be, accepted by us.'[31] The chances of removing the subject from the field of partisan politics were thus very slim. However, the Cabinet decided that the Queen's offer might be accepted only after their proposals were laid before Parliament.[32]

At a Cabinet meeting in November Derby warned his followers of the risk of their being 'outbid' by the Opposition, but they decided unanimously not to ignore the issue.[33] On November 8th they adopted Derby's plan to proceed by resolutions, and agreed to thirteen of them.* These called for increasing the number of county and borough electors by reducing the qualifying tenements in both places, and by adding franchises not dependent on such value. The occupation franchise was to be based on rating. While more direct representation would be given labour, 'it is contrary to the Constitution of this realm to give any one class or interest a predominating power over the rest of the community'. There should be a redistribution of seats, but no borough was to be wholly disfranchised save for corrupt practices. Seats so gained would be distributed to unrepresented places which were qualified by 'population, property or special circumstances'. A commission was to be formed to revise and enlarge the borough boundaries, and to obtain other required information. County registration was to be assimilated to that which prevailed in the boroughs, new polling places were to be constructed, and the use of polling papers was to be permitted. Derby had favoured the last since about 1861 as a sort of innocuous substitute for the ballot.[34]

These resolutions were general in detail, partly because of Cabinet disagreements as to their details, partly because sufficient information to make them more definite was lacking. For instance, they decided that each borough should have a certain minimum population, but they lacked statistics which would permit a definite figure to be determined, and the matter was much discussed during the closing weeks of the year. Disraeli still was

* *Disraeli Papers*, Derby XII. (Resolutions provisionally adopted, November 8th, 1866). These resolutions were drawn up by Derby. Actually there were thirteen of them, but, in writing them, he skipped number eleven, so that the total appeared as fourteen!

restless and anxious for the Cabinet sessions to end quickly. Writing Derby on November 18th, he felt they might pass the resolutions, but he was not certain how they might justify the commission. What specific problems would it study? Bribery might be one, but he was at a loss to think of others.[35] Derby admitted the difficulty, but declared a commission was 'our only chance of escaping shipwreck, and, from what I hear, it is a very good one'.[36] By November 25th it had been unanimously decided to proceed by resolutions preparatory to the appointment of a commission, but the work of that body was still uncertain.[37]

Where to find work for the commission? About this time the idea which was to change the whole course of the Conservative Party took hold of Derby. Just when and how the concept of a 'Conservative democracy' took shape is not clear,* but by December 1866 Derby was toying with it.[38] In an undated letter to Disraeli about this time, Derby used the phrase which Gladstone admitted 'bowled us over'.[39] 'I suppose it would be absolutely impossible', wrote Derby, 'to introduce into a Reform Bill, in any shape, the principle of plurality of votes. But I have had many suggestions to the effect of giving voters of (£10) & upwards two votes, of (£20) three: in which case we might with safety go as low as Household Suffrage for single votes.'[40] Thus was the magic phrase 'Household Suffrage' introduced into party councils. Derby did not, of course, advocate pure and simple household suffrage without safeguards, but he realized the magnetic possibilities of the phrase, and sought a safe way to appropriate it for his party. In a letter of December 22nd, he again took up the problem of the commission, which he felt was needed as a 'buffer'. He pointed out to Disraeli that it might inquire into the enlargement of the boroughs for one thing, and then con-

* After the disastrous election of 1868, the *Quarterly Review* wrote: 'The phantom of a Conservative democracy was a reality to many men of undoubted independence and vigour of mind. A vague idea that the poorer men are the more they are influenced by the rich: a notion that those whose vocation it was to bargain and battle with the middle class must on that account love the gentry: an impression . . . that the ruder class of minds would be more sensitive to traditional emotions . . . all these arguments . . . went to make up the clear conviction of the mass of the Conservative party that in a Reform Bill more Radical than that of the Whigs they had discovered the secret of a sure and signal triumph.' 'The Past and Future of Conservative Policy', *The Quarterly Review*, CXXVI-CXXVII (1869), 284-5. As was noted earlier, Malmesbury was convinced of the conservatism of the labouring class as early as 1853.

tinued: 'But I would suggest, as a subject of inquiry for them that which has never been touched, the effect which will be produced by a Lodger franchise, say of £10 a year . . . The same inquiry might extend to the Savings Bank Franchise: and of all possible Hares to start, I do not know a better than the extension to Household Suffrage, *coupled with plurality of voting*.'[41] Disraeli, however, was unimpressed, and wrote Cranborne: 'I have throughout been against legislation, and continue so. Lord Derby, about the time you were here, thought it inevitable, but, as you know, his views are now modified.'[42] Just what Disraeli meant by the last sentence is uncertain, for it conveyed an erroneous impression. Derby, in fact, the following day wrote him another long letter on Reform.[43]

Certainly by the new year, Derby was convinced that household suffrage, balanced by plurality of voting was the only way out of their dilemma. Thinking, as he always did, in terms of debate, Derby could not see how, once the £10 franchise was given up, they could arbitrarily select and defend any position short of household suffrage.[44] Unlike Malmesbury, who apparently was first to believe that the working man was innately conservative, Derby was unwilling to adopt the fascinating slogan without the plural vote. However, by January 10th the Government still had outlined only a very general course and the details of the measure finally to be proposed were not clear. Following the Derby plan, they would introduce resolutions specific enough to leave 'all details to be dealt with as matters only of degree',[45] and then a Royal Commission, drawn from both sides of the house, would be appointed to study the whole question and make recommendations. Reform would be mentioned in the Speech, but the resolutions would not be revealed until February 11th.[46] Such a bipartisan approach would have resulted, if adopted, in a compromise solution of the problem. Several weeks later Derby spoke with Delane of the powerful *Times*, who expressed himself in favour of the government plan.[47] Derby learned, however, that one of the important Adullamites, Robert Lowe, opposed it.[48] Opposition might also be expected both from the anti-government Liberals, who wished to overturn the Administration on a specific proposal, and from some Conservatives who feared that the debates on the resolutions might result in a radical bill.

Derby's efforts to solve the question had meanwhile won the cordial approval of the Court. Hoping for a public sign of this support, Derby urged the Queen to be present at the opening of Parliament, and Her Majesty in the hope of strengthening the Administration, agreed. At the same time, she asked that the request should not be repeated year after year. Derby wrote gleefully to Disraeli regarding the Court: '. . . we are not only on velvet, but we may look on it at present as *Partisan*; and we can have their intervention when, and as, we choose'.[49] Striking a more sombre note, he added: 'I wish we could calculate on the "Patriotism" of the Leaders of Opposition with as much confidence as the Queen does – but it may do them some good to be made aware of H.M.'s feelings.'[50]

Later in January Derby again fell ill, and his chagrin at not being able to attend Cabinet meetings for about ten days retarded his recovery.[51] The Cabinet sessions continued without him, however, and Disraeli finally sent him another set of Reform resolutions tentatively adopted about the end of the month.[52] Actually very little had been decided. Rather strangely, the opposition to a bold scheme of franchise was stronger among some of the newer men in the party, especially Cranborne and Carnarvon, than among, save Peel, the older men. Cranborne early took a highly conservative position with regard to the extension of the borough franchise; Carnarvon, while ready to accept household suffrage by February 2nd, insisted on a large number of safeguards.[53] Early in February Disraeli sent Derby some statistics on the subject, which made him pause. 'I return the papers you left me', he wrote. 'They are conclusive to my mind that without plurality of voting we cannot propose Household Suffrage, which would give the Working Classes a majority of nearly 2:1. Even Gladstone repudiated the idea of giving them *any* majority – and our friends would not, and I think ought not, to listen to it for a moment.'[54] At the same time, Derby felt there was a general tendency 'in favour of plurality in some shape or other', but, as always, he was ready to compromise even on the single safeguard he valued so highly. Some indication that his own party would not support plurality came to him in a letter from Disraeli, dated February 4th, wherein Walpole was represented as being decidedly against the scheme.[55]

Before the opening of Parliament both Russell and Grosvenor asked for previews of the Speech. Derby, as always, granted Russell's request, but he was reluctant to recognize the Adullamites as a party by such a gesture, and feared they might misinterpret the paragraph on Reform.[56] The correspondence does not reveal whether or not he granted the request. However, on February 5th Derby appeared before the Lords and talked of many things. He dwelt for some time on the importance of maintaining good relations with 'the great Republic on the other side of the Atlantic', and then replied to Russell's observations on the non-progress of Reform since 1832. Stressing that no administration could carry a Reform bill by its own strength, Derby called for 'mutual compromise' and 'mutual forbearance' in discussing the plan Disraeli would lay before the Commons the following Monday.[57] The following day Derby expressed his satisfaction at the attitude of Parliament, but noted they were 'very hot on Reform without delay'.[58]

On February 6th the Cabinet met at Downing Street to place their Resolutions in final form. At this meeting, apparently for the first time, Derby advised, as Resolution Five, household suffrage accompanied by plural voting based on the assessed value of the house the voter occupied.[59] General Peel immediately announced that he would resign rather than accept household suffrage in any form. Disraeli observed colourfully that 'his eye lights up with insanity' any time the phrase was mentioned.[60] For twenty-four hours, Peel hung suspended between official and private life, while Derby and Disraeli feverishly exchanged letters. Derby was forced to admit – '*I* have utterly failed'[61] – and sent him to Disraeli. Peel warned Disraeli that, if the phrase 'household suffrage' were used, 'the whole of our back benches would rise and leave us, as one man', but the Commons' leader managed to soften him up considerably before returning him to Derby.[62] The Prime Minister was able to report finally: 'I have this instant seen Peel. He *consents* and *remains!*'[63] The price of Peel's remaining, however, was a modification of Resolution Five which finally read: 'That the principle of plurality of votes, if adopted by Parliament, would facilitate the settlement of the borough franchise on an extensive basis.' This represented a minor triumph for Derby, as it contained his basic ideas for a sound settlement, but its wording, if read by anyone who did not know the background of its adoption, seemed quite ambiguous. To Peel, it obviously did not mean that household suffrage was recommended.

On February 11th Disraeli redeemed the promise of the Government by producing thirteen resolutions for the consideration of the House. These Resolutions were substantially the same as those drawn up by Derby on November 8th, indicating how little progress had been made during the intervening period. Added was number five on plural voting, mentioned above, and number nine, alluded to in Disraeli's letter of November 18th, which suggested that provision be made to prevent fraud and bribery at elections. These two might help justify the creation of a commission which Derby had thought of vital importance during the preceding autumn. Disraeli's introductory speech was unusually ineffective, and, under Opposition attacks, he promised, apparently without the consent of his colleagues,[64] to present the outlines of a Government bill on February 25th, the day previously fixed to move the Resolutions. The bi-partisan approach was thus quickly abandoned under pressure from the hostile Opposition.*

This change allowed the Government only two weeks to compose their differences and agree on a Reform Bill. Derby and Disraeli worked in close concert, and apparently sought to determine the trends of public opinion from letters received, and from conversations with lobbyists and the like.[65] When the Cabinet met on February 16th they had obviously decided, with deference to Peel's strong opinions, not to propose household suffrage with safeguards immediately, perhaps hoping that the rising temper of the country might help break down resistance within the Cabinet. Disraeli's proposal contemplated a £5 rated franchise, a £50 savings bank franchise, an educational franchise, and a franchise based on direct taxation.[66] But General Peel now decided he opposed any reduction of the borough franchise, creating a new crisis.[67] After the meeting Derby sent Disraeli to the Queen to seek her aid, and to learn her attitude towards possible Cabinet changes. Her Majesty was wholly co-operative, and offered to contact Peel. Disraeli explained that Derby felt it was his own responsibility to keep his men in line, but he readily accepted the offer on Derby's behalf. He assured her, for Derby, that his superior would not quit office until a settlement was reached.[68] Derby, then, at this time apparently promised both Disraeli and the Queen to see the matter through.

* Gladstone's biographer blamed the failure of this plan on the lack of confidence the House had in Disraeli's character. Morley, *Gladstone*, II, 231.

The Queen's intervention momentarily saved the Government, and on February 19th Peel called on Derby and agreed to support any Reform measure he brought forward. This apparently emboldened the two leaders to suggest their plan for household suffrage, limited by personal payment of rates, a set term of residence, and possibly dual voting, at a Cabinet meeting of February 19th.[69] Disraeli promised to produce some statistics on the plan the following Saturday, and the Cabinet assented, though Peel explained he agreed only because he had been the only dissentient.[70] Accordingly, on February 23rd they discussed the plan, and Derby was able to report to the Queen that his Cabinet was unanimously behind the measure.[71] It seemed for the moment that the Government would be able to introduce a comprehensive plan based on an intelligible principle.

On Sunday, however, Cranborne studied the proposals more closely, and concluded that sixty per cent of the constituencies would be thrown into the hands of the new voters. After contacting Carnarvon, Cranborne wrote Derby stating his intention not to support a measure which would ruin the Conservative Party. It was a blunt, quite unpleasant, communication. 'Under ordinary circumstances', he wrote, 'I should apologize to you for not having discovered the difficulty before. But in the present case I cannot blame myself on this account . . . The error of attempting to frame a Reform Bill during the weeks previous to its production is one that in my opinion cannot be redeemed.'[72] Undoubtedly Cranborne had some cause for complaint. The original plan for resolutions and a royal commission had been designed to protract the preparation and passage of a bill, and Disraeli's sudden promise to bring in the outlines of a bill had scuttled this plan. But they had been having Cabinet meetings on Reform since November, and there is no reason to believe that a few extra days, weeks or even months would have secured unanimity.

Derby received the letter early on February 25th, the day Disraeli was to present their proposals. He sent it hurriedly to Disraeli with the note: 'The enclosed, just received, is utter ruin! What on earth are we to do?'[73] Disraeli replied: 'This is stabbing in the back. I will come to you as soon as possible . . .'[74] Fifteen minutes after receiving Cranborne's letter, Derby received a similar communication from Carnarvon. A Cabinet meeting was held at St. James's Square at noon, and Derby later described it as of 'the most unpleasant character'.[75] Cranborne, supported by Carnarvon and Peel, was the moving spirit in the revolt, and stood tenaciously by his views. Derby was scheduled to address a meeting of the party at two o'clock, and up to fifteen minutes before then he was faced with the prospect of announcing the disruption of the Cabinet.[76] At the last moment, Stanley, who certainly could not have approved such a plan, suggested they revert to an old compromise embracing a £6 borough, and a £20 county franchise.[77] In this crisis Derby decided to sacrifice his own opinions to save his Cabinet, and this plan, later dubbed the 'Ten Minutes' Bill' was adopted as the Government Reform Bill. Thereafter, Derby rushed to the party rally, and there explained the situation to his followers. He found to his chagrin that the household suffrage plan, which he candidly admitted favouring, was very well received by the members, but the 'Ten Minutes' Bill' created no enthusiasm.[78] Disraeli, of course, had the greater burden, being called upon to introduce the plan into the hostile Commons.* He could hardly do so enthusiastically, and the Opposition, such as Bright, were quick to fall on the 'wretched proposition', as the Radical leader called it. Some Conservatives were almost as dissatisfied as the Opposition, and Disraeli later told the Queen he had great difficulty in preventing some of his own men from introducing the household suffrage measure.[79] Another critical moment had been reached. To proceed with the 'Ten Minutes' Bill' meant ruin.

The attitude of the rank and file of the Conservative Party now became of great importance. Disraeli felt that they were ready for the larger measure, and no doubt this was true in many cases. Some were ready to reduce both the county and borough franchises providing they could secure a firmer hold on the county representation by eliminating the liberal influence in the counties. This could be done by extending the borough limits to include the suburban areas, and by introducing the old plan to prevent those who owned property in the boroughs from voting in the counties.[80] Undoubtedly, in other minds, the idea of a 'Conservative Democracy', which assumed the Conservative leanings of the borough workers, was uppermost. Several days later Bright told Disraeli that at the rate some of the Conservatives were going, he would

* Technically, Disraeli did not introduce a bill, but merely stated the Conservative proposals while moving the committee for the Resolutions.

soon have to hold them back, and Disraeli replied that they represented a 'considerable section' of his party.[81]

However, Derby could not overlook the influence of many Conservatives who were quite reluctant to accept the household franchise. On February 28th he wrote Disraeli: '. . . I am afraid, especially if there is a secession, that our own party will not be united in our support'.[82] He must have recalled the effect of his own secession from the Peel Cabinet in 1846, and perhaps feared a repetition of the incident. These were trying days, even more than those of 1845. The future of the party was squarely in his hands. He could pursue a bold course and perhaps risk a disruption of his party; or he could retreat to the position they had held since 1846. There was, of course, a question of honour involved. Derby never was, and never would be, an advocate of pure democracy, and he knew many of his followers, like Northcote, did not really want a far-reaching bill, but merely hesitated to 'divorce the Conservative Party from the current of affairs'.[83] Would the honourable course be to withdraw, and allow someone who had a greater faith in democracy, such as Bright, to take responsibility for the measure? Reviewing his own career, however, he found ample evidence of his own attachment to the spirit of Reform, and, more specifically, that he had never opposed Reform as such. Perhaps in the long run a wide extension would actually have a conservative influence—who could tell? In that case, even a measure which appeared radical would really be conservative. There was no way of knowing, for no one could predict how labour would vote. The tension of the situation was constant and enervating. Gathorne-Hardy wrote, '. . . I fear the mortification and annoyance had a permanent effect on him'.[84] During those exhausting days Derby no doubt recalled with satisfaction that in 1846 he had taken no part in the damnation of Sir Robert Peel.

The resourceful Disraeli, aided by Stanley, decided that a demonstration by the rank and file of the party might aid Derby in reaching a decision. The Prime Minister on February 26th had faint hopes that the intervention of the Queen and a party demonstration might bring Cranborne to support the larger measure, and he also toyed with the idea of having the Queen contact Gladstone, but nothing came of it.[85] The following day he visited the Palace, and the Queen found him in 'terribly low spirits', convinced that the 'Ten Minutes' Bill' would be opposed both by Liberals and

Conservatives, and half-inclined to consider going on with the household suffrage measure even at the risk of breaking up his Government.[86] At a Cabinet meeting that afternoon they agreed, in view of the fact that Gladstone was ready to introduce a hostile resolution to compel it, that they should abandon their Resolutions and go ahead with their bill.[87] It was, however, a quiet and unenthusiastic session. Returning home Derby found a note from Lord Grosvenor, who presented him with a rather vague Resolution he thought might be supported. Derby turned it over to Disraeli with the comment: 'I propose to tell him that in my opinion the time for Resolutions is gone by; and that we must introduce our Bill & stand by it.'[88]

The following day various individuals contacted Derby in an effort to influence his decision. Dudley Baxter, whose opinions on Reform Derby respected, advised Derby that there would be considerable 'Beer-barrel influence' under the wider plan, and Derby was inclined to agree with him.[89] The Queen also feared the household suffrage plan, and tended to favour the 'Ten Minutes' Bill'.[90] On the other hand, there were many important voices in favour of household suffrage. Disraeli wrote that the Adullamites at a meeting had declared for household suffrage and plurality.[91] At the Carlton meeting about a hundred members declared for rated, residential suffrage with three years' residence. 'If this is the general feeling (and they represent it as universal)', Derby wrote Disraeli, . . . 'I think it is a strong argument in favour of meeting our fate on the bolder line. . .'[92] But he still feared that a secession might disrupt the party. The following day he received a letter from Malmesbury, who strongly urged him to go ahead with household suffrage regardless of the opposition to it.[93]

Determined to present a bill which might pass and strengthen his party, and influenced no doubt by Disraeli, Malmesbury and Stanley, Derby made his far-reaching decision on March 1st. That day he wrote Cranborne and the others that he would recommend household suffrage as a substitute for the 'Ten Minutes' Bill' at the Cabinet meeting of March 2nd.[94] At this meeting Cranborne was much disturbed and refused to accept the change.* Carnarvon

* According to his biographer, Cranborne still spoke with deep emotion on the subject a dozen years later. Several days after the secession Derby met Cranborne's wife at a gathering. 'Is Robert still doing his sums?' Derby asked grimly. Lady Gwendolen Cecil, *Life of Robert, Marquis of Salisbury* (London: Hodder & Stoughton, 1926), I, 236-7.

and Peel joined him in opposition. Derby could do no more than inform the Queen of the defections, and receive her approval of his course. That course had caused him much soul-searching. 'Lord Derby is to be pitied,' wrote Gathorne-Hardy, 'but feels it a profound duty to the Queen to go on, and I for one will go with him.'[95] Weakened in numbers, but firmer in purpose, the Government was at long last ready to present its bill.

On March 3rd Derby consulted with Disraeli on the subject of reconstructing the Government, and the matter was arranged by taking the Duke of Richmond, the Duke of Marlborough and Henry Corry into the Cabinet. Next day Derby made his explanation in the Lords, and alluded rather vaguely to the two bills considered. He insisted the real issue was one of detail, not of principle – how many of those excluded from the vote should have it given to them, and how to prevent the electoral body from being swamped by any one class. In solving these details, he insisted his Government had every right to 'take the House of Commons, as it were, into council' on the subject.[96] Carnarvon also gave his account, and went more into detail than Derby felt was necessary.

Now that they had committed themselves to household suffrage, the next problem was the nature of the checks to be applied to it. Derby stressed plural voting, but many of his party thought that this scheme could not be adopted. Cairns wrote Disraeli on March 6th: '. . . I think it is clear that there is a great indisposition to accept in any shape, plural or dual, or cumulative voting . . .'[97] On March 9th another dangerous split opened in the Cabinet. The Duke of Buckingham, Gathorne-Hardy and Walpole were very reluctant to give up the idea of the dual vote, and at one point during the discussions, Derby handed Disraeli a note: 'If we do not take care, we shall have another breakup. Duality will defeat us – abandonment of it will destroy us.'[98] This note suggests that Derby had been won over to Disraeli's reasoning on the subject, and believed there was little chance of carrying the dual vote. Nothing, however, was decided upon immediately. The Duke of Buckingham visited Derby the following day, a Sunday, and declared, without the dual vote he did not see his way clear to support the bill.[99] Derby relayed the information on to Disraeli, along with some information regarding a former colleague: 'Peel has declared that he is no party to any agreement not to divide on the 2d Reading. He says he does not wish to say anything if he can help it; but that if anybody divides, he will, in any case, vote with them: and that if the dual vote is withdrawn, and no one has moved the rejection of the Bill, he will do so himself! It is indeed a regular debacle on all sides!'[100] A fear that the secessionists might create an opposition faction within the party no doubt prompted Derby to call a meeting of the party before the bill was introduced. He informed Disraeli of his intention the same day.[101] Late that night Derby received conciliatory letters both from Buckingham and Marlborough, and these brightened an otherwise dreary day.[102]

During the next four days the Cabinet gradually constructed a Reform Bill. It was finally decided to enfranchise all who had a residence of two years and personally paid poor rates. This, of course, was a modification of the earlier plan, which required three years' residence, but Derby realized at least as early as March 3rd that the three-year provision could not be maintained. He noted in a letter to Disraeli that this would disfranchise some people qualified under the old Act.[103] Disraeli estimated 115,000 would be enfranchised under the modified plan, and 50,000 could become eligible if they took over their rate payments from their landlords. Derby insisted a second vote be given to those who paid both rates and direct taxes, but was not ready to stake his Government on the issue.[104] It was thus a large bill, but one based on an intelligible principle – that those who paid taxes should have a voice in the government.

Rising from an illness earlier that week,[105] Derby explained the bill to a large meeting of his followers on March 15th. He declared that a two years' residence and payment of rates were its essential points, and suggested the dual vote might not be carried.* The reception of the plan was very encouraging, and it seemed the party might give it almost unanimous support.[106] Derby had thus far taken the lead, and had borne the weight of the important decisions. Now the load was transferred to Disraeli's shoulders.

* This follows M&B, *Disraeli*, II, 253. According to this source Derby explained that 'The dual vote would be proposed, but he admitted the Government were not strongly wedded to it.' Compare with: Buckle, *Victoria*, I, 407-9. (Disraeli to Grey, March 15th, 1867). This writer has no explanation for the discrepancy. It seems, however, that the former account must have been taken from some unidentified memorandum on the meeting.

The Opposition lay in wait for the minority leader. Gladstone had a carefully kept file of Derby's, Disraeli's and Stanley's utterances on Reform, and a number of possible plans of his own.[107] One undated memorandum on the subject reads as follows:[108]

> That a plan for the Reform of Parliament which would fix the suffrage in Boroughs, and the limit downwards of liability for the direct payment of rates at five pounds ratable value, with a franchise for lodgers in due proportion, and with every facility which is at the command of Parliament for the registration of those householders, being otherwise qualified, who by law bear local taxation in the form of rent; which would place the occupying franchise in the Counties at twelve pounds ratable value; which would materially enlarge the proposed scale for the redistribution of Seats; and which would make a moderate addition to the number of representatives for Scotland without adding to the whole number of members of this House: would afford a just basis of settlement of the question.

Bright's desires were outlined in a conversation with Disraeli on March 1st. 'I advised him . . . that £5 rating franchise or household suffrage would save him in the boroughs, and that £10 or £12 would do in the counties.'[109] Save in the counties, neither of these plans was more liberal than the one offered by the Conservatives. The opposition to the bill, then, was largely a matter of detail and party politics.

On March 18th Disraeli introduced the bill into the Commons, and immediately a hard fight loomed ahead. Ralph Earle, one-time intimate of Disraeli, wrote Derby the same day that he could not support the bill and must resign his office.[110] This, however, was a minor defection, and Peel's prediction that the whole back bench of the Conservative Party would bolt at the mention of household suffrage was not borne out. But Disraeli was hard-pressed to stave off the partisan attacks of Gladstone, and on March 24th he wrote Derby: 'It is very trying, and no doubt we shall, both of us, always remember the year 1867.'[111] The Chancellor of the Exchequer, however, managed to have his bill read a second time. Just before his 'marvellous & memorable speech', as Disraeli himself called it, Derby sent a note of instruction and encouragement:[112]

> I hope it has not been forgotten, and, if it has, that it will not be, that Sir R. P. declared last year that there was no safe standing-point short of Household Suffrage! Last night was excellent.

> Hardy has quite vindicated our selection of him, and has placed himself in the front rank, *as a debater* . . . P. Talbot sat by Delane all through the debate and the latter said 'Gladstone has done you more good than all your Cabinet together.' Shall you close tonight? If so, excuse me for saying I hope you will be as short and pithy as possible, striking the Key-note which I understand to have been agreed upon between us, of willingness to consult the opinion of *the House*, but refusal to submit to the dictation of one assumed Leader of a Party. If you are going to speak, don't trouble to answer, but request somebody to write or to come up.

It is apparent that during the initial stages of the battle, Derby helped decide on the tactics to be used in the Commons. On March 25th Hardy had been unexpectedly delegated to follow Gladstone in the debate, and Derby, who had made the choice, sent him a warm note of appreciation thereafter.[113] Disraeli's speech also called forth Derby's highest praise:[114]

> I cannot let the day pass over without offering you my cordial congratulations on your splendid achievement of last night. I hear from all quarters that it was the finest speech you ever made; and you seem to have carried the House bodily away with you. In fact, you have won our game for us; and in writing the Queen this morning, to announce your 'triumphant success', I told H.M. that I now, for the first time, entertained a sanguine hope of carrying a Bill through in the course of the present session . . . The most dangerous rock I now see ahead is the proposal for a £5 rating, and excluding those below the line from the option of claiming to be rated. That proposal will, I am afraid, carry both 'Caves' with it.

The 'rock' which Derby saw ahead rapidly became a reality. Gladstone tried to substitute the £5 rating franchise for the larger measure proposed by the Conservatives, but found the Liberals would not follow him. 'Some malcontents on our side met this afternoon;' Bright wrote, 'conspired to defeat measures of Mr. Gladstone . . . They have done their utmost to defeat him and the Liberal Party.'[115] Gladstone, however, continued to press his ideas, and there was another great division on April 12th and another defeat. Following it Bright recorded woefully: 'We are destroyed by deserters from our Party, some honest and misled, some far from honest.'[116] The methodical Gladstone made a list of forty-five Liberals who deserted him on that division, and the ten Liberals absent because of 'disaffection'. He reduced them to four groups: Lord Grosvenor's followers, Advanced Liberals who favoured household suffrage, some who desired to save the bill or the Government, and some who feared dissolution or had 'worse' motives.[117] By April 19th Gathorne-Hardy noted that the disunity of the Opposition was complete.[118] These failures probably resulted from the lack of a real plan supported by Gladstone and Bright which was as logical and defensible as household suffrage. Nevertheless, it was a hard fight, and Derby wrote the Queen on April 12th:[119]

> He hopes that your Majesty will have approved the tact and temper with which the Chancellor of the Exchequer has conducted the harassing controversy in which he is engaged in the House of Commons; a controversy the more harassing, inasmuch as the disorganized state of the House places the decision of every question in the hands of a certain number of gentlemen, on whose vote it is almost impossible to calculate beforehand, who have little or no concert even among themselves, and who really hardly know what it is they desire. . . .

The following month some highly important changes were made which liberalized the bill considerably. Early in May Disraeli gave up the two years' residence qualification and it was reduced to a single year. An even more important question, however, arose towards the middle of May. The compound householders did not pay their rates directly,* and it was originally intended to deny them the vote unless they assumed the payment of rates personally. As a group, they numbered about half a million people, and thus their case was of first-rate importance. J. T. Hibbert proposed an amendment early in May designed to give them the vote without being directly rated, but Disraeli was able to beat him on the ground that it subverted the principle of his bill, which called for direct payment of rates. Shortly thereafter, however, another member offered an amendment whereby occupiers were made directly responsible for paying the rates, and this opened the door to a swarm of new voters. Disraeli accepted the amendment, and it was probably one of those which Derby later said had been accepted without sufficient discussion and even without his being consulted.

* Derby explained the position of this group later. Collecting rates from the compound householders was a sort of modified tax farming. The landlord made a contract for his tenants and paid the rates himself. He went on, then, to recover the rates from the tenants, and was allowed to keep a certain portion of the rates for assuming the risk. *Hansard* (third series), CLXXXVIII, 1790.

Later, when the question of redistribution was taken up, a motion was introduced to deprive each borough whose population was less than ten thousand, rather than seven thousand, as the Conservatives planned, of their second member. The Government resisted this change, but was beaten on the division when seventy-two of the Conservative members supported the motion.[120] This provision deeply affected the agricultural interest, and the fact that it passed indicates there was some deterioration in the discipline of the Conservative Party. As finally constructed, the measure was so large that Derby later had to admit he did not know how many people would be enfranchised as a result of it.[121]

Derby's attitude towards these later changes is not clear. Up to the end of March he participated in all of the decisions on the bill,* but after that he seems to have faded from the scene. From March 30th until April 6th he was forced to be absent from Cabinet meetings where strategy was discussed.[122] He missed another highly important session on April 13th, and three days later he wrote Disraeli he was leaving town and hoped to return in 'better force'.[123] At that time, Derby was evidently quite satisfied with the bill. In May, accompanied by Disraeli, he attended the Royal Academy dinner, where the two leaders made rather mediocre speeches.[124] About this same time the Prime Minister conducted the negotiations which placed Walpole, who had shown up badly during the Hyde Park riots, in the Cabinet without portfolio, and brought in Gathorne-Hardy as Home Secretary.[125] That he was considerably enfeebled, however, is indicated by a letter from General Grey to the Queen, dated May 7th, which observed: '. . . Mr. Disraeli is evidently the directing mind of the Ministry, and . . . he is the person to whom any representation can now be most effectively made.'[126] Derby's health and control of the party, then, during the weeks when these decisions were made, seems to have been precarious. At the time of the secessions Hardy noted that the events then had a 'permanent effect' on Derby, but his collapse apparently did not take place till late March.[127] During May he was able to resume his leadership in the Lords, and carried on with fair efficiency. He also wrote Disraeli on a number of

* A letter written later that year noted that the 'real attack' came in March. It must have been rather late in the month, however, for Derby's ineffectiveness seems to date rather to April than March. *Disraeli Papers*, Derby XII. (Emma Derby to Disraeli, September 26th, 1867).

minor governmental matters, and on May 15th he was involved in the problems of the boundary commission.[128] Three days later, however, Disraeli made his important decision on the compound householders, and his letter of May 18th to Gathorne-Hardy contained an implication that there was no one to turn to for advice in the matter.[129] This would indicate that Derby was once again *hors de combat*, though he was present in the Lords on May 20th.

In view of this evidence, it is apparent that Derby had little control over the bill in the Commons during April and May, and was unable to use his influence to keep the party in line. Probably he would have preferred to exclude the compound householders, and to keep the two years' residence qualification. And there could be no question but that he wanted the original redistribution provision, for the agricultural interest lost about fifteen seats by the change. Other Conservatives might have been ready to put their trust in the new borough voters, but it is doubtful that Derby would have been willing to go so far. The amount of time he spent studying the problems of the boundary commission, however, indicates he might have hoped some polite form of gerrymandering would create solid Conservative constituencies in the counties.

Gladstone expected the Conservatives counted on the Lords to modify the bill, and the Queen, though an advocate of moderate Reform, had the same idea. On June 25th she wrote the Prime Minister:[130]

> She feels that it is impossible to recede from whatever concessions to popular feeling the Government has already made. All she would earnestly urge upon Lord Derby, is, to allow any amendments which may be proposed in the House of Lords, with a view to avert the danger which many people apprehend from the great increase of democratic power, to receive a fair consideration from the Government. She cannot believe that, even in the House of Commons, some modification of a measure, which even the most advanced Liberals regard with some degree of alarm, would not be willingly accepted.

Derby, however, held out little hope to the Queen. He admitted some modifications of the original plan had been adopted without sufficient discussion, even without his being previously consulted, but he stressed that these changes sprang from his minority position, and because there was no recognized Opposition leader with whom to deal. He went on:[131]

> On the whole, although one or two provisions have been inserted which Lord Derby would rather have seen omitted, he is inclined to hope that, as a whole, the arrangement which has been hitherto made, may be looked on as satisfactory . . . Your Majesty, however, will not fail to see that it will require very nice judgment to decide what amendments, if pressed, it may be possible to accede to, without running the risk of their rejection by the House of Commons, and the consequent loss of the Bill. . . .

Two days later he was again confined to bed with gout and rheumatism.[132]

The Reform Bill received its first reading in the Lords on July 16th. Two days later resistance to it formed around the son of the former great Reform Prime Minister, Lord Grey, and some understanding with Russell was reached to amend it in committee. When, on July 18th, Grey laid his amendment on the table, Derby hastily wrote Disraeli:[133]

> . . . I have immediately sent out as strong a Whip as possible against it. But I learn that the whole of the Opposition will support him and he has been tampering, and, with the aid of Carnarvon, not unsuccessfully, with our people. It is therefore quite in the Cards that we may be left in a minority, in which case it is very important not only that we should consider our course of proceeding, but that I should know the language which I must hold at a meeting of our Party which is summoned for tomorrow at 3 o'Clock . . . It is *essential* that I should see you.

Between the two the details of their countering moves were worked out.*

The afternoon of July 19th a large meeting of important peers was held at Derby's residence, where they heard their chief's plea for unity. Reviewing the history of Reform, Derby declared that the events of 1859 had proved there must be a reduction of the borough franchise. Gladstone's bill of 1866, lost by its author's imperiousness, would not have been a final settlement, but a stepping-stone to new demands. Russell, Derby observed, was

* The tone of this letter shows a marked dependence on Disraeli, much greater than Derby's letters of four months before. Only occasionally did Derby assume such an attitude. The Grey Amendment declared that the bill was unacceptable in the form drawn up by the Commons, but that the Lords would give it a second reading and amend it in committee.

wrong to resign over his defeat on Reform, but once he, Derby, came to power, he was ready to resign if Reform were not taken up. It became his object '. . . to act so as to place the Tory party permanently in power & not to place them in a position to be beaten as soon as they had served the purpose of the opposition'. Then he reviewed the story of the Cabinet dissensions, and the factors which created the bill. In recommending it to his followers, Derby declared it was the most conservative measure that could be adopted, that it was based on an intelligible principle, and that it had the unanimous support of the Commons. While acknowledging the power of the Lords to discuss the bill, he vigorously denounced the Grey amendment, and said he would not send the bill into committee with such a stigma attached to it. The adoption of the Grey resolution meant a rejection of the bill, and this would lead to the fall of the Conservative Government. Derby's speech, which was occasionally interrupted by applause, was followed by some comments from their lordships. Carnarvon and Rutland were hostile to the bill, but the sentiment was generally in favour of beating down the Grey resolution.*

At Rockhampton on Sunday, July 21st, Derby prepared his speech for the following evening. In reviewing their plan for redistribution, he suddenly discovered they had apparently overlooked a seat given to London University, and had therefore added one seat to the total English representation. Hastily Derby wrote Disraeli,[134] and shortly thereafter the latter replied, pointing out that South Lancashire counted for only one, and not two seats, as Derby had figured. To have made such an error indicated Derby's uneasy state of mind, and he wrote apologetically: 'It was stupid in me not to recollect that S. Lancashire only counts for one seat. I am very nervous about what I have to do tonight, though Grey appears to have collapsed. . . .'[135]

The evening of July 22nd Derby introduced his Reform Bill into the Lords with a long and telling speech. The first part was spent in reminiscences, recollections of the rotten borough system, and of Grey's desperate attempts to amend the franchise in 1832. Praising the Reform Bill of 1832, Derby admitted that the new one

* This paragraph is based on some fragmentary minutes found in: *Disraeli Papers*, Reform Bill XIV. At what appears to have been an earlier meeting, Derby apparently threatened to resign if his peers did not support the measure. Malmesbury, *Memoirs*, II, 371. (Undated entry).

probably would not improve the legislature, but he accused Russell of upsetting the previous settlement and making a new Reform inevitable. In justifying his own introduction of a measure, Derby showed that his party had never committed itself against Reform. Then he stated briefly and frankly his political motives in introducing the bill:[136]

> I did not intend for a third time to be made a mere stop-gap until it would suit the convenience of the Liberal party to forget their dissensions and bring forward a measure which would oust us from office and replace them there: and I determined that I would take such a course as would convert, if possible, an existing minority into a practical majority. As our political opponents had failed in carrying a measure, the carrying of which was of vital importance to the interests of the country, and the postponement of which, added to the public inconvenience and embarrassment year after year, and the agitation for which was standing in the way of every measure of practical improvement and practical legislation, I felt it to be my duty to undertake this difficult task — a task which, as I thought, it was all but impossible to fulfil: and despite of any taunts of inconsistency, despite of any opposition to endeavour towards the close of my political career to settle one great and important question of vital importance to the interests of the country.

Derby then went on to discuss the terms of the measure. He explained that once the £10 borough franchise were abandoned, the only way to end agitation was to adopt household suffrage, accompanied by residence and rate-paying requirements. While he regretted the defeat of the dual vote proposal, and the lowering of the residence requirement from two to one year,* he did not recommend that the Lords try to re-establish these safeguards. In his opinion the permanently established ratepayer would make an 'intelligent and honest voter', and was superior to the £6 or £7 householder who did not pay rates. While he explained the problem of the compound householders in some detail, Derby did not clarify his opinion of this important change.† Going on

* During the discussions on the residence requirement it had been pointed out that the delay between the application for the vote and the actual registration would be about six months, so that the voter would have about 18 months' residence requirement in any case. For this reason the two-year residence provision was not insisted upon. *Hansard* (third series), CLXXXVIII, 1788.

† Derby, however, would have liked to permit the landlords, if they chose, to pay the rates, and allow the tenants to waive their rights, but the Commons would not

to the redistribution provisions, Derby explained that the enfranchisement for the first time of some large towns would remove a large number of voters from the county constituencies, and that the lowering of the franchise would remove many of the freeholders then voting in the counties into the boroughs. These provisions were at least mildly conservative in nature. In summing up, Derby called the measure 'large, extensive and Conservative', and pointed out that it was likely to put the matter to rest for many years.[137] He therefore called upon the Lords to resist the Grey amendment.

Carnarvon rose to complain that the county constituencies would be disturbed.[138] Granville followed with heavy sarcasm, and, while expressing doubt concerning its authenticity, told a story of one of Derby's followers who visited the Prime Minister and complained of the radical nature of the bill. Derby had simply replied: 'Don't you see how it has dished the Whigs?'* Granville also charged Derby with exercising a coercive influence over the Lords through his control of Scotch and Irish representative peers.[139] The debate continued into a second night, and at that time Derby complained of Granville's 'dish the Whigs' charge, and pointed out that, during Victoria's reign the Conservatives had created only fifteen peers, while the Whigs had been responsible for sixty-five.[140] Russell spoke on the second night and complained that Derby, while planning 'great democratic measures' had encouraged his followers to resist the £7 franchise.[141] But the movement against the bill collapsed. Blaming Russell for not joining him, as he had promised, Grey agreed not to go on with his amendment.[142] The bill, in fact passed its second reading with little difficulty. As one authority pointed out, the Lords accepted the Reform Bill from Derby in much the same way as they accepted the alteration of the Corn Laws from Wellington.[143] Had the measure been presented by a Liberal government it would undoubtedly have encountered considerable opposition.

Lord Derby again fell ill late in July, and it fell to Malmesbury to guide the bill through the early stage of the committee. His orders were to resist amendments, but one of his own party, Lord Cairns, was able to carry through a proposal to allow

* Ibid., pp. 1857-8. The expression 'dish' was commonly used. See also: Hodder, *Shaftesbury*, III, 218. (*Diary*, March 9th, 1867).

---

agree. He predicted that, under the bill, there would be some difficulty in collecting the rates. *Hansard* (third series), CLXXXVIII, 1790-1.

minority representation in the large cities.[144] In three-member constituencies, the voter was to be given only two votes, which was expected to aid the minority party in securing one of the seats. Derby did not like 'three-cornered constituencies', and was not enthusiastic over the change, but the amendment was subsequently accepted by the Commons. Lord Grey proposed to modify the redistribution provisions to make twenty-three more seats available for distribution, but, as his party would lose by the change, Derby left his sick-bed on August 1st to resist the amendment, and was successful by a twelve vote margin.[145] He supported Salisbury's motion to allow the use of polling papers, and, though it was carried by the Lords, it was later rejected by the Commons.[146] Russell proposed to lower the lodger franchise from £15 to £10, and Derby wrote Disraeli: 'Shall I give him a helping hand, if I can manage to do so without offending our friends?'[147] Disraeli agreed, and the proposal was carried. A rider, which would have given the lodger franchise to resident members of Oxford and Cambridge universities, was later rejected by the Commons. By and large, however, there were no major attacks on the bill in the Lords.

On August 6th the bill was read for the third time. Russell rather grudgingly approved it, but he could not resist recalling how Derby had once, owing to the fickleness of a democratic electorate, lost his seat to 'Orator' Hunt.[148] The Prime Minister rose to thank the House for its co-operation in passing the measure, and concluded with his own frank, and famous, appraisal of the measure:[149]

> No doubt we are making a great experiment and 'taking a leap in the dark', but I have the greatest confidence in the sound sense of my fellow-countrymen, and I entertain a strong hope that the extended franchise which we are now conferring upon them will be the means of placing the institutions of this country on a firmer basis, and that the passing of this measure will tend to increase the loyalty and contentment of a great portion of Her Majesty's subjects.

As finally passed, the Reform Bill of 1867 was an important step along the road to democracy in England. All rate-paying householders could vote, as could the £10 lodgers in the boroughs, and the £12 occupiers in the counties. Conservative influence in the counties remained very strong, and they stood by the party fairly well in 1868, gave them a sweeping victory in 1874, and not until 1880 was there a serious defection there. Following the enfranchisement of the rural workers in 1884, the rural vote swung towards the Liberal camp. The effect of the Reform Bill of 1867 on Conservative fortunes in the boroughs was to bring defeat in 1868, and a victory in 1874.

At the time of its passage, no political leader knew what to expect from the bill. Gladstone, Russell and Bright were uncertain about it, but nevertheless tried to claim credit for its passage, though it went far beyond their modest measure of 1866. Actually the father of the bill was the spirit of the times, for British political evolution had been working towards a democratization of the franchise for many years, and by 1867 public sentiment favoured a large change. The main question was merely whether it should be passed by the Conservatives or the Opposition. If credit can go to individuals for it, Derby's services should be recognized for demanding that Reform be brought up, for having projected the original household suffrage idea, and for having used his wide influence as an arbiter of conservatism to secure its passage, though he surely doubted the wisdom of some of the clauses of the final act. It was a supreme undertaking for an invalid statesman in the evening of his life, and it would have been impossible without the services of Disraeli, whose parliamentary manœuvring kept the Conservatives in power. To the Liberals must go the credit for having carried it far beyond its original provisions.*

To Gathorne-Hardy, however, must go the credit for expressing in writing the thoughts then clouding the minds of all the political leaders. 'What an unknown world we are to enter, but I believe more safely, or at least as safely, and more permanently than a £5 franchise would enable us to do. If the gentry will take their part they will be adopted as leaders. If we are left to demagogues, God help us!'[150]

The passing of the Reform Bill of 1867 brought with it the

* According to one authority, if the bill had been passed with the safeguards proposed by the Conservatives, the electorate would hardly have been greater than that contemplated in Gladstone's bill of 1866, and the dual vote would have strengthened considerably the upper classes. Derby, as we have seen, had little hand in liberalizing the measure, but merely accepted it. See: Charles Seymour, *Electoral Reform in England and Wales* (New Haven: Yale University Press, 1915), pp. 258-79.

unresolved question of whether or not, from the standpoint of political ethics, the Conservative Party should have passed it. Lord Clarendon wrote that all the liberals were alarmed at the 'leap in the dark', and he felt Derby had destroyed the constitution.* Privately Russell condemned the measure as a 'democratic version of Bright's scheme', and wrote Gladstone that it had been carried by a series of brilliant lies.[151] Lord Dalhousie observed that 'Derby has set himself to prove that dishonesty is the best policy . . . Where we have lifted the sluices of democracy an inch; he and Dizzy have raised them a foot. My only hope is that they will be the first to be washed away in the flood.'[152] Robert Lowe wrote privately: 'Derby and Dizzy utterly deceived everyone and did so avowedly for the most sordid motives, what worse can be said of them than they said of themselves.'[153]

Some periodicals were particularly bitter. *Fraser's Magazine* wrote:[154]

> They, the Derby-Disraelites, stand arraigned for having obtained office under false pretences, and for having drifted or blundered into what they themselves describe as the most perilous of courses, from a determination to retain office at the sacrifice of principle, conviction or consistency . . . That they go on calling themselves Conservatives after what has recently taken place, is one of the most extraordinary facts connected with them.

It went on to describe an incident at the Carlton Club. A messenger boy with a sense of humour stopped by and asked: 'Is this the Reform Club?' The angry reply was: 'No, you rascal, the Revolution Club.' Then it concluded: 'Party discipline may compel votes: it cannot compel conviction, hide regret or cover shame.'[155] The most scathing denunciation of Derby, however, was made by his former colleague, Cranborne. Writing for the *Quarterly Review*, he observed:[156]

> This species of 'obloquy' Lord Derby experienced in 1852 on the subject of Protection, and again in 1859 on the subject of the county franchise: and by the readiness with which he has executed a still more startling change this year, he appears not to have disrelished the sensation. But the charge recorded against him by

* Maxwell, *Clarendon*, II, 333 and 351. (Clarendon to Lady Salisbury, June 19th, 1867). While this letter containing the 'leap in the dark' expression is dated June 19th, Derby used it in Parliament in August. Derby was fond of the expression and must have used it in private before his well-known speech in Parliament. As was noted above, he used it many years before in another connection.

recent events is far graver than that of any change of opinion, however rapid. It is that he obtained the votes which placed him in office on the faith of opinions which, to keep office, he immediately repudiated. It is that — according to his own recent avowals — he had made up his mind to desert these opinions at the very moment he was being raised to power as their champion . . . It is true, as the Duke of Argyll observed, that Lord Derby, in his determination not to become a stop-gap, has become a weathercock.

These charges should not be dismissed lightly, and the view of Derby's activities contained in them might be summed up about as follows. Derby and Disraeli were committed to a party which had been traditionally opposed to the extension of democracy, and their followers had a right to believe they would stand by this principle. While their giving up the resolutions might be explained readily enough, when they brought in a measure calling for household suffrage, they emphasized that safeguards such as the dual vote and the residence qualification would render it safe, and gave the impression that they would stand by these safeguards. Yet they quickly abandoned these important provisions for no better reason than that they were determined somehow to pass a bill and to retain office. Subsequently they invented the story of deciding, at the time Derby took office, to take steps to convert 'an existing minority into a practical majority' as a means of covering up the fact that they were forced to accept a bill they did not want. Under these circumstances, the best that could be said of them was that they might have sensed a willingness in their party to grant a large reform for political reasons, and, by various misleading devices, accomplished this end.

In explaining Derby's part in this sequence of events, and in partial answer to these charges, one might be permitted to indulge in some speculation. Derby obviously had been deeply annoyed in the past by the cavalier treatment both of his Administration and his party by the Opposition — his speech of February 8th, 1855, and his letter of December 15th, 1856, to Malmesbury indicate that. No doubt he also resented the treatment given his Reform measure of 1859. During the 1860s two other factors appeared. Derby's fear of the masses, so marked during the period 1846-52, lessened as a result of his intimate observation of their conduct during the cotton famine; and opposition to his leadership within the party increased considerably. This opposition was particularly strong among the newer elements in the party, and was much in evidence just prior to Derby's assumption of office for a third time.

It might well have been that Derby, in assuming office in 1866, hoped in some way to vindicate his leadership. About the only way of doing this was to reform the franchise in a manner which would give his party, almost stationary for twenty years, a numerical majority in the Commons, and his ministerial statement of July 9th indicated both that he might deal with Reform, and that his measure on the subject might be more radical than those offered previously. He believed, however, that the Conservatives had no right to originate such reforms, but could take them up only in response to a genuine demand. During the summer of 1866 that demand became apparent, and, as we have seen, he immediately took up the subject with Disraeli. To that extent his statement of July 22nd, 1867 – 'I determined that I would take such a course as would convert, if possible, an existing minority into a practical majority . . .' – was undoubtedly accurate.

But the 'course' he determined upon was entirely different from the one he actually took. He may well have hoped that his Government would fall (as his letter of September 16th, 1866, to Disraeli indicates) on some 'great leading principle' and that an election would be held which would convert his minority into a majority. However, it seems probable that he thought his new strength would come from those who feared an extensive measure such as was advocated by Bright rather than from the working classes, as is implied in his statement of July 22nd, 1867.

Things, of course, did not go as he had anticipated. Disraeli probably was opposed to bringing up the Reform question because he feared Derby would not support a strong measure of Reform, and apparently had little faith in Derby's plan to fall on a leading principle. But, after the failure of the resolutions, Derby gave his word both to Disraeli and the Queen to see the matter through, and this permitted the opportunist Disraeli a considerable freedom of movement. Derby's real spiritual crisis, however, came with the resignations from his Cabinet, the patching-up of the Government, the introduction of the 'Ten Minutes' Bill', and the inevitability of defeat resulting from the last. That this was a genuine crisis is shown by Gathorne-Hardy's remarks – 'Lord

Derby is to be pitied', and 'I fear the mortification and annoyance had a permanent effect on him'.

While Lord Derby had steadfastly refused the advice and guidance of others in matters of honour, he evidently struggled with himself at this time. If he continued in office the chances were that the conservative household suffrage measure would be liberalized far beyond his original intentions. Wellington and Peel in 1829 had, indeed, sponsored a measure they had previously opposed, and the latter in 1846 had passed legislation which represented a reversal of his earlier opinions. Derby had recognized their right to change their minds. Disraeli's arguments that many Conservatives wanted a suffrage bill, and that such a bill might prove their political salvation also carried weight.

Once he decided to go on, Derby seems to have accepted the changes, the sweeping away of the safeguards, without really fighting for them. The idea of a deal with the Opposition probably crossed his mind, but the 'disorganized state of the House', mentioned in his letter to the Queen of April 12th, made such a thing difficult. The current of affairs in the Commons simply swept by Derby. Had Palmerston, or even Russell, been in the Lower House at the time, Derby would undoubtedly have been able to exercise some control of the measure through a *sub rosa* understanding with them.

Under the existing circumstances the bill came out of the Commons in a form that neither of the Conservative leaders really understood. In spite of the various explanations sometimes advanced, Disraeli's part in the passage is still difficult to understand. Once Derby had promised to go on, Disraeli could operate behind the shield of his associate's honour, for the responsibility for the measure was ultimately the Prime Minister's. While he liberalized the bill, Disraeli's activities, or lack of them, at the next election buttress the suspicion that he did not fully realize the implications of what he had done.

On the other hand, some defence can be made of Derby's right to pass the bill. His principle regarding the franchise had always been that it should be withheld only if the prospective voters could not be trusted to use it wisely. Undoubtedly he was more convinced of the trustworthiness of the householders in 1867 than he had been twenty years before. If Derby had not passed the bill, then who, by his public and private pronouncements, was qualified to pass it? According to Russell's definition of the Whig principles on the subject, he could hardly have honourably passed the measure.* Gladstone, as was noted above, in framing his bill of 1866 was quite as interested in excluding people as including them, and he had certainly not identified himself with household suffrage. While some Radicals believed that every adult male had the right to vote, Bright in the past had not gone so far as Derby did. If anyone had the right, by virtue of his privately expressed opinions at least, to pass the bill, it was Edward Stanley, who, during the 1850s, apparently favoured both universal manhood suffrage and the ballot. Be this as it may, it is a fact that the same Parliament which rejected Gladstone's bill in 1866 passed a much more radical one in 1867. Thus not only Derby, but many others suddenly changed their opinions, and one can hardly doubt that all sought to gain political advantage from a measure which the spirit of the times seemed to make inevitable.

Not all of his contemporaries regarded Derby in low esteem after the passage of the bill. Writing Disraeli in August, Derby explained: 'I have, very much *contre cœur*, accepted an invitation, sometime in October, to a Conservative "Banquet" in Manchester!! and I am threatened with another in Liverpool.'[157] On October 23rd he received a 'triumphant reception' in Liverpool, and Derby described the Manchester gathering as a 'very great success and very enthusiastic'.[158] Robert Lowe, however, considered Derby's speech at Manchester as trite and morally low.[159] But the receptions of Derby and Disraeli in the large cities, and the chagrin of the Opposition, all seemed to point to a new era of Conservative popularity and power. In the autumn of 1867 Derby could hope that both his party and British institutions had been put on a broader and firmer basis as a result of his measure. During the next two years, however, these hopes changed to doubt, then to disillusionment.

NOTES

[1] Malmesbury, *Memoirs*, II, 351-2. (Derby to Malmesbury, April 22nd, 1866); Gathorne-Hardy, *Cranbrook*, I, 187. (*Diary*, May 9th, 1866).

[2] M&B, *Disraeli*, II, 174. (Disraeli to Derby, June 25th, 1866).

[3] *GP*, BM 44112. (Bright to Gladstone, June 24th, 1866).

* According to Russell the Whig principle was that people should be qualified by property and education for voting; the Radical principle was that every adult male subject to law should vote. Russell, *Recollections and Suggestions*, pp. 291-2.

[4] Malmesbury, *Memoirs*, II, 356. (*Diary*, June 22nd, 1866).
[5] Ibid., p. 357. (*Diary*, June 27th, 1866).
[6] *DP*, Derby XII. (Derby to Disraeli, June 27th (?), 1866); Buckle, *Victoria*, I, 343. (Derby to Victoria, June 27th, 1866).
[7] Gathorne-Hardy, *Cranbrook*, I, 188-9. (*Diary*, June 29th, 1866); Lang, *Northcote*, pp. 158-9. (*Diary*, June 28th, 1866).
[8] Maxwell, *Clarendon*, II, 317-18. (Derby to Clarendon, June 28th, 1866).
[9] Buckle, *Victoria*, I, 348. (Derby to General Grey, June 29th, 1866).
[10] *DP*, Derby XII. (Derby to Disraeli, 7.20).
[11] Ibid. (Derby to Disraeli, 7.00 p.m.).
[12] Ibid. (Derby Memorandum, June 30th (?), 1866).
[13] Ibid.
[14] Hodder, *Shaftesbury*, III, 210-12. (Derby to Shaftesbury, June 29th, 1866). (Shaftesbury to Derby, June 29th, 1866).
[15] Ibid., p. 214. (*Diary*, August 9th, 1866).
[16] Malmesbury, *Memoirs*, II, 309-10. (*Diary*, January 9th, 1864).
[17] Maxwell, *Clarendon*, II, 321. (Russell to Clarendon, July 2nd, 1866).
[18] Buckle, *Victoria*, I, 353. (Derby to Victoria, July 1st, 1866).
[19] Gathorne-Hardy, *Cranbrook*, I, 187-8. (*Diary*, May 20th and June 28th, 1866).
[20] Lang, *Northcote*, p. 157. (*Diary*, March 25th, 1866).
[21] Gwendolen Cecil, *Salisbury*, I, 263. (Cranborne to Shaw-Stewart, April 17th, 1867).
[22] *Hansard* (third series), CLXXXIV, 726-44.
[23] Malmesbury, *Memoirs*, II, 360-1. (*Diary*, July 9th, 1866).
[24] *Hansard* (third series), CLXXXIV, 1370-1.
[25] *DP*, Derby XII. (Derby to Disraeli, September 16th, 1866).
[26] M&B, *Disraeli*, II, 186-8.
[27] Ibid., p. 188. (Disraeli to Derby, September 24th, 1866).
[28] *DP*, Derby XII. (Derby to Disraeli, September 27th, 1866).
[29] Ibid. (Derby to Disraeli, October 9th, 1866).
[30] M&B, *Disraeli*, II, 191-2. (Victoria to Derby, October 28th, 1866).
[31] Morley, *Gladstone*, II, 223. (Gladstone to Brand, October 30th, 1866).
[32] Buckle, *Victoria*, I, 371-2. (Derby to Victoria, November 1st, 1866).
[33] Gwendolen Cecil, *Salisbury*, I, 225; Buckle, *Victoria*, I, 371-2. (Derby to Victoria, November 1st, 1866).
[34] *DP*, Hunt XIII. (Derby to Hunt, January 18th, 1861).
[35] M&B, *Disraeli*, II, 193-5. (Disraeli to Derby, November 18th, 1866).
[36] *DP*, Derby XII. (Derby to Disraeli, November 18th (?), 1866).
[37] Buckle, *Victoria*, I, 378. (Victoria's Journal, November 25th, 1866).
[38] *DP*, Derby XII. (Derby to Disraeli, December 2nd, 1866).
[39] Morley, *Gladstone*, II, 225.
[40] *DP*, Derby XII. (Derby to Disraeli, undated).
[41] Ibid. (Derby to Disraeli, December 22nd, 1866).
[42] M&B, Disraeli, II, 197. (Disraeli to Cranborne, December 26th, 1866).
[43] *DP*, Derby XII. (Derby to Disraeli, December 27th, 1866).
[44] *Hansard* (third series), CLXXXVIII, 1785.
[45] Buckle, *Victoria*, I, 388-9. (Derby to Victoria, January 10th, 1867).
[46] Gwendolen Cecil, *Salisbury*, I, 225.
[47] *DP*, Derby XII. (Derby to Disraeli, undated).
[48] Ibid. (Derby to Disraeli, undated).
[49] Ibid. (Derby to Disraeli, Saturday night).
[50] Ibid.
[51] Ibid., Malmesbury XIII. (Emma Derby to Malmesbury, January 21st, 1867).

[52] Ibid., Derby XII. (Derby to Disraeli, Saturday).
[53] Ibid., Carnarvon XII. (Carnarvon to Disraeli, February 2nd, 1867).
[54] Ibid., Derby XII. (Derby to Disraeli, February 2nd, 1867).
[55] M&B, *Disraeli*, II, 224. (Disraeli to Derby, February 4th, 1867).
[56] *DP*, Derby XII. (Derby to Disraeli, February 2nd, 1867).
[57] *Hansard* (third series), CLXXXV, 35-41.
[58] *DP*, Derby XII. (Derby to Disraeli, February 6th (?), 1867).
[59] Gwendolen Cecil, *Salisbury*, I, 225-6.
[60] M&B, *Disraeli*, II, 226. (Disraeli to Derby, February 7th, 1867).
[61] *DP*, Derby XII. (Derby to Disraeli, February 7th (?), 1867).
[62] M&B, *Disraeli*, II, 226. (Disraeli to Derby, February 7th, 1867).
[63] *DP*, Derby XII. (Derby to Disraeli, February 7th (?), 1867).
[64] Gwendolen Cecil, *Salisbury*, I, 227-8.
[65] Ibid., p. 228.
[66] Malmesbury, *Memoirs*, II, 365. (*Diary*, February 16th, 1867).
[67] M&B, *Disraeli*, II, 229. (Disraeli Memorandum).
[68] Ibid.
[69] Gwendolen Cecil, *Salisbury*, I, 230-1; Malmesbury, *Memoirs*, II, 366. (*Diary*, February 19th, 1867).
[70] Ibid.
[71] Malmesbury, *Memoirs*, II, 366. (Undated entry).
[72] Gwendolen Cecil, *Salisbury*, I, 233. (Cranborne to Derby, February 24th, 1867).
[73] *DP*, Derby XII. (Derby to Disraeli, 6.45 a.m.).
[74] M&B, *Disraeli*, II, 234. (Disraeli to Derby, February 25th, 1867).
[75] Buckle, *Victoria*, I, 400. (Derby to Victoria, February 25th, 1867).
[76] Malmesbury, *Memoirs*, II, 366. (Undated entry).
[77] M&B, *Disraeli*, II, 234.
[78] Buckle, *Victoria*, II, 400. (Derby to Victoria, February 25th, 1867).
[79] Ibid., pp. 401-2. (Disraeli to Victoria, February 26th, 1867).
[80] 'Ministerial Prospects', *Fraser's Magazine*, LXXV (1867), 131-42.
[81] Walling, *Bright*, p. 296. (*Diary*, March 1st, 1867).
[82] *DP*, Derby XII. (Derby to Disraeli, February 28th, 1867).
[83] Lang, *Northcote*, pp. 164-5.
[84] Gathorne-Hardy, *Cranbrook*, I, 202.
[85] *DP*, Derby XII. (Derby to Disraeli, February 26th, 1867).
[86] Buckle, *Victoria*, I, 402-3. (Victoria's Journal, February 27th, 1867).
[87] Gathorne-Hardy, *Cranbrook*, I, 200-1. (*Diary*, February 27th, 1867).
[88] *DP*, Derby XII. (Derby to Disraeli, February 27th (?), 1867).
[89] Ibid. (Derby to Disraeli, February 28th, 1867).
[90] Ibid. (Derby to Disraeli, March 1st (?), 1867).
[91] M&B, *Disraeli*, II, 242. (Disraeli to Derby, February 28th, 1867).
[92] *DP*, Derby XII. (Derby to Disraeli, February 28th, 1867).
[93] M&B, *Disraeli*, II, 245. (Malmesbury to Derby, March 1st, 1867).
[94] Gwendolen Cecil, *Salisbury*, I, 235.
[95] Gathorne-Hardy, *Cranbrook*, I, 201. (*Diary*, March 3rd, 1867).
[96] *Hansard* (third series), CLXXXV, 1285-1300.
[97] *DP*, Cairns XII. (Cairns to Disraeli, March 6th, 1867).
[98] Ibid., Derby XII. (Derby to Disraeli, March 9th, 1867).
[99] Ibid. (Derby to Disraeli, March 10th (?), 1867).
[100] Ibid.
[101] Ibid.
[102] Ibid. (Derby to Disraeli, 11.30 p.m.).

[103] *DP*, Derby XII. (Derby to Disraeli, March 3rd, 1867).
[104] Buckle, *Victoria*, I, 407-9. (Disraeli to Grey, March 15th, 1867).
[105] *DP*, Derby XII. (Emma Derby to Disraeli, March 13th, 1867).
[106] Buckle, *Victoria*, I, 407-9. (Disraeli to Grey, March 15th, 1867); M&B, *Disraeli*, II, 253.
[107] *GP*, BM 44755 (Unbound).
[108] Ibid.
[109] Walling, *Bright*, p. 286. (*Diary*, March 1st, 1867).
[110] *DP*, Derby XII. (Earle to Derby, March 18th, 1867).
[111] M&B, *Disraeli*, II, 256. (Disraeli to Derby, March 24th, 1867).
[112] *DP*, Derby XII. (Derby to Disraeli, March 26th, 1867).
[113] Gathorne-Hardy, *Cranbrook*, I, 204. (*Diary*, March 26th, 1867). (Derby to Hardy, March 25th, 1867).
[114] *DP*, Derby XII. (Derby to Disraeli, March 27th, 1867).
[115] Walling, *Bright*, p. 301. (*Diary*, April 8th, 1867).
[116] Ibid., p. 302. (*Diary*, April 13th, 1867).
[117] *GP*, BM 44755. (Unbound).
[118] Gathorne-Hardy, *Cranbrook*, I, 205. (*Diary*, April 19th, 1867).
[119] Buckle, *Victoria*, I, 418. (Derby to Victoria, April 12th, 1867). This and several subsequent direct quotations from the same work are taken by permission, from G. E. Buckle's *The Letters of Queen Victoria*, published by John Murray.
[120] Malmesbury, *Memoirs*, II, 369-70. (Undated entry).
[121] *Hansard* (third series), CLXXXVIII, 1789.
[122] *DP*, Derby XII. (Barrington to Disraeli, April 7th, 1867).
[123] Gathorne-Hardy, *Cranbrook*, I, 206. (*Diary*, April 13th, 1867); *DP*, Derby XII. (Derby to Disraeli, April 16th, 1867).
[124] Burghclere, *A Great Lady's Friendships*, pp. 122-3. (Lowe to Lady Salisbury, May 6th, 1867).
[125] *DP*, Derby XII. (Derby to Disraeli, May 7th, 1867). (Derby to Disraeli, 7.20).
[126] Buckle, *Victoria*, I, 424-5. (Grey to Victoria, May 7th, 1867).
[127] Ibid., pp. 421-2. (Grey to Derby, April 26th, 1867); Malmesbury, *Memoirs*, II, 369. (*Diary*, March 26th, 1867).
[128] *DP*, Derby XII. (Derby to Disraeli, May 15th, 1867).
[129] M&B, Disraeli, II, 274-5. (Disraeli to Hardy, May 18th, 1867).
[130] Buckle, *Victoria*, I, 434-5. (Victoria to Derby, June 25th, 1867).
[131] Ibid., pp. 435-6. (Derby to Victoria, June 26th, 1867).
[132] *DP*, Derby XII. (Emma Derby to Disraeli, June 28th, 1867).
[133] Ibid. (Derby to Disraeli, July 18th, 1867).
[134] Ibid. (Derby to Disraeli, July 21st, 1867).
[135] Ibid. (Derby to Disraeli, July 22nd, 1867).
[136] *Hansard* (third series), CLXXXVIII, 1782-3.
[137] Ibid., pp. 1774-803.
[138] Ibid., p. 1838.
[139] Ibid., pp. 1861-2.
[140] Ibid., p. 2026.
[141] Ibid., p. 2018.
[142] Ibid., p. 2031.
[143] George M. Trevelyan, *The Life of John Bright* (Boston: Houghton Mifflin Co., 1913), p. 379.
[144] Malmesbury, *Memoirs*, II, 373. (*Diary*, July 29th, 1867).
[145] *Hansard* (third series), CLXXXIX, 526-39.
[146] Ibid., p. 707.

[147] *DP*, Derby XII. (Emma Derby to Disraeli, August 4th, 1867).

[148] *Hansard* (third series), CLXXXIX, 942.

[149] Ibid., p. 952.

[150] Gathorne-Hardy, *Cranbrook*, I, 212. (*Diary*, August 9th, 1867).

[151] Maxwell, *Clarendon*, II, 338. (Russell to Clarendon, October 18th, 1867); *GP*, BM 44294. (Russell to Gladstone, February 26th, 1868).

[152] Maxwell, *Clarendon*, II, 334. (Dalhousie to Halifax (?)).

[153] Burghclere, *A Great Lady's Friendships*, p. 148. (Lowe to Lady Salisbury, November 2nd, 1867).

[154] 'The Conservative Transformation', *Fraser's Magazine*, LXXVI (1867), 654-69.

[155] Ibid., p. 668.

[156] 'The Conservative Surrender', *The Quarterly Review*, CXXII-CXXIII (1867), 281-97.

[157] *DP*, Derby XII. (Derby to Disraeli, August 19th, 1867).

[158] Ibid. (Derby to Disraeli, October 24th, 1867). (Derby to Disraeli, October 26th, 1867).

[159] Burghclere, *A Great Lady's Friendships*, p. 147. (Lowe to Lady Salisbury, October 23rd, 1867).

CHAPTER XII

'IRISH LAWN FOR SALE'*

WHILE the passage of the Reform Bill marked the end of Derby's effective party leadership, he by no means wished to retire from the headship. As he put it, the doctors had 'patched' him up on particular occasions during 1867, and the fact that he had survived many sieges of illness indicated he might expect to carry on. But in September 1867 he was struck by one of the most severe and painful attacks of gout he had ever experienced. 'I fear', wrote his son Frederick, 'the last few days of Reform have something of this to answer for, as he was not half cured when he went down to his place in the House. It was, however, a worthy occasion for that amount of risk.'[1]

The debilitating effects of forty-odd years of public life, as well as a full and vigorous private life, left Derby in 1867 a shell of his former self.† For the first time serious thoughts of retirement entered his mind. Writing Disraeli of his plight he observed: '. . . time cannot be far distant when I must seek for restoration to health in absolute withdrawal from public service'.[2] Under these circumstances, Disraeli was anxious to learn Derby's plans for him in such an event, and he replied politely: 'I am selfish in hoping you will not quit public life, as my career will terminate with yours . . .'[3] At the moment, however, Derby did not reveal his intention to make Disraeli his political heir.

For about a month Derby's condition changed from time to time. On September 20th Emma Derby wrote Disraeli for her husband that 'That restless woman' the Queen of Holland had 'invaded' England and planned to visit him on the 28th. 'She says she requires no party,' Derby continued, 'but I know that her

* Suggested by: *Punch*, LVI-LVII (1869), 260. 'Commercial Intelligence — Irish Lawn is at a discount.'

† In common with most of his class Derby loved wine, and this probably had some effect on his general health. The story was told of a wine merchant who tried to sell Derby his sherry as a cure for gout. Derby is quoted as having replied: 'I have tasted your sherry and prefer the gout.' Horace G. Hutchinson, *Private Diaries of the Right Honourable Algernon West* (London: John Murray, 1922), p. 202.

great wish is to meet the celebrities, and specially the Male celebrities, of the country.'[4] The Prime Minister felt hardly up to the task of entertaining her, and he was right, for the day after writing Disraeli, Derby was unable even to talk.[5] The visit nevertheless went off as scheduled, and Derby played host as best he could. The description left by the Queen, however, reveals his precarious state of health. 'When I was at Knowsley, he was carried up and down stairs, not from *pain*, but from *weakness*, and it was positive *exertion* to lead me from the drawing room to the dining room. At dinner his colour would get ghastly white, like a corpse . . . he seemed like a candle burning out. His feverish eyes, his ghastly paleness, were at times quite frightful.'[6]

By early October, however, Derby had improved considerably, and once again could transact business and write his own letters. Business rendered imperative an autumnal session of Parliament, and he wrote Disraeli of his plans for it. The middle of the month he gave a large party for his followers,[7] and thereafter attended receptions at Liverpool and Manchester. But early November again found him ailing. Gathorne-Hardy wrote: 'The Cabinet without Lord Derby, who again has the gout. It becomes a very serious matter.'[8] Nevertheless, Derby was present at the opening of Parliament on November 19th and spoke effectively in defence of his Administration. Lord John Russell, who had recently had one of his perennial fainting fits,[9] was also there and still able to criticize his long-time rival. During these closing years, their arguments in Parliament became even more animated, if, perhaps, frequently less logical and effective. During the autumnal session Derby was usually in his place in the Lords until Parliament was adjourned on December 7th.

A number of problems disturbed the peace during these months. King Theodore of Abyssinia had refused to release some British captives, and the Government was compelled to send an expedition against him. The Fenian society in Ireland was particularly active, and they extended their deeds of lawlessness into England at this time. 'I incline very much', wrote Derby in October, 'to the opinion that the less we meddle with Ireland the better.'[10] When the situation grew acute in December and news reached the Government of elaborate plots, Disraeli recommended that Habeas Corpus be suspended in areas of England where police failed to keep order, but Derby replied the British public would not stand for it.[11] Derby thought the Fenian disturbances might strengthen them politically, but feared they might cause an 'indiscriminate proscription of the Irish Roman Catholics'.[12] They led, however, to something entirely different, for they caused Gladstone to take up the cause of the reform of Irish institutions.

Early in January the Government was involved in an internal squabble over a proposed education measure. The Duke of Marlborough thought he had been authorized to draw up a bill, but Disraeli opposed his measure both because it did not go far enough and because the time was not right for such a proposal. Derby supported Marlborough, and furnished the Cabinet with his own ideas on the subject.* He proposed to grant funds to all religious bodies that maintained schools, hoping that this would increase the hold of the various churches over education. 'I believe', he wrote late in January, 'the consequence will be that nine-tenths of the Schools will connect themselves with some religious body.'[13] Certainly on the subject of education Derby's ideas were quite constant over his career, save, perhaps, for his Irish schools' system, which was designed to meet an unusually complex problem.

With the new year came a letter from Disraeli presenting the compliments of the season, and a brief discussion of political affairs. Derby replied cordially with the hope that increased trade might improve their financial prospects.[14] During the first half of January it seemed that Derby would be able to meet Parliament the next month, and he even looked forward to the coming election.[15] He was also able to play host to a Royal Party at Knowsley.[16] Then came the collapse. On January 12th the gout returned, and he was unable to meet the Cabinet the following week. 'He is pretty free from pain,' Barrington wrote on January 19th, '. . . and he goes through the ordinary routine business with me, *without mental friction.*'[17] The emphasis on his mental state hints that Derby may have occasionally suffered from some sort of derangement, possibly resulting from arteriosclerosis, during these years. Perhaps, however, this 'friction' resulted from artificial causes, for, in taking a certain medicine, opium was also administered with some frequency.[18] Derby's letters during the period 1867-69,

* This paragraph is based on: *Disraeli Papers*, Derby XII. (Derby to Disraeli, January 29th, 1868). There is also an undated memorandum in this collection containing Derby's thoughts on education.

some written in his own hand, others dictated to his wife or son, were quite lucid, and his speeches in Parliament were coherent, though he occasionally made errors and misrepresentations. This indicates that the 'mental friction', which might have been the 'new symptom' referred to by Earle in 1862, was transitory and possibly drug-inspired. The following year, however, Granville strongly intimated that Derby was weak both mentally and physically.[19]

The rest of January was an ordeal for the Prime Minister, and his thoughts again turned to resignation. Writing to Disraeli on January 26th, he styled himself 'everything that a Prime Minister ought not to be'.[20] Once again there was a slight recovery during which he busied himself with a favourite project — the British Navy,[21] but on February 6th he wrote the Queen's secretary: '... the increasing frequency of my attacks must lead me to look forward to the time as not far distant when I shall be compelled to request Her Majesty to relieve me from duties which I shall be no longer able to perform with credit to myself or advantage to her service'.[22] The Queen discouraged his resignation, noting that Disraeli badly needed his authority during the coming session,[23] and Disraeli, in spite of the inconvenience to himself in the situation, tended to agree. About this time he observed that during Derby's illness the Opposition, out of courtesy, tended to be quiet, but might resort to violent action if he resigned.[24]

For the moment Derby set aside his thoughts of immediate resignation, and wrote on February 13th that, if his colleagues would overlook his inefficiency, he was willing to remain.[25] This letter indicated that he would continue through the session and thereafter Disraeli would succeed him. The news was not unexpected. Disraeli had already sounded Granville regarding the possibility of his co-operation in the Lords.[26] To no one, save Disraeli and the Queen, did Derby make known his intention, and it apparently never entered his mind to thrust his son into the leadership. His inability to meet Parliament decided Derby in favour of resignation; the attitude of the Queen made him hesitate for a time, then a serious attack on February 17th made him return to his original intention. Two days later he wrote Disraeli: 'I had hoped that I might have been enabled to struggle through the present session; but, as matters stand, my attempt to do so would not only be a certain failure, but would involve a risk of life which

I am not justified in incurring.'[27] The tone of his letter seemed final, and Disraeli immediately expressed his willingness to accept responsibility for directing the party.[28]

After receiving Disraeli's reply, Derby tendered his resignation to the Queen, but indicated that the formal change-over should take place when he was well enough to visit the Queen personally.[29] In these circumstances, Disraeli was unable to proceed with the formation of his government. Hoping to secure a more definite word, Stanley contacted his father for an explanation. Derby's reply was mysterious: 'Glad there are no difficulties. Will write by post. Do nothing formal till you hear. A few days indispensable to me.'[30] Later that same day, February 24th, Derby explained more fully his situation in a letter to Disraeli. The Queen had not yet authorized certain peerages for his friends, and he wanted to remain in power until he could communicate the good news to them.[31] The Queen's letter of February 24th, which accepted Derby's resignation and expressed a hope that he would remain in the Cabinet without office, did not mention the peerages.[32] Rather peevishly, Derby replied:[33]

> Lord Derby, with his humble duty, has the honour to acknowledge the receipt, this afternoon, of the command contained in your Majesty's letter of yesterday, in obedience to which he cannot hesitate in laying at your Majesty's feet his instant resignation of the office which . . . he has hitherto held. He had hoped, before doing so, to have been honoured by some notice of the humble request which he preferred to your Majesty in his letter of Friday last, that he might be permitted to recommend to your Majesty, for the honour of the Peerage, some few gentlemen whose political support has been of the greatest value to the Government. . . .

Concluding his letter Derby explained that his health would not permit him to sit in the Cabinet, but he guaranteed to use his influence to strengthen the Government. Later that day the Queen, rather reluctantly for fear of setting a precedent, granted Derby the favour she had refused Russell, and agreed to the creations.[34] Derby then immediately telegraphed his resignation to Disraeli. On receipt of the news, Stanley conveyed it privately to Gladstone,[35] and later that day Stanley in the Commons, and Malmesbury in the Lords, made the official announcements. Russell immediately rose to speak warmly of his opponent.[36]

The incident closed with an exchange of letters between Derby and Disraeli. Writing on February 27th, Disraeli was very magnanimous, noting '... I consider myself, and shall always consider myself, only your deputy'.[37] To this Derby replied: 'One line ... to assure you that, so far as I am concerned, there is no danger of any sentiment of estrangement arising between us, who for more than twenty years have worked together with unreserved and unbroken confidence. But I cannot accept for you the position which you are willing to accept for yourself, of being considered as my deputy. You have fairly and most honourably won your way to the highest round of the political ladder, and long may you continue to retain your position!'[38] The former Prime Minister then explained he would give his opinions, if asked, but would not be affronted if Disraeli did not act on them.

The letters were a pleasant incident in the relationship of the two men. It was unfortunate that the patronage question arose at the last moment, but perhaps it was natural enough. Derby was always anxious to reward those who had served him well, both from a sense of loyalty and for political reasons. As Disraeli observed the preceding January: 'You have done very well for your friends: 3 Garters, 4 Bishoprics, 8 Lord Lieutenancies, and almost the whole Bench in the three kingdoms.'[39] His skilful use of his patronage powers had added considerably to Derby's influence, and he planned originally not to create more titles until just before the election, when 'we must have a batch'.[40] Thereafter relations between Derby and Disraeli were as cordial as before, though, because of their changed position, both had to be rather diplomatic. In a sense Derby continued to be, as Argyll put it, the 'Guardian Angel' of the Government,[41] but after surrendering his position, he merely made suggestions which Disraeli accepted or politely rejected.* In the autumn of 1868, Disraeli received Derby's usual sign of approval, a 'haunch of Red deer venison', just as the year before, and again in 1869. In his last letter to Derby, Disraeli still addressed him as 'My dear Chief'.

Derby, nevertheless, was loath to retire, even though Russell

* That Derby had been Prime Minister in fact as well as in name is attested to by the Queen, who later noted he had been 'entirely master' of his Cabinet. Arthur Ponsonby, *Henry Ponsonby, Queen Victoria's Secretary* (New York: The MacMillan Co., 1943), I, 195. (Victoria to Ponsonby, April 15th, 1885). He was interested in all branches of the government, and much departmental correspondence went through his office. See: *Disraeli Papers*, Stanley XII. (Edward Stanley to Disraeli, February 21st, 1868).

and others might feel Disraeli was 'only the heir of triumphant worry'[42] which Derby hitherto had shared. It was always hard for such men to retire. Wellington, much as he admired Peel, felt somewhat uncomfortable when he took a subordinate position. Palmerston died beside his dispatch box. Derby, after enjoying great prominence, saw in retirement that he would be like some of his old thoroughbreds, with their exciting days behind them, turned out to pasture.

Perhaps another reason for Derby's hesitation in surrendering the reins of government was the mounting threat to his pet ward, the Irish Church. In 1865 Gladstone had thought the question was remote and without bearing on the practical politics of the day. But the Fenian disturbances apparently convinced him that Ireland needed a wide programme of reform. By November 1867 he was willing to 'suppress' the Irish Church, and by the middle of the following month he had formulated a comprehensive programme embracing educational reform, land reform, and a reform of the religious institutions of Ireland.

Nothing could have been more calculated to prolong Derby's political activities than this programme. In 1865 Derby had written Disraeli frankly regarding his reasons for upholding the Irish Church. 'I feel sure that you will agree with me it [a motion hostile to the church] should be resisted to the uttermost, and with all our strength: 1st Because the Abolition of that Establishment would be fatal to our hold on Ireland, and an injury to Ireland itself; next, because an attack on that branch would be only the prelude to one on the English Church; and lastly, because any slackness on our part would infallably lose us a large amount of Protestant support in Ireland, without gaining us any from the R. Catholics.'[43] These were, clearly stated, the national, religious and political considerations which motivated Derby's last political battle.

Writing Disraeli on March 3rd, 1868, Derby expressed little concern over the land question, which he felt could not be solved, but he was much alarmed over the prospects of the Irish Church. Recalling that his successful resistance to the appropriation clause during the 1830s had been based on the principle that Parliament had no right to alienate the property of the Church, or any other corporation, Derby thought the same line should be followed in

1868, though many now considered this position untenable. Hoping that Gladstone would not be able to decide on a definite programme, he advised Disraeli to sit still until he discovered what attack the Opposition would mount.[44] Disraeli's ideas on the subject were rather nebulous, but he apparently hoped Parliament would oppose disendowment if the Roman Catholic Church were to share in the Church's property.

It seemed probable that Gladstone, bidding for Catholic votes in the election, would carry some abstract resolution on the Irish Church. In such a case Derby advised that Disraeli retain office and challenge Gladstone to air his scheme before the election. The tactic anticipated by Derby was not long in coming. On March 16th Gladstone called for the disestablishment of the Irish Church, and on March 23rd produced three resolutions calling for its disestablishment, its gradual disendowment, and placing the Crown's interest in the Church Temporalities at the disposal of Parliament.

Disraeli decided to try to amend the resolutions by affirming that 'considerable modifications' in the Irish Church Temporalities might be expedient, but that the matter should be left for the next Parliament. Derby arrived in London on March 24th, and conferred with Disraeli shortly thereafter. He objected to the phrase 'considerable modifications', and doubted that Edward Stanley could introduce the amendment effectively, but Derby conceded that his 'opinions are not those of the majority', and that Disraeli had good reasons for using the phrase.[45] Derby's prediction regarding Stanley proved correct, and friend and foe alike considered his speech inferior. Hardy, who was much closer to Derby on the subject than Stanley, spoke very effectively, and earned Derby's highest praise and blessing for his efforts.[46] For a time Derby had some hope of success,[47] but early in April Gladstone beat the Government by forty-eight votes.

On April 3rd the Queen visited Derby at St. James's, and spoke very critically of Gladstone's position on the Church.[48] Her Majesty and Derby united in urging Disraeli not to resign over a defeat on the issue, and the Prime Minister followed their advice. During the rest of the month Derby kept in close touch with his old subordinate and gave advice regarding parliamentary tactics. Disraeli, probably as a courtesy gesture, offered Derby the Lord Lieutenancy of Middlesex, but the latter declined because he lacked the local knowledge necessary to discharge such an office.[49]

Meanwhile, after returning to London, Derby immediately became active in the Lords, where he was a sort of unofficial leader of the Conservative Party. On April 23rd another of Gladstone's church reforms, this time the abolition of compulsory church rates, came up for discussion. Under the terms of this bill all legal proceedings for the recovery of church rates were abolished, but voluntary assessments were allowed to be made and to be considered as valid contracts. Before speaking on the subject, Derby wrote Disraeli that, if the Government did not object, he would vote against the bill, but would not call for a division against it.[50] Disraeli apparently requested Derby to compromise. For the first time since the preceding December, Derby rose to address the House. While condemning the measure, which had a tendency to put the Established Church on the same footing as other Churches, Derby grudgingly agreed to a second reading.[51] Lord John Russell, who had also abdicated his party leadership, still remained, as Derby put it, the 'objector in Chief in the Lords'.[52] After welcoming Derby back to the fold, Lord John went on to tear up his speech as best he could.[53]

While considerably shaded by the contest between Gladstone and Disraeli in the Commons, Russell and Derby nevertheless had some interesting parliamentary encounters during these months. On April 27th Derby gave notice for the following evening of a question on the resolutions being discussed in the other House. Expecting that the Orders of the Day would take longer than they did, Derby was somewhat late in arriving the following night. Derby's question was a rather obvious one — would the resolutions being discussed in the Commons be referred to the Lords? In putting the question, he drew a fine distinction — he would not comment on the merits of the resolutions, but only on the effect their passage by the Commons would produce. He predicted that the subject of disestablishment would find the two Houses irreconcilably at variance, and would stir up bitter religious animosities. Then he reviewed Russell's alleged four changes of opinion on the subject during the last two years, and recalled their battles on the issue in the 1830s.[54] Russell replied that a bill would at length be presented to the Lords, and, dubbing Derby's conduct 'somewhat extraordinary', he went on to present a different interpretation of their former contests.[55] Shortly after the debate Robert Lowe reported to a friend: 'Lord Derby, I think, argued his case very ill in the Lords the other night, grossly misrepresenting the facts when the facts would have served the purpose as well, besides having the advantage of being true.'[56] This charge was made often during Derby's declining years. What might be called 'tactical misrepresentations' were, however, quite common in their lordships' House, and Aberdeen once remarked that only one debater there (whom he did not specify) was always perfectly fair in quoting his opponents.[57] Derby, however, had issued his open declaration of war. While he and Russell were arguing their cases, the resolutions meanwhile passed the Commons and Disraeli decided, when business permitted, to dissolve Parliament.

Having failed to dislodge the Government with his resolutions, Gladstone introduced a Suspensory Bill, designed to suspend Irish ecclesiastical appointments and the creation of new interests in the Irish Church. Disraeli was unable to deal with the bill in the Commons, and on May 29th Derby wrote that he would dispose of the bill in the Upper House.[58] Derby was quite willing thus to thwart the will of the Commons, knowing that the public would not become excited over such a tactic with an election in the near future. Late in May Derby left London for a time, but returned for their lordships' debate on the Irish Church, which began on June 25th.

The speeches in the Lords were characterized by unusual heat and ill-feeling. Granville, Russell, Clarendon, Argyll and the Earl of Kimberley spoke for the Opposition, while Derby, Grey and Malmesbury upheld the cause of the Irish Church. Derby's speech came on the first night of the debate, and it was not conciliatory. Roundly denouncing the 'dictation of a would-be Minister, who, I must be forgiven for saying, appears to be ready to sacrifice the cause for which he at one time held it to be his high and holy privilege to defend and uphold', Derby based his argument on the concept *Nullum tempus occurrit Ecclesiae* — time shall not injure the rights of the Church. In upholding this idea he went so far as to condemn the confiscation of the monastic lands by Henry VIII. William of Orange, whom Derby dubbed the 'Deliverer', Lord Palmerston and the Coronation Oath were all summoned in to buttress his case. This measure, he claimed, was far too important to be decided upon by a dying Parliament, and he called on the House to show their independence by throwing out the bill. He admitted, however, that his course was not a popular one, and that no one could be wholly indifferent to the feelings of his fellow-countrymen, but, Derby added: 'I have never yet courted popularity for the sake of popularity.'[59]

The Opposition speakers trained their guns on the centre of resistance to disestablishment. Lord Kimberley asked: 'He constructed a Conservative Government – to do what? To bring in a measure in the very teeth of Conservative principles.'[60] Argyll was particularly bitter. Commenting on a portion of Derby's speech, he observed: 'It is perfectly natural that men in whose hands the noble instrument of party government has been for more than two years so much degraded, by whom it has been entirely dissociated from all definite political opinions, and therefore from all public principle – it is perfectly natural that they should denounce party government.'[61] Of all the members, he declared, 'who require to have their quotations very closely looked after, the noble Earl is the chief'.[62] Lord John Russell averred that Derby spoke with some of that 'unfairness which I think is apt to characterize him'.[63] Also drawing on the arsenals of the past, Russell hinted strongly that some of the early members of the Derby family, far from being staunch Protestants, had sought to place Mary Queen of Scots on the throne. His own family, the Bedfords, however, had opposed the Derbys in the sixteenth century and opposed them still in 1868.[64] Regardless of the slurs and insinuations regarding his political character, however, Derby and Grey were able to defeat the measure on June 29th, after three nights of debate, by a margin of ninety-five votes.

The Lords had done, to Derby's way of thinking, their simple duty. The parties now could appeal to the people. The fate of the Irish Church, which Derby regarded with such anxiety, was thus placed into hands which had only the year before received the vote from him.

Late in July Derby left London to spend the rest of the year at Knowsley. To that place, in September, on the invitation of Derby, came the Prime Minister to consult on various matters of importance. Derby certainly could not have expected more considerate treatment from his successor. Disraeli had submitted the speech proroguing Parliament to Derby for his suggestions, and was always careful to satisfy requests for patronage. Derby kept these down to a minimum,[65] but he did ask that a newly vacant Lay

Lordship at the Admiralty be given his younger son, Frederick Stanley.[66] Disraeli complied immediately. On matters of Church patronage, of which there were a great deal just then, Disraeli frequently consulted his former chief, and the latter agreed with Disraeli's policy of trying to recognize all the parties of the Church.[67] The Prime Minister's hope of reconciling the various Church factions, however, was not realized.

Derby's eldest son, Edward, continued to cause parental worry. Edward was despondent over their prospects and felt the elections were hardly worth fighting. Writing to Disraeli late in September, Stanley voiced sharp disagreement with the party policy on the Irish Church: 'Does any man suppose, who has considered the matter at all, that it is possible to save the whole of the endowments – to maintain the thing as it stands? I will answer for it that two-thirds of the conservative party are not of that opinion. There are very few of them . . . who are not in favour of a compromise.'[68] Stanley, in fact, thought the only solution to their internal difference was for the Government to be defeated.[69] Under these circumstances, Derby was disturbed about an address his son was to make to his constituents, and feared his utterances on the Irish Church would reveal the Cabinet split. Once again Derby appealed to Disraeli to 'use to the utmost your personal influence' with Stanley.[70] The Prime Minister, likewise alarmed, appealed to Stanley not to 'stab me in the back'.[71] In deference to the opinion of his father and his friend, Stanley spoke rather ambiguously on the Irish Church and advocated reform rather than disestablishment and disendowment.

The election did not go well with the Conservatives. Malmesbury wrote in November: 'Everything proves what a Radical bill Lord Derby and Disraeli have brought in . . . The elections are going on as badly as possible all over the country, so our fate is decided.'[72] Spofforth, whom Derby called an honest man, but rather injudicious in his choice of candidates,[73] was removed from managing the elections in favour of a party committee, but otherwise the Conservative campaign was lethargic. The Conservatives failed to contest some seats with the liberals,[74] and Disraeli did not undertake a speaking tour such as Gladstone and Bright carried on. They apparently realized, as Disraeli did not, that the Reform Act necessitated a more vigorous approach to the electorate.

The Conservatives lacked a basis on which to appeal to the country. While they used Protestantism, this did not attract the Low Church party or the Dissenters. The Irish Church question was of little help because Gladstone did not divulge the extent of his scheme for disestablishing and disendowing that Church. The Conservatives did not take credit for the Reform Bill, and appeal to the voters on that ground, possibly for fear of alienating the more conservative wing of their own party. Under these circumstances, the election brought a resounding defeat for the Government. Derby anticipated the outcome, but it was nevertheless a disappointment.[75] There was some satisfaction, however, in seeing his own county go overwhelmingly Conservative, and in having his son, Frederick, returned to Parliament.

Following the election it was obvious the Government could not continue. Disraeli and Stanley were agreed that they should resign before Parliament met, but this novelty did not appeal to Derby, who felt it might discourage the party.[76] Instead, he proposed that they place a paragraph on the Irish Church in the Speech which would invite amendment to hold out reform of that institution as against its abolition.[77] In that way, they could go down in defence of the Church, and no doubt Derby thought this might still attract some Protestants. Disraeli, however, decided against the plan, but instead sent a circular to the members of the party, expressing the reasons for his resignation and committing the party to a continued fight on behalf of the Church. On second thought, Derby agreed with Disraeli. 'My father charges me', wrote Edward Stanley, 'to tell you that on farther consideration of all the circumstances, he is satisfied that we did right in resigning when we did: and he wishes you to know this, as he had previously expressed a contrary opinion . . .'[78] Derby had once again fallen ill, and was unable to write himself. During that winter Derby was bedridden most of the time, and spring found him feeble. His physical condition seems to have deteriorated rapidly thereafter.

While the great enemy of disestablishment thus slipped gradually into senescence, the proponents of the measure grew stronger. Gladstone, now in the most vigorous period of his career, coupled to his usual earnestness of purpose and his missionary-like faith in his cause a determination to humble the Conservative Party, and possibly also the House of Lords, which had humiliated him at the time of the struggle over the paper duties. His cause was strong, and he knew that the Conservatives could not rest their case on any liberal principle. Supporting him were the Scotch Presbyterians, the English and Welsh Nonconformists, and the Roman Catholics, all of whom had no love for the Anglican Church. On the other hand, the defence of the Church was weak, for the Established Church was divided into factions. With more than a hundred majority in the Commons, Gladstone, in undertaking his huge and complicated project, had no fears of the sort which harassed Disraeli when he undertook the reform of the electorate. There was, however, one fear in his mind. Bright wrote in January: 'if anything should happen to estrange a ''Protestant'' section on our side of the House, the Lords will take courage and horribly mangle or even reject the Bill — in the belief that you dare not refer the question again to the Constituencies with a scheme for giving considerable funds to the Catholic Church'.[79] The stumbling-block, then, was not the disestablishment of the Church, for which there would be widespread support, but the disposal of the property of the Irish Church. Bright particularly feared that the Scotch members, fifty-three of them, might balk at any attempt to give the Catholic Church a major share of the spoils.

Gladstone, however, went to work, and between his symbolic tree-cutting activities and translating of Homer, he was able to produce a bill which was presented to the Commons on March 2nd. His measure went far beyond the expectations of some Conservatives.[80] It provided for the disestablishment and disendowment of the Irish Church; i.e., the severance of the connection of the Irish Church with both the English Church and the Government, and the disposal of its sixteen million pounds worth of properties. About half of this sum went to satisfy the claims of the Irish Church itself, and the rest was to be appropriated for relief purposes. Only Gathorne-Hardy offered effective opposition to the scheme in the Commons, for Disraeli, though he adhered to the party's principles on the subject, was never at his best in defending the Irish Church. The bill was read for a third time on May 31st, and thereafter faced a hostile House of Lords.

Meanwhile, Derby had returned to his place in the Lords in March, where he continued to wrangle with Russell, but his attendance was irregular. Disraeli apparently toyed with a plan to scuttle the measure in the Upper House, but the prospects were not encouraging. Cairns probably referred to the Irish Church Bill when he wrote Disraeli on May 1st: 'I spoke very seriously with Lord Colville last night as to our numbers. He says that he is not prepared to say we cd. *not* throw out the Bill: we *might* do it: he is not clear that we could: but if we did, it would be a *greatly* reduced majority. This is, to my mind, equivalent to saying that, practically we *cannot* do it.'[81] Cairns adopted a conciliatory position on the issue together with a small section of the Conservative Party. Disraeli next supported a movement, led by the Archbishop of Canterbury, to allow the bill a second reading in the Lords and thereafter to amend it. Lord Derby, who was the heart and soul of the Opposition even though he disclaimed such leadership, refused to go along with this compromise and it failed.* Accordingly, early in June a small meeting of peers was held at Marlborough's residence and the Conservative peers, including Derby, resolved to oppose a second reading of the bill.† Gladstone realized that the forces against him were formidable, and, with his knowledge if not at his request, the Queen appealed directly to Derby to prevent a collision between the two Houses. The gist of the Queen's letter was that she did not approve the disestablishment of the Church, but feared the opposition of the Lords might bring disaster to the aristocracy.[82]

Derby's reply to his Queen revealed his own state of mind:[83]

> Lord Derby does not affect to conceal from himself the serious peril of a collision with the House of Commons, especially under the guidance of the present head of your Majesty's administration; but on the other hand he sees in the passing of this measure consequences so infinitely more serious, that he will not venture to contemplate them, still less to hint at them to your Majesty . . . Lord Derby is therefore humbly of the opinion that in a matter of such deep moment and when a step once taken cannot be retraced, some further time should be allowed for the deliberate judgment of the country, and that the House of Lords should not be called upon to give a vote on so vital a question in opposition to their known opinions, with more haste than ever attended any measure, within his recollection, of importance at all comparable . . . his own

* In a letter quoted in Monypenny and Buckle, which I have not been able to find, Derby is quoted as having said 'no consideration on earth' would cause him to compromise on the measure. M&B, *Disraeli*, II, 446.

† Disraeli apparently did not attend this meeting, though strongly urged to do so by Lord Cairns. *Disraeli Papers*, Cairns XII. (Cairns to Disraeli, May 12th, 1869).

> individual opinion, he may add [is] that there is a great probability that a majority of the House of Lords may support a Second Reading of the Bill, in hopes that some substantial amendments may be introduced in Committee . . . Lord Derby is bound to say that no amendments would remove his individual objections to the whole principle of the Bill; but he ventures to add that, if there is one way more certain than another to ensure its rejection, it is the language of menace and coercion which is sought to be applied to the House of Lords; and to which if they were to submit, their influence in the State would be forever and deservedly lost.

In 1869, then, Derby chose to play the part of Wellington in 1832, and to place himself as an immovable obstacle in the path of the bill. As his letter indicated, however, he did not feel he was thwarting the will of the people in so doing. To him the issue was of such importance that he felt it should be subject to decision at another election.

Debate in the Lords began on June 14th, but Derby did not speak until the third night. As usual, he attracted a large crowd and all the good places in the gallery were taken early, but the gathering did not hear the same man who had forty-five years before spoken in defence of the same Church. 'His voice was feeble,' wrote Malmesbury, 'he looked pale and ill, and his manner had lost its energy.'[84] *Punch* reported briefly: 'The Earl of Derby, in a speech of touching earnestness, assailed the Bill with all his force.'[85] It was a voice from the past, the swan song of an artist whose speaking had charmed, thrilled, amused, and often piqued his countrymen for many decades.

Lord Derby termed the bill a complete revolution striking at the foundations of all property, and a betrayal of the Irish Protestants. To dramatize the effect it would have on the Church of England, he quoted earnestly from Sir Walter Scott's *Guy Mannering*:[86]

> My lords, may I venture upon an illustration of a very simple kind with which your Lordships are probably acquainted, and which none of your Lordships can have heard without having been touched by its simple pathos. The language represents the feelings of a poor gypsy when she and her tribe were driven from their homes in which they had for many years found a shelter, and driven out by a man to whom they had long looked for protection . . . The noble Duke opposite [the Duke of Argyll] will pardon me if I fail in giving the right accent:
>
> 'Ride your ways, Laird of Ellangowan! Ride your ways,

Godfrey Bertram. This day have you quenched seven smoking hearths; see if the fire in your ain parlour burn the blyther for that. Ye have riven the thack of seven cotter houses; see if your ain roof-tree stand the faster . . . There's thirty hearts there that wad hae wanted bread ere ye wanted suckets, and spent their lifeblood ere ye had scratched your finger.'

Might not, he asked, the Irish Protestants also say: 'Go your ways, Ministers of England! Ye have this day, so far as in you lay, quenched the light of spiritual truth in 1500 parishes. See if your own Church stand the faster for that.'[87] Duped and betrayed, he pictured the Irish Protestants, whose property had been guaranteed by the Coronation Oath, casting their lot with the Catholics for a dissolution of the Union. After an exchange with Clarendon, Derby went on to criticize the Catholics for declaring their own church property inalienable, but refusing to recognize this principle in connection with other Churches. He declared:[88]

> Now, in the first place, let me ask in what part of the world in which the Roman Catholic religion is the dominant power does it admit for a moment the notion of the principle of religious equality? It is a principle, they say, which may be all very well for the Protestants; but they condemn, under the authority of the Holy Father, not only the principle of religious equality, but absolutely that of religious toleration. In Ireland, and in Ireland alone, we find the Roman Catholics joining in the cry for religious equality, which, if they had the upper hand, they would not for a moment countenance.

Asserting that the whole principle of the bill was in error, Derby would not single out any specific sections of it for criticism. He concluded with one of the most appealing perorations in English oratory:[89]

> At the same time, my Lords, I do not deny that I entertain the strongest opinion on the principle of the Bill — an opinion which I have steadily upheld for a period longer than I am willing to recollect. My Lords, I am now an old man; and like many of your Lordships, I have already passed the threescore years and ten. My official life is entirely closed; my political life is nearly so; and, in the course of nature, my natural life cannot now be long. That natural life commenced with the bloody suppression of a formidable rebellion in Ireland, which immediately preceded the Union between the two countries. And may God grant that its close may not witness a renewal of the one and the dissolution of

> the other! I do not pretend, my Lords, to be able to penetrate the veil which hides from mortal vision the events of the future; whatever may be the issue of this great controversy — whatever may be the result of your Lordships' present deliberations — I say, for my own part, even if it should be that for the last time I now have the honour of addressing you, that it will be to my dying day a satisfaction to me that I should have been enabled to lift my voice against the adoption of a measure of which, I believe the political folly is only equalled by its moral injustice.

On this nostalgic note, Lord Derby rested his case.

The Earl of Kimberley, who followed, noted the 'touching remarks' with which Derby had concluded his address.[90] But a single speech, however appealing, could not overbear the weight of the majority committed to the bill. Lord John Russell, hoping to destroy the effect of Derby's warning that a dissolution of the Union might result from the bill, pointed out that the Earl's record as a seer was not too good. He had, in fact, predicted ruin would follow repeal of the Navigation Laws.[91] On the division, thirty-six Conservatives, enough to have given Derby victory and perhaps to have forced a general election on the issue, deserted their old leader, and the bill was carried.

When the bill went into committee attempts were made to save for the Church as much of its property as possible. Their lordships proposed that the Church be given thirteen million pounds, but Gladstone was unwilling to meet that figure.* Derby insisted that a disestablished and disendowed Irish Church could not compete with the Catholic Church,[92] and hoped a quarrel over the distribution of property would deadlock the two Houses. One day, while the battle still raged, Derby received a letter from Gladstone, sending a book of his translations from the Greek.[93] This was the supreme test of Derby's rule that political differences should not affect the personal relations of gentlemen, and only a hint of his irritation over the Irish Church question crept into his acknowledgement:[94]

> I have to thank you very sincerely for your kind note of yesterday, and for the Volume which accompanied it. How, among your various occupations, you have found leisure to write the latter, passes my comprehension. I accept it however thankfully,

* Gladstone had to meet the claims of the Presbyterian Church, which lost its subsidy, the *regium donum*, and Maynooth College, which also lost its grant. Together these claims, however, did not amount to more than about one-sixteenth of the property.

not only because the subject is one of such interest, more because your sending it to me is a proof that in your mind political differences have not been allowed, however wide they may be, to interfere with the feelings of personal esteem with which, on my part, I am, Sincerely yours.

During those tense days, when it seemed Derby's prediction that the two Houses would be irreconcilably at odds on the measure would be borne out, Lord Cairns worked to find some *via media* between the positions of the two Houses. He contacted Derby early in July, but the latter remained wholly intransigent and Cairns was deeply worried.[95] The deadlock seemed hopeless until July 22nd when Lord Cairns, on his own initiative, worked out a compromise with Lord Granville. Most of their lordships breathed a sigh of relief when it was announced, but not so Lord Derby. On hearing Cairns, the former Premier immediately rose and said loudly: 'I shall go away.' He whispered something to Lord Salisbury, and, passing by Lord Cairns, added: 'I have nothing left but to go away.'[96]

And so they both faded out that night, the Established Church from Ireland, and Derby from political life.*

Though he usually ignored the splendour of his natural surroundings, the Earl of Derby could not help but notice the beauties of Knowsley that especially lovely autumn. There was a new atmosphere of peace there, both in the environment and within the Earl himself. He was now too infirm to be turned from his meditations by thoughts of hunting, and the political battles on the horizon no longer concerned him very much. Cairns's compromise, which had ruined his plan for a general election on the subject of the Church, had been, in effect, a repudiation of his leadership in the Lords.[97] While this annoyed him considerably at the time, a second thought convinced him it was useless to continue a struggle which was obviously hopeless.[98] For the first time in almost fifty years he could assume a detached attitude towards politics, for the future could hold no continuation of his career.† But he was not

* Some sixty-two amendments to the bill were passed by the Lords, of which the Commons accepted thirty-five. Derby and fifty-five others signed a protest against the bill, charging, among other things, that the right of Parliament to confiscate such property was doubtful.

† During the last two years of Derby's life, his name, which came up so frequently before, virtually disappeared from the correspondence of the various leading statesmen, indicating the sharp decline in his importance.

removed from his memories.

Of this he was certain. Over his long political career he had made many friends, and many enemies; he had accomplished much for the good of his country, and he had made mistakes. Only twice did he hold the line uncompromisingly, first against the Repeal of the Corn Laws, and secondly against the Disestablishment of the Irish Church. That the first would eventually ruin British agriculture, and that the second would finally end the Union – of these things he was certain.

The innumerable details of his career, during these last days, seemed to form themselves into a generalized pattern. He had supported the Reform Bill of 1832, which expanded the influence of the middle class in Parliament, and the new voters had rendered decisive aid to Russell, Palmerston and Gladstone, his chief opponents. By emancipating the slaves of the West Indies, he had helped undermine the proud agricultural aristocracy there. He had helped emancipate the Catholics, admitted the Jews to Parliament, failed to maintain the universities as a special Anglican preserve, and consented to the removal of oaths protecting the Church. His whole career seemed to be a process of gradually compromising the special privileges of his class, and changing the old society into something new and less attractive. But he had no grudges or hard feelings towards anyone, or any class. As a sincere Christian, such malice had no place in his life; as a sportsman, it was not his way to condole with himself or others regarding his losses.

In September his son, Edward, came home for a lengthy visit. In the past Derby had always tried to avoid political subjects at home, and now more than ever there seemed reason to ignore them. But he spoke frankly regarding the future. Ireland would probably break away before long.* The House of Lords would probably come under attack by both the middle and lower classes, and possibly the Monarchy itself would be challenged. Republican sentiment was growing, and the Conservative Party was on the wane.† So

* Derby mentioned his Irish estates in 1869; Bateman's work, published in 1876, does not list these holdings. *Hansard* (third series), CXCVI, 719. Bateman, *Acreocracy*, p. 56. Possibly the family divested itself of its estates there about this time because of Gladstone's Irish legislation.

† The only evidence of Derby's state of health and mind after his defeat found by this writer is a letter from Edward Stanley to Disraeli: 'I cannot report very well of my father: he has become more of an invalid in his habits, goes out but little, and is seldom quite free from gout in some form: but he has on the other hand no severe

he had little advice, and less inspiration, to offer Edward, but he was not sure the former would have been accepted even if he had it to give. While Stanley was still there, the post brought a letter from Disraeli, who, for a change, had little to say about politics. Actually nothing much could be said, but his former lieutenant promised to write '. . . sometimes, if I have anything to say . . .' Not the least of Derby's satisfactions was the recollection of helping a brilliant young man, whom so many of the gentlemen of the time snubbed because of his racial background.

In October the Earl of Derby, who had never been wholly free from gout for many months, fell ill again. On October 12th came a false report of his death. The flag on the town hall at Liverpool was lowered, and the church bells tolled, but these respects were premature. About that time, however, the doctor administered a dose of opium equal to that taken when Derby had been in better health, and he never recovered from the shock.[99] The final pages of his life were a story of peaceful decline, day by day, until he passed away on Saturday morning, October 23rd, 1869.

In recording his death the *Annual Register* noted: 'Concerning his wisdom as a statesman and his capacity as a political leader much difference of opinion will prevail',[100] and this has proved to be correct. Liberal newspapers and journals left a mountain of criticism, dwelling on his changes of party, his alleged changes of opinion, and his so-called 'unstatesmanlike' temperament, most of which is so general that it is difficult to refute. His friends differed only slightly regarding the accomplishments of his political life. Disraeli summed it up with characteristic brevity: 'He abolished slavery, he educated Ireland, and he reformed Parliament.'[101] Malmesbury added to these the recognition of the French Government in 1852, in which he himself had played a part.[102] Actually, Lord Derby was responsible for a huge mass of legislation, some of it his own, some of it being shared with Disraeli.

Much of Derby's legislation, and his compromises, represent, by and large, the adjustment of the old agricultural society to the new social and economic situation created by the Industrial Revolution.

attacks and his spirits continue good. He thinks badly of the political future, but speaks of it without excitement or annoyance.' *Disraeli Papers*, Stanley XII. (Edward Stanley to Disraeli, September 16th, 1869).

The expanding middle and labouring classes, the concentration of larger and larger wealth in the cities disrupted the old agricultural monopoly and the special privileges of the landed aristocrats and gentry who had been identified with it. Derby certainly aided in the readjustment of British institutions to these changed conditions, striving at all times to retain for his own class as many of its privileges and as much of its power as he could in the changing world. In this respect, his career forms a wholly consistent pattern from beginning to end.

Certain criticisms of his leadership are no doubt fair and founded in fact. He affected at times a light-hearted attitude towards politics; he offended large numbers of people unnecessarily; he refused to provide the inspiration which direct contact with the rank and file of his party would have afforded. Yet to explain the stationary nature of the Conservative Party during his term as its leader solely on the basis of these defects of leadership is not quite fair. Between 1846 and 1852 his party was so closely identified with the dying cause of Protection that no amount of leadership could have caused it to grow. From 1852 until the 1860s there was in the Conservative Party the dead weight of a strong Ultra-Tory faction which resisted any domestic reforms that might have made the Conservative Party more attractive to newcomers. At the same time the Radical movement in England did not seem dangerous enough to scare people of substance into the Conservative Party. Derby undoubtedly followed the wishes of the majority of his supporters when he remained in opposition and aided Palmerston in resisting the reforms of the more radical wing of his party.

Faced with this situation there was perhaps only one avenue of escape for Derby. By making the Conservatives the 'patriotic party', he might have attracted some converts by a strong foreign policy. To a considerable extent, that is what Disraeli did after him. But in Derby's time two factors prevented such a tactic — first, that Palmerston had already identified himself with this approach, and second, that Derby was by nature isolationist and anti-imperialistic. His pleas on behalf of the Greeks or Chinese, his reluctance to take Hong Kong, and his tenderness towards the Maoris did not have a widespread appeal in a nation which then dominated international affairs. Being committed to isolationism and the preservation of the *status quo* at home, Derby had few grounds to appeal to the British voters. His position has certain obvious parallels in modern American history.

Lord Derby has had the misfortune to be remembered for his faults rather than his virtues, even though of the latter there were many. On learning of his death, Gladstone wrote Stanley:[103]

> In a moment like this, differences of political opinion are lost to view. I can recollect only the extraordinary brilliancy of his endowments and of his career, and the more than kind public notice from him which was my earliest encouragement in Parliamentary life, and which, whether we agreed or differed, he never failed to follow up by marks of kindly recollection . . . The whole country will share your sorrow, but I am well assured that where Lord Derby was best known, there he will be most lamented.

To this Stanley replied: 'God grant that in our English public life, political rivals may always be able so to think, and so to speak, of one another.'[104] During his career the Rupert of Debate had inflicted many wounds, but he accepted the slashes in return without rancour. He fought for his ideas, but always recognized the right of others to hold (in his words) 'a contrary view', and submitted to that view when the will of the majority was made clearly known. In this approach to politics, one might perhaps discern the nature of the British genius for parliamentary government.

NOTES

[1] *DP*, Derby XII. (Frederick Stanley to Disraeli, September 13th, 1867).
[2] Ibid. (Derby to Disraeli, September 10th, 1867).
[3] M&B, *Disraeli*, II, 303. (Disraeli to Derby, September 14th, 1867).
[4] *DP*, Derby XII. (Derby to Disraeli, September 20th, 1867).
[5] Ibid. (Emma Derby to Disraeli, September 26th, 1867).
[6] Burghclere, *A Great Lady's Friendships*, pp. 173-4. (Queen of Holland to Lady Salisbury, February 11th and 22nd, 1868).
[7] Malmesbury, *Memoirs*, II, 374. (*Diary*, October 14th, 1867).
[8] Gathorne-Hardy, *Cranbrook*, I, 247. (*Diary*, November 8th, 1867).
[9] *DP*, Derby XII. (Derby to Disraeli, October 6th, 1867).
[10] Ibid.
[11] Ibid. (Derby to Disraeli, December 17th, 1867).
[12] Ibid. (Derby to Disraeli, December 15th, 1867). (Derby to Disraeli, January 3rd, 1868).
[13] Ibid. (Derby to Disraeli, January 29th, 1868).
[14] Ibid. (Derby to Disraeli, January 3rd, 1868).
[15] Ibid. (Derby to Disraeli, January 12th, 1868).
[16] Buckle, *Victoria*, I, 488-9. (Derby to Grey, January 9th, 1868).
[17] *DP*, Derby XII. (Barrington to Disraeli, January 19th, 1868).
[18] Ibid. (Barrington to Disraeli, January 22nd, 1868).
[19] Buckle, *Victoria*, I, 610-11. (Granville to Victoria, June 17th, 1869).

[20] *DP*, Derby XII. (Barrington to Disraeli, January 26th, 1868).
[21] Ibid. (Barrington to Disraeli, January 30th, 1868).
[22] Buckle, *Victoria*, I, 492-3. (Derby to Grey, February 6th, 1868).
[23] Ibid., pp. 493-4. (Grey to Derby, February 8th, 1868).
[24] Ibid., pp. 494-5. (Grey to Victoria, February 13th, 1868).
[25] M&B, *Disraeli*, II, 316-17. (Derby to Disraeli, February 13th, 1868).
[26] Fitzmaurice, *Granville*, I, 520. (Granville to Gladstone, February 13th, 1868).
[27] M&B, *Disraeli*, II, 318-19). (Derby to Disraeli, February 19th, 1868).
[28] Ibid., p. 319. (Disraeli to Derby, February 20th, 1868).
[29] Buckle, *Victoria*, I, 496-8. (Derby to Victoria, February 21st, 1868).
[30] M&B, *Disraeli*, II, 321. (Derby to Edward Stanley, February 24th, 1868).
[31] Ibid., pp. 322-3. (Derby to Disraeli, February 24th, 1868).
[32] Buckle, *Victoria*, I, 501. (Victoria to Derby, February 24th, 1868).
[33] Ibid., pp. 503-4. (Derby to Victoria, February 25th, 1868).
[34] Ibid., pp. 504-5. (Victoria to Derby, February 25th, 1868).
[35] *GP*, BM 44141. (Edward Stanley to Gladstone, February 25th, 1868).
[36] *Hansard* (third series), CXC, 1096-7.
[37] M&B, *Disraeli*, II, 324. (Disraeli to Derby, February 27th, 1868).
[38] Ibid. (Derby to Disraeli, February 28th, 1868).
[39] Ibid., p. 310. (Disraeli to Derby, January 1st, 1868).
[40] *DP*, Derby XII. (Derby to Disraeli, January 12th, 1868).
[41] *Hansard* (third series), CXCIII, 171.
[42] *GP*, BM 44294. (Russell to Gladstone, March 2nd, 1868).
[43] *DP*, Derby XII. (Derby to Disraeli, March 10th, 1865).
[44] Ibid. (Derby to Disraeli, March 3rd, 1868). (Derby to Disraeli, March 6th, 1868).
[45] Ibid. (Derby to Disraeli, March 25th, 1868). (Derby to Disraeli, March 21st, 1868).
[46] Gathorne-Hardy, *Cranbrook*, I, 272. (Edward Stanley to Hardy, October 29th, 1869.)
[47] *DP*, Derby XII. (Derby to Disraeli, March 28th, 1868).
[48] Ibid. (Derby to Disraeli, April 3rd, 1868).
[49] Ibid. (Derby to Disraeli, April 14th, 1868).
[50] Ibid. (Derby to Disraeli, April 20th, 1868).
[51] *Hansard* (third series), CXC, 1124-7.
[52] *DP*, Derby XII. (Derby to Disraeli, March 6th, 1868).
[53] *Hansard* (third series), CXC, 1142-4.
[54] Ibid., pp. 1425-35.
[55] Ibid., pp. 1435-43.
[56] Burghclere, *A Great Lady's Friendships*, p. 184. (Lowe to Lady Salisbury, April 30th, 1868).
[57] *Hansard* (third series), CXCIII, 177.
[58] *DP*, Derby XII. (Derby to Disraeli, May 29th, 1868).
[59] *Hansard* (third series), CXCII, 2092-114.
[60] Ibid., p. 2116.
[61] Ibid., CXCIII, 171.
[62] Ibid., p. 177.
[63] Ibid., p. 235.
[64] Ibid., p. 237.
[65] *DP*, Derby XII. (Derby to Disraeli, November 28th, 1868).
[66] Ibid. (Derby to Disraeli, July 15th, 1868).
[67] Ibid. (Derby to Disraeli, November 3rd, 1868).
[68] Ibid., Stanley XII. (Edward Stanley to Disraeli, September 24th, 1868).

[69] Ibid., Derby XII. (Derby to Disraeli, November 3rd, 1868).
[70] Ibid. (Derby to Disraeli, October 29th, 1868).
[71] M&B, *Disraeli*, II, 431. (Disraeli to Edward Stanley, November 10th, 1868).
[72] Malmesbury, *Memoirs*, II, 386. (*Diary*, November 18th, 1868).
[73] *DP*, Derby XII. (Derby to Disraeli, August 2nd, 1868).
[74] Ibid. (Derby to Disraeli, September 14th, 1868). (Derby to Disraeli, October 29th, 1868).
[75] Ibid. (Derby to Disraeli, October 29th, 1868). (Derby to Disraeli, November 14th, 1868).
[76] Ibid. (Derby to Disraeli, November 22nd, 1868).
[77] Ibid.
[78] Ibid., Stanley XII. (Edward Stanley to Disraeli, December 10th, 1868).
[79] *GP*, BM 44112. (Bright to Gladstone, January 9th, 1869).
[80] Malmesbury, *Memoirs*, II, 391. (*Diary*, March 2nd, 1869).
[81] *DP*, Cairns XII. (Cairns to Disraeli, May 1st, 1869).
[82] Buckle, *Victoria*, I, 603-4. (Victoria to Derby, June 7th, 1869).
[83] Ibid., pp. 606-8. (Derby to Victoria, June 9th, 1869).
[84] Malmesbury, *Memoirs*, II, 401. (*Diary*, June 17th, 1869).
[85] *Punch*, LVI-LVII (1869), 259-60.
[86] *Hansard* (third series), CXCVII, 20.
[87] Ibid., p. 21.
[88] Ibid., p. 30.
[89] Ibid., pp. 40-1.
[90] Ibid., p. 41.
[91] Ibid., p. 182.
[92] Ibid., CXCVIII, 293-4.
[93] *GP*, BM 44140. (Gladstone to Derby, July 1st, 1869).
[94] Ibid. (Derby to Gladstone, July 2nd, 1869).
[95] *DP*, Cairns XII. (Cairns to Disraeli, July 10th, 1869).
[96] Buckle, *Victoria*, I, 521. (Granville to Victoria, July 22nd, 1869).
[97] Malmesbury, *Memoirs*, II, 409. (*Diary*, July 22nd, 1869).
[98] Gathorne-Hardy, *Cranbrook*, I, 271.
[99] Malmesbury, *Memoirs*, II, 411. (*Diary*, October 18th, 1869).
[100] *Annual Register* (1869), p. 202.
[101] M&B, *Disraeli*, II, 451.
[102] Malmesbury, *Memoirs*, II, 412
[103] *GP*, BM 44141. (Gladstone to Edward Stanley, October 24th, 1869).
[104] Ibid. (Edward Stanley to Gladstone, October 27th, 1869).

INDEX